Journey to Centennial SARASOTA
SECOND REVISED EDITION

Cover photo: Clyde Butcher
"Venice Beach"

By Janet Snyder Matthews, Ph.D.
Epilogue by Allan H. Horton
With a foreword by John D. MacDonald

Sesquicentennial Productions, Inc.
Sarasota, Florida

Fourth of July fireworks.

Second Revised Edition design and pre-publication layout by
Coastal Printing, Inc. Sarasota, Florida.

Second Revised Edition Copyright 2007 by Janet Snyder Matthews, Ph.D.
All rights reserved.

Narrative Copyright 1985, 1989 by Janet Snyder Matthews, Ph.D.
First Published 1985 by Continental Heritage Press
within the American Portrait Series.
Contemporary photography by Chuck Kennedy
for Continental Heritage
Second impression 1989 by Pine Level Press.
Printed in the United States of America

Library of Congress Catalogue Card No.: 97-061782
ISBN 978-0-9621986-3-2

Prize-winning Steinmetz photo at Point of Rocks, "Commercial Fishermen, Crescent Beach, Florida," 1949, for *Saturday Evening Post* article by John Mahoney entitled "Late Date with a Mackerel."

in memoriam
to Harvey and Esther,
Maryan and Nappy,
James R. Snyder,
Arthur M. Wood, Sr.

Contents

Advisors and Partners in Progress	iv
Foreword by John D. MacDonald	vi
Introduction	vii
I. The Land And Its First People	17
II. The Spanish Crown	23
III. An American Outpost in Indian Country	31
IV. Cowboys and Indians	37
V. The Civil War and Frontier Violence	45
VI. The Ormiston Colony	53
VII. A City Is Born	61
VIII. Sarasota Enters The Twentieth Century	79
IX. Boom And Bust	105
X. Circus Town By The Gulf	127
XI. The Prosperous Years	145
Retrospective	158
Epilogue	163
Partners In Progress	172
Bibliography	239
Index	241
Acknowledgments	245

SESQUICENTENNIAL PRODUCTIONS

Sesquicentennial Productions, Inc. was established in 1994 to elevate public awareness of Florida's history and to inform Floridians of their diverse cultural heritage.
Sesquicentennial Productions, Inc. is a corporation described under 501(c)(3) of the Internal Revenue Code.

The Second Revised Edition of *Sarasota: Journey to Centennial* is the second in a Sesquicentennial Productions series. Proceeds are devoted to furthering the study of archaeology and history throughout Florida. Our Advisors have agreed to offer advice in the selection of ongoing research and publication projects.

ADVISORS

Elizabeth Barzell, Winston E. Barzell, Charles R. Baumann, Alice Harllee Boylston, Lisa Carlton, Judy Miller Collins, E. Keith DuBose, Bob Graham, Katherine Harris, Allan H. Horton, Althea Henry Jenkins, Wendel F. Kent, Elizabeth Lindsay, Dan Miller, Glenda Miller, John Ringling North II, Shirley Ringling North, Arva Moore Parks, Edgar H. Price, Jr., Jerrell H. Shofner, Carole Clark Smith, Sandra Sims Terry

PARTNERS IN PROGRESS

This second-in-a-series volume would not have been possible without the commitments of the following Partners in Progress. These underwriting corporations and individuals' own histories and those of the organizations they sponsored add a significant dimension to the Second Revised Edition of *Sarasota: Journey to Centennial*. Through Spring and Summer of 2007, their stories were drafted, edited and finalized. They appear on pages 172 through 238. These reflections on their histories stand as a separate valuable source of information for residents, visitors and future generations interested in the Sarasota region of 2007.

Historic Spanish Point
Archaeological Consultants, Inc.
A.G. Edwards & Sons, Inc.
The ADP Group, Inc.
Ball Construction, Inc.
Beall's, Inc.
Cyrus Bispham & Family
Boone, Boone, Boone, Koda & Frook
Center for Sight
City of Sarasota
City of Venice
Clyde Butcher Gallery
Community Foundation of Sarasota County
Kevin Daves
Diocese of Venice in Florida
Education Foundation of Sarasota County, Inc.
   Sponsored by Jim and Shirley Ritchey
The Episcopal Church of the Redeemer
FCCI Insurance Group
First Baptist Church of Sarasota
First Presbyterian Church
   Sponsored by Charlie and Dee Stottlemyer
Frederick Derr & Company, Inc.
The Glasser/Schoenbaum Human Services Center
Gulf Coast Community Foundation of Venice
Herald-Tribune Media Group
Hi Hat Ranch
Icard, Merrill, Cullis, Timm, Furen & Ginsburg, P.A.
The Jelks Family Foundation
   Sponsored by the family of Katharine Nau
Kerkering, Barberio & Co.
Longino Ranch, Inc.
The Mabry Carlton Ranch
Matthews, Eastmoore, Hardy, Crauwels & Garcia, P.A.
Manatee Community College
   Sponsored by Walter Serwatka and Constance Holcomb

Michael Saunders & Company
Mote Marine Laboratory
   Sponsored by Frederick Derr & Company, Inc.
Myakka Valley Ranch
The Pat Neal Family
Northbrook Cattle Company
Northern Trust
The Out-of-Door Academy
   Sponsored by Stanley Meuser and Veronica Meuser
The Perlman Music Program
   Sponsored by Jan and Lamar Matthews, Jr.
Pines of Sarasota
   Sponsored by Dr. Robert E. and Lelia Windom
   Arthur M. and Viola L. Goldberg
   John W. and Pamela Overton
Professional Benefits Inc.
Purmort & Martin Insurance Agency, LLC
The John and Mable Ringling Museum of Art
   Sponsored by John Ringling North, II
   and Shirley Ringling North
Ringling College of Art and Design
Piero Rivolta
The Ritz-Carlton, Sarasota
Sarasota Conservation Foundation
Sarasota Family YMCA
Sarasota Memorial Healthcare Foundation, Inc.
   Sponsored by Northern Trust
Schroeder-Manatee Ranch, Inc.
Seibert Architects, P.A.
SunTrust Bank, Southwest Florida
Syprett, Meshad, Resnick, Lieb, Dumbaugh & Jones
Toale Brothers
United Way of Sarasota County, Inc.
The Urology Treatment Center
Wendel Kent & Company, Gator Asphalt Company
   & Quality Aggregates Incorporated
Wilson Jaffer, P.A.

Photo by Susan Henry

Manatee County Historical Society

A stroll on Indian Beach in the early 1920s.

Photo by Allan H. Horton

Waterfront drive along Sarasota Bay, 2007.

Photo by Chuck Kennedy

Waterfront drive along Sarasota Bay, 1997.

Photo by Chuck Kennedy

Hobie cat regatta at Lido Beach.

This Moment of Paradise

Sarasota is the arbitrary name we humans have put upon the center of a geographic area with a fascinating geological history. Prior to the Pliocene Epoch, the peninsula was a part of the sea bed of a great warm ocean.

In the Pliocene Epoch, eleven million years ago, it rose up out of the sea, very slowly, a long broad ridge of the limestone remains of sea creatures. Thousands of years of torrential rains carved out great rivers which carried materials out toward the Gulf, depositing them where the flow became slower, thus beginning the formation of the barrier islands along this coast.

When the most recent Ice Age began, the glaciers that covered much of the world's surface used up so much of the available water that the sea levels dropped 300 feet. One could have walked west from Sarasota for many miles before reaching the new shoreline.

The melting began 25,000 years ago, and took 15,000 years to melt the glaciers back to their present size and location. The water roaring off the continental shelf in the melt created the barrier islands of the northern Gulf, off Mississippi.

Our keys off Sarasota County are older, and for the most part, except for the transient later deposits at the ends and on the beaches, are as solid as the mainland. These gross whims of nature, in a mindless turbulence, created this particular piece of the world we now celebrate, made of it a place of bays and inlets, beaches and vistas.

We have been here a hundred years.

In geological time the waters will again cover the peninsula and again recede, only to return again. So let us cherish this moment of paradise, relish these years of sun and beauty, and do what we can to keep it pristine.

Siesta Key

John D. MacDonald
October, 1985

Photo by Susan Henry

Introduction

*I*n 1987, acting as a consultant for the City of Sarasota in a team headed by archaeologist Bob Carr of Miami, we worked to discover the location of Fort Armistead. Architect Becky Spain came across a murky black-and-white line drawing entitled 'Encampment of the 1st Infantry at Sarasota Bay, 1841." It illustrated a Florida magazine article that dealt neither with Sarasota nor the First Infantry.

Sources confirmed the presence of Army Captain Seth Eastman at the post, and a large number of his paintings at the nation's capitol, but still no connection to the mysterious unattributed illustration. In 1994, under pressure to locate a visual image of the fort for a WWSB-Channel 40 series directed by Jeanne Eklund, "Our Historic Hometown," Sarah Turner, archivist for the Architect of the Capitol, surveyed her Eastman files. A 1959 Smithsonian exhibit catalogue included the title, attributed the 4-by-7-inch watercolor to Seth Eastman, on loan by Peabody Museum. The Peabody generously loaned the negative in time for the TV production.

Last winter, preparing for this Revised Edition, we visited Minneapolis where a recent exhibit of Eastman works had included what a friend called "lots of sweet little watercolors." The collection owner, W. Duncan MacMillan, directed us to call Patricia Condon Johnston of the Afton Historical Society Press. We met Mrs. Johnston at the new Minnesota History Center in St. Paul, where she brought along her 1995 publication underwritten by MacMillan, *Seth Eastman, A Portfolio of North American Indians*. She is a generous, walking encyclopedia on Eastman and his work, which largely took place at Fort Snelling among the Dahcotah Indians a century earlier and not so far from where we sat that chill October Monday. She sent me on to the Minneapolis Public Library, where Eastman's little black leather sketch book resides in a special collections vault. The center spine, where the Florida material once lay, is broken and pages are missing. The rest is history.

The Artist

*S*eth Eastman is "the foremost pictorial historian of the American Indian in the nineteenth century," according to Patricia Condon Johnston. A century and a half ago, Eastman depicted the earliest known visual records of Sarasota Bay. He painted and sketched there several years before the first landowners arrived.

The Maine-born cadet began formal art training in 1826 at the U.S. Army Military Academy at West Point. As a second lieutenant, he subsequently served with the First Infantry at forts Crawford and Snelling in Wisconsin and Minnesota, where his fascination with Native American lifestyle began. The 21-year-old lived with *Wakaninajinwin*, daughter of a Sioux chief. They parented a child, Nancy Eastman, who was raised as a ward of the Indian agent, along with other officers' children. (Years later, Nancy's son, Dr. Charles Alexander Eastman [*Ohiyesa*], a Dartmouth-educated author and attending physician after the 1890 massacre at Wounded Knee, warmly recounted what he had been told about his grandfather's affection for the baby left behind at Fort Snelling.)

In 1833, Eastman returned to West Point as Assistant Teacher of Drawing. For seven years, he taught painting and topographical mapping. He was promoted to first lieutenant, then captain. His 1839 *Treatise on Topographical Drawing* became the standard Army manual on the subject. He studied privately with Academy instructors, C.R.Leslie and Robert Walter Weir, painter of the epic mural decorating the Rotunda of the nation's Capitol. For four years he exhibited annually at the National Academy of Design in New York City. Eastman married Mary Henderson, the teenaged daughter of the Academy's Assistant Surgeon. She became an author.

With Company D of the First Infantry, Eastman was sent to Fort Fanning on the Suwannee River prior to assignment at Sarasota Bay in Fall of 1840. In Florida, the 32-year-old Eastman "began . . . the transition from . . . landscape painter . . . to an Indian painter," wrote Sarah Boehme, curator of the Whitney Gallery of Western Art at the Buffalo Bill Historical Center in Cody, Wyoming.

"Eastman watercolors are important for several reasons," according to Larry Curry, author of *The American West, Painters from Catlin to Russell*. "As a watercolorist, Eastman worked in a medium with which American artists subsequently created some of their greatest works. It was not until the second half of the nineteenth century that the potential of watercolor was fully realized in the hands of Winslow Homer. Thus Eastman's achievement is all the more remarkable. Working in the 1840s, a time when most artists were using the medium in a rather timid way, he began to anticipate its ultimate power. . . . Eastman to a surprising degree let the medium express itself. . . . his style very likely could not have evolved without extensive direct use of the medium in the open air. Even without the more ambitious oil paintings of Indian life, this achievement would have justified his effort as an artist."

Untitled, self-portrait

Seth Eastman, Untitled, figure with house

Only a half dozen or so of Eastman's small Florida watercolors are known, although a journalist in 1846 implied there were more and that they focussed on Seminole lifestyle. They pre-date practical outdoor photography, though later in his career he photographed images and painted from them.

In Fall of 1841, Eastman returned to Fort Snelling as post commander, prolifically sketching scenes of the upper Mississippi. Mary Henderson Eastman authored *Dahcotah, or Life and Legends of the Sioux around Fort Snelling* (1849), illustrated by her husband. She recorded a disappearing culture, stories told by people she knew, whose language she spoke. Three years later Mary authored *Aunt Phylis's Cabin, or Southern Life as It Really Is,* a response to Harriet Beecher Stowe's *Uncle Tom's Cabin.* Mary's novel sold 13,000 copies in two weeks.

Reassigned to the Bureau of Indian Affairs in Washington, Major Eastman produced nearly 300 plates to illustrate Henry Rowe Schoolcraft's six-volume Congressionally-funded *Historical and Statistical Information Respecting the History, Conditions and Prospects of the Indian Tribes of the United States.* (Unsuccessful competitors included George Catlin, an outspoken critic of federal Indian policy that favored expansionism over the rights of Native Americans.) As the publication was released, in Florida the last deported Seminoles boarded a steamer at Egmont Key.

In 1860, Eastman was one of the incorporators and first trustees of the National Gallery. A joint resolution of Congress and a special order of President Andrew Johnson in 1867 commissioned Eastman paintings for the Capitol. Nine were completed by 1869 to hang in the room of the House Committee on Indian Affairs. In 1870 the House Committee on Military Affairs commissioned 17 pictures of forts, including Fort Jefferson in the Dry Tortugas and Fort Taylor in Key West. On August 31, 1875, Brigadier General Eastman slumped over at his easel and died.

Eighty four years later, the Smithsonian Institution produced *The Art of Seth Eastman, A Traveling Exhibition of Paintings and Drawings.* According to James McDermott, it was the first Eastman show ever assembled.

Dysentery and fever ran rampant through Fort Armistead. Nearly a dozen died. By Spring, a third of the men were feverish and disabled. The assistant surgeon suspected the drinking water. He also blamed the soldiers for habitually wading into Sarasota Bay to fish. Ironically, Eastman's sketchbook includes a pencil sketch of a cleverly suspended jug for "cooling" drinking water—out of the reach of insects.

Seth Eastman, *A monkey for cooling water. Fla. 1840.*

A somewhat mysterious Eastman oil, included in the McDermott book, depicts an identical water jar inside a tent in which a smiling Seminole chief, perhaps erroneously identified as Osceola, is guarded by a fully-uniformed Army sentry.

The Army issued a few "wall tents" to officers at Fort Armistead, but at least one penned a complaint regarding his lack of same. Perhaps the controversial tents influenced Eastman's choice of this bit of lifestyle at the post.

Seth Eastman, *Encampment of the 1st Infantry at Sarasota, Fl.* 1841.

Fort Armistead

The Second Seminole War was in its fifth year in 1840, when Captain Eastman was assigned to a new post at Sarasota Bay (at today's Indian Beach). The land still belonged exclusively to the federal government. The site stood on prehistoric Indian middens and the abandoned fish rancho of an Hispanic American. Several officers slept in a palmetto-thatched house already standing on the site, but most personnel slept in tents.

By December 10th, Eastman assumed command of the post and 332 military personnel. Civilians constructed buildings, drove mule teams and wagons, and captained vessels the Army leased. Steamers and sailboats transported everything— nails and lumber, corn and olive oil, horses and medicines, papers and pens, pasta and wines, and occasionally Commanding General Walker K. Armistead who traveled from Fort Brooke (Tampa).

Continued on page 14.

Eastman identified the deserted village on elevated ground, perhaps a hammock on a lake shore in the upper Big Cypress, where wartime forced Sam Jones's band to flee at the first sign of the approaching Army. The artist recorded an upright wooden rack for drying hides or food preparation; a mortar and pestle for grinding corn, nuts and roots; temporary homes called chickees made from readily available palm and palmetto.

Seth Eastman, *Sam Jones's Village in Florida.* 1840-1841.

Garcilasco de la Vega became one of America's earliest published writers, and *Florida of the Inca,* first published in 1605, has been characterized "the first truly American work."

LA FLORIDA
DEL INCA.
HISTORIA
DEL ADELANTADO,
HERNANDO DE SOTO,
GOVERNADOR, Y CAPITAN GENERAL
del Reino de la Florida.

Y DE OTROS HEROICOS CABALLEROS,
ESPAÑOLES, E INDIOS.
ESCRITA
POR EL INCA GARCILASO
DE LA VEGA,
CAPITAN DE SU MAGESTAD, NATURAL
de la Gran Ciudad del Cozco,
CABEÇA DE LOS REINOS, Y PROVINCIAS DEL PERÚ.
DIRIGIDA
A LA REINA
NUESTRA SEÑORA.

VAN ENMENDADAS EN ESTA IMPRESION,
muchas erratas de la Primera: Y añadida Copiosa Tabla
de las Cosas Notables.

Y EL ENSAIO CRONOLOGICO,
QUE CONTIENE, LAS SUCEDIDAS,
hasta en el Año de 1722.

CON PRIVILEGIO: En MADRID.

~~~~~~~~~~~~~~~~~~~~~~~~~~~~~~~~~~~

En la OFICINA REAL, y à Costa de NICOLAS RODRIGUEZ FRANCO, Impresor
de Libros. Año CIƆ IƆCCXXIII.
Se hallaràn en su Casa.

ENGRAVING BY JACQUES LE MOYNE DE MORGUES. SPECIAL COLLECTIONS, UNIVERSITY OF SOUTH FLORIDA

Florida warriors of the 16th century traveled waterways in massive dugouts.

Circus performers and artistic directors at work in winter quarters.

Sarasotans love their boats, at home here at the City Marina.

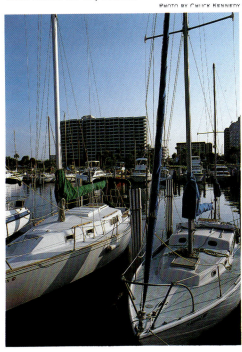

Mama and Papa Ringling started it all — five of their seven sons began a circus empire.

Felix Pinard captured Sarasota's early coastal residents in a classic pose for the photographer.

Ca' D' Zan, the showplace home of Mable and John Ringling North.

The Sarasota County Government administration building on Ringling Boulevard, 2007.

During Sarasota's first "Sara de Soto" pageant in 1916, Mayor Harry Higel presented the key to the city to I.R. Burns, who represented the great conquistadors, while Higel's daughter looked on.

Seventeen deported Seminoles arrived from the Territory of Arkansas (today's Oklahoma). Traveling with an Army officer, they were paid to pursue and negotiate with Seminole chiefs, secreted away in villages along Peas Creek (Peace River), Charlotte Harbor, and in the Big Cypress. The Oklahoma Seminoles risked their lives. Several were executed by the desperate chiefs.

General Armistead ordered the command to reconnoiter south to Charlotte Harbor, to scout on foot and on horseback and map the country. They followed an old Indian trail from the fort to Peas Creek.

By April of 1841, Fort Armistead's post returns totaled nearly 600. Another 100 Seminoles camped there. Even the famed Holata Micco, Chief Billy Bowlegs, negotiated at Sarasota Bay. But sickness overwhelmed the post and forced its abandonment. Among the stricken, Captain Seth Eastman was assigned to sick leave at Norfolk, Virginia where he recuperated several months.

One hundred twenty years later, John McDermott authored *Seth Eastman, Pictorial Historian of the Indian,* including a half dozen or so little Florida pieces. They reflect a penchant for depicting the commonplace, the lifestyle, the detail. Fort Armistead encompassed a bakehouse, a blockhouse, a guardhouse, a stockade, a hospital, a graveyard. But Eastman painted the tents—the quarters where the men grumbled and slept, gossiped and rested.

The discovery of Eastman's historic winter in Florida opens a door, a door to the earliest known visual records of the Sarasota region. The watercolors of Fort Armistead and Sam Jones's village and several pencil sketches are included here. Others have been mentioned by McDermott and may be tracked down one day.

Janet Snyder Matthews
August, 1997

PHOTO BY CHUCK KENNEDY

Preservation of this irreplaceable environment has become a priority of the 1990s in Sarasota.

Condos grace the Sarasota bayfront.

Serious suntanning, Florida style.

Roseate spoonbills.

Frederic Remington, on assignment for *Harper's Monthly* magazine, captured the essence of the local cowboys of the late 1880s.

UNIVERSITY OF SOUTH FLORIDA LIBRARY

Scene in Grounds at Mrs. Potter Palmer's Home, near Sarasota, Fla.

Perched atop an ancient Indian mound overlooking Little Sarasota Bay, Mrs. Potter Palmer's tulips and shell walkway graced the Hill Cottage, circa 1918.

PHOTO BY CHUCK KENNEDY

American egret in mating plumage.

PHOTO BY CHUCK KENNEDY

The exclusive and lovely St. Armands Circle.

16

1. The Land And Its First People

The Frenchman Le Moyne visited Florida's East Coast in the early 16th century. He depicted heavily tattooed chiefs and moss-draped maidens.

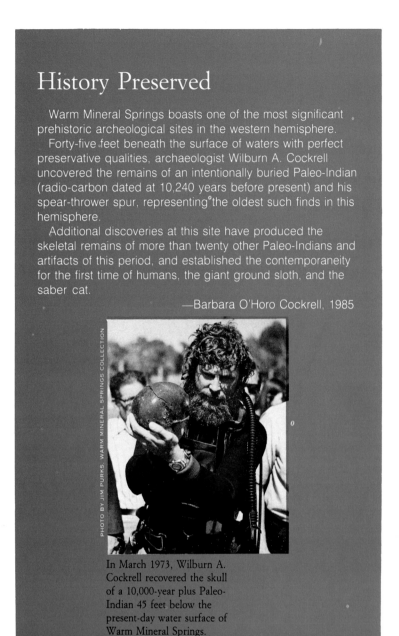

History Preserved

Warm Mineral Springs boasts one of the most significant prehistoric archeological sites in the western hemisphere.

Forty-five feet beneath the surface of waters with perfect preservative qualities, archaeologist Wilburn A. Cockrell uncovered the remains of an intentionally buried Paleo-Indian (radio-carbon dated at 10,240 years before present) and his spear-thrower spur, representing the oldest such finds in this hemisphere.

Additional discoveries at this site have produced the skeletal remains of more than twenty other Paleo-Indians and artifacts of this period, and established the contemporaneity for the first time of humans, the giant ground sloth, and the saber cat.

—Barbara O'Horo Cockrell, 1985

In March 1973, Wilburn A. Cockrell recovered the skull of a 10,000-year plus Paleo-Indian 45 feet below the present-day water surface of Warm Mineral Springs.

Fossil remains discovered at Venice were restored and exhibited at the Smithsonian Institution.

The land of Florida is a youngster compared to the rest of the United States, probably the final land mass to emerge as oceans receded and the peninsula arose millennia ago.

Each successive geological era marked the emerging plateau. Great waves once washed westerly across the entire peninsula, depositing layers of sedimentary marine limestone. The porous strata were destined, in time, to erode and dissolve in waters of another age, producing shafts for underground springs and the mysterious waterways of an aquifer beneath the soil deposited during a succeeding age.

A cross-Florida peninsular waterway (the Suwannee Straits) once flowed from the Atlantic to the Gulf. Mountainous bluffs rose up along the emerging Gulf coast. To the north, great ice sheets repeatedly formed and melted, imprinting in the strata permanent records of their forces and of flora and fauna living and breathing in the midst of change so protracted that comprehension of it overwhelms the cultural ego of modern man.

Sarasota lies within the Coastal Lowlands which ring the Florida peninsula, one of six regions formed during the geological eras. Sarasota on the Gulf coast — a "drowned coastline" — backs up to the Central Highlands region, distinguished by rolling hills punctuated by thousands of lakes. From the direction of those comparative inclines, Sarasota's waterways flow to the Gulf.

Even as Florida-the-plateau appeared above sea level, it was surrounded by a continental shelf equal to the present land area of the state. Through evolution's ages, the Gulf coast waters rose and fell, skimming shallowly across the broad shelf, a calmer version of the traumatic Atlantic coastal wave patterns — a gulf of gentler waves, fewer tides. The geological contours of inland Sarasota exhibit beach ridges, or marine terraces, formed by the wave action of previous Pleistocene (Ice Age) sea levels. These elevated former shorelines form Sarasota's only hills and ridges.

In the center of the city, at Five Points, is a Pleistocene ridge, from which a surprising incline slopes down Main Street to the bayfront. Another rises at the intersection of Cunliff Lane and Osprey Avenue, extending northerly to the area of present-day Sarasota Memorial Hospital. Another Pleistocene shoreline is apparent where the Municipal Auditorium stands high above the land sloping away to the west. Pleistocene shores probably formed the elevations of present-day Bee Ridge, Tatum Ridge, and Lockwood Ridge.

FLORIDA PHOTOGRAPHIC COLLECTION, FLORIDA STATE UNIVERSITY

Le Moyne saw Florida Indians at work tilling fields and planting crops.

Creating a Culture

The original inhabitants of the peninsula, Paleo-Indians, migrated overland from northeastern Asia about the time of the final ice sheets and receding waters of the Pleistocene period. They hunted along lakes, rivers, and sinkholes for ancient mastodon, camel, deer, and horses. Over the passage of thousands of years, as the climate changed and some of these animals were doomed to extinction, descendents of those early Ice Age hunters learned to fashion a greater variety of stone and bone weapons and came to be described as Archaic peoples. Always, they left the story of their life style — their spearpoints and knives, the bones of their victims and themselves — upon the face of the lands they trod, including Sarasota County.

These earliest Paleo-Indians lived on the land of Sarasota as long ago as 8200 B.C. Over the millennia, a series of descendant cultures occupied the region, their successions often distinguished and labeled by the mode of construction and decoration of their pottery. The archeological periods became known as Orange, Manasota, Weeden Island, and Safety Harbor.

These Ice Age descendants learned to fish the Sarasota waters, hunt wild animals in coastal forests, and gather berries and fruits produced by plants and trees which also thrived upon the once submerged land.

Near these coastal food sources, Post-Archaic period men and women built up more permanent homes — seasonal villages constructed of native materials. As centuries passed, they constructed mounds and middens upon which village complexes perched.

Sarasota's mounds and villages have been the subjects of study at Englewood, Laurel, Osprey, North Port, Verna, Old Myakka, and Harbor Acres. An imposing temple mound, constructed for ceremonial use, stood just north of present-day Whitaker Bayou and along U.S. 41. Indian mounds once lined the coast of the modern city and are responsible for the mysterious bumps and contours in many residential lawns along the bayfront and the islands.

The last mound builders of the Sarasota area, called "Tocobagas," met the Spanish *conquistadores* in the 1500s. Their domain encompassed the coastal region lying roughly between present-day Tarpon Springs and Sarasota.

On massive, pryamid-shaped temple mounds the elite of the Tocobaga chiefdom built circular houses framed in wood, the walls and roofs thatched in palmetto fronds. The common folk lived at lower levels near garden plots and on smaller shell middens. The mounds and middens provided dry escapes from seasonal rains, as well as lookout stations. From the heights, smoke from signal fires could be seen for miles.

A ceremonial moment among Florida's early people, as depicted by Le Moyne, included a 16th century Venus in her sedan chair.

Like their forefathers, the Tocobagas were expert fishermen. They learned to hollow out the giant Florida cypress trees for dugouts. Near the shore, they built rock enclosures to trap fish at low tide. They wove fishnets of grass and spears of cane. They hunted manatees with pikes, alligators with spears and clubs, and went after deer armed with powerful bows and arrows. Their martial skills were to frighten Europe's best-equipped soldiers, and the spearpoints they fashioned of fishbone or sharpened cane penetrated the Spaniards' shirts of mail. Their arrows were equal in power and accuracy to European crossbows.

The Tocobagas considered man's spirit to be apparent in his shadow, in the pupil of his eye, and in his mirror image. The villagers buried the bones of their dead after the flesh was removed, bundling the bones together and burying them with the skulls and prized possessions in a special burial mound. Villagers fasted four days before the burial of a chief, whom they thought to be divinely guided.

Since the language of the Tocobagas was not written and, in fact, varied from chiefdom to chiefdom, the temple mounds, middens, and burial mounds would one day become the record of their culture. Built over centuries, they contained massive amounts of shells as well as the remains of game and fish dinners, the pits of berries, bones of birds, and broken pieces of pottery. The Tocobaga villagers moved their cooking fires and camps from one spot to another as the refuse piles grew. Later, when the explorers from Europe arrived, beads, mirrors, iron tools, and trinkets became part of the mounds.

The Tocobagas pulled their hair high into pompadours. They wore no clothing, but tattooed their bodies with dyes and ornamented themselves with jewelry of bone, shell, or fish bladders. Skilled artisans, they shaped clay into useful

A circle of fire, set by Florida's indigenous people, the Timucua Indians, allowed them to trap and kill game.

The Indians barbecued fish and game.

containers, worked wood into benches, boxes, totem poles, and plaques, and made farming tools from shells and stone. They learned to cure and paint beautiful cloak-deerskins which were much admired by the Europeans. They fashioned pearl necklaces and bracelets prized by powerful chiefs.

The various Tocobaga villages paid allegiance to one or more powerful chiefs. One inland chief was reportedly located in the fertile, higher inland area they called Ocale, and the local people may have migrated to and from Ocala. They also had contact with Indians of the south peninsula and as far away as the Bahama banks.

The Tocobagas were often at odds with the fierce Calusas to the south in the Charlotte Harbor region and waged war with neighboring chiefdoms. They sometimes "trophied" their victims — returning victorious to their villages where they hung the limbs and scalps from posts. Others of their vanquished they captured as slaves and brought home alive. They also killed hapless Europeans whose ships were driven ashore in the shallow Gulf during storms, sometimes in ceremonial sacrifices.

But in spite of their fierceness, the local Indian peoples were destined for destruction. When the Europeans arrived in the sixteenth century, they found the Floridians powerful and populous. But within two centuries, they would be decimated and destitute, doomed by an awesome conflict of cultures. Their strength was sapped by slavery and warfare and, far more importantly, by disease and imported intestinal microparasites, invisible carriers of sweeping epidemics and death.

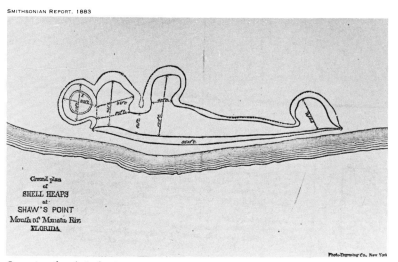

Centuries after their demise, the Indian mound builders' creations remained objects of curiosity for newcomers to Florida.

2. The Spanish Crown

The ordeal of Juan Ortiz, the Spanish slave held among the local Ocita Indians, was the forerunner of later legendary colonial American scenarios.

Bartolomé de Las Casas became Spain's most outspoken crusader against slavery of the New World peoples. He published works throughout Europe regarding the "Black Legend," holding the Spanish responsible for the deaths of multitudes of New World peoples, sealing, he claimed, the doom of the Spanish empire.

AN
ACCOUNT

Of the First

VOYAGES and DISCOVERIES

Made by the SPANIARDS in *America*.

Containing

The most Exact Relation hitherto publish'd, of their unparallel'd Cruelties on the *Indians*, in the destruction of above Forty Millions of People.

With the Propositions offer'd to the King of *Spain*, to prevent the further Ruin of the *West-Indies*.

By *Don Bartholomew de las Casas*, Bishop of *Chiapa*, who was an Eye-witness of their Cruelties.

Illustrated with Cuts.

Mural at Warm Mineral Springs depicts Ponce de León's fatal wound suffered in battle with west coast Indians.

When Christopher Columbus landed at Hispaniola in the fall of 1492, he set patterns which were to influence successive ventures of the Spanish crown. Columbus, empowered as a representative of the crown, operated with great authority over the land he claimed for Spain. Because he thought he had discovered a new route to India, the islands became the "Indies" and the New World people "Indians." He took some of the "Indians," whom he considered heathen, as slaves.

The Spanish rulers, Isabella and Ferdinand, were concerned for the souls of these primitive people and decreed that leaders who followed Columbus to the New World would present the Indians with a choice between Christianity or their own faith. Those who accepted Christianity were to be treated as subjects of the crown; those who refused were to be treated as enemies of the faith, and therefore not entitled to the protection accorded subjects.

Although enslavement of Indians was officially prohibited, Spanish colonial labor practices in mines and plantations from Hispaniola to the West Indies, Honduras, Peru, and Mexico, were exploitative of riches and people. As the matter of subjugation, virtual enslavement, and widespread death of New World people continued to vex the crown, the controversy resulted in a formal debate between the best and brightest of Europe.

But Sarasota's New World people saw only the intent and strength of invaders. Natives of the coast apparently had had contact with slavehunters long before first recorded contacts. When Ponce de León arrived on the Gulf coast near Charlotte Harbor in 1521, he found instantly hostile Calusas, a few of whom reportedly spoke words in Spanish. Ponce de León himself died from wounds inflicted by the Gulf coast warriors.

Nevertheless, the riches rumored to lie in La Florida *inspired the crown to enter into a series of ventures to colonize.*

Pánfilo de Narváez

Pánfilo de Narváez, the son of Spanish colonials in Cuba, was the first to strike a mutually attractive deal with the crown and to reach local shores. Appointed by Charles V to become sixth governor of *La Florida*, the experienced *conquistador* landed in the Tampa Bay region on Thursday before Good Friday, 1528. Though he had started out from Spain with 600 colonists and military troops, his forces had been reduced by desertion and a hurricane during the previous winter in Cuba. His 400 expeditioners in five vessels were blown ashore prematurely by storm winds from the north coast of Cuba and arrived in a precarious state, with neither interpreter nor knowledge of a safe port for their vessels. Their main supply ship still awaited them in Havana.

Although Narváez was the first chronicled European to visit the region which includes Sarasota, when he reached local shores in 1528 he learned, as had Ponce de León, that he was not the first European to make contact with the Indians of this coast. He found them immediately wary, fierce, and strong. Visiting a village with his men, he discovered the remains of Europeans, wrapped in painted deerskins, in boxes which had been manufactured in Spain. The Indians maintained that the victims had been forced ashore by shipwreck.

Narváez exercised his royally delegated authority. In rapid order, he hoisted flags to claim the land for the Spanish crown and forced the Indians to submission, insisting they direct the way to supplies of food for his hungry expedition. His show of force included execution of the mother of the local chief. Narváez ordered her thrown to the ferocious war dogs, trained Spanish greyhounds. He also ordered punitive mutilation of the chief, Hirrihigua. Narváez had the unfortunate leader's nose severed from his face.

Narváez also demanded to know the whereabouts of gold. The local people repeatedly let Narváez and his officers know that the local villages had no gold and directed them to a distant village they called Apalachee, far to the north. They glowingly described that place as loaded with gold, just what the Spaniards had come so far to find. Narváez led his men overland with inadequate food supplies and ordered his vessels to sail up the coast in search of a port where they might rejoin forces.

By summer, Narváez and his men had reached the vicinity of present-day St. Marks River in the panhandle. Though they routinely plundered the Indian villages for maize, the expedition was reduced to near starvation, beaten down by the continued attacks of skilled Indian marksmen and weaked by sicknesses. In desperation they built escape vessels from wood cut in the surrounding forests and iron from their meager expeditionary stores, as well as the hair and hides of their horses which they butchered for food.

Narváez and his skeleton force set out along the Gulf coast in five clumsy boats bound for Mexico. Only four men survived to reach that Spanish stronghold after a struggle lasting eight years.

Hernando de Soto

A famous, rich conquistador, descended from generations of Iberian nobility, became the next to try Florida for Spain. His expedition was spectacular, a splendid force of Spain's elite, augmented by skilled artisans, numerous servants and associates, and arrayed in the finest equipage. Gulf coast history was destined to sparkle a little more because of the legendary expedition of Hernando De Soto.

Only a decade after the disastrous Narváez expedition, De Soto had returned to Spain after twenty years of successful conquests in Panama, Nicaragua, and with Francisco Pizarro in Peru. He petitioned the crown for a contract *(asiento)* for his own expedition to a New World territory, requesting the region north of Pizarro's contract. Instead, Charles V offered him a contract for *La Florida,* encompassing the territory far north of present-day Florida and extending as far west as the Rio Grande.

Meanwhile, another veteran of New World missions appeared at court with an exciting piece of intelligence. Cabeza de Vaca, an officer who had amazingly survived the Narváez expedition to reach Mexico, would divulge his information about Florida only in private audience with the king. Such mystery only heightened interest in De Soto's contract, and an unusual number of investors and soldiers hurried to join the expedition. It was a sellout. Many were turned away.

The royal contract set out precise responsibilities for both parties. De Soto was required to sponsor a fleet and to purchase provisions for his army for a year and a half. As governor of Florida and Cuba, he was granted authority to appoint and pay salaries to judicial and military officers. De Soto himself was to receive a salary from the king, taken from profits made on Florida finds. He was personally granted official titles and privileges in Florida and allowed to import into Cuba 200 slaves duty-free. In return, he was to establish stone fortresses and colonies in Florida and see to evangelizing the heathen. The king was obligated to supply horses and equipment, arms and munitions, and 500 men. His royal share was to be 50 percent of the treasure discovered in graves or temples, and a sixth of the general loot. Officers and accountants of the king were to accompany the expedition, as were members of the clergy who would spread the message of Christianity among the Indians.

Within a year from the granting of the *asiento,* De Soto had purchased and generously outfitted seven vessels. With his bride, Doña Isabel de Bobadilla, and their personal entourage, he prepared to sail on the annual New World voyage of the Spanish fleet with an expeditionary force numbering more than 700.

As the entire twenty-ship fleet sailed out of the harbor of San Lúcar in spring 1538 amid great celebration and fanfare, De Soto commanded from the flagship, the 800-ton *San Cristobal.*

After a voyage of 5,000 miles and eight weeks, the fleet arrived safety at Santiago de Cuba, the base for final preparations. Fall and winter passed while the large army and investors conducted business, including the acquisition of horses and perishable commodities for the Florida expedition. De Soto sent out a reconnoitering party under the command of his officer and the king's accountant, Juan Añasco. Añasco was charged with locating a safe Florida port for the fleet and an Indian village to accommodate the army. When he returned, mission accomplished, Añasco brought along Indians he had captured on the coast, Indians who told the Spaniards that there was indeed gold in Florida.

De Soto's fleet finally departed Havana in mid-May 1538, Doña Isabel remaining behind with her entourage and the other officers' wives. As the fleet set sail for the north and what seemed a promising future, she retained power of attorney to act on her husband's behalf in business interests.

On Sunday, May 25, after a voyage of seven days, the fleet sighted the entrance to the large bay chosen by Añasco (southwest passage, Tampa Bay). Beyond the pass, they saw the Indian villages. The commander faced the not inconsiderable challenge of maneuvering his fleet to the chosen landing place (probably present-day Shaw's Point on the Manatee River). Five days passed while headway was laboriously made through the shallow, sandy-bottomed pass.

Inside the broad bay, the coast lay before them in a parade of beaches, mangrove-lined shores backed by virgin forests. Indian mound villages rose up, smoke signals occasionally lined the horizons. The signal smoke was the only evidence of man, for no Indians came forth to greet them. The Indians had learned their lessons well. They knew the ways of the invaders and all the arrival of their great sailing vessels presaged. The villagers and their chiefs relayed messages and waited warily.

Like Narváez before him, De Soto hoped the cities of gold lay where the Indians indicated. Six weeks after landing, he struck out for the rolling hill country to the north and east, toward the rich and fertile lands of Ocale, and wrote of his high hopes to officials in Cuba. A small party stayed behind to mind the gardens and keep the peace with Indian allies.

The Indian peoples of the Tampa-Manatee-Sarasota region were not destined to host these Spaniards for long, but their lives were to be forever changed. The formidable strength and great populations of these people were to begin a period of decline. Anthropologists use the second year of the De Soto expedition to mark "the end of the prehistoric aboriginal period in the Southeast."

De Soto died of fever three years after he arrived in Florida and was buried in the river he had called Rio Grande (the Mississippi). Like the men of the Narváez expedition, the once resplendent force under De Soto was reduced to wearing skins and struggling for survival.

The old wooden marker stood on Longboat Key to commemorate the 1538 arrival of De Soto's advance reconnaisance of the coast under expedition officer Juan Añasco.

Hernando de Soto.

A 16th century galleon, typical of the transports that carried the famous Spanish expeditions across the Atlantic.

The conquest of the New World was romanticized in some literature, often depicting the conquered as willing subjects of the noble Spanish conquistadors, over whose helmeted, plumed heads angels hovered smiling down from heavenly realms.

Bishop Bartolomé de Las Casas worked with Father Luis Cancer de Barbastro to organize a peaceful mission to convert Florida's Indians.

Father Luís Cáncer de Barbastro

The next chapter in the arrival of Spain to her land of *La Florida* occurred ten years later and was very different from the splendid arrival of De Soto. This effort was to be peaceful rather than warlike, humble rather than proud, and single-mindedly devout. The expedition was the result of the heartfelt conviction of Spanish priests that the peoples of Florida deserved more than they were getting, that a mission to bring the word of God was overdue.

The influential Bishop Bartolomé de Las Casas worked with Dominican fathers for several years to gather support and funding for such a mission. In Spain, Las Casas, who had devoted his life to the causes of New World peoples, laid plans together with Father Luís Cáncer de Barbastro who was working among colonies in the New World and who had been involved in a permanent mission in Guatemala. For several years, letters were carried to both sides of the ocean by the annual fleets.

When at last all was in order, in 1549, the king sent an order to the Viceroy of Mexico to outfit a ship and personnel for an evangelical mission to be established in a part of Florida not yet visited by a Spanish military expedition. The priests felt that their best hope for success lay with Indians whose hearts and minds were receptive, unblemished by hatred and revenge.

Accordingly, the ship *Santa María de la Encina* set out in spring 1549 for Cuba from the mission at Vera Paz, Mexico. Aboard with Father Cáncer were Fathers Gregorio de Beteta, Dominic de Santa María, Juan Garcia, Juan de Peñalosa, and lay brother Diego de Fuentes. In Cuba, the mission acquired an interpreter, an Indian woman of the Gulf coast who had arrived in Cuba as a result of the De Soto expedition. She was a converted Christian whom the priests called Magdalena.

Under Captain Juan de Arana and his crew, the unarmed caravel made its way up the coast. Off the coast of present-day Clearwater, the beauty of the shore compelled a few sailors to take the ship's small sailboat (*chalupa*) and head for land. As they approached, Indians appeared. The sailors panicked and headed back, shouting "Indios! Indios!"

On a venture ashore on May 30, the priests carried trinkets for the Indians, who embraced them enthusiastically and knelt with the priests in prayer. Through their interpreter, Magdalena, the priests learned that they were only a short distance from the village of the chief, the same one which had been occupied by De Soto.

When it was time to return to the ship, the Indians refused to release Magdalena, Father Peñalosa, and Brother Fuentes. Others returned to the *chalupa* with Father Cáncer for presents of shirts and food. One Indian sailed back to the *Santa María* with the priest for more.

Returning again to shore, the priest could not see the members of his party — only a few Indians who swam out with fish to trade. Taking with them a sailor who had waded ashore, the Indians departed into the forest. Next day, Fathers Cáncer and Gregorio returned to the spot, but found no one and decided to go on to the chief's village.

Nearly two weeks passed while captain and crew maneuvered their deep-draft caravel into the bay and toward the Indian village, finally anchoring miles off the shallow shore. In the third week of June, Fathers Cáncer and Garcia went ashore for water and celebrated mass on Florida shores. In time, a crowd of Indians appeared asking for shirts and machetes. Some appeared hostile during the exchanges. One insisted upon receiving the priest's cross, kissed it, and held it for others to kiss. Among the group, the priests recognized Magadalena, who was now naked. She called to them that the missing clerics were at the chief's house. She told them that the Indians had initially thought the missionaries were part of an armada, but she had convinced them that there were four priests and that they had come solely to teach "the things of heaven." She added that half a hundred Indians had gathered.

To indicate kindness and good will, Father Cáncer returned to the *Santa María* for more gifts. The Indians once again eagerly accepted presents and demanded more. Agreeing to meet the Indians again next day, Father Cáncer returned, much encouraged, to the ship.

Once aboard, he suffered the shock of a terrible truth. In his absence, a slave of the Indians — a Spaniard captured ten years previously during the De Soto expedition — had escaped by canoe to the vessel. His name was Juan Muñoz, and he spoke the dialect fluently. Muñoz brought news that the Indians had killed both clerics and were holding the sailor for a slave.

Father Cáncer was still determined to win the hearts of the savages. Even if no one would accompany him, he would go ashore to do that for which he had come.

The caravel's sailors threatened mutiny. Food supplies were perilously low, fevers were running through the crew. Muñoz feared for his own life, wanted only to escape, and refused to serve as interpreter for Father Cáncer. Fathers Gregorio and Dominic wanted to try again, but in a new location. However, their superior was adamant and optimistic. His mind made up, the priest worked on his report to the Viceroy of Mexico, penning carefully the events of this Florida mission.

After several unsuccessful tries, Father Cáncer was taken ashore on the morning of June 26 by a crew of sailors, accompanied by Father Gregorio and Muñoz. As the party neared land, they spotted Indian lookouts in the trees. Reaching the beach of the Indian village, they saw the Indians heavily armed with bows and arrows, clubs and darts, and obviously agitated. They were insisting on the return of their slave, Muñoz.

Despite the pleas of his brother to reconsider, the priest slipped over the gunwale into waist-deep water and waded ashore. In the midst of the Indians, he knelt and prayed, raising a hand toward heaven. Then he arose and walked toward the mound. A single villager embraced him and took him by the arm. Other Indians roughly hustled the priest up the side of the mound, slapping his hat from his head, and began to club him. As the blows sent him to the ground, the Indians continued their attack. The party aboard the *chalupa,* able to hear and see all, set sail for the ship, while Indians ran to shore firing arrows after them.

The caravel reached Mexico in mid-July. Father Gegorio de Beteta completed the fallen priest's report and submitted it to the Viceroy of Mexico, a first-hand testimony of a sincere and costly effort to evangelize the Floridians without force.

Pedro Menéndez de Avilés,
Adelantado de la Florida,
Comendador de Santa Cruz de
la Zarza, Orden de Santiago.

Pedro Menéndez de Avilés

Two decades after Father Cáncer's martyrdom, another major Spanish effort was made to establish a colony in the region. This one was a mixture of armed force and godly intent, a composite of the legendary figure of Pedro Menéndez de Avilés, the king's general of the Armada of the Indies and the founder of St. Augustine.

After establishing that fortress on the Atlantic coast, Menéndez turned his attention to the Gulf coast, beginning with the Indians of present-day Charlotte Harbor, where he met with Carlos, chief of the Calusas. The two leaders agreed upon establishment of a Spanish Christian mission at the chief's village (thought to be present-day Mound Island in Estero Bay).

Menéndez was convinced of the existence of a cross-Florida waterway linking the St. Johns River and St. Augustine to the Gulf. He wanted alliance with the coastal peoples in order to discover the waterway's opening and protect it for Spanish traffic. Chief Carlos assured Menéndez that such a waterway existed to the north. Menéndez convinced Carlos to accompany a Spanish detachment to ally the people of the Tampa Bay region, headed by the powerful leader Tocobaga, or Tocobaga Chile.

On a moonless night in March 1567, Menéndez, Carlos, and Spanish soldiers sailed quietly along the coast aboard dugouts guided by a Calusa Indian. The convoy reached Tocobaga's village and Menéndez met with the powerful chief, who was able to assemble 1,500 subchiefs in only two days. For an interpreter, Menéndez enlisted the services of Hernándo Escalante Fontaneda, a Spaniard held by Carlos as a slave since his shipwreck as a 13-year-old schoolboy.

An alliance was agreed upon, and when he departed, Menéndez left behind 30 Spanish soldiers to begin a second Gulf coast colony and keep the peace.

In January of the following winter, a priest assigned to the missions, Father Rogel, sailed into the region from Havana with critically needed provisions. Accompanied by a nephew of Menéndez, the priest was surprised neither to see nor hear any sign of life in the village as they approached. Once in the village, the party discovered two recently murdered Spanish soldiers and subsequently learned that all the others had also been killed by the Indians. In a report to officials in Havana, the priest blamed food shortages and lusty, abusive Spanish soldiers. He recommended that future missions enlist the services of married men accompanied by their wives.

Both Gulf coast missions existed amid traumatic events, and then only briefly. That among the Calusas lasted the longer of the two, but did not survive through 1569. While the culture of the coastal peoples experienced a slower demise, extending over several centuries, by the eighteenth century it virtually had become extinct.

STATE PHOTOGRAPHIC COLLECTION

Theodore de Bry Leod's beautifully engraved 1594 map of western America reveals how little the Spaniards knew about Florida a century after Columbus started the ball rolling in his *Nuevo Mundo*.

3. An American Outpost In Indian Country

Daguerrotype of Holata Micco (Chief Billy Bowlegs) which appeared in the London *Illustrated News* in 1840, only months before the Seminole chief conferred with the base commander at Fort Armistead. Posing with the elusive chief: left to right, Sarparkee Yohola, Fasatchee Emathla, John Jumper, Abraham the interpreter, Holata Micco, Chocote Tustenuggee.

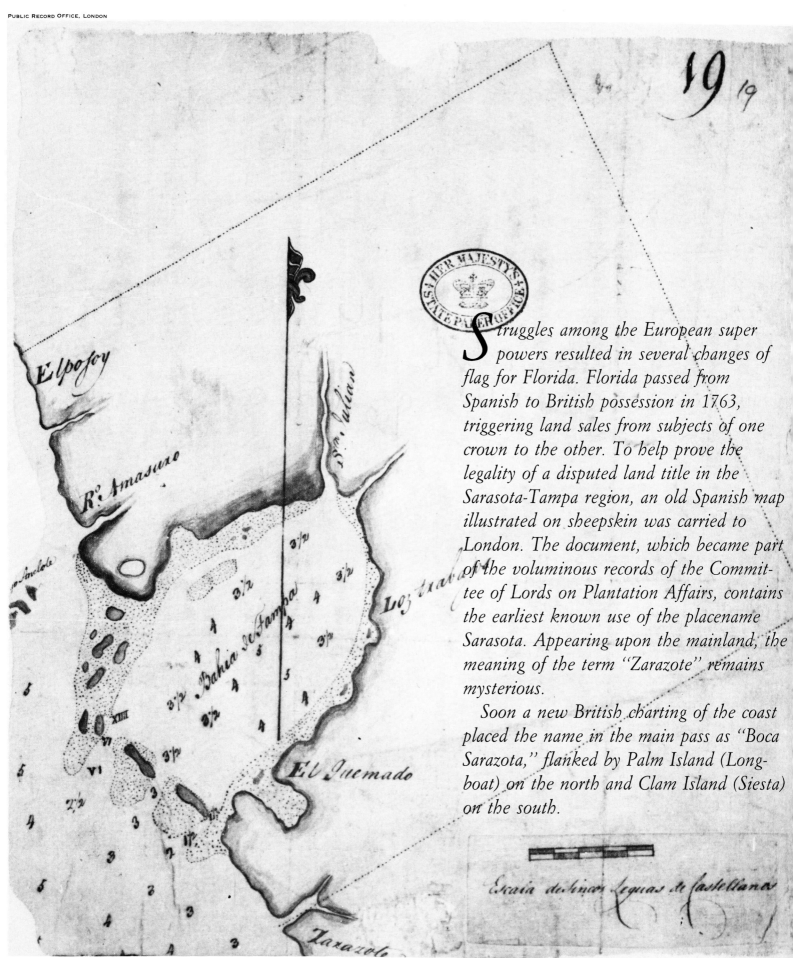

Struggles among the European super powers resulted in several changes of flag for Florida. Florida passed from Spanish to British possession in 1763, triggering land sales from subjects of one crown to the other. To help prove the legality of a disputed land title in the Sarasota-Tampa region, an old Spanish map illustrated on sheepskin was carried to London. The document, which became part of the voluminous records of the Committee of Lords on Plantation Affairs, contains the earliest known use of the placename Sarasota. Appearing upon the mainland, the meaning of the term "Zarazote" remains mysterious.

Soon a new British charting of the coast placed the name in the main pass as "Boca Sarazota," flanked by Palm Island (Longboat) on the north and Clam Island (Siesta) on the south.

One of the earliest uses of the word Sarasota appears as Zarazote on a Spanish map found in London.

Rancho life on the bay

Though debate raged an ocean away, daily life along distant, wild Sarasota bays continued unaffected, the Gulf having become the traditional home of seasonal fishermen. Each fall, a congenial group arrived from such population centers as Havana to the shores around Sarasota and Tampa bays and Charlotte Harbor. Their fish camps, or *ranchos,* dotted the shores. The clustered houses, circular and palmetto thatched, usually perched atop Indian mounds, former villages of the Tocobagas.

On the wild coast so removed from markets, the fishermen cultivated fields in which they planted garden crops — corn, squash, melon, sweet potatoes, peas, beans, tomatoes, and herbs. From distant homes, they brought citrus and peaches and set out trees.

The *ranchos* remained in operation until the last of the seasonal runs of the great schools of mullet through the bays, usually in late spring. Using salt purchased in bulk in Havana, the fishermen pressed and brine-cured split mullet as the commercial staple, although the catches included pompano, carp, turtle, sole, trout, and drum. They used burned corn cobs to smoke-cure roe and stacked the cured fish in storage houses. When a full cargo was prepared and loaded aboard the *rancho* schooner, a fisherman and crew set sail for Havana, where the market was particularly receptive during the lenten season.

The fishermen were Spanish-speaking natives of Spain, Cuba, the Canaries, and other Caribbean islands. They were usually illiterate, their schooling restricted to the unlettered language of the sea and its resources. The Gulf was their highway, its coastal shores their community, its Indians (recently immigrated Seminoles, a British corruption of the Spanish word *cimarron* , or "wild") became their hired laborers, their winter companions, and the mothers of their children. The mixed-blood families increased and multiplied among the fisheries.

Though the industry appeared lucrative, changing governments paid little attention. Even under surveyor George Gauld, who was hired by John Perceval, second Earl of Egmont, to chart the coast, the fisheries did not command great attention. Bernard Romans, a later surveyor of British Florida, estimated that the fishermen's numbers approached 400 and their base export totaled at least a thousand tons. Romans recommended regulation of the industry to better tax advantage by Britain, but his employers apparently perceived more compelling colonial demands for their administration.

By 1783, when Florida reverted to Spain, a handful of major *ranchos* appeared on a chart commissioned under a Spanish naval officer to indicate prominent features of the coast. These established operations were joined by additional *ranchos,* some before 1810.

Sarasota Bay attracted a handful of the fishermen, who built homes and planted fields in little settlements with names like Angola and Oyster Bay. Antonio Gomez arrived in 1812 and established his *rancho* at the northeast end of the bay. Jose Maria Godoya settled in the same year with his family on land he cleared himself, and was joined within six years by Pedro Jose Artiaga. On either side of the Oyster River (perhaps at Whitaker or Hudson bayous) lay the fish camps of Jose and Joaquin Caldes. Jose, on the north side of the river, arrived in 1814. On the south side, Joaquin and his family were cultivating their spot by 1812. Both the Caldes men referred to their location as Angola. North of Oyster Bay lay the *rancho* of Andrew Gonzales, his wife, and four children.

All six fishermen were well-acquainted with the other fishermen located on islands in the mouths of Tampa Bay and Charlotte Harbor. The circle formed a distinctive Gulf coast community, and when Florida's flags changed a final time, from Spain to the United States in 1821, each of the Sarasota men claimed ownership of 640 acres.

The fisheries continued their progress under the American government. In 1831, when the question of tax revenues arose once again, the customs collector at Key West, young William Whitehead, was sent to personally assess the situation. Whitehead was amicably disposed toward the industry and its fishermen, especially Jose Caldes, who then operated a fishery at Caldes Island (Useppa) in Charlotte Harbor. Whitehead praised the rancho coffee, observed its quaint houses, barking dogs, naked children, and Indian wives, and informed the U.S. Department of Treasury that the traditional industry should be permitted to continue without interruption.

Perhaps the largest, most lucrative fishery was established by an American, a former Baltimore sea captain named William Bunce, first at the mouth of the Manatee River, then at Palm Island. The complex produced an annual net income of $6,000 and included approximately 40 houses, a store, boat houses, spacious storage houses, and fields. Bunce employed Seminoles and fishermen with Indian families. The life style of the mixed-blood people was uniquely adapted to the coastal fishing communities, but as the American government began to extend itself into its new southern wilderness, the tension increased between Americanized interests and the Indians. The fishery people complained about lack of protection and, on occasion, asked the military for help against Indian raids upon their range cattle.

The remarkable Juan Gomez, a coastal fisherman, lived more than 100 years. His name appears on Fort Armistead records of civilian employees.

Model of the 30- to 40-ton *Emma M. Lowe,* a typical 1830s fishing smack.

A slave named Luis

In December 1835, the tension between the Americans and Indians culminated in events which triggered a war.

At Sarasota Bay, a 30-year-old slave named Luis operated a trading post at the *rancho* of the Pacheco family, traditional fishermen. The son of full-blooded African slaves, Luis was considered most valuable. Intelligent and educated, he read and wrote in four languages, knew the Indian dialect, and was a carpenter, a trade practiced by his father before him.

Around Christmas, the Army hired Luis to serve as interpreter for what was to be a routine march from Army headquarters at Fort Brooke (Tampa) to Fort King (Ocala).

Summoned by his mistress, Señora Pacheco, Luis arrived at Fort Brooke two days before Christmas, 1835. There he was instructed to set out on the road to Fort King to catch up with Major Francis Langhorne Dade, a proud, 43-year-old career officer. Dade's command had marched out that afternoon, waiting neither for its interpreter nor reinforcements which were due in from Key West.

Late that same night, Luis caught up with the command, 100 enlisted soldiers and eight officers. During the next few days, he was sent forward to check the trail for signs of Seminoles. He found more than a few, including a death threat in the form of a cow slaughtered in the road. The warning was disregarded. In fact, the command was so

Coastal expeditions of the Second Seminole War involved the joint operations of marines, sailors and soldiers in swamps and coastal waterways in search of elusive Seminoles.

The sloop of war U.S.S. *Vandalia* defended local waters during the Second Seminole War.

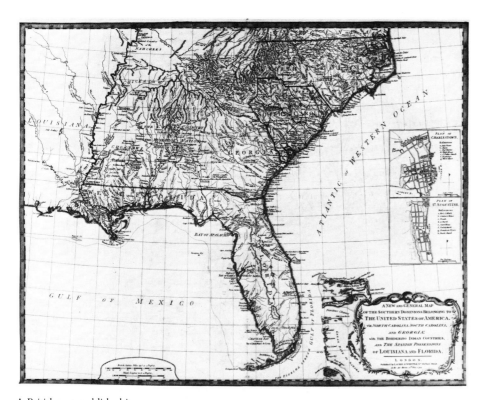

A British map published in London in 1794, representing the two colonies — East and West Florida — during Florida's 20-year British period.

The Second Seminole War brought the 100-ton U.S. *Concord* to local waters in April 1836, only months after the Dade command was ambushed between Fort Brooke and Fort King.

A fort for one season

Dade's Massacre, as it came to be called, and Osceola's corresponding ambush at Fort King triggered the outbreak of Florida's Second Seminole War, which lasted a long seven years. The war brought great numbers of troops to Tampa Bay. Hundreds of Americans and immigrants were introduced to coastal hammocks and swamps over which they trod upon crude trails or aboard a miscellany of marine craft. Revenue cutters and new-fangled steamers were pressed into duty.

Spanish fishermen routinely guided the military forces into mysterious, shallow coastal waterways in search of Indian war parties and hidden camps. But in 1838, the army did an incredible about-face at the Bunce *rancho* when General Thomas Jesup ordered the capture of all the fishery people who had *any* Indian blood and immediate deportation to Arkansas Territory with a waiting group of Indians. The fishermen, away at the time, returned to find their families missing. In dismay they protested to Washington. The petition was answered by Secretary of War Joel Poinsett, who indicated that only at the close of hostilities might the families be returned. But Thomas Jesup, who maintained that the people had been antagonistic to his Indian policies, had administered the coup de grace.

The highwater mark in military excitement during the Second Seminole War at Sarasota Bay came in the war's final years, during the winter of 1840-41. The commanding General of the Army of Florida, Brevet Brigadier General Walker K. Armistead, established a coastal post closer to the Indian villages and camps extending along Peas (Peace) Creek and south to hideaways in the Big Cypress Swamp south of the Caloosahatchee. The post was to be Armistead's new southern division headquarters for the Army of Florida.

Accordingly, Zachary Taylor's First Infantry under Major Greenleaf Dearborn proceeded with companies in fall 1840 from Fort Brooke to Sarasota Bay. In early November, Dearborn's command embarked upon a steamer and two days later reached its destination, the *rancho* of Manuel

relaxed that advance and rear guards marched dangerously near the main body, and one drizzling, cold morning some men buttoned their overcoats over their ammunition packets.

On the sixth day of the march, the morning of December 28, the command crossed the Withlacoochee River. Three miles beyond the river the trail entered the flat open spaces of inland pine country south of Fort King (the present-day Dade City area). Luis and an officer, Captain Fraser, had dropped back to check out a lone grey horse by the side of the road. Finding nothing of interest, they were returning to the advance guard when the Sarasota slave heard a single shot. Major Dade called out "My God!" as he drew his hand to his chest, then toppled from his horse. Suddenly the air was filled with gunfire. An Indian ambush had been set loose by the signal shot fired by Seminole Chief Micanopy at the commanding officer. Survivors fumbled to reach ammunition and load weapons, while about them fully half the command lay at their feet.

Luis fell to the base of a tree in a vain search for cover. The entire advance guard had been felled and he was caught in crossfire. In terror, he beat his head against the tree and prayed.

One young warrior raised his rifle to kill the slave, but was stopped by an old Indian who commanded, "Don't kill him." Another group was restrained by the son of Chief Jumper, who ordered, "That's a black man. He is not his own master. Don't kill him." A third time the slave prevented another Indian executioner by insisting that the chief's son had ordered him spared. One, who promised to return and kill him, was shot in the ensuing fray.

Luis was taken back to the cabin of a black slave of the Indians. When news spread of his survival, it was claimed among the Indians that he had supernatural powers, that he had made himself invisible, for they had sworn to leave no one living.

Chief Osceola, who was destined to become the single most celebrated warrior of that long war, told Luis, "You are a lucky Negro. . . . We Indians claim to save no one."

BY KEN HUGHES. © 1976 MATTHEWS

Luis Pacheco, a slave at the Sarasota Bay trading post of Antonio Pacheco, miraculously survived the Dade Massacre.

Andrew P. Canova wrote of the Seminole War in his book *Adventures in South Florida*. The militiaman wrote colorfully of comrades whose homes were early Sarasota Bay settlements.

Fort Brooke, circa 1837, served as a supply depot for forts later established at Sarasota Bay, Manatee River and Charlotte Harbor.

Olivella, a Spanish fisherman and Clerk of Circuit Court for Hillsborough County.

The Sarasota post was situated on the mainland north of present-day Whitaker Bayou and had been the site of historic fisheries. Along the shore, on terrain marked by bluffs and aboriginal Indian mounds, the First Infantry set about its business. A blockhouse, bakehouse, and guard house quickly rose up amid a village of Army-requisitioned tents.

Detachments were sent inland and by steamer to Charlotte Harbor to find Indians. Their mission was to pressure the Seminoles into surrender and deport them to the reserved lands west of the Mississippi. The Sarasota post became one of the Florida bases from which Indian "delegates" from Arkansas Territory attempted to find their brothers to sell them on the wondrous life there.

To operate its fortification, the Army hired carpenters, sailors, wagon drivers and teamsters. Some were Spanish fishermen, others were newcomers to the coast or new immigrants to America. Sailboats and steamers were often leased from private owners, as traffic came and went from the landing. During the winter, the post rolls showed several hundred men. By April, the population had reached an all-time high of 600 soldiers and 100 Indians waiting deportation.

Though the location proved effective for contact with Indian camps, fevers and dysentery ran rampant. Often the numbers of sick nearly equaled those who were hale. The post quartermaster hired a crew of civilians to build a hospital. Within seven months, a dozen soldiers had died. Others had been taken to the hospital at Fort Brooke. Reluctantly, General Armistead ordered the post evacuated in May.

Fort Armistead became a wooden silence. The gardens soundlessly went to seed. Boards bleached in the sun. The stockade, hospital, blockhouse, guardhouse, bakehouse, graves and markers, pipes and buckles, buttons and beads — all that was Fort Armistead — slowly settled into the earth. Its very existence was rarely mentioned, then forgotten, as years passed by and those who remembered were gone.

Frontier Defenses

At the outbreak of the Third Seminole War, the local frontier people found themselves vulnerable in the extreme. Typically living on isolated lands, they were forced for safety to "cluster" together in the areas of concentrated population. Accordingly, State Senator Hamlin Snell and Bill and Mary Jane Whitaker and their young child left Sarasota Bay, camping for many months with other families at the Manatee River in Dr. Branch's "fort," buildings intended for use as a sanitarium.

Sarasota and Manatee politicians and citizens of influence petitioned friends in government to send more troops to drive the Indians out of Florida. Sarasotan Hamlin Valentine Snell, president of the Senate, took pen in hand to describe the situation to the powers that be:

"Our settlement consists of about one hundred and twenty whites, and about three hundred slaves, but from the plantations and settlements being on both sides of the river, which is a mile or more wide, it is impossible for the citizens to afford to each other that protection which would be necessary in case of attack."

—Senator Hamlin Valentine Snell

PAINTING ATTRIBUTED TO JAMES R. LAMBDIN, NATIONAL PORTRAIT GALLERY, SMITHSONIAN INSTITUTION

General Zachary Taylor, "Old Rough and Ready," headed the First Infantry, U.S. Army, headquartered at Sarasota Bay in 1840-41 at Fort Armistead.

Whitaker children, circa 1880.

4. Cowboys And Indians

Captain Isaac Alderman Redd, circa 1850, a veteran of Florida wars. Redd settled inland when open cattle ranges stretched toward the Myakka River valley.

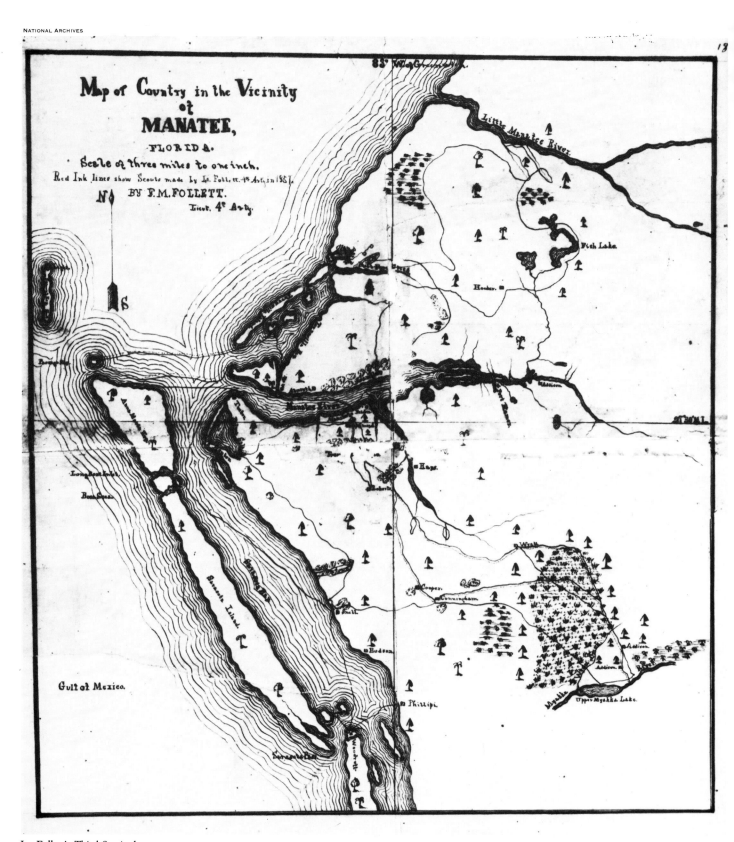

Lt. Follett's Third Seminole War map charted the local frontier and identified locations of coastal settlers as well as the inland homes of cattlemen.

At the close of the Second Seminole War, the Congressional Armed Occupation Act of 1842 brought cowboys, planters, fishermen, grocers, ditchers, coopers, boatbuilders, shoemakers, slaves, surveyors, and real estate developers to the new frontier, formerly Indian country.

Congress offered 200,000 federal acres "free" to citizens who would personally occupy a parcel for five years, build dwellings, clear and cultivate five acres, and promise to defend the lands from the Indians if necessary. The offer pertained to the inland sector extending from south of Palatka to Tampa and Sarasota bays. The opportunity provided by the act, signed into law in August 1842, was good for just one year.

At Sarasota Bay, three claims were registered for 160 acres each by two Spanish fishermen — Mañuel Olivella and Jose Elzuardi — and Benjamin Fuller.

Fuller claimed his quarter-section at present-day Bowlees Creek, while Elzuardi and Olivella laid claim to the bayfront stretching north from present day Whitaker Bayou. Olivella had occupied his rancho *area prior to the war — the* rancho *which had become Fort Armistead. He was Clerk of Court for local Hillsborough County. Elzuardi, who had married a lighthouse keeper's daughter and eventually resided with his large family in Key West, had served in the Florida legislature.*

Although none of the Sarasota claims proved successful, the tradition of fishermen continued as the primary commercial occupation along the coast. Fish ranchos *continued to thrive along the bay. One prominently appeared on the north end of present-day Siesta Key/Bay Island, and another lay across bay waters along the south side of present-day Hudson Bayou.*

Pioneer cowboys

The cattle industry also was old in Florida, a land well-suited to support range cattle. Most plantations and farms had at least a few head, and some settlers raised cattle on a larger scale as their main income-producer. Spanish fishermen in the Sarasota Bay region had owned cattle even prior to the Second Seminole War.

Cowboys headed to the new frontier driving stock cattle purchased in Florida's older frontiers to the north and moved them out to natural grazing lands, the Myakka and Peace River valleys. Gone from home for months at a time, the cattlemen worked and camped the open ranges from February to October, separating, marking, and branding calves and driving them to market.

To the site of earlier *ranchos* came two brothers from Middle Florida — Hamlin Snell, a territorial legislator from Calhoun County, and his younger brother, William Whitaker, who as a Tallahassee schoolboy of 18 had fought in the Second Seminole War. Snell was in his 30s, Whitaker in his 20s, when they came to Sarasota Bay.

Whitaker went into the cattle business, acquiring his herd in 1847. He was one of the first newcomers to actually own land in the Sarasota area. Cowboys like Whitaker and his neighbors lived in Indian country as much as they lived in their own homes along the coast. Back in the settlements, frontiersmen pursued the fishing industry, land acquisition, and plantation agriculture, but the inland cattle industry was destined to thrive and expand on the lands where Indians had freely hunted and grazed their own cattle until the Second Seminole War.

The cattlemen became solitary figures by occupation and routine. Self-reliant in the wilds, the cowboy learned to "read" the inland, to detect Indian signs as well as those of cattle. His usual weapons were the tools of his trade — his horse, his hound, his saddlebag, cookpot, rope, hat, and pocket knife. Stories circulated about cowboys who killed — practically barehandedly — panthers and bears, alligators and rattlesnakes. Even among fellow settlers, the cowhunter was regarded as tough, rugged, and fierce on occasion. The cowboy became a hero, and in time of Indian conflict, was the fighting force upon which fellow settlers counted for victory.

Casey's Key

Army Captain John Charles Casey's tenure as an officer was commemorated permanently as a place name because of his association with the first government chart of the coast. The survey, which required a three-year effort, credited Casey's assistance and placed his name upon the southernmost Sarasota Bay inlet (site of present-day Venice Inlet). From that location, the name slipped onto the island to the north in a succeeding military map, which labeled the island Casey's Key, which it has remained.

PAINTING BY KEN HUGHS. © 1985 JANET SNYDER MATTHEWS

Depiction of Captain John Casey's 1849 meeting with Billy Bowlegs' emissaries, a vain attempt to forestall conflict with the Seminoles.

A war stopped at the bay

A 20-mile buffer separated Indian lands from Florida coasts. Peas Creek officially divided the grazing lands of the cattlemen from those of the Indians. The Indian camps lay along their open ranges, while their major villages were located in South Florida's great swamps below the Caloosahatchee River. Though the Seminoles came among bay settlers to trade skins or to travel on official business with the Indian agent at Fort Brooke, their former cattle grazing and hunting lands had been permanently restricted, as was their weaponry. Their only source of guns and gunpowder was government-sanctioned trading posts. Some white settlers perceived a certain alien element in the Indian presence, while others downright mistrusted and feared them.

Florida had become a state in 1845, and occasionally flexed its legislative muscle. The 1849 legislative session imposed a penalty of "stripes" (whipping) upon any Indian who left the reserved lands — even for a meeting with the Indian agent. Army officers who disregarded the state law and gave "passports" could be fined hundreds of dollars. Some of the newcomers exercised political pressure from time to time to hurry the government into driving all the Seminoles out of Florida, thereby opening the remaining Indian lands for settlement.

In 1849, a succession of events far from Sarasota Bay produced a threat of war which touched close to home. In June, Indian agent Captain John Casey made an excursion to Caloosahatchee to talk with the acting head chief of the Seminoles, Holata Micco (Billy Bowlegs). Casey, a veteran of Indian wars in Florida and Mexico, had served at Fort Brooke during the war and was in critical health as a result of tuberculosis. On his excursion to the Caloosahatchee and up Peas Creek, Casey took a sloop and a small boat, guns, rifles, provisions, and presents of calico, as well as three soldiers, an interpreter named John, and a guide, Jose Phillipi Bermudez. Bermudez had been part of the Bunce *rancho* during the war and had lost two wives and five children when the Army deported Bunce's *rancho* people to the West. Phillipi, or Felipe, as he was usually called, lived at Sarasota Bay.

For several weeks, Casey and his entourage traveled about Charlotte Harbor waterways, lighting signal fires for Indians and leaving symbol messages and presents, with no results. The third week of July, Casey's party sailed back to Tampa Bay and Fort Brooke, only to learn that an Indian war party had attacked two settlements in their absence — one at Indian River and another on Peas Creek.

Panic spread among the settlers. Many abandoned their investments and planned to leave permanently. Others camped together in defendable, stockaded positions, abandoning fields and homes.

The citizens organized a call for state and federal action, choosing Hamlin Snell to petition Washington. Hamlin and other settlers wrote to President Millard Fillmore asking for military protection. "We are situated on the extreme frontier of an almost entirely wilderness country," they wrote, "inhabited only by savage tribes of hostile Indians, having no military post nearer than forty miles." General

David Twiggs, commanding Army forces in Florida, was meeting with the settlers and acting simultaneously. He had already asked that troops be ordered to Florida.

Influential citizens petitioned the governor for special state militia companies to defend the new frontier. Governor William Mosely commissioned two companies which moved into strategic positions. A total of six were organized. Hamlin Snell and Joseph Woodruff, another Sarasota settler, were among those who volunteered for military service against the Indian Nation.

In spite of all indications to the contrary, John Casey felt certain the Indian Nation was not at war, that the two attacks were perpetrated by a few Indians acting independently. Holato Micco had left a peace symbol at Phillipi's Rancho in Sarasota which Phillipi relayed to Casey at Fort Brooke. Accordingly, the officer prepared to comply with the head chief's sign of peace and organized a journey to Sarasota Bay. General Twiggs agreed to hold off all military movements against the Indians pending the outcome of Casey's mission.

Casey made contact with three Seminole leaders, emissaries of Holato Micco, who explained that the attacks had been the work of several young renegade Indians, not an act of war. Though the chief's emissaries were authorized only to arrange a meeting between Holata Micco and Casey, they reluctantly agreed, at Casey's insistence, to a meeting between the chief and General Twiggs if Casey would be present. Casey told them that the general insisted on bringing armed troops, but pledged his word that the chief would not be captured. The meeting was scheduled for September 18 at Charlotte Harbor.

Because of the full cooperation of the chief and his leaders over the following period of weeks, the renegade Indians were captured and war was averted, at least for the time being.

The 1849 attack upon Peas Creek Trading Post came unexpectedly at the dinner hour, killing Mr. Payne and Dempsey Whidden, and sending the McCullough family wandering for days to reach safety from the renegade Seminoles.

I Could Live In Peace

"The sun, which is warm and bright as my feelings are now, shines to warm us and bring forth our crops, and the moon brings back the spirits of our warriors, our fathers, wives and children. The white man comes; he grows pale and sick, why cannot we live here in peace? . . . I could live in peace with him, but they first steal our cattle and horses, cheat us, and take our lands. The white men are as thick as the leaves in the hammock; they come upon us thicker every year. They may shoot us, drive our women and children night and day; they may chain our hands and feet, but the red man's heart will be always free."

—Coacoochee, March 5, 1841
from Mahon, *Second Seminole War*

Coacoochee (Wild Cat), circa 1840.

FLORIDA PHOTOGRAPHIC COLLECTION

War for real

When the census taker went through the Sarasota neighborhood in 1850, Snell and Whitaker had expanded to two households, planted an orange grove, guava trees, and cultivated their fields. Both were listed as planters, though they lived with fishermen from the Bahamas and Georgia. Snell's household included Nassau-born William and Wade Rigby, one a carpenter, the other a fisherman. The household also included a fisherman and a sailor, Daniel and Mañuel Hassel, natives of Santa Cruz and the Canary Islands. Georgia-born Joseph Woodruff, a veteran of the Mexican War, listed himself as a clerk. Woodruff had sold a 160-acre Military Bounty land warrant to Whitaker, which Whitaker used in 1850 to purchase the homeplace; he bought an additional 44 adjacent acres for $1.25 each. The settler's newly acquired mile of bayfront extended from present-day Indian Beach Drive south to Tenth Street.

The year following his land purchase, Whitaker married Mary Jane Wyatt, the daughter of river settler William Wyatt, a well-known political figure of territorial Florida. With his wife, Nancy, Wyatt had come to the newly opened frontier with an entire family of cattlemen and planters. Mary Jane was the youngest child. Educated in Illinois, she was 19 when she and Whitaker were married by Reverend Franklin Branch. Theirs was the first wedding listed in the Manatee Methodist Episcopal Church register.

The Sarasota neighborhood to which William brought Mary consisted in the mid 1850s of Phillipi, whose *rancho* lay to the south along the mainland shore, and a neighbor named Hudson who lived at a bayou between the Whitakers and Phillipi. Toward the inland were the Coopers and the Oglesbys, a family of cattlemen, and the household of Owen Cunningham, an Irish laborer.

While his brother and new sister-in-law stayed home to raise crops, citrus, and cattle, Hamlin Snell continued his political career. He was elected to represent the 18th District in the legislative sessions of 1852 and again in 1854, when he was voted president of the Senate. In that session, the new settlement along the river and bay broke away to form a new county called Manatee, and Snell was among three citizens charged with the selection of a county seat. In fall 1856, Snell was elected the county's first delegate to the legislature and went on to become Speaker of the House in that same session.

The state legislature continued to press for further restriction of the Seminoles. Many legislators urged the federal government to deport them all. Holata Micco was invited to visit Washington and meet with the President on several occasions. Though the chief of the Indian Nation had been continually pressured, and the reserved lands were once again reduced drastically in size, he insisted upon the Seminoles' willingness to abide by white laws and reiterated his refusal to take his people and go.

The federal government surveyed deep into Indian country, detailing previously secreted Indian villages, connecting trails, and the locations of canoe landings in the Everglades. Army posts were built inside Indian lands. Pressure upon the Seminoles was neither subtle nor disguised.

In December 1855, deep in Indian country, a party of U.S. Army Corps of Engineers under Lt. George L. Hartsuff was completing a dozen-day survey to locate Indian fields and villages. On the last night before heading back to Fort Myers, the nine-man team camped with wagons, mules, and equipment only three miles from the village of Holata Micco. Before dawn, the sleeping survey crew awakened to blazing rifles and the war whoops of warriors. Led by the chief, 30 Seminole warriors began their last stand against forcible eviction from Florida. In a matter of minutes, four men were dead, four others wounded.

Newspaper headlines screamed out against the barbarity of the Indians. Leaving only a few slaves or employees behind on homesteads, most Sarasota Bay settlers moved to a fortified encampment at the Manatee River near the home of Dr. Franklin Branch. Citizens held emergency meetings and elected committees to petition state and federal authorities for military protection.

Sarasota Bay men signed into local militia units to defend the settlement and scout across cattle country looking for signs of Indians. Local units were headed by cattleman John Parker, cattleman and planter William Hooker, and cattleman John Addison, who lived at the river with his sons and families. Whitaker, Woodruff, Snell, Isaac and David Redd, and the Oglesbys were among those who signed up. Whitaker served as an officer in Parker's company, as did Woodruff.

In spring, the conflict — called the Third Seminole War — struck very close to home. Hamlin Snell left the Manatee settlement on a run to Sarasota for provisions to feed the encamped families. As he neared the bay, he sensed danger ahead. Climbing a tree for a better vantage point, he saw all the buildings in the Whitaker-Snell clearing ablaze in the full spring afternoon. Neighbor Owen Cunningham lay dead in one of the blazing cabins. By dark, more Sarasota clearings blazed brightly. The house of Joseph Woodruff and those of inland cattlemen Oglesby and Cooper were also torched.

For safety's sake, that night some of the women and children were taken aboard the vessel *Elizabeth Ann* in the river. Next day at Branch Fort, Mary Whitaker gave birth to her second child and first son, Furman Chairs, named after Whitaker's Tallahassee friend, planter Furman Chaires.

The local newspaper blazoned the news of the attack on Snell by the savages. In Tallahassee, Governor James Broome wrote to Secretary of War Jefferson Davis protesting the undefended situation of this important group of settlers and their investment in the frontier.

Exactly four weeks after the attack at Sarasota, Indians headed toward the newly constructed plantation house of Virginia and Dr. Joseph Braden, where Furman Chaires was among the family and friends present for dinner. At twilight, the war party stealthily made its way to the porch

Portrait of Hamlin Valentine Snell which hangs in the Florida Senate.

Holata Micco, Chief Billy Bowlegs, posed for an ambrotype dressed ceremonially in his beaded shot bag, turban and ostrich feathers. From a ribbon he hung the silver likeness of Millard Fillmore, presented by the President to the chief.

before they were spotted by a servant. Dr. Braden blew out the lights and proceeded upstairs to the front windows, meanwhile arming Chaires, his son, and another male guest. When all were in place, Braden called out, asking the identity of the men. A volley of shots answered. As the settlers returned the Indians' fire, the warriors withdrew to the plantation cabins where they abducted some slaves, packing children on mules along with blankets, food, and plunder.

Next morning, Braden sent a message to Hamlin Snell who alerted militiamen stationed inland, while William Whitaker rode alone nearly 50 miles inland to Fort Meade for reinforcements. Local cowboys organized a militia under John Addision, with John Whidden as tracker, and followed the Indians for several days, catching up to them at Joshua Creek where several Indians were killed and others injured. The cowboys took two scalps; Addison presented one to Dr. Braden, the other to militia leader and cattleman William Hooker.

The war continued in and about the settlements that year. A farmer at the Alafia River was killed while plowing his fields. Farther south, two oystermen were murdered, and the slave of an oysterman named Hudson was missing. Their boats had drifted to shore, burned to the waterline. Indians plundered and burned the clearings and buildings of cowboys at every opportunity. At a summer skirmish, three cowboys — Alderman Carlton, Lott Whidden, and William Parker — were killed.

As large numbers of regular troops and citizen militia companies converged on the area, the war was fought farther south. Operating out of the wartime hub of Fort Myers, military groups extended into the Indian villages and the Everglades, burning villages and capturing the Indians' hidden supplies of food and ammunition. Phillipi and an Indian woman, Polly, hired out to the Army as guides.

In December 1857, Hamlin Snell headed a mounted six-month company of volunteers mustered into federal service by a former legislative colleague. Two months later, Snell was a special delegate assigned to a group of Indians brought back from the West to induce the Seminoles to leave.

To convince Chief Billy Bowlegs (Holata Micco) to emigrate, the federal government offered $7,500 to Bowlegs personally, $500 to each warrior, and $100 for each woman and child. In his vulnerable situation, it was an offer he could not refuse.

In May 1858, Billy Bowlegs with his wives and slaves and his band of 38 warriors willingly sailed aboard the steamer *Grey Cloud* bound for reserved lands in the Territory of Arkansas (present-day Oklahoma). The steamer set out from Egmont Key, where the chief's sister and 40 other Seminoles had been incarcerated awaiting deportation. When the steamer reached New Orleans, Bowlegs was followed about for days by a reporter for *Harper's,* who filed an extensive article on the chief, whom he saw as wealthy with gold and happy (happily out of it) with whiskey.

The settlers returned to their long-abandoned fields and groves. Mary and Bill Whitaker rebuilt a cabin for their growing family. Whitaker was appointed tax assessor and collector. Snell ultimately was appointed deputy customs collector and resided in Tampa, where he was elected mayor in 1861.

5. The Civil War And Frontier Violence

Confederate Secretary of State Judah Benjamin.

45

Yet another war descended upon the Sarasota Bay families within three years of Billy Bowlegs' deportation. In 1861, Florida seceded from the Union, following the lead of South Carolina and Mississippi. The armed conflict that was to come laid a heavy hand upon local citizens and affected their daily lives.

Florida was called upon to supply her quota of armed companies to the Confederacy, no small task in a state sparsely populated with whites. Local men signed into a company headed by the son of the veteran Indian fighter John Lesley — Company K of the Fourth Florida Regiment — which served in defense of the Tampa Bay region for a time. By fall 1861, some soldiers were stationed at the mouth of the Manatee River, rationed on corn meal as a substitute for flour, and on beef and pork purchased locally.

But within six months, the force was reorganized. It was soon needed far from home, and the homefolk marched to join General Braxton Bragg's army. Also ordered off to join that army was the Seventh Regiment, whose Company K and Company E ("South Florida Bulldogs") included local men such as William Lowe and Joseph Woodruff. (This was the fourth war in which Woodruff had fought.) They were to see action in some of the worst battles of the war — at Nashville, at Murfreesboro the day after New Year's 1863, at Vicksburg, and at Chickamauga. In late 1863, the Fourth Regiment fought at Missionary Ridge where all but 18 of 172 men were captured, wounded, or killed.

The Cowboy Cavalry

Once again, the cowmen were called upon in the face of war, this time as part of a unique Florida force commonly called the "Cowboy Cavalry," organized to provide the Confederacy with one of the main commodities needed from Florida — beef. In late spring and summer, when edible native grasses covered the lands along the route, cowboys drove cattle northward through interior Florida nearly to the Georgia line to the railroad terminus at Baldwin. A half thousand head went out a week. Each drive required six weeks. As the war progressed, the Cowboy Cavalry was also directed to combat the increasing numbers of deserters and stragglers who roved the inland cattle country as rustlers and Union suppliers to the federal companies stationed at Fort Myers. The Cowboy Cavalry also was responsible for guarding the coast after the regular Confederate troops had been called to distant duty.

During the first few years of war, Florida supplied an estimated 25,000 head of cattle; records indicate that a Confederate commissary agent expected 9,500 head the winter of 1863. An officer of General Bragg's army wrote, "We are now dependent upon your State for beef." Florida's quota was raised as supplies from the other Southern states were exhausted, and in 1864, Florida was asked to supply 25,000 head of cattle as well as syrup, fish and hogs.

A continual wartime threat upon coastal families was posed by the Union blockade. Early in the war, President Abraham Lincoln had ordered southern ports closed in order to cut off supplies into and revenue-producing exports out of the South. The Gulf Blockading Squadron monitored the coast from Cape Canaveral to Pensacola, including the Tampa-Sarasota Bay sector. Initially, the blockade constituted little hindrance to local mariners who continued their runs to Havana with sugar, molasses, fish, and assorted local products. Vessels often made the return run loaded with weapons and ammunition for Confederate troops.

STEAMSHIP HISTORICAL SOCIETY COLLECTION, UNIVERSITY OF BALTIMORE LIBRARY

The *Lizzie Henderson* regularly plied Gulf waters in the late 1800s transporting local cattle to Cuba, loading at such places as Shaw's Point on Manatee River.

But as the Union Navy increased in strength, the force grew ever more oppressive upon the local economy. In time, even seasoned veterans of Gulf commerce like Frederick Tresca, Mary Whitaker's brother-in-law, were without vessels. Local families had none of the manufactured commodities they needed — coffee, flour, oil, saddles, knives, fabrics, thread and needles, buttons, machinery, tools, hardware, rope, wire, nails, bricks, medicines, shoes, hats, paper, matches, letters, books, magazines, newspapers, paint, children's toys, ammunition. Prices on scarce goods skyrocketed. Families were soon reduced to using only the things they could produce themselves. They made coffee from parched corn, flour from repeated grindings, shoes from leather cured from hides. Their clothes became old, faded, or homespun.

With so many menfolk at war, the cowboys off to drive cattle up the distant inland, and many slaves gone or going, women often administered the fields and livestock as well as home and hearth. Unable to earn income, they faced hardship in every direction. Leisure was quickly absorbed by a return to an anxious and primitive existence.

The local situation was additionally depressed by the increasing arrival of troops detached from the Union blockade. Soldiers came ashore to destroy local industry — to chop or blast away grist and sugar mills, to confiscate livestock and produce to feed Union forces.

In the rivers and bays, Union blockade forces lay in wait for barges and sailboats attempting to get out with messages or small amounts of products. Vessels were confiscated after one warning, and if captured, crews were forced to swear allegiance to the Union or taken to jail at Key West, a Union stronghold throughout the war. Soon, local men were entirely without craft of any kind. The settlers learned to hide everything — occasionally even a small boat — deep in the tangle of woods and palmettoes in the back country where Union forces seldom ventured. And when they did, outlooks were posted to warn the households with a signal. At the signal, portable possessions were grabbed up and carted to the woods. China, silver, even precious foodstuffs, were often buried underground.

Union landing parties often approached the Whitaker buildings, which were on a high clearing visible from the pass and broad bay, to confiscate citrus, hogs, and crops from the field. On one occasion, Mary Whitaker faced the commanding officer and, eye to eye, challenged his intention to burn her house. She allegedly stopped him with one sentence: "Sir, I want to look into the eyes of a man who can stoop so low as to burn the home of a helpless woman and her family."

On another occasion, a Union soldier took the rifle of young Furman Whitaker, the boy who had been born in an Indian war fort and lived through another war before he was 10. The boy told his mother of this great loss, and she insisted that he himself go straight to the officer and ask for return of his property. Young Furman successfully recovered his weapon.

Nellie Abbe Whitaker and Furman Whitaker.

Running the blockade

Furman Whitaker and his cousin Will Tresca later were also privy to a most sensational wartime event. The Civil War had come to its penultimate end with Jefferson Davis' cabinet headed southward from Richmond on Sunday, April 2, 1865, anticipating the imminent invasion of the Confederate capital by Union forces. When the cabinet members reached Charlotte, news came of the assassination of Lincoln on April 14.

Near Washington, Georgia, President Davis and the Confederate Secretary of State, Louisiana planter and former U.S. Senator Judah Benjamin, were among those who parted company. Agreeing to meet again if possible in the trans-Mississippi district, Davis headed through south Georgia, where he was captured and jailed on May 10. A reward was offered for capture of the remaining cabinet members, whose only hope was to reach the sanctity of a neutral port such as the British Bahamas. All the coastal blockade forces were alerted and security was tightened.

Late in May, a dark-haired, twinkly eyed, spirited man arrived in the Sarasota Bay area. It was Judah Benjamin. After a tense time and close calls with a blockade detachment at the Gamble plantation house, Benjamin had been spirited by loyal Confederates to the Tresca home south of the Manatee River and nine miles from Sarasota Bay. There he stayed secretly for several weeks. Will Tresca knew the man as a memorably well-dispositioned Mr. Howard — a visitor in their home who showed "love for the children." Will's mother sewed secret pockets in Mr. Howard's vest and waistband where he might carry gold without attracting notice. The distinguished visitor offered a few carefully selected local seamen $1,500 in gold to get him to safety. The risk was great, but Will's father, French-born Frederick Tresca, had been master of commercial vessels on the Gulf coast for some 30 years. Like Benjamin, who had been born in St. Croix and lived many years in New Orleans, Tresca spoke French fluently.

On a day late in June, a crude two-wheel spring wagon set out from the Tresca home on the road to Sarasota. Driven by Ezekial Glazier, pioneer river settler who had been the local delegate to Florida's Secession Congress in

Anatomy of a Homestead

Early in 1882, Oscar Payne, a young cigarmaker from Marietta, Ohio, arrived in Sarasota to search for federal acreage upon which to homestead. When he had located an available tract and made a few improvements, he headed north for Gainesville where, for a few dollars, he personally filed his claim at the General Land Office to nearly 160 acres lying along Phillippi Creek at present-day Hyde Park. The tract was typical pineland — land of the "scattering pine" some called it.

Returning to Sarasota, Payne built a temporary palmetto-thatched house. Later he erected a three-room frame house and a chicken shed. Once the place was habitable, his mother agreed to leave her Marietta home and live with Oscar on his distant homestead. Payne grubbed out trees and fenced about five acres for fields. He planted citrus, potatoes, cowpeas, and "garden truck." For cash income, he worked as a day laborer for other farmers, sometimes for several months at a time.

After five years, Payne could "prove up" his claim. At the Land Office, a 30-day notice of "proving up" was placed "in a conspicuous place." Payne's final proof had to be made before the Clerk of the Circuit Court at the county seat of Pine Level (now in De Soto County, but then the Manatee County seat). The Pine Level *Times* published the notice for six weeks running.

On May 29, before Clerk Robert Griffith, Payne's neighbors — Peter Crocker, A.J. Tatum, W.W. Brown, and W.J. Drumright — testified that Payne had resided, cultivated, and otherwise fulfilled the intent of the Homestead Act.

On January 27, 1890, after eight years of isolation, frontier labor, and hardship, the homesteader — now 37 — won final approval to receive his "free" land.

Three months later, Oscar Payne was issued a patent from the U.S. Land Office to become the first private owner of a piece of Sarasota.

1861, the wagon was accompanied by a carefully chosen armed guard — Jeff Bolding, a freed Whitaker slave. The wagon was filled with freshly butchered beef, but under the beef, a layer of palmetto leaves completely camouflaged the escaping Secretary of State. The humble little party proceeded warily along the trail toward Sarasota Bay.

At the bay was a sixteen-foot open boat which had been hidden deeply in the woods during the war by river settler and native Bahamian John Curry. Also waiting at the bay was Captain Tresca and a lone crew member, 29-year-old Hiram McLeod, whose sister and niece lived at Gamble plantation. McLeod had been a coastal fisherman and assistant lighthouse keeper at Egmont lighthouse before the war. Limping and disabled by wounds received with the Confederate navy in Wilmington and with the army at the Battle of Murfreesboro, McLeod had returned home from the war only weeks before Benjamin's arrival.

The daring little group shoved off and set sail southward. Off the coast of Charlotte Harbor, they were spotted and pursued by a Union blockade vessel and forced ashore to spend the night on a mangrove island near Gasparilla Pass amid heavy mosquitoes and terrible anxiety. After 23 days and risky stops in the Keys and Biscayne Bay, the group successfully braved the tight blockade and tropical storms to deposit Benjamin in Bimini on Monday, July 10. Benjamin eventually reached England where he established a new legal career and lived until his death. He has been called "America's most outstanding 19th century Jew." Tresca, Curry, Glazier, Whitaker, and McLeod had taken a great risk and did not discuss the event freely. It was part of a terrible time that left permanent scars on those who survived it.

SMITHSONIAN INSTITUTION ARCHIVES

Eliza Graves Webb and John Webb homesteaded on a bayfront quarter section they named Spanish Point and later renamed Osprey. The native New Yorkers emigrated at the close of the Civil War with a family of five to take advantage of the healthy climate and the Congressional Homestead Act of 1862.

Homesteaders and cattle kings

At the close of the Civil War, another land-oriented governmental measure influenced a major wave of settlers into the area which would equal in effect that produced by the Armed Occupation Act exactly 20 years earlier. The Homestead Act, passed by a wartime Congress in 1862, had inspired the popular slogan, "Vote yourself a farm." After the war, Republicans descended upon the region with money to invest in big dreams about the well-publicized (and highly romanticized) profits of south Florida agriculture. Coastal settlements were enlarged by the influx of Yankees and winter snowbirds.

New Yorkers John and Eliza Webb and their large family arrived at the Manatee River in spring 1867 and looked along the bay for federal land on which to establish a homestead. In the fall, they settled upon a complex of Indian middens they called "Spanish Point" (at present-day Osprey). To the north, their nearest neighbors were the Whitakers, eleven miles away.

To the south, the Webb family was soon joined by the family of Jesse and Caroline Knight, frontier Floridians and parents of 15 children who, over a period of years, bought from the state nearly 600 acres for about 90 cents an acre. The Knight men had been frontier cowboys earlier in Hillsborough County and followed a married daughter to the Sarasota region after the war. Their lands lay in the area to become Nokomis and Venice, on both sides of present-day Dona and Roberts bays and Shake It Creek. They called the area Horse and Chaise for a landmark growth of trees along the shore, but their interest was in the inland ranges and cattle. Jesse's brother, Joel, drove cattle herds farther south, nearer Charlotte Harbor. The Knight men were among those sometimes referred to as "Cattle Kings."

Though the Webb and Knight families were isolated, they were not singular. In 1871, Robert Rickford Roberts, a farmer in his early 40s, established a homeplace on the south end of the bay and became a neighbor of the Knight and Webb families. Two years later, he brought his widowed sister and her two children to his 120 acres, where he had built two houses. Roberts cleared, ditched, and picket-fenced six acres and planted bananas, sugar cane, corn, potatoes, and tobacco in "marketable quantities." The bayside waterway adjoining his land became known as Roberts Bay. Jesse Monroe Clower arrived a few years later and settled north of the Webbs on the bay. Clower Creek bears his name.

In fall 1881, a native Iowa farmer, cattleman, and day laborer named John Slemans Blackburn came with his wife and a son. He built a palmetto-thatched house and filed claim to 188 bayfront acres for $35.20. He also built a sloop, which was the family's sole transportation to market or church. Two years later, John's son, Benjamin Blackburn, homesteaded 80 acres a mile and a half south, filing for $12. Benjamin, in his early 20s, built a frame house and enclosed his bayfront land in a wire fence. Blackburn Point, Blackburn Road, and Blackburn Bay bear the family name.

The offer for federal homestead land attracted settlers to the remaining tracts for more than 50 years. When it was available, many settlers added to their federal homesteads with purchases of state lands.

Inland, scattered settlers more often were descendants of the earlier wave of pioneer settlement. Many were occupied with the cattle industry which had survived the war. Disparities were apparent between the incoming educated families and those depressed by the war's overwhelming reverses. Among the distinct classes, there was often a general sense of community, but also a sense of social and economic division.

At the same time, the frontier county of Manatee had outgrown its organized authorities. Created before the last Indian war and stretching from Tampa Bay to Charlotte Harbor and from the Gulf to Lake Okeechobee, the hub of the community had once been Manatee Village, where citizens had solidly clustered. But during the Reconstruction period after the Civil War, Florida authorities had strategically moved the county seat to a neutral geographical center, and a town called Pine Level had grown up in the middle of nowhere — a real frontier town with a saloon, a sawmill, a newspaper, and advertised stage connections. Though crude dirt roads were constructed to the new county seat, it was a two-day journey for coastal and inland settlers to the courthouse for necessary business matters — such as proving up homestead claims. Most settlements springing up across the frontier were not only far from the courthouse, they also were many miles from the sheriff at Manatee.

The Sara Sota Assassination Society

In the 1880s, violence was not uncommon across the frontier — sometimes a carryover of cowboy justice, sometimes a result of friction among fractious men or bullies harrassing law-abiders. Sarasota was no exception, and the climate of violence played a part in one of historic Sarasota's most infamous crimes — the murder of its first postmaster.

Charles Abbe had come to Sarasota from Kansas, where he and his wife, Charlotte, had raised their children. Abbe had purchased from the state several tracts of land along the bay in present-day downtown Sarasota, and following the high school graduation of their daughter, Nellie, had moved to Sarasota in 1877 with his wife and daughters. They built a house on the highest point of one of the recently purchased tracts (present-day Osprey Avenue near Sarasota Memorial Hospital) and began to acquire adjacent lands from the state and from private owners. Though their first reaction was dismay, soon the Abbe daughters, Nellie and Carrie, had acclimated themselves to the frontier. Nellie fell in love and married Furman Whitaker.

The Abbes were hard workers. Carrie taught Sarasota schoolchildren in a little house on a bayfront tract (present-day McClellan Park area). Charles raised citrus crops and started a pineapple "plantation" on Longboat with Bill Whitaker. He managed farming operations for absentee landholders and traveled north to tout Sarasota to prospective buyers and visitors at summer fairs. He also wrote a Sarasota column in the local newspaper (published at Tampa). He and Charlotte started up a little store and took boarders into their home to raise money, and ultimately they had a block of bayfront lands from Hudson Bayou to present-day Southside School. The Abbes' dream was to build a hotel on their enterprising development which they advertised as "Helena."

Abbe, a Republican, was political and outspoken. Republicans were in power nationally after Reconstruction and still controlled federal patronage in the South. Charles Abbe accepted an appointment as U.S. Commissioner for the federal courts in 1882 and bore responsibility for involvement in related judicial proceedings.

In 1878, Charles had applied for — and gotten — the first post office for the Sarasota region, to serve a total population of 40 families. As postmaster, he could count on regular income. He also had the privilege of naming the post office — and thereby the community. Though he nearly named it Helena, he stuck with the historic name of the bay, and soon mail was arriving addressed to residents of "Sara Sota."

Charles Abbe after seven years of life in Sarasota became one of the local citizens whose very life was threatened by an unlikely plot — not by a bully or an angry settler, but by a handful of men who apparently resented Abbe's authority and achievement. Alfred Bidwell, a storekeeper a

Charles Elliott Abbe, Sarasota's first postmaster, died by the bay at the hands of a group dubbed by the New York *Times* in 1885 the Sarasota Assassination Society.

Charlotte Scofield Abbe succeeded her husband for a time as Sarasota's postmistress.

Mary and Alfred Bidwell built their new house near Hudson Bayou in the early 1880s only a few years before Bidwell was convicted of ringleading the vigilante assassination group.

the bay by Abbe's lands, and Leonard Andrews, a doctor and homesteader from Iowa, apparently instigated with others a secret organization disguised as a "Democratic club" in spring 1884, a presidential election year. Though most solid citizens reportedly responded negatively to membership invitations, the ringleaders were successful in recruiting a number of locals including a few homesteaders, a thug or two, one reputed murderer, and a handful of young, uneducated farm laborers who were flattered by the attentions of the doctor and the storekeeper. They found out too late that it was not a political club. Called the Sara Sota Vigilance Committee, members took an oath of secrecy and promised to protect one another and do the business of the society — even if that business were murder. Resignation was categorically forbidden.

Bidwell and Andrews assigned several young bloods to their first murder in summer 1884, providing the boys loaded guns and a warning that the ammunition would be fired into them if they failed to do as ordered. They ambushed a Bee Ridge settler, Harrison Riley, while he rode his horse along a new road to the Sarasota post office. With 27 buckshot through his body and his throat slit, the victim soon lay dead in the palmettoes along the road (present-day intersection of Ashton and Proctor roads). Encouraged by their first success and by the lack of an investigation, the leaders planned more crimes.

Two days after Christmas 1884, Charles Abbe was gunned down as he walked up the sandy main road from the bay to his house (present-day Cunliff Lane). Charles Willard, the murderer, was drunk on holiday moonshine. The gun he fired belonged to another neighbor, Joseph Anderson. Abbe fell dead, and the murderer and his

Mary Jane Wyatt Whitaker and Bill Whitaker lived through Indian wars, hurricanes and the War Between the States as they raised a large family at the Yellow Bluffs by Sarasota Bay.

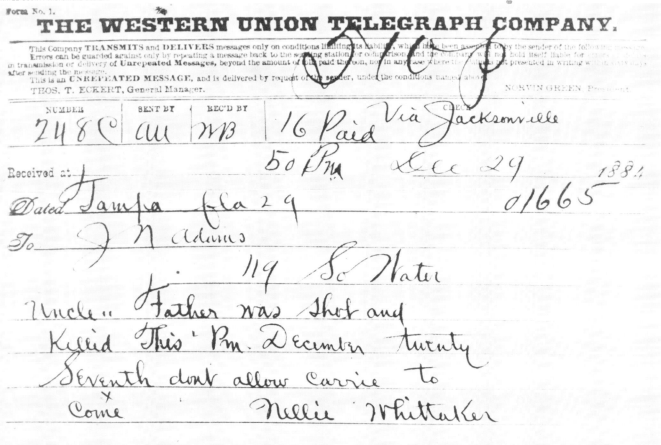

Nellie Louise Abbe in a school graduation pose in Lawrenceville, Kansas, only months before the Abbe family settled at Sarasota Bay.

Reeling from shock, Nellie Abbe Whitaker telegrammed word to her sister Carrie in Chicago that their father had been murdered in Sarasota.

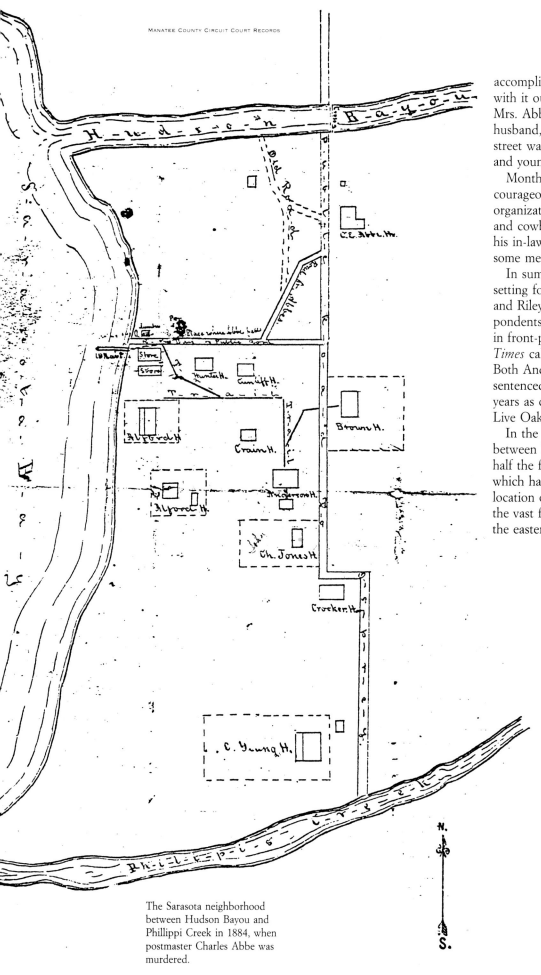

The Sarasota neighborhood between Hudson Bayou and Phillippi Creek in 1884, when postmaster Charles Abbe was murdered.

accomplices dragged the body to a waiting boat, sailed with it out Big Pass, and threw it overboard in the Gulf. Mrs. Abbe frantically searched the bayfront for her husband, with the help of Richard Cunliff, for whom the street was later named. A homesteader at Phillippi Creek and young Emil Whitaker rode to Manatee for the sheriff.

Months of investigation spurred local citizens to courageously testify to the existence of the secret Sarasota organization. The first was a young Tatum Ridge farmer and cowboy named Henry Hawkins. He was backed up by his in-laws, the Tatums. There were many arrests, and some members agreed to testify.

In summer 1885, the courthouse at Pine Level was the setting for two Circuit Court trials in the murders of Abbe and Riley. The scandalous revelations brought correspondents from the Jacksonville *Times Union* and resulted in front-page stories as far away as New York, where the *Times* called the group the Sara Sota Assassination Society. Both Andrews and Bidwell were convicted of murder and sentenced to death. Many society members worked for years as convict-lease prisoners in turpentine camps near Live Oak, Florida.

In the scattered Sarasota Bay neighborhood lying between Hudson Bayou and Phillippi Creek, more than half the families were directly affected by the murders which had rocked Sarasota and ultimately changed the location of the business center. Two years after the trials, the vast frontier county of Manatee was divided in two and the eastern portion became a new county named De Soto.

Mary Sherrill, circa 1890, and her mother boarded with the Webb family during the winter of 1892 hoping to improve Mary's health in the healing Florida sunshine.

6. The Ormiston Colony

The men thatched lean-tos in their clearings and continued the labor of their unexpected pioneer effort.

The economic depression of Florida's postwar period fostered an event that promised to impact greatly large sections of the state, including the Sarasota region. When Governor William Bloxham struck up his famous 1881 deal with Hamilton Disston, son of the Philadelphia industrialist, vast tracts of the state's acreage ultimately were acquired by a few private corporations. Disston sold half of his four million acres to Sir Edward J. Reed, M.P., who was internationally known for his development projects for foreign governments. In only a few years, British and American developers' communities had sprung up across southwest Florida, ushering in the era of the big speculator — an essential end to land policy once influenced by Jacksonian democracy. In Sarasota alone, title to hundreds of thousands of acres was held by a handful of corporate interests. Great tracts were resold to investors in Great Britain who, along with Disston's firms, sought to market smaller tracts to smaller buyers at a profit.

A city on paper

The city of Sarasota was established by British developers. Its original population appears to have been the brainchild of a Scot, John Selwin Tait. Tait organized a "middle class colony" in 1885 for Florida. His timing was good. Thousands of Europeans were migrating, interest in faraway places was high, and the 1873 collapse of mid-Victorian prosperity had triggered a decade of economic tensions and doubts. Particularly affected were small British industries and merchants — the "middle class" — and anxiety over markets and materials prompted many to relocate in faraway places of promise. *The London Times* carried a series of reports in 1885 by a special correspondent in Florida who extolled the virtues of climate, price, and the economic opportunity to be had by "British hands and brains, and by British capital." John Tait also had written a series of letters in daily papers on the subject of an emigration colony. Responses compelled him to head up such a project himself. He wrote that he had agreed to do so reluctantly, and only with the co-responsibility of an able council.

Tait's promotion of the "Ormiston Colony" originated in Edinburgh during the summer of 1885 when he offered the sale of units within the colony and announced endorsement of impressive patrons of the enterprise. Tait's promotional packet hyped Florida's good weather and instant promise, pronouncing Sarasota's location to be "the most beautiful and one of the healthiest."

Tait's appeal suggested the life style of gentlemen farmers and was aimed at merchant-class readers of British papers. The offer included a temporary town house, a 40-acre country farm, and special group rates for travel. The colony would depart Scotland in three stages — the first was the immediate emigration of the original group. A second group was to emigrate a year later, while members of a third group were to hold their 40-acre farm plots *in absentia* and pay the colony council to develop and manage the little farms. Tait fully expected each colonist to recover his investment after the first year.

Tait made a deal for his colony with "a highly responsible Scotch Company," Florida Mortgage and Investment Company Limited. FM&I was headed by a directing board of five from Scotland and England and held 50,000 acres in Florida concentrated in the Sarasota Bay vicinity. The board was represented by solicitors in Edinburgh, a lawyer in Philadelphia, and retained a manager in Florida. It was a matter "of great gratification," Tait wrote, "to deal with one's own people" rather than "a foreign Corporation." He described the company as "a wealthy institution of the highest standing." FM&I was "fully alive to the advantages which such a colony would bring," Tait wrote.

The company's solicitor in Edinburgh, Sir John Hamilton Gillespie, was a company director and stockholder and also a patron for the colony. His credentials were impressive — he had been a Writer to the Signet for some 40 years and had been knighted just two years before he patronized the organization of the colony. He was a director of Edinburgh Academy, a member of the Royal Company of Archers (the sovereign's bodyguard for Scotland), and the Royal Caledonian Hunt. Sir John was not the only FM&I director who doubled as a patron of the colony. Of the seven principal patrons, all but two were directors.

ARCHERS HALL, EDINBURGH, SCOTLAND

Sir John Hamilton Gillespie — attorney, Writer to the Signet and Secretary to the Royal Company of Archers, Queen's Bodyguard for Scotland — served as solicitor and director of Florida Mortgage and Investment Company.

A bright picture

People who read the glowing advertisements for the proposed Sarasota colony had little basis on which to judge the merits of the package. Tait and the company thought of that, too. The circular included impressive testimony on the quality of the lands from an 1884 report to FM&I made prior to purchase from Hamilton Disston. The lands had been examined by the State Engineer of Florida, H.S. DuVal, accompanied by FM&I's general manager in Florida, Piers E. Warburton, a former British naval officer with land appraisal and management experience. DuVal cited the healthfulness of the climate, the industry of established settlers, steamer lines along the coast, and new Southwest Florida railroads under construction and soon to reach the Sarasota region. The "experts" predicted a marvelous future for the new town, which was so located as to become the "foremost place as an American Sanatorium." Tait's circular also included an endorsement by J.J. Dunne, vice president of Hamilton Disston's Florida Land and Improvement Company, as well as an FM&I shareholder. "The great attraction . . . is the bay," Dunne enthused. He called the place "A Sportsman's Paradise."

On September 22, 1885, W. James Ceasar, secretary for FM&I, sent Tait a map of company lands within a radius of five miles of the newly platted "Town of Sarasota." Ceasar was authorized to offer Tait a maximum 6,000 acres at £2,10s. The company required a £20 deposit for each 40-acre plot. FM&I would take individual mortgages at eight percent for the balance, to be paid in eight half-yearly installments. The company reluctantly agreed to give a homesite in town to each bona fide settler. The company also agreed to bear half the expense of building roads leading into its new town of Sarasota. Finally, the company limited Tait's farm selections to the area north of a certain line (roughly present-day Stickney Point Road) and excluded parcels within the town of Sarasota. Tait was limited to selection of no more than 240 acres from each government section (640 acres).

The promotional literature painted a bright picture of a new town about to spring up as gracefully and naturally as a seedling nudging up out of the soil. Every possible doubt was anticipated. Even transportation, the unmanageable gremlin of southwest Florida's commerce, was to be tamed.

By October 1885, John Tait had announced 90 sales to "well-to-do families of exceptionally high standing." He was to be off in fifteen days for America to pick the 40-acre farm plots for his colony. Twenty-five surveyors had already been hired to "grade and classify" Tait's personal selections. The company also had agreed to throw in a lot in town for each buyer.

For the first group of emigrants, the company promised a package, including a house rent-free for six months which the colonist must agree to purchase at the end of that period, arrangements for transportation from Cedar Key to Sarasota, and a store in the new town to serve the isolated colony. Tait indicated that the hotel and pier were under construction and that "suitable dwelling accommodations" would be available for settlers on arrival.

The glowing offer advertised in Scotland contained two promises which were never kept — the farm plots to "adjoin and surround — within touch — three sides the Town of Sarasota," and dwellings provided for six months. But the developer's failure to meet these two conditions may not have been the colony's greatest problem. Tait's circular sounded an ominous premonition of a natural event destined to becloud his manmade venture: "The locality selected is below the frost line and there is no fear that the labour of years will be destroyed in a single night." John Tait should have picked *any* other year.

Sarasota's colonists traveled across the ocean from Glasgow on the S.S. *Furnessia* of the Anchor Line.

A rough passage

The first Ormiston Colony group departed Glasgow the day before Thanksgiving 1885 on the 5,495-ton S.S. *Furnessia*. The ship was accommodating, but passage proved rough. Off the Nova Scotia coast, mechanical failure forced the use of sail power and the ship drifted off course. Seas swept over the main deck, restricting all but the upper deck passengers to cabins or bunks. The *Furnessia* arrived in New York harbor in fifteen days, four days late. John Tait met the colonists in New York and ensconced them in the Continental Hotel, an economical place. "The most amazing city I had ever seen," wrote 19-year-old Alex Browning, who with his parents and four siblings had left Paisley, where his father had owned a sawmill and turned out vans and lorries. Alex thought the lights of New York made their home town seem, in contrast, "a deserted village."

After a few days sightseeing, the colonists boarded a smaller steamer, *State of Texas* of the Mallory line, bound for Florida's Fernandina, just below the Georgia line where the cross-peninsular railroad began. As the steamer progressed on its way, the passengers began to respond to the warmer air, shedding woolens for lighter things. On arrival at Fernandina, the colonists had their first look at tropical wonders — palm trees, Spanish moss, citrus groves, and crates of fruit at the wharf gave an industrious look to the town. The optimism was echoed in the conversation of citizens who hosted the colonists to impromptu home-cooked dinners (at a reasonable fee) and urged them to remain in Fernandina and settle.

Soon a railway engine chugged across the peninsula on a chartered run from Fernandina to Cedar Key. From the slow-moving, narrow-guage train, they watched the inland towns through which they passed — often only a row of board buildings decorated by "slouchy" men wearing "slouchy hats" and accompanied by their hound dogs. The colonists passed cattle they described as "tickey," and an occasional ox cart driven by a black boy with his whip. From time to time, a Florida cowboy raced the train or an alligator slithered off the railbed into a pond. At one of the train's regular stops for wood and water, a colonist bought a crate of oranges to pass among the dusty, thirsty travelers. At another stop, the ladies gathered palm fronds and decorated the interiors of the cars. The young Browning boy thought the fronds silly, but noticed one practical benefit — they "gave the flies another place to roost" rather than upon the faces of his drowsing companions.

Upon their arrival at the bustling port city of Cedar Key, the colonists received their first tidings of the ill about to descend upon their sturdy Scot heads. A local sawmill was only just beginning to turn out lumber to build the wharf and boarding house for the new town of Sarasota — the buildings which Tait thought were under construction in early October!

Alarm turned to dismay. A few of the single men and John Tait sailed to Sarasota with the first schoonerload of lumber. The remainder of the colony stayed behind at Cedar Key. Hotel bills escalated along with anxiety. On the

The Scottish colonists reached the St. Johns River on November 11, 1885, when one of them sketched the harbor before setting out across Florida by rail.

hotel porch, the ladies knitted as the days rolled by, their needles clicking ever more furiously.

Four days before Christmas, impatience won out. The families at last boarded the steamer *Governor Safford* bound for Sarasota Bay. Somehow mothers and children found a place to curl up for the night in the single cabin, while the men slept outside on deck between stacks of luggage. Kerosene lamps faintly lit the way around lumpy forms of sleepers.

The day before Christmas Eve, the *Governor Safford* entered the mouth of Tampa Bay and passed Egmont Lighthouse. At last, in late afternoon, the colonists cast their eyes upon the town of Sarasota and the venture for which they had cut ties to the past and to which they had committed their futures. As the steamer pulled closer to the shore of virgin oak, cedar, and rising pinelands, they saw a makeshift dock at the bay shore. At its foot was one single structure, "the Company Store . . . the only building in sight." No streets, no homes, only a stumpy sand trail led up the slope. The trail was Main Street.

A bitter blow

Amid the press and shock of dashed hopes the colonists found the warm, welcoming faces of strangers. The local families knew better than anyone the task ahead and softened the blow with what they could share. The Whitaker family, the Riggins, Abbes, Tuckers, and Tatums — they were there when the families from Scotland stepped ashore. The memory of that, in some cases, would outlast the rest. Even so, only a few were to overcome the hardships ahead to make Sarasota home.

Children clustered around mothers while fathers tried to get the word on plans for their tired, hungry families. John Tait met with them, as well as A.C. Acton, a newly immigrated Britisher who represented the company as a manager. Some families were taken in by the local settlers, some were designated to bunk in the company store. Another group set out for the vacant, porch-wrapped log homestead house built by Cedar Key's Captain Albert Willard a few years earlier in the wooded bayfront nearby. The manager for the company store, Tom M. Weir, passed

Some newly arrived Sarasota colonists were forced to camp out in the rough, setting up makeshift tents and axing out a clearing.

Some of the young men among the colonists reached Tampa only a few days after they reached Florida, then hurried on to Sarasota to help with the behind-schedule building of the new town.

In the shade of his broad-brimmed European hat, a colonist rowed along the pristine Hillsborough River.

58

ut bedding and cots to those families who had none in their luggage.

Tents were pitched along the bayfront. Alex Browning's mother turned out scones and pancakes over an open fire and boiled water for tea on a kerosene burner. Later, around a large community bonfire, the men smoked their pipes while the locals told the newcomers all about the land to which they had come. Alex Browning noticed that Sarasota's young men made special efforts to impress the pretty, red-cheeked Scotch girls.

Hamlin Whitaker taught the tricks of cast netting the plentiful staple, mullet, and showed colonists how to clean and fry the split fish on stakes set over a firebed. His young brother Emile brought bread baked by their mother, Mary Jane Wyatt Whitaker, and demonstrated for the girls the art of baking bread in a pot over a campfire.

The colonists' ultimate grim surprise was not manmade, but handcrafted by Mother Nature. The mild winter temperatures which had enticed the Scots to discard their heavy woolens took a dive. The winds turned from south to north and a cold rain fell as temperatures dropped. Then, snow fell on Sarasota. Even the natives were taken completely by surprise — they had never seen snow at Sarasota Bay.

During the bitter freeze, giant mangrove trees died along the bay. Soon dead fish began washing onto oyster bars, tens of thousands rotting in deep layers stretching along like hedgerows. Their stench filled the air. Many judged the colony an awful mistake and left. Others called on John Tait in the night with shotguns, but he had abandoned his dream, too. When his visitors arrived, John Tait was already gone.

Sarasota, circa 1886, as seen from the roof of the De Soto Hotel. In the background are freshly painted new cottages along sandy roads newly carved out of virgin forest.

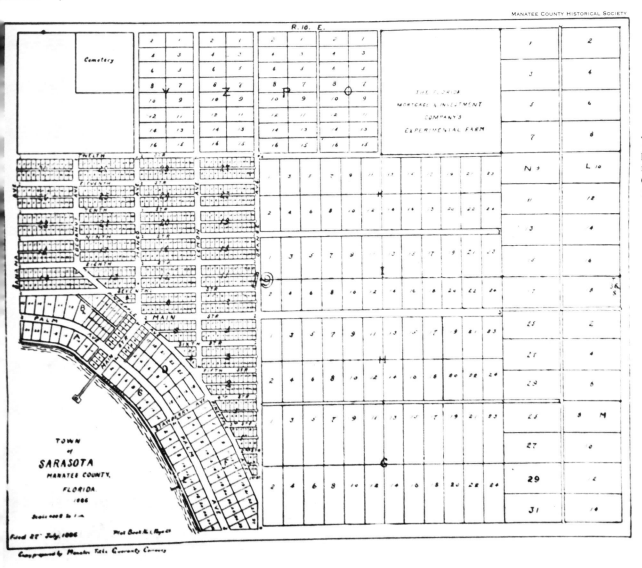

The town of Sarasota was platted out in 1885 and registered with the Clerk of Court for Manatee County in 1886.

The Jane Gault and John Browning family, circa 1890, one of the families of Scots that arrived with the Ormiston Colony in 1885.

7. A City Is Born

MANATEE RIVER JOUR

BRAIDENTOWN, M ... FLORIDA, THURSDAY, MA

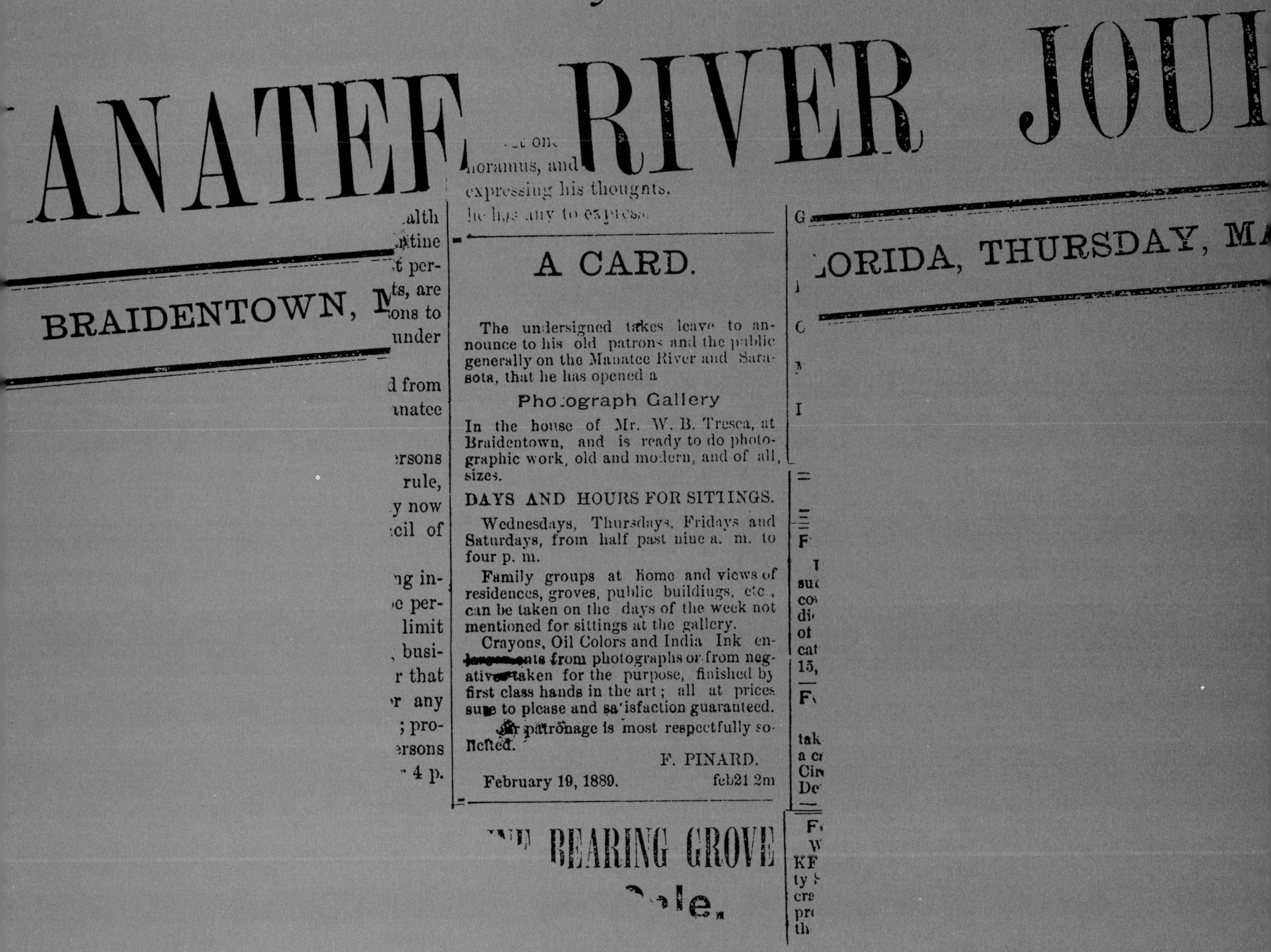

A CARD.

The undersigned takes leave to announce to his old patrons and the public generally on the Manatee River and Sarasota, that he has opened a

Photograph Gallery

In the house of Mr. W. B. Tresca, at Braidentown, and is ready to do photographic work, old and modern, and of all sizes.

DAYS AND HOURS FOR SITTINGS.

Wednesdays, Thursdays, Fridays and Saturdays, from half past nine a. m. to four p. m.

Family groups at home and views of residences, groves, public buildings, etc., can be taken on the days of the week not mentioned for sittings at the gallery.

Crayons, Oil Colors and India Ink enlargements from photographs or from negatives taken for the purpose, finished by first class hands in the art; all at prices sure to please and satisfaction guaranteed.

Your patronage is most respectfully solicited.

F. PINARD.

February 19, 1889. feb21 2m

BEARING GROVE

Felix Pinard advertised in the February 19, 1889 *Manatee River Journal.*

*O*ver the next year and a half, after the arrival of the Scottish immigrants in 1885, FM&I pumped capital into its development. For land and interest spent, their total was nearly £50,000. A thousand went for surveying and another thousand on surveying, grading, and draining. In the first few months, the company spent £3,000 on improvements to the town of Sarasota, the village of Fruitville, an experimental farm, a hospital, and a cemetery.

First Street between Central and Pineapple, looking west, circa 1886.

A frontier life style

The company laid out its town. The north-south ways were to be named for fruits that appealed to the European investor, with names such as Pineapple, Strawberry, Lime, Mango, Cocoanut, Pineapple and Banana. The east-west streets were to be numbered consecutively from the intersection of Pineapple and Orange. Men painstakingly grubbed trees to clear for narrow, sandy roads. Main Street was constructed beyond the town's central intersection, the meeting of Pineapple, Mango, and Main (today's Five Points) and into the inland pineland. From Five Points, Main Street was cleared of stumps to the eastern edge of the company's town (vicinity of Lime Avenue). A ditch along the roadway drained the bed and provided dirt for the road's crown.

Shallow-draft vessels transported building materials from the Gulf ports of Pensacola, Pascagoula, and Appalachicola, as well as Cedar Key. Captain Lewis Roberts, formerly of Key West, supervised the ferrying of materials to shore. From the schooners, men tossed lumber overboard. The boards were floated to mule-drawn wagons pulled into the bay until the mules stood in water touching their bellies. Like the company mules, the laborers worked waist-deep in cold December waters.

Crews of carpenters and workers had arrived from Lakeland with Captain Roberts to build the town's hotel and a boarding house. First, the two-story boarding house was built at the hub of the town plat (site of present-day Southeast Bank). A manager, Joe Vincent, arrived with his wife, Rosy, and their five young children to fill the boarding house with the sounds of their musical family.

One of the first bayfront construction projects was a community dock, which extended out from the foot of the sandy Main Street. Colonists who could work hired on to build the wharf. The laborers earned two dollars a day and forged a link in a chain of subsistence. Young Alex Browning was one of those who signed on. "One of my first jobs was setting the piling. . . . This was done by sharpening the end with an axe, wedge, shape and rock it back and forth, while we were in the water from knee deep to shoulder deep." At the end of the dock, a square 50-foot extension supported construction of a company warehouse from which supplies were trucked ashore to the company store over a 2 x 4 railway.

Cottages promised for colonists went up on the town block bounded by Mango (now Central) and Cocoanut (between present-day Third and Fourth streets). The cottages were built as "portables" for the colonists, some of whom signed on to work with the company laborers.

The workers also put up a 16 x 24 foot school. Two more cottages went up on Main Street, one at Five Points to be used as a town church. There, also, the laborers sank an artesian well to supply water for the town.

In one of the new cottages, the company manager, Mr. Acton, had his office. There the colonists drew lots for their farm acreage. Some were dismayed to find that their 40 acres were very far from town. John Browning, father of Alex, drew his farm in the present-day Fruitville area, on the crude road to the Pine Level courthouse and near the area of the company's Village of Fruitville. The trek over nearly roadless areas required tedious time and effort. Others learned to their horror that their plots were suited only for grazing cattle rather than for the production of citrus and crops upon which their economic hopes had been founded.

Despite all the traumas, some colonists threw themselves into the awesome manual labor required of settlement. They learned to drive ox teams and to crack whips as well as any Florida "Cracker." Several contracted to clear the 40-acre company experimental farm. Others continued to work on road crews, clearing roadways and burning out stumps. The town was, wrote young Alex Browning, a "busy place, with the ring of axes and the crash of falling pine trees, accompanied by the songs of negroes, and burning brush." Laborers were grateful for pay despite aching muscles, blisters, and calluses. They put in a ten-hour day for a few dollars and considered it "good wages."

On the east and north sides of the platted town, the company soon had a clearing for its experimental farm (in the vicinity of present-day Sixth Street and Washington Boulevard) and Rosemary Cemetery (at present-day Central and Ninth).

Three handsome sons: Walter, Jim and Luther Mason.

Gazing in 1886 from the roof of the Belle Haven Hotel one could look down upon the first fruits of the municipal building boom — the Whitaker Smith Livery Stable, the office and home of Dr. Wallace and the twin two-story frame buildings, one of which served for church services.

ROSEMARY CEMETERY.

SARASOTA, FLA., *Jan'ry 16* 1905

Know All Men By These Presents:

THAT *C.V.S. and Rose Wilson* has paid the sum of *Ten* Dollars, and has become the owner of Lot No. *Nine* in Block "*A*" of Rosemary Cemetery, Sarasota, Fla., subject to the Regulations of the Cemetery. This Certificate is evidence of such ownership, and accepted by the purchaser under said Regulations.

IN WITNESS WHEREOF, The Mayor of the Town of Sarasota has herewith set his Hand, and caused the impression of the Seal of the Town of Sarasota to be made hereunto, at the Town Hall in the Town of Sarasota, the day and year above written.

ATTEST: *C.V.S. Wilson*
Town Clerk.

J. Hamilton Gillespie
Mayor of the Town of Sarasota.

Rest In Peace

When Florida Mortgage and Investment Company laid out its Town of Sarasota, the plan included a cemetery on the north edge of town. Rosemary Cemetery became the final resting place of many Sarasotans. Landmark names of original town fathers would ultimately stand on granite stones within the plot.

In 1905, after incorporation of Sarasota, when C.V.S. and Rose Wilson paid $10 to buy a lot, the deed was officially signed by Mayor J. Hamilton Gillespie as well as the town clerk, who in this instance also happened to be the buyer, Mr. Wilson.

The town seal — prominently featuring its original mullet — was affixed to the historic document.

A shining beacon

In that banner year of 1886, the crowning achievement of Florida Mortgage and Investment Company soon stood proudly upon the bayfront, by the dock at the foot of the new Main Street. It was the De Soto Hotel, a shining beacon to entice visitors to visit long enough to become interested in investing in the future of the new Gulf coast town. The hotel stood three stories high, surrounded by a two-story veranda and capped by a flag-flying, twelve-window observatory. From the artesian well at Five Points, water was pumped into a storage tank, from which the hotel drew water. From her rooftop, the new town's commercial photographer, Frenchman Felix Pinard, photographed Main Street and all its new buildings.

Soon the De Soto Hotel was joined near the bayfront by another imposing structure — an expansive house for the company's new manager, John Hamilton Gillespie, son of Sir John Gillespie, illustrious company director and colony patron. Like his father, Gillespie was an attorney, a Writer to the Signet, and a member of the Royal Company of Archers. He had served with the Midlothian Artillery Brigade of Volunteers in Australia.

The new home Gillespie and his wife planned was built of lumber, with doors, sashes, and hardware shipped in from Apalachicola. Their yard was to be entirely enclosed by a planed and sanded picket fence.

Gillespie was a lay reader for the regular Episcopal services held in the company's house at Five Points. There he alternated Sundays with Preacher Redd from Tatum Ridge and Mr. Ange, who lived by Phillippi Creek and delivered what Alex Browning called "a regular old hardshell sermon."

Aside from his lifelong efforts in the church, Gillespie was absolutely consumed with passion for the game of golf. He had learned the game in Scotland at St. Andrews. Within the expansive enclosure of his home, the young aristocrat built a golf tee and, in a natural clearing up the slope (at the site of the present-day Sarasota post office), laid out a golf course using a cowpath for a throughway. He later laid out a nine-hole course and a clubhouse in the city, which encompassed the present-day Sarasota county courthouse, the administration building and jail, and the historic A.C.L. railroad station, and extended easterly several blocks beyond Lime Avenue. Its borders touched on Links and Gillespie avenues. The remains of Golf Street are a few blocks away.)

Newcoming immigrants were not the only investors in the company's new town. Natives of Sarasota Bay also invested heavily in the future of the town. Three Whitaker sons, whose parents had been at Sarasota Bay for 40 years, set up businesses on Main Street. Charlie and Furman Whitaker built a store across from a drug store operated by a newly arriving Scot, Dr. Robert Wallace. Their brother, Hamlin, built a livery stable. Hamlin slaughtered a steer every week and sold it among the people in Sarasota and Bradentown on the Manatee River. The brothers bought citrus, produce, and livestock from the settlers, retailed among the coastal buyers, and exported the rest to market.

They bought shares in the company along with other locals such as Myron Abbe, George Riggin, and W.G. Wilson.

During its initial two years of operation, Florida Mortgage and Investment had expenditures and assets of £106,000. More than £5,000 alone was spent on the De Soto Hotel and its furnishings — more than the cost of all the other cottages, buildings, and portable houses combined. The new hotel on the recently constructed Main Street was impressive by any standards, attracting more and more tourists. Many returned annually for two or three months to the sportsmen's paradise to shoot birds, catch fish, and sail the waters of the bay. Still others came to fight tuberculosis, chillblains, or rheumatism. Sarasota's sun was healing and her accommodations inviting and well-advertised in newspapers at home and abroad.

The company published a 28-page brochure in St. Louis called "De Soto Hotel in Sara Sota on the Gulf," extolling the virtues of the area. The sale of company land was advertised along with resale parcels throughout the state. Railroad connections from Gainesville and Jacksonville were detailed.

Activity in Sarasota centered around the De Soto Hotel. Steamers carried passengers and freight between the hotel and the Tampa terminus of the railroad, departing from the wharf right at the hotel's front door and the foot of Main Street. The sidewheeler *Kissimmee* ran weekly with passengers. Tampa traffic also traveled aboard the *Mary Disston,* known locally as "Dirty Mary." Local entrepreneurs plied the Gulf in small commercial craft, running cargoes from the bay to market at Key West. Pigs, chickens, sweet potatos, and melons were hauled aboard local craft with such names as *Phantom, Wild Goose, Guide, Ruby, Vision, Lizzie, Florence,* and *Margaret Ann.*

In 1888, when the De Soto Hotel was about to enter its third winter tourist season, a raging epidemic of yellow fever hit the coasts. Thousands in Florida were struck, many died. Citizens across the state feared an adverse effect upon the coming winter tourist season, and quarantines shut down all commerce. Not until Christmas did the first crates of oranges and barrels of fish go out of the area.

The yellow fever epidemic of 1888 was followed within a handful of years by the national panic of 1893, brought on by excessive speculation in railroads and monetary uncertainty. The Sherman Silver Purchase policy drove gold out of circulation, while a simultaneous crisis in England resulted in a flow of gold out of the United States. In Florida, the panic ushered in a sudden halt to capital investments in massive development enterprises. Suddenly, buyers stopped buying, investors stopped investing, and the projections of the mid-1880s became meaningless numbers calculated for another time. Even the grandaddy of it all, Hamilton Disston's corporate enterprise in Florida, came to a paralyzing slowdown, and then to a grinding stop with the sudden death of the entrepreneur in 1896.

PHOTO BY FELIX PINARD. FLORIDA PHOTOGRAPHIC COLLECTION. FLORIDA STATE ARCHIVES

The first Mrs. Hamilton Gillespie, Mary, before the Gillespies' Palm Avenue house built near the Belle Haven.

The heart of Sarasota's bayfront development in 1886, the De Soto Hotel was the pride and joy of Florida Mortgage and Investment Company.

Captain Will Hamlin's *Phantom* takes on cargo at Webb's packing house. Formerly the *Ella M. Little* of Homosassa, she was rebuilt in Frank Guptill's boat yard at Spanish Point and sailed out of Casey Key in commercial traffic for decades.

The steamer *Mary Disston*, built at Kissimmee in 1884, carried mail, freight and passengers and was better known as "Dirty Mary" according to colonist Alex Browning in his colorful memoirs.

The sidewheeler *Gussie* which ran from Manatee River to Cuba in the 1880s was one of the largest cattle transports in the early local industry.

Felix Pinard, a handsome young Frenchman, arrived in Sarasota shortly after Florida Mortgage & Investment started its development; he became Sarasota's first commercial photographer. For years he photographed the young town, whose barefoot families posed proudly for his camera against their homemade quilts. Pinard's surviving photographs provide a poignant glimpse of a town struggling to become a twentieth century entity.

67

Guests at the downtown Belle Haven fed chickens from the steps, while a kitten padded its way among the rockers lined up on the shady veranda.

Pinard photographed Sarasota's downtown bayfront after the town was laid out by the developer. Back in the trees stands the glorious new home of the company manager, J. Hamilton Gillespie.

At the bayfront Belle Haven Hotel, sportsmen proudly roped ten tarpon to the porch rail.

The original Gulfstream Avenue was a deeply rutted, narrow track along the beach front.

The steamer *Mistletoe*, chugging along in Sarasota Bay, carried passengers on regular runs to and from Tampa.

Dr. Leffingwell and Dr. Warren posed by Sarasota Bay with crossed rods and three prize tarpon.

Pinard often photographed a favorite subject — his wife, Helen Drew, and their children, Francis and Josephine.

The Vincent children, known throughout the young community as a musical family, posed with instruments in hand.

Bicylists visited Sarasota Bay in the season, their life style a vivid contrast to that of many locals.

The family of L.D. Hodges, before the ubiquitous backdrop of a handmade quilt.

Even though the weeds grew hub deep, the antebellum Braden plantation house on the Manatee River remained a favorite place to see and photograph during the final years of the 1800s.

The Main Street boardwalk carried the visitor over deep sand directly to the front steps of Vincent House. Pinard caught the Whitaker mules grazing on the boarding house grass.

Mother and baby, all dressed in Sunday best, posed in the front yard of their inland homestead.

The Inn, site of an 1894 Baptist Convention, said to be Sarasota's first.

Pinard homesite by the bayfront on Gulf Stream Avenue.

THE PHOTOGRAPHS ON THESE PAGES ARE BY FELIX PINARD, COURTESY OF FLORIDA STATE ARCHIVES, FLORIDA PHOTOGRAPHIC COLLECTION.

A "bye word" in Florida

Hamilton Gillespie remained in Sarasota to nurse along the corporate interests in which his father continued to play a major role as director and solicitor. Although the directors had established their town and surrounding subdivisions, the resulting revenues were never what the company prospectus had envisioned. The bad start with the colony and the freeze could be blamed for much, but investors close to the situation cited another cause for the continuing failure of the town to blossom and grow — young John Hamilton Gillespie. The Whitakers, Riggins, Myron Abbe, and other stable townspeople had thrown in their economic lot with the company's. They owned stock and were agitated when investments looked bad. In a singular letter printed and circulated to shareholders, they castigated Gillespie and asked that he be removed for mismanagement, charging that he was "totally unfitted and incapable, both mentally and morally" and that he "used his position for his own ends and interests in direct opposition to those of the Shareholders." They suggested that Gillespie's actions were those of one "temporarily insane" and that he quarreled in "a most outrageous manner" with nearly everyone who arrived in town. They charged that through his widely-known misconduct, Gillespie's name had become "a bye word on the West Coast of Florida."

The local petitioners also included colonists such as the M'Auslans, Stewarts, and Anton Kleinoscheg, as well as Robert Wallace, the town's doctor. Their position was supported by Piers E. Warburton, then a resident of Acton in Polk County. Warburton, who had been FM&I's general manager twice and once worked over Gillespie as assistant manager, asserted that the removal of the young Scot was "absolutely necessary."

Ultimately, two of the Whitaker boys went on to invest in a future elsewhere. Only one adult son, Hamlin, remained as a businessman in the town venture that had not lived up to expectations.

The Austrian flag at Cunliff Lane

While some of the colonists had worked for the company in constructing the town of Sarasota, others engaged precisely in what they had come to do. One who did both was Anton Kleinoscheg, not a Scot but an Austrian.

Kleinoscheg, who came from an aristocratic family of wine producers with vineyards in Austria, bought a farm plot near Phillippi Creek, where he planted grape vines from home and dreamed of a successful commercial operation. When the young Austrian became ill with fever, a local family, ignoring its own troubles, took pity on the newcomer. He was taken in by Sarasota's postmistress, the widow of Charles Abbe, and her daughter, Carrie, a former Chicago schoolteacher.

Once recovered, Kleinoscheg returned to his fields. Even though he had ditched his clearing, the rainy season flooded the area and destruction lay across the face of his work. But some good came with the bad. Kleinoscheg and Carrie Abbe fell in love and were married. They built a house at the foot of present-day Cunliff Lane — the sandy wagon trail which had once been the main bayfront street of the settlement. Their new home stood across the wagon trail from the store of Alfred Bidwell, convicted leader of the vigilantes who had murdered Carrie's father, and within a hundred feet of the place where Charles Abbe had died.

Over the house, Kleinoscheg daily flew an Austrian flag, climbing a ladder built on the side of the house to raise and lower his national banner. He and Carrie lived there, farmed, fished, and worked to restore his health until the devastating winter of 1894.

During that year, immediately following the international panic of 1893, a natural disaster again struck south Florida. The temperature dropped to below 20 degrees early Sunday, December 29. Temperatures fell to 10 degrees in the state's citrus beltway across the central northern counties. The freeze was followed by mild weather which

Cunliff Lane in the late 1880s was a sandy road leading to the tidy Kleinoscheg home by Sarasota Bay.

encouraged new growth in damaged groves. Then, toward the end of the first week of February, temperatures at Tampa Bay dropped to 22 degrees and fell below the freezing mark during the two days to follow. Little children at Sarasota Bay were thrilled to see snow lying on the limbs of trees when they awoke one morning. Their parents and grandparents did not share their enthusiasm. In Jacksonville, trees split wide open. In Orlando, icicles hung from ripe fruit and heavy limbs. Near Gainesville, citrus towns such as Windsor were destined to become ghost towns within a few years. Florida's citrus belt moved farther south permanently.

Anton Kleinoscheg had lost his gamble on Florida and made plans to return with Carrie to his family estate in Austria. He had lost his health and his investment. He had not, however, lost his sense of humor. He carved the image of a palm frond in wood from one of his trees destroyed by the freeze. Into the smooth surface, the poet carved his little poem of parting:

> *The tree that furnished this splinter*
> *died of a cold last winter.*

Anton and Carrie Abbe Kleinoscheg, circa 1890.

Garrett "Dink" Murphy poses with family and friends on his Myakka cattle ranch. The ranch was purchased by Mrs. Potter Palmer and later became part of Myakka State Park.

Pioneer cattleman Garrett "Dink" Murphy, hunting dog at his feet, barefoot children swinging legs over a wagon by his side, poses with family, game and sportsmen at his Myakka ranch.

Flanking the mule, the wagon and the crate of oranges, workers pose on their ladders in the 1890s.

Frederic Remington depicted a frontier cowboy ambush in typical cattle range country of the Sarasota-Manatee-DeSoto region.

A Florida "Cracker" on the humble porch of his log cabin.

The spectre of war

A few years after the great freeze, Hamilton Gillespie still was in the midst of routine activity at Sarasota. He continued his enthusiasm for golf, working for Tampa developer Henry Plant on his new course and hoping to work for Henry Flagler, whose investments transformed Florida's east coast. From time to time, the company sent someone to assess progress; often the report was negative. The company's fortunes looked especially bleak after one such visit when Gillespie wrote home to his mother in Scotland. He discussed his golf game ("I won at Kissimee again"), prospects of tournament playing, and of a coming war which frightened the market and completely stopped sales.

The spectre of war loomed over the coast of Florida the same year as the great freeze, when a revolt of Cubans against Spanish rule threatened to involve the United States. The revolution was at Florida's back door. And two years later, in the midst of the 1897-98 tourist season, it threatened her economy as well as her sense of well-being. Businessmen generally feared that U.S. entry into the war might retard recovery from the panic of 1893. But the combined forces of a barbarous conflict in Cuba and yellow journalism in New York propelled the country toward intervention. The United States entered the Spanish-American War in April 1898. West coast Floridians feared a Spanish invasion. That month, Hamilton Gillespie wrote his mother, "We here are very exposed . . . I fully expect if war comes that every house in the place will be burnt."

The company manager saw no hope for military protection for the town. "I have applied to the authorities for protection but I think they have not enough protection for themselves, far less for us."

Regarding land sales, Gillespie was even more despondent. "It is impossible to *give* land away until peace is restored."

The Scot-turned-Floridian related well to his adopted home. In his relating of the war, he echoed a pride in the fierce cowboy tradition, a pride that had been familiar half a century earlier during the Seminole wars: "I see they expected to put the cowhunters first into Cuba. I expect they can't trust the Regulars. Too soft. So I may get to the front."

The war was suddenly very close. By the end of May, 23,000 troops had bivouacked in Tampa. The U.S. gunboat *Helena* cruised offshore. Panic was high. A strange steamer heading unexpectedly into Big Pass occasioned an alarm from the Belle Haven observatory and sent citizens fleeing to the surrounding woods. The vessel proved to be American.

Though Sarasotans feared an invasion of Spanish troops, what they got was an American one. Great numbers of soldiers descended on Florida ports, inundating coastal suppliers with their presence and the logistical challenges of space for the men and the commodities arriving to feed and equip them.

Richard Jeffcott's Gulfstream Avenue home, 1899, was surrounded by a plank and wire fence to keep out roaming cattle and wildlife.

8. Sarasota Enters The Twentieth Century

Group of young people at Osprey, circa 1900. The Spanish Point homestead was a favorite gathering place for the Little Sarasota Bay community.

Many coastal settlers found Indian mounds on the lands they claimed for settlement.

Mary Jane Wyatt Whitaker, pioneer settler.

A springboard wagon hitched to a team of oxen trundled settlers across South Florida's frontier trails.

*T*he Spanish American War had brought tens of thousands of military personnel south to Tampa. Ordered out to Cuba, they had been transported across the waterways of Tampa Bay — even the Rough Rider Teddy Roosevelt. In the course of the conflict, highly hyped by the press, many more died of disease than foreign bullets and, as always, Cuba's affairs directly affected her Gulf coast neighbor, Florida. Because of the conflict, great numbers of Americans had seen Florida. Long after bad memories of the war had faded, many men returned.

The war left in its wake renewed hope for return to normalcy and economic growth. The state's turn-of-the-century population showed a 42 percent increase in just a decade. As Floridians increasingly distanced themselves from the pioneer era, progressive changes were apparent, particularly in coastal communities. In the company town of Sarasota, enterprising residents began to see the advantage of self-government, of incorporating their town as a municipality. And in the summer of 1902, voters met and took action.

On August 14, citizenry set out municipal bounds of incorporation and elected officers. The boundaries were those of the original town platted seventeen years earlier by Florida Mortgage and Investment. Electors added four parcels lying along the bay and Hudson Bayou so that the new municipality lay roughly between the bay on the west and the present-day Seaboard Railroad tracks on the east. On the north and south, the boundaries extended from present-day Tenth Street to Hudson Bayou.

The 162nd Infantry Company at Fort Dade on Egmont Key, at the time of the Spanish American War.

Boat and picnic outings were favorite leisure pastimes for residents as well as tourists.

Privies and profanity

After a two-month period of legal notice, qualified voters again came together on October 14 to elect Sarasota's first municipal officers: five aldermen — J.B. Turner, Dr. J.O. Brown, G.W. Blackburn, W.J. Hill and Harry L. Higel — and a clerk, B.D. Gillett. T.F. Blair was elected marshal. Sarasota's first mayor was to be none other than J. Hamilton Gillespie, the aristocratic Scot who had come to Sarasota sixteen years earlier to manage corporate development interests. On his arrival, Gillespie had been a thin, wiry fellow in his 30s. Now, as mayor, he was approaching his 50th year and posed quite properly as a portly figure.

Sarasota's Mayor Hamilton Gillespie, like his father before him, held membership in Scotland's Royal Company of Archers.

On Monday following elections, October 20, Sarasota's first officers held their initial meeting and Dr. Brown was unanimously elected president of the council. At the second meeting, October 27, the council adopted 26 rules and procedures, including the stipulation that each alderman should rise to address the chair and might speak only when recognized. A member who left the meeting without permission might be fined five dollars.

The council paid $38.50 to publisher C.V.S. Wilson of the Sarasota *Times* to print the new ordinances in his weekly newspaper for four consecutive issues. Sarasota's publisher had several decades of experience. The New York-born Wilson had been publishing in Florida since shortly after the Civil War. He had left Central Florida after twenty years to move with his family to the village of Manatee, governmental seat for the Manatee-Sarasota region, where he established the Manatee *Advocate* shortly before the yellow fever epidemic of the late 1880s, which claimed his wife. A year later, his son died. A widower with five children, some years later Wilson had married Rose Phillips, and the two had brought his presses to Sarasota and began publishing the *Times* from an office at the foot of Main Street.

The council's ordinances covered a broad range of subjects and reflected the turn-of-the-century life style of city fathers and their peers. Standards were set for items ranging from privies to profanity. The mayor, whose authority extended to calling special council meetings and elections, issued warrants against offenders. After arrest by the marshal, offenders were heard in proceedings before Mayor's Court, which presided over violations of municipal ordinances.

Persons could be fined or imprisoned at hard labor for violations of ordinances relating to profanity, fighting, blocking the sidewalk, or driving a wagon over a bridge "faster than a walk." Fire safety played a prominent role in a town whose buildings were constructed exclusively of wood, and citizens risked a $50 fine or twenty days in the calaboose for entering a stable with "an open or uncovered light." Merchants were required to store no more than three kegs of powder and then only in tin containers. They were prohibited from displaying or selling explosives or flammable liquids after twilight, called "early candlelight." Ordinances prohibited burning trash within 60 feet of houses or businesses and regulated a cautious approach to installation of stovepipes. A permit from Mayor Gillespie was required of Sarasotans who wished to set off "fireworks, rockets or fireballs."

While tourists and investors were most welcome, Sarasota's council turned a jaundiced eye upon unemployed visitors — "persons having no visible means of support" — and categorized those as vagrants. An ordinance prohibited their sleeping in citizens' privies, unfinished buildings, and "other outhouses," or from hitching rides on railroad cars (a relatively easy thing to do since the train's top in-town speed was restricted to six miles per hour).

On the streets of Sarasota, acceptable behavior was carefully prescribed. Businesses located on shaded streets were required to install hitching posts for horses, while owners of mules and oxen were prohibited from tying the animals to trees. Any woman whose "reputation for chastity and virtue is bad" was prohibited from what the councilmen called "plying her vocation." Houses of prostitution, sale of "lewd books" and presentation of "lewd plays," gambling on keno, wheel of fortune, or pool, as well as operation of "bawdy houses" were punishable by fine or imprisonment. Citizens were forbidden to disrupt worship services by means of noise, nudity, indecent behavior, or profanity. The only businesses that might operate on Sunday were those of Sarasota's barbers, and then only in the morning until 10 o'clock, and drugstores, which might be open all day but only for the sale of medicines.

Sarasota residences lining Orange Avenue, circa 1905, were advertised widely for winter season rentals.

City fathers also took a dim view of abuse of animals and considered the overall aesthetics of their municipal environment. They ordained a $50 fine against anyone who "cruelly beats, tortures, maltreats or abuses" not just the beast of burden, but also the "dog, cat, or other animal or bird." Residents were expected to refrain from penning hogs in town and from leaving carcasses to the whims of Mother Nature's due process. They were required by ordinance to regularly clean out privies and transport "contents" to some unnamed place — at *least* every fifteen days.

Enforcement of everything from public morality to inspection of privies fell upon Sarasota's Marshal Blair, who was empowered to arrest. In the case of fire danger, he was required to act fast, giving violators only twelve hours to correct substandard situations.

Leaving organizational matters behind, Sarasota's officers convened for the third regularly scheduled meeting and finally were able to turn their attention to pressing administrative matters. Meeting at the home of J.P. Turner, the council considered its first municipal building project, the need for which had been legislatively created — "the matter of building a calaboose." Harry L. Higel and George Blackburn were appointed to get plans and estimates. During the following several weeks, the council accepted the mayor's offer to "advance" $200 for construction costs and agreed to give a note for principal plus interest. W.F. Rigby bid $105 to build it, and Gillespie selected the site — the north side of Cedar Point (present-day Golden Gate Point area).

Over the next few months, the new municipality was supported by Mayor Gillespie on numerous occasions through gifts. All the new ordinances — 27 of them — were entered in a handsome red leather-bound volume presented as a gift by Gillespie to the town.

The council's sixth meeting addressed the matter of bondedness and payment of officers. Bonds for clerk and marshal were set at $200 each. The clerk was to receive $10 for writing and recording ordinances and two and a half percent on all collections, while the marshal was initially to be paid $10 for his work as sanitary inspector and $5 monthly thereafter. He was also to get a dollar for each arrest he made, and a percentage on all collections for licensing.

A Fortuitous Accident

South Carolina-born Leonard Reid's lifetime residency in Sarasota was an accident.

Reid had sailed in December 1900 aboard a fishing boat out of Savannah bound for Cuba. The boat had found its way to Sarasota on New Year's Eve, a holiday, and Reid was one of those who attended a party ashore. Afterward, proceeding to the bayfront, he discovered that the fishing boat had pulled out without him.

Fishermen introduced Reid, who was in sudden need of a job, to the aristocratic "Colonel" Hamilton Gillespie, who hired Reid to drive his carriage, supervise his grounds, and work and live at "Roseburn," the home Gillespie had built on Morrill Street. The household held an elevated place of social and political status in Sarasota, and Reid became a legendary part of it all.

Reid married Perry-born Eddie Coleman that same year, in 1901. They eventually acquired property in Sarasota and raised a family of four — Ray Field, James Leonard, Ethel, and Viola.

Reid had intended to go fishing in Cuba, but stayed a lifetime in Sarasota.

The municipal dock at the foot of Main Street in 1899, three years before Sarasota was first incorporated.

When Mrs. Gillespie set off with her parasol and her sister Louise, they were entrusted to Mayor Gillespie's right arm, Leonard Reid. The dog, Tiny, perched proudly alongside the top-hatted Reid.

Leonard Reid was educated at Savannah Normal School before his arrival in Sarasota.

At the turn of the century, modern commercial photographers still found some families living in poverty in Florida's remote piney woods.

"Roseburn," the Victorian home of Mayor J. Hamilton Gillespie and Mrs. Gillespie, the former Miss Blanche McDaniel of Bradentown. In that house (demolished in 1984 to make way for an apartment complex), the first Sarasota Town Council held its first meeting.

Boardwalks and a burying ground

In addition to the caboose, the council faced the need for bridging. Sarasota's streets crossed arms of Hudson Bayou and natural waterways flowing into the bay. The councilmen ordered bridges built at spots on Palm Avenue near the home of Gillespie's neighbor, E.W. Morrill, for whom Morrill Street was later named. Like Gillespie, Morrill was referred to as "Colonel" by the townsmen.

The council addressed the question of tidying and lighting the town. It purchased three kerosene lamps at a total cost of less than $12 from Sarasota merchants Highsmith Turner and Co. To their cost was added $5 a month to be paid to the marshal for "filling, cleaning, lighting, and extinguishing the street town lamps." Property owners themselves bore the cost of new sidewalks. Those on the south side of Main Street were required to build walkways ("a good and substantial sidewalk, seven and a half feet wide") while the store owners on the north side were required only to keep their existing boardwalk "in good order."

Attention next turned to a municipal burying ground, Rosemary Cemetery, set aside by Florida Mortgage and Investment in its original plat. The council voted its thanks to Mayor Gillespie for his gift of the cemetery to the municipality, while Colonel Morrill proposed to survey and stake it for $35. Within a few months, the survey complete, the cemetery lots were ready for sale. For $10, $20, or $30, buyers might gain a small lot, a large one, or one of those in the center of each block.

The new municipality of Sarasota embraced significant modernizations quickly. Two new businesses promptly called on the council for permission to conduct modern utilities. In December 1902, six representatives of Sarasota Ice, Fish, and Power Company asked for a permit to make ice, store and handle fish, and operate electric lights in town. Two months later, Peninsula Telephone petitioned to construct and maintain a telephone exchange. Lights, telephones, ordinances, and sidewalks — in a few short months, Sarasota's first councilmen had put the machinery in gear to move forward in keeping with America's turn-of-the-century outlook and the municipal slogan cast on its seal: *May Sarasota Prosper.*

Eliza and Frank Guptill's home atop an Indian mound hosted winter guests. It later became part of Mrs. Potter Palmer's winter estate.

Interior of the Frank and Luzzie Guptill home where the young people of the Little Sarasota Bay community gathered for Saturday night dances.

Colonel Hamilton Gillespie brushed up on his golf swing at his home on South Palm Avenue.

In 1908 Dr. Jack Halton opened The Halton, his sanitorium on Gulfstream Avenue, in a building developed by Mayor Hamilton Gillespie.

Badger Pharmacy, circa 1907, a gathering place for Sarasotans for decades.

The home of Councilman Harry L. Higel stood at the foot of Main Street in 1905. The downstairs housed the office of Dr. Jack Halton.

Main Street Sarasota, circa 1909.

In 1903, only a year after Sarasota was incorporated, Main Street between Five Points and Orange Avenue was a quiet stretch slumbering in the heat of the afternoon sun.

Don't Stop The Presses

After four decades of newspaper publishing in Florida, more than two of them in the Manatee-Sarasota communities, C.V.S. Wilson left his business in the capable hands of Rose, his wife. Rose had been operating the business during her husband's illness and would continue turning out the Sarasota *Times* until she sold out years later during the boom in 1923.

Four weeks before his death in September 1910, Wilson itemized the equipment he bequeathed. The inventory of Sarasota's only newspaper plant consisted of the following:

"One Fairhaven two-revolution cylinder press; one Chandler & Price job printing press; one Washington-Hoe printing press; one paper cutter; one imposing stone; cases, racks, desks, type and all printing and other material now a part of the Sarasota *Times* newspaper and job printing outfit . . . in office building on . . . Main Street . . . together with the books and accounts and good-will of newspaper and job printing business."

— C.V.S. Wilson, August 26, 1910

C.V.S. and Rose Wilson, publishers of the Sarasota *Times*.

The golf clubhouse built by Hamilton Gillespie at the west edge of the nine-hole course at South Links and Golf Street in 1905.

The woman golfer teeing off at Colonel Hamilton Gillespie's golf course certainly has the undivided attention of a dozen caddies and golfers, including Colonel Gillespie, fifth from left.

Sarasota Gun Club in 1907. Front: *(left to right)* R.I. Kennedy, Zeke Messer, Clarence E. Hitchings, J.W. Harvey. Back: C.C. McGinty, George W. Blackburn, C.M. Jones, Jake Chapline Jr., Asa Chapline, Hamden S. Smith.

City Livery Stables and home of Eliza Grantham at the northeast corner of Main and Lemon, circa 1906.

Dr. Jack Halton's Minstrel Show performed regularly, to the delight of Sarasota residents and winter guests.

General merchandise store of Clark and Calhoun and the J.C. Calhoun residence on Main Street, 1903.

School house built in 1905, on the block across from present-day First Baptist Church, served as the high school. It later became an elementary school when the new brick high school was built facing Main Street.

Advent Of The Syndrome

"Misses Kathleen Lacey and Katherine Southgate received slight injuries in an auto accident Wednesday afternoon. Miss Lacey, who was driving her father's car, on turning the corner at Main Street and Gulf Stream Avenue, turned out to avoid a wagon and crashed into a telephone pole, breaking the wind-shield and damaged the car. She was thrown against the steering wheel, but not as much injured as Miss Southgate, who received cuts on the throat and one knee from the broken glass.

"The young ladies were taken to Dr. Joe Halton's office, where Miss Southgate had several stitches taken, which she bravely stood. The shock to both was severe, but there is a thankful feeling that the accident was not more serious."

—from the *Sarasota Times*, October 15, 1914

Those infernal machines

Statewide, Florida was coming of age in a modern world of technical turning points, and Sarasota was carried along with the tide. During the next decade, Sarasota's officers added ordinances dealing with sidewalk licensing, issuing of bonds for construction of a municipal sewer system, and street paving. In 1910, a tax was levied to widen Main Street. A reinforced concrete seawall was to run along the bay from the Main Street pier to Banana Avenue. Regulations were passed for operation of "motor cars . . . propelled by steam, gasoline or electricity" (ten miles per hour in town). Mayor Gillespie and the council levied taxes for the sinking fund to pay interest and principal on the bonded indebtedness.

Facing continuing capital outlay, in May 1913 an act of the state legislature incorporated the City of Sarasota while abolishing the corporation of the Town of Sarasota and empowered the city to issue and sell bonds in the face of an indebtedness of $15,000. Accordingly, under direction of the newly incorporated city's Mayor Harry L. Higel and council President Hugh K. Browning, bonds at $500 were issued for $15,000.

Sarasota was leaving her horse and buggy days behind. As city fathers legislated in-town speeds for automobiles, they were only a few years behind state regulations which restricted auto drivers to a maximum speed of four miles per hour at bridges and curves and mandated a complete stop at the request of a person in control of a horse. Although Florida's early drivers were subject for a short time to preemptive equestrian traffic, the automobile was soon to change permanently the face and habits of America, and dramatically so in Florida.

A good roads movement grew to prominence in Florida after the Panic of 1907. And in 1909, when Governor Albert W. Gilchrist came into office, the good roads issue was joined by another even more definitive to Sarasota's future — massive projects of land drainage. The succeeding administration concentrated on highway safety along with eradication of cattle ticks which caused the dreaded tick fever, yet another major problem confronting agricultural Sarasotans.

Public work day on November 6, 1913, reflected the community's collective efforts to build Gulf Stream Park along the bayfront.

Dr. C.B. Wilson posed in his 20-horsepower Reo roadster in front of his South Orange Avenue home in 1909. Wilson bought the car in Tampa and made it home in just five hours — including a lunch stop.

Looking toward shore, 1914, from the municipal dock.

Highways constructed from northern centers were ribbons of asphalt stretched in beelines to southern coasts once difficult to reach. The car was the rage for about-town travel, but even though "Road 120" was complete from Chicago to Birmingham and points southeast, the railroad remained king. Sarasota was served by an entity of the Seaboard Airline Railway to the Manatee region. When the affluent headed for Florida, they did so in the comfort and style of the train.

Chicago was a major industrial hub whose citizens had frequent occasion to glance toward Florida. The buying power of the new industrialists and capitalists was evident in newspapers such as the Chicago *Tribune*. During the winter season, pages prominently included classified ads for groves and developments in California and Florida, while social pages flaunted the transcontinental mobility of famous and affluent Chicagoans such as Mrs. Marshall Field and Mrs. Potter Palmer.

During the winter season of 1910, Mrs. Potter Palmer, widow and international celebrity, traveled with her brother, father, and two sons to Sarasota. Though their visit was a short one, it was confirmation of an investor's hunch. Ultimately, Bertha Honoré Palmer and corporate Palmer interests involving her brother, Adrian Honoré, and her sons, Potter Jr. and Honoré, acquired thousands of acres with and through Joseph Lord, a Chicago-based lawyer and large-scale investor in Sarasota lands since the 1880s.

Palmer corporations ultimately held easily a fourth of the land of present-day Sarasota County. Mrs. Palmer purchased large blocks along the new Seaboard Coast Line Railway extensions to Venice, as well as bayfront and Gulfside tracts near the town of Sarasota. A block of nearly 80,000 Palmer acres stretched northeasterly from Osprey and surrounded upper Myakka Lake. Mrs. Palmer established a showplace winter estate at Little Sarasota Bay on lands which included the old homestead of the Webb family (present-day Osprey, historic Spanish Point, and The Oaks subdivision) while her sons established a home called Immokalee on Phillippi Creek nearer town (present-

Mrs. Potter Palmer, an elegant businesswoman, influenced a continuing pattern of Chicago investment in South Florida.

Armistice Day celebration at Five Points in 1919.

Stanley and Sara Field's glorious winter estate was typical of those built along the shores of Sarasota Bay during the Roaring Twenties. In 1957, the Fields' house and part of its grounds became the private Field Club.

Fire At Five Points

Fire broke out at Five Points on Monday night, March 8 1915, at 2 a.m. Sleeping citizens, awakened by the fire alarm, soon discovered it was a big one.

Sarasota's downtown professional and business commu was hard hit. The fire destroyed the office of Dr. Joseph Halton who, though he lost equipment and a library, set u practice across the street in the Bank of Sarasota. Proprie of the Palms Theatre, Edgar Maus, reopened in Hover Arcade at the bayfront.

Other businesses displaced included Western Union, Crescent Pharmacy, Krebbiel's Pharmacy, and Mrs. E.L. Frazier's bakery.

Town of Sarasota's first fire station and firemen, circa 1912.

ay Landings subdivision). Potter Jr. purchased a large inland block at Osprey.

Bertha Palmer consolidated coastal tracts in the vicinity of Casey's Key and Casey's Pass (present-day Venice Inlet), the mainland stretching south, and the peninsulas which jutted along Shake It and Hatchet creeks. Southward from municipal Sarasota, the Palmer lands stretched for miles. Surrounding inland Myakka River, Mrs. Palmer acquired choice pioneer ranches to form her 30,000-acre Meadowsweet Pastures (a major portion of present-day Myakka State Park) where she introduced modern cattle raising methods. She imported purebred stock, fenced the ranges, and constructed vats to dip her cattle — years before the state legislature passed an act in 1923 requiring dipping to eradicate the dreaded tick fever. The inland ranch became an important segment of the forward-reaching Myakka Drainage District, supported by Governor Gilchrist, who knew well the problems of the river's wetlands, having once represented De Soto County in the legislature.

Bertha Honoré Palmer invested heavily — both personally and corporately — in the family's Florida venture, joined actively by her brother and both sons. She carefully developed her ranch and her estate at Osprey to demonstrate the potential market value of Florida real estate. In the area she came to regard as home, she and her sons developed vegetable, citrus, and real estate ventures called Bee Ridge Farms, Bee Ridge Homesites, and the prominent Sarasota-Venice Company. The Bee Ridge project alone covered a twelve-square-mile tract. The Palmer interest in Sarasota attracted a wave of investors imbued with an aura of affluence and aristocracy, and continued a distinctive pattern set decades earlier by Hamilton Gillespie.

Mrs. Potter Palmer transformed the former homestead area of the Webb family into a winter estate complete with walkways and formal gardens.

The Acacias, another Palmer family home.

The old Belle Haven, looking more imposing than ever, circa 1910.

The magnificent Palmer estate house, The Oaks.

The Bay Island Hotel on the north end of Siesta Key.

Some fourteen miles from The Oaks, the Acacias graced the bluff the pioneer Whitaker family had called "Yellow Bluffs."

The 18-hole golf course opened in 1927 to replace Colonel Gillespie's downtown course; the star attraction was Bobby Jones, for whom the course was named.

Immokalee, the home of Potter Jr. and Honoré Palmer.

The railroad as king

The promise of the Sarasota region in which the Palmer family saw such potential depended largely upon railroads that connected the outside world to Sarasota production centers. Though a woodburning locomotive had chugged down a rail line to reach Sarasota from the Manatee River in 1892, the company had not survived the economic traumas of the 1890s. Sarasota had been served again in 1903 by a line from Palmetto Junction to Sarasota. Ultimately acquired by the Seaboard Air Line Railway moving south from Tampa, the line was extended by the Seaboard from its Fruitville station to Venice in 1911.

Railroad commerce created communities where there had been none. In 1918, the new town of Manasota arose where the Manasota Lumber Company cut and milled Florida's native long-leaf pine. Eventually, lumbering company interests constructed a railroad to connect with the Seaboard at Venice. The company town included a commissary, a movie house, 1,500 homes, and two churches.

The growth of the railroad was a reflection of Florida's governmental climate. Building on the state's sensational appeal to American capitalists, the legislature in the early '20s passed, and Florida's voters approved, a prohibition on state taxes on income and inheritance. Thus encouraged, the development boom, including rail expansion, continued statewide. In Sarasota, meanwhile, a competitive line entered the Seaboard's territory. The Tampa Southern owned by the Atlantic Coast Line Railroad, reached Sarasota in 1924 from Tampa, Palmetto, and Bradenton. Travel was both comfortable and brisk between Sarasota and once-distant cities. Daily passenger trains included dining cars, coaches, and Pullman sleepers to carry Sarasotans to Chicago, or anywhere between Chicago and Fort Myers, while yet another train operated between New York and Naples.

Flag stops on the line were at Fordville, Palmerville, Utopia, Myakka River pump house, Honore, Sidell, and Parkland. Running through the inland, the modern locomotives also pulled cars loaded with Sarasota's agricultural exports — vegetables, citrus, turpentine, logs, lumber, and pine sap for the production of turpentine, a booming new industry in Sarasota's flat pine lands.

Seaboard Air Line depot, 1903, a year after Sarasota was incorporated.

Black laborers on the railbed of, ultimately, the Seaboard Air Line Railway paused to pose for photographer Felix Pinard.

A Venice in Florida

The railroad was king in more than a transportation sense; it opened the lands along its roadbeds for large-scale developments. The Seaboard Air Line Railway stretched from Tampa down the coast to Sarasota in a race with the Atlantic Coast Line, as both headed south toward Naples.

The City of Venice, located in a massive concentration of lands acquired by Palmer entities, was the result of immense railroad capital lured to Sarasota Bay — that of the Brotherhood of Locomotive Engineers, an organization of some 91,000 members in Canada and the United States with a chain of banks stretching across the country from Boston to San Francisco.

Acquiring an 80-square-mile tract, the BLE put considerable resources behind its Florida investment. The concept was comprehensive — a planned resort including a city and a corresponding 25,000-acre farm development. The city was serviced by the Seaboard, while the farm acreage was to be serviced by a canal dredged into the inland to transport produce. Included in the concept was a separate inland residential community for black residents.

The BLE hired nationally known planners John Nolen and Associates of Cambridge to lay out a master plan for the bayfront city. Construction proceeded under Walker and Gillette architects of New York. The BLE put together a team of experienced professionals — a construction firm based in New York and Chicago, nationally known civil engineers, a graduate of the Harvard School of Land Architecture to head the landscape department, and a nursery superintendant lured away from New Orleans city

Frank Higel, a Philadelphian and former Union officer, purchased land in the Horse and Chaise coastal area from pioneer Robert Roberts of Roberts Bay.

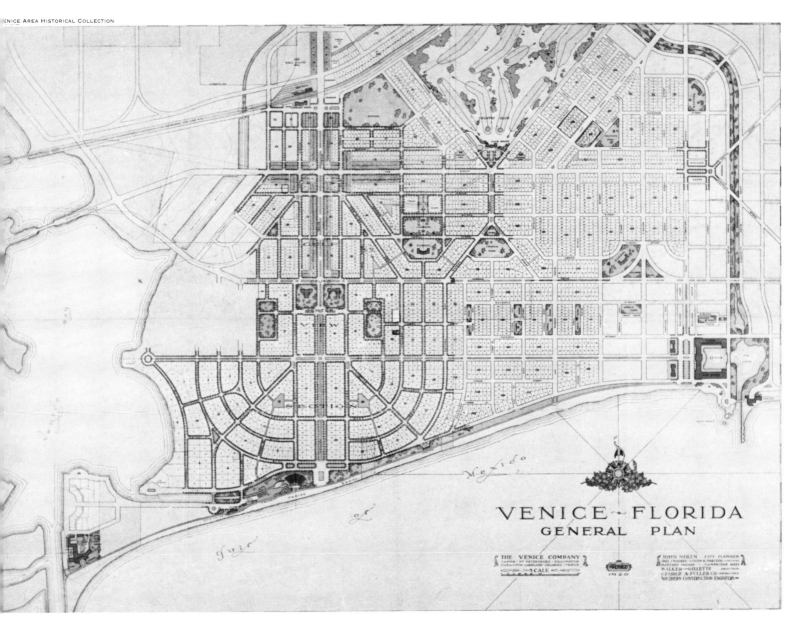

John Nolen's 1926 plan for Venice was for a sophisticated town for the largely undeveloped area that pioneers had called Horse and Chaise.

Dr. Fred Albee, whose sanitarium at Venice-Nokomis brought another element of fame to the area, was an active entrepreneur during the real estate boom.

parks. The BLE Realty Corporation maintained architectural control through an architectural department. Buildings, roadways, parkways, vistas, and promenades were aimed at creation of a total effect.

Once the plan was underway, the union invited news editors from around the country to visit the new planned community. The union's officers planned national meetings in Venice, attracting prospective buyers and visitors from far and wide. The Venice Hotel opened in July 1926, one of three built by the BLE; others opened under private backing. The Seaboard station, which carried in carloads of guests, was moved to a new location a quarter-mile east and constructed in the adopted architecture the company called "northern Italian." Florida's Governor John Martin visited Venice, welcomed the BLE to the state, and pronounced the city "More than amazing — it is magnificent."

In January 1927, Governor Martin appointed the first mayor of Venice, Edward L. Worthington, to preside with a council of the newly incorporated town. The new mayor boasted that Venice was "the only completely planned community in Florida, and the only one of its kind in the entire country." He added, "It is bound to go ahead because it presents precisely the kind of opportunities that people are looking for."

The BLE recruited and paid an army of workers, and the town of Venice took shape in record time. Palm-lined medians, grassy lawns, and stuccoed walls quickly transformed flat Florida piney woods into cosmopolitan boulevards fronting on private and public courtyards. News of the attractive and highly advertised development soon reached population centers of the country and the hype quickly reached fever pitch. The editor of the Jersey City *Journal* wrote that he bought a farm along Venice Boulevard three hours after he arrived in town.

Venice industries included toy and tile manufacturers, printers and publishers, real estate agents, lumber and building companies, novelty mills, an ice plant, and a marine ways machine company. The instant community included schools, playgrounds, a golf course, tennis courts, ball fields, and a bandstand roofed in palmetto thatch at the civic center. Visitors were encouraged to cruise the Gulf in motor launches, to play golf or pursue archery on the greens, to water ski, sail, or participate in the annual June National Tarpon Tournament sponsored by the Venice Tarpon Club.

Venice's new central parkway, Venice Boulevard, ran from Myakka River to the Gulf.

Venice had everything. Nearby at Venice-Nokomis, another building in the northern Italian architectural style took form — Albee Sanitarium. The imposing structure was to be a year-round health resort — "one of the largest . . . in the world," according to the Venice *News,* which reported that the sanitarium was soon to be enlarged by Dr. Fred H. Albee, "the world's foremost bone surgeon." Albee's brother, Stephen, represented Nokomis as a director of the new Venice Chamber of Commerce.

Sometimes visitors arrived en masse — seven Pullman cars filled with Minnesotans, on one occasion. The guests accepted the hospitality of the BLE to survey the array of homesites, businesses, and farms. They looked over crops of watermelon, asparagus, artichokes, tomatoes, raspberries, grapes, and citrus. They visited the union's ten-acre "strawberry demonstration farm," its five-acre "poultry demonstration farm," and its 160-acre model dairy farm. Sportsmen hunted quail, duck, dove, snipe, deer, and turkey and headed toward the Big Cypress for bear and panther.

The BLE game plan bore quick fruit. With such dedicated effort, sales were brisk. In the case of the trainload of Minnesotans, it was afterward reported, "All but one bought Venice farm or city property."

Prospective buyers, union members, and beachgoers gather for a photo in 1927 at Venice Public Beach.

St. Augustine roadbed under construction as businessmen and horsemen inspect Dr. Albee's real estate office building, newly moved from Nokomis.

Interior of a farm home, advertised by the BLE to appeal to a broad variety of American buyers.

The Venice pioneer family of Wilson and Laura Virginia Stephens on their porch. The Stephens homesite was completed in 1897 and was one of those dotting the area to become present-day Venice.

In front of Laurel School, children of local families — Blackburn, Roberts, Reagan, Stephens, Phillips — join hands with Mrs. T.W. Yarborough, wife of the school superintendent.

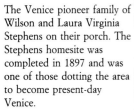

The home Frank Higel built for his family in the present-day Venice area.

Venice Public Beach during the boom, site of present-day Sandbar Beach Hotel. The sunbathers often wore suits monogrammed "V" for Venice.

VENICE AREA HISTORICAL COLLECTION

VENICE AREA HISTORICAL COLLECTION

The Venice Golf Course in 1927.

The *Robin,* a cruise boat purchased by the BLE to ply local bays and the Gulf, at Casey's Pass where the recent effects of dredging and filling are obvious along the shore.

The Venice Hotel courtyard was the scene of glittering gala events of the boom period.

Photo by Jay Brown. Venice Area Historical Collection

The cosmopolitan Venice included the Park View Hotel and its corner coffee shop, all set for business with water decanters, matches, and fresh flowers on every table.

The reading room at Venice's Park View Hotel, where John Philip Sousa once performed during the Venice boom.

The Venice Post Office, 1926. To the left is the housing building constructed by Mrs. Potter Palmer when the railroad was extended to Venice.

The new Venice Pharmacy, at the corner of Nokomis and Venice Avenue West.

The Venice Tile Company produced hollow clay tiles and floor tiles used prevalently in the new city's Mediterranean style construction projects.

The Venice Ice Company, one of Venice's boom time industries, was located along the railroad in present-day Nokomis.

The inland dairy on Jackson Road, 1926, a prominent part of the BLE demonstration farm.

The Tampa to Miami Trail

When Governor Martin publicly praised the developers of Venice, he also touched on a subject dear to the heart of every west coast developer. Martin, who had been in office two years, announced his intention to complete the Tamiami Trail during his administration. The long-elusive dream of Florida's investors was a cross-Florida highway linking the two coasts by a modern automobile route. The plan had hit snag after snag for a decade. The proposed road was to run from Tampa through Sarasota, Venice, Fort Myers, and Naples. Then, incredibly, modern man proposed to build a hard road across the heretofore impenetrable Big Cypress Swamp and the Everglades to hook up with Miami's Dixie Highway. The dream, dubbed the Tamiami Trail, had been planned on paper, but road construction had been relegated to individual counties. Not until the booming mid-'20s did its realization seem attainable. In 1926, a state road department assumed responsibility and, as the governor had promised, the Trail was officially opened two years later — during Martin's administration.

But hard roads in Sarasota County were not new. To accommodate the craze for the automobile, Sarasota roads had been constructed during the Teens along range and township lines as public rights-of-way. Sharp, right-angle turns characterized the path of the distinctive roadway — solitary and singular, nine-foot-wide ribbons of asphalt through wild expanses of pristine piney woods. The roads were constructed in sections, starting at the Manatee River. Although their width allowed only one car to pass at a time, they had been a source of great excitement.

Ultimately, this repeated roadbuilding linked Sarasota with her communities to the south. And when the work ended, proud Sarasotans called the road the Velvet Highway.

Road grader.

Setting curb forms.

The Velvet Highway

The hard roads constructed across piney woods and hammocks during the 1910s often formed sections of the Tamiami Trail when it was completed in the late '20s.

In the summer of 1918, in the present-day Osprey and Venice area, a work crew cleared and graded the right-of-way under a contract let to pioneer Dr. Furman C. Whitaker. The crew worked with a big tractor and with a palmetto plow invented by Henry Webb, Iowa-born black businessman and landholder.

After some experience with contracting for clearing land and building houses, Webb began experimenting with designs for a machine which would sever and remove the tenacious palmetto. His patent application was filed in January 1917, approved in May, and the plow itself soon put into use. Prior to its 1918 employment on road sections at Osprey and Venice, the equipment was impressed for government service and taken to Arcadia to clear airfields constructed there for World War I flight training. Webb's equipment later returned to civic enterprise, building roads south of Venice.

Some Sarasota folk still refer to clearing a field as "webbing."

Henry Webb.

9. Boom And Bust

John Ringling's causeway was under construction in 1925. The dredge pumped away even at night, creating a fill called Golden Gate Point.

In municipal Sarasota, the reigning king of development was John Ringling, Iowa-born circus magnate. Ringling was attracted to Sarasota by friends and business associates, among them Charles N. Thompson, once with the Buffalo Bill Show and former manager of Forepaugh-Sells Circus, which the Ringling circus had acquired a few years earlier.

Thelma Thompson, daughter of Charles N. Thompson, clowns at the family's own Shell Beach railway siding, constructed on the Atlantic Coast Line tracks in the midst of undeveloped Sarasota County.

The entrepreneurs of Shell Beach

Ringling and his wife, Mable, followed the heavily traveled trail to Sarasota and purchased in 1912 Thompson's own white frame home, wrapped in spacious porches. Its 1,660-foot dock stretched out to deep bay waters. The house lay in Thompson's own bayfront acreage which he had acquired, platted, and named Shell Beach Subdivision in the 1890s. Thompson had attracted a core of notable investors who constructed impressive Mediterranean Revival homes on a few estate-sized lots in the subdivision (along present-day Bayshore Drive). On Thompson's homesite, the Ringlings would construct in 1926 their own Venetian palace, Ca' D' Zan — House of John.

The Ringlings were flanked on the bayfront by Ellen and Ralph Caples on the south, who lived in the log house purchased in 1901 from another circus man, W.H. English, and which was later replaced with an Italian Renaissance house. Ralph Caples, a veteran railroad man and general agent for the New York Central Railroad, was a major investor in Sarasota properties. He had purchased several large residential parcels along the bayfront, one of which he sold to Ringling. Caples became a representative of John N. Willys, president of the Willys-Overland Automobile Company. He was destined to direct the campaign train of Warren G. Harding, the Republican presidential candidate, during the 1920 presidential race. And one day, Ringling would design a grand plan to bring Harding to a Sarasota retreat.

On the north, John and Mable's estate adjoined that of John's brother, Charles. Charles and his wife, Edith, had constructed their own palatial pink marble residence to incorporate a home for their daughter, Hestor, and her husband, Louis Lancaster. The Lancaster home was attached to the main house by a covered promenade and tea house. (The estate is within present-day New College of University of South Florida campus complex.)

John Ringling, the youngest of the five Ringling circus brothers, was the front man. He sized up a town in advance and arranged everything from public relations to percentages. Following the lead of Ralph Caples and others, Ringling appraised the opportunities of Sarasota and rapidly invested in real estate. He acquired islands, city parcels, and a great chunk of the inland. On a par with his personality, John's visions were diverse and daring. He envisioned Gulffront resorts and gambling casinos, bayside residential subddivisions, yacht basins, city business centers, and inland oil wells. Ultimately, his corporate associations included Ringling Isles Real Estate Development Company, St. Armands-Lido Realty Corporation, Trust Company of Sarasota, and Sarasota Oil Company.

Charles N. Thompson at Buffalo Bill Cody's business office. The circus men traveled in the same circles and eventually wintered in the same southern city.

John and Mable Ringling bought a bayfront home built by Charles N. Thompson in his Shell Beach subdivision.

Philanthropists By The Bay

Marie and Bill Selby moved to Sarasota Bay in 1908, soon after their marriage. Bill had seasonally hunted and fished in Sarasota, staying in the old Belle Haven Hotel at the foot of Main Street. Bill's father, Frank, an Ohio farm boy, had founded Selby Oil Company which owned wells in Oklahoma and Texas and maintained a business office in Tulsa.

Bill, a six-foot sportsman, routinely dressed in rough cowboy clothes, complete with hat and boots, and frequented Roth's newsstand and Badger's Drug Store at downtown Five Points — a daily pasttime for Sarasotans of his day. The Selbys enjoyed hunting and fishing trips together, and Bill continued a lifelong pattern of fishing excursions in summer and hunting and fishing at Okeechobee in winter. Marie was interested in her gardens and music. They lived quietly.

A year before Selby's death from leukemia in 1956, he instituted a charitable trust with assets in excess of $10 million — the William G. and Marie Selby Foundation which supports hundreds of local and statewide bequests for institutions, scholarship grants to more than 500 students a year, and distribution of an annual total in excess of a million dollars.

When Marie Selby died in 1971 at age 86, she bequeathed and endowed their bayfront home and acreage in trust for the Marie Selby Botanical Gardens, which was opened to the public in 1975. It eventually included the adjacent two-story brick and columned house constructed by Christy Payne, son of C.N. Payne, another Sarasota benefactor and oilman.

In their adopted southern home, many structures and projects bear the Selby name and carry it on.

John and Mable Burton Ringling at home.

Interior views of Charles and Edith Ringling's bayfront winter estate house. The house was designed by Clas, Shepherd and Clas of Milwaukee, and constructed of pink marble by crews of Wisconsin workers.

Sarasota bayfront road in Indian Beach area, circa 1920.

Indian Beach Road, circa 1920, looking west from the turn at present-day 27th Street.

Ringling the isles

Ringling conceived a grand plan, called Ringling Isles, to encompass a development accessible by automobile from the city to his island properties. In 1917, he purchased Cedar Point (present-day Golden Gate Point) where dredging and filling began five years later. The development complex included Bird Key, St. Armands, Coon and Otter keys, and the south end of Longboat. The Ringling Isles project attracted investors such as Owen Burns, a Marylander who supervised construction while pursuing development of his real estate interests in municipal Sarasota (including Burns Court, Washington Park, and El Vernona Hotel, later John Ringling Hotel).

At a cost approaching a million dollars, John Ringling enterprises bridged the bay to Bird Key. During construction, nearby residents found it difficult to sleep as pile drivers worked even into the night. And a year after it was finished, the citizenry turned out to applaud as John Ringling gave his bridge to the city. From Bird Key, Ringling continued the roadway on to St. Armands Key — misspelled but named, nevertheless, for the island's Louisiana-born homesteader, Charles St. Amand.

The Ringling Isles plan included a shopping circle, a casino called Lido, and a subdivison called John Ringling Estates. Adjoining the circle at St. Armands was Lido Beach on the west, while to the north — across a birdge over New Pass to south Longboat — a newly finished 18-hole golf course was played by a champion, Chick Evans, who pronounced it "one of the finest" he had ever seen.

Visible from afar were the first few floors of the $3 million Ringling-conceived and broadly underwritten grand hotel, the Ritz Carlton.

Ringling's complex tamed the sandspurred islands with paved boulevards and promenades, imported statuary, street lamps, imported palms and shrubs, and miles and miles of concrete curbings.

Though the financial kingdom they shared was known worldwide and produced enormous revenues, John and Charles Ringling competed to the point of apparent animosity. The brothers purchased yachts to cruise Sarasota Bay and outdid each other in size and accommodations. John built a downtown bank in the heart of the bayfront city at Five Points, while across the street on Main, Charles established Ringling Trust and Land Title Guaranty and Mortgage Savings Bank. John acquired Owen Burns' El Vernona Hotel (John Ringling Towers) and Charles built his own ten-story hotel on the opposite side of town, along the new Tamiami Trail.

The Trail was still a sandtrap for construction trucks in the midst of Mayor Gillespie's old golf course when Charles constructed the Sarasota Terrace Hotel (present-day Sarasota County Administration Building). He and his wife, Edith, conveyed adjacent land for the new county's courthouse, and platted out a subdivision surrounding the hotel and courthouse. On either end of his Courthouse subdivision, Charles looped a roadway to and from Main Street and named it Ringling Boulevard.

John Ringling's causeway was the first linking of the city to the islands in Sarasota Bay. A filled causeway stretched to connect tiny Bird Island with the project.

Looking toward the city dock along Gulf Stream Avenue, about 1920.

A Marvel Of Modern Miracles

In the '20s, John Ringling's causeway reached Bird Island, winter home of the singular New Edzell castle, constructed by Thomas M. Worcester and his wife, a painter who died before completion of the three-year building project. It was named for "her ancestral home" — Scotland's Edzell Castle. When Thomas Worcester socially opened the house in February 1914, it was accessible only by boat and featured many modern marvels — its own electric plant, electric and acetylene gas lights, steam heat, and hot and cold running water in every room.

Worcester's visiting nephew once reflected upon his impressions of contrasts on first arrival at Sarasota Bay's New Edzell:

"Uncle Tom met us at the train, carried our bags, and walked us down to the city dock. We got in a boat and went straight out into the dark. . . . I'll never forget that transition from the heart of New York City to a desert island."

—Charlie Pickett

View of grounds through arched porte cochere of the Charles and Edith Ringling house.

Drilling for oil

The two circus kings also entered into joint Sarasota ventures. In December 1922, years before they built their palaces on the bay, John and Charles purchased 67,000 acres of Sarasota real estate called "the Woodward tract." The vast parcel extended from the Palmer ranch along the Myakka River to the southern end of fledgling Sarasota County. Five years later, after Charles' death, John gave the tract the same kind of promoter's creative attention he had given the bay islands project. Ringling sold others on his ideas and raised capital backing among shareholding investors. In summer 1927, Sarasota newspapers prominently advertised the imminent drilling of test wells to discover local oil fields.

Five-year leases were offered at $10 an acre to prospective buyers. The touch of the master showman was evident in the scheme, which relied prominently upon a three-ring show. First, the optimistic analysis of a geologist. Second, the geologist was backed up by the American Petroleum Institute, and third and finally, the report of a committee composed of highly placed officials of various American oil companies — no fewer than eight presidents, one director, a general secretary, and one chairman of the board. Said an ad in the local newspaper, "When the A.P.I. thinks there is OIL in Florida, it's about time to wake up."

The idea of oil in Florida was not new. Exploration had begun in Pensacola as early as the turn of the century. And just as the arrival of the railroad and the automobile had opened Florida to the rest of the country, so the resultant pattern nationwide had created an unprecedented commercial need for oil. All over the country speculators were drilling for oil, and some were finding it. In addition to Ringling, Sarasota had a number of oilmen in residence, some of whom were highly visible investors and developers, while others maintained a low profile.

Pennsylvania-born Calvin Payne had been an oil driller, producer, and corporate executive. With his wife, Martha, Payne arrived in Sarasota when he was in his 70s, ultimately financed construction of Payne Terminal on Sarasota's bayfront at Sixth Street, and established Payne Park by the courthouse complex next to Charles Ringling's hotel on Washington Boulevard. Early in the 1920s, Payne sold 60 acres, half to the city and half to the county, specifically for "Fair Grounds and other park purposes."

Among other oilmen attracted to Sarasota was Bill Selby and his wife, Marie, who built a house on the bayfront along Hudson Bayou. Bill's father, Frank, had founded Selby Oil which had acquired substantial holdings in Standard Oil of California, Standard Oil of New Jersey, and Texas Oil Company, which became Texaco. Bill and Marie kept a low social profile.

The Boom and the Sarasota look

The mood of Sarasota's movers and shakers was infectious. Assessed 1923 values had tripled in only one year, while building permits reflected the same unprecedented rises. By 1925, the sale of documentary stamps had quadrupled those of the previous year; bank resources and building permits had tripled. The population of greater Sarasota had jumped from 3,000 in 1920 to 8,000 in 1926. The real estate boom was vibrant and visible. Building after building rose up in expensive, distinctive style and excited a population whose investment enthusiasm knew no bounds.

Precisely in the middle of the 1920s, real estate developer and former mayor A.B. Edwards built his downtown Edwards Theater at the corner of Pineapple and First (present-day restored home of Sarasota Opera Association). Two months after opening, *Martha* and *Carmen* were performed onstage by the 125-person San Carlo Opera Company which swept into town in eight railroad cars. A Womans Club on nearby Palm Avenue had become a center for feminine civic service activities.

The "phenomenal growth" in 1923 prompted the city in 1924 to engage John Nolen, city planner of Cambridge, to design a comprehensive plan. By dark, Main Street (part of which Nolen labeled Victory Avenue) was lighted from Lemon to the bay by "ornamental posts and globes." The Francis Carlton Apartments were under construction in late summer 1924. On the city's bayfront, the Hover Arcade straddled the foot of the Main Street wharf entrance and housed city and county governments until the courthouse was constructed. Two blocks south at Strawberry Avenue, Fish House Spur jutted into the bay, a dock and track which eventually housed John Ringling's personal railroad car each season. (Strawberry Avenue became an extension of the Ringling Boulevard of Charles Ringling's Courthouse subdivision.) On Palm Avenue, the Mira Mar Hotel and auditorium complex had been completed in six months to house the affluent winter guests of the 1923-24 season, while Mira Mar casino stood on Sarasota Beach. The Mira Mar Hotel, in a choice spot on the site of Mayor Gillespie's 1886 home, was joined in the mid-'20s by Sarasota's "first skyscraper," Sarasota Hotel at the northeast corner of Palm and Main.

Within a few years, Adair Realty and Trust, an Atlanta-based realty company, built a ten-story building at the

From the roof of a third "skyscraper," the photographer captures J.H. Lord's proud new bank building and arcade at Five Points during the building boom.

PHOTO BY BURGERT. FLORIDA PHOTOGRAPHIC COLLECTION, FLORIDA STATE ARCHIVES

southwest corner of Palm and Main. American National Bank Building was built on the choice site of the 1886 Belle Haven Hotel which had for decades distinguished Sarasota's bayfront and housed affluent visitors. Across the street on the northwest corner of Palm and Main, the Watrous Hotel had been sold and plans were underway to enlarge it.

Nearer the Ringling estates at the intersection of Indian Beach and Bradenton roads, J.G. Whitfield was about to erect a three-story hotel to be called Bay Haven Inn (present day Ringling Art School). A Tennessee-born winter resident, Whitfield planned each of its 70 rooms to contain a private bath and steam heat. Eleven shops were planned, along with a lobby and courtyard.

In the midst of the boom, Sarasota public and private projects shaped an architectural theme which reflected the tenor of the time. One of the professional definers of Sarasota's Spanish style was New York architect Dwight James Baum. Baum set up an office in Sarasota in the mid-'20s and designed many structures, including the Ringlings' Ca' D' Zan, the El Vernona, the Casa Bona (present-day Belle Haven), and a number of residences at St. Armands.

But the central city building Baum designed was influenced by the California Spanish Colonial mode. In the heart of the city, next to Charles Ringling's hotel, the cornerstone was laid in May 1926 for a courthouse and county government building. The courthouse plan incorporated two identical wings (one for government, one for the judiciary) joined by connecting colonnades which met at a 100-foot, functional observation tower. A reflecting pool graced most of the ground surface of a courtyard which, like the entire complex, fronted on Main Street. Despite delays in arrival of supplies and a hurricane, Sarasota's architecturally arresting courthouse was completed the following February at a cost of more than a million dollars.

CITY BUILDING, SARASOTA, FLORIDA.

The Arcade Building at the foot of Main Street, circa 1925. The Sarasota County Commission first met here in 1921 in space rented from the city.

MERLE EVANS COLLECTION

Back Row L. to R.
Tommy Glenicke, F. Mathews, Hershell Berts, F.W. Moore, Emil Mobius, Frank Stephens
Merle Evans, Phillip Garkow, Robert Sturgell, Geo. Davies, Wm. Spielberg
Pete Schmidt, Clinton Evans, Harold Hillman

Front Row L. to R.
Frank Kenney, Joe Simons, W.D. White, Fred Kusman, Carlos Pease, Guy Fuller
Geo. Bishop, W.H. Plummer, A. Miglionico, J.W. Pratt

Before the circus came to Sarasota for winter quarters, the circus band played for the 1926-27 tourist season. The Mira Mar Hotel and Casino are to the rear.

PHOTO BY BURGERT, FLORIDA PHOTOGRAPHIC COLLECTION, FLORIDA STATE ARCHIVES

Sarasota Hotel and J.H. Lord's bank building were the only new high-rise buildings in sight from lower Main Street in October 1926.

It seemed everyone was in real estate in 1925 and 1926. Tuckers Sporting Goods near Five Points hung a prize tarpon above the sidewalk and advertised real estate in the window.

Yachtsmen competed in the Sarasota Yacht Club's annual regatta and posed with Marie Selby on the terrace of the Selby home in March 1928.

Sarasotans turned out at Five Points en masse for the unveiling of a war memorial and flag pole on the tenth anniversary of the World War I Armistice.

Louise Higel, circa 1923, on the first tee of Hamilton Gillespie's golf course. Louise contributed greatly to the preservation of Sarasota's heritage by her clippings and photo albums assembled over a lifetime.

Gillespie's golf course in 1922. The holes had expanded to eleven and seven more were scheduled for construction. Players wore the ever-present knickers of the era.

John Ringling's Bank of Sarasota at Five Points, 1922.

Sarasota's police force posed at the bayfront by their one car — a 1927 Hupmobile.

PHOTO BY T.F. ARNOLD. MANATEE COUNTY HISTORICAL SOCIETY

View from Tower, Edison Keith's Home.

Edson Keith built his grand winter home on historic Phillippi Creek across the waterway from Immokalee.

Mango Avenue Hotel, circa 1920.

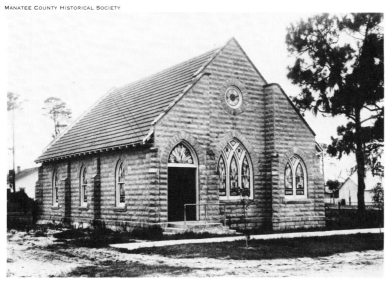

The First Presbyterian Church on Orange Avenue, circa 1920, before the real estate boom produced the present-day Mediterranean Revival sanctuary by the Tamiami Trail.

The Hotel Watrous on lower Main Street was one of Sarasota's most modern buildings until it was joined during the boom by neighboring "skyscrapers" as well as the competitive Mira Mar Hotel just down the street on Palm Avenue.

A master in school design

Sarasota's school system began to consolidate communities and to replace some of the smaller community schools. To accommodate the increase in Sarasota's school age population, John Nolen had recommended in his plan construction of five white schools — a central high school and four elementary schools — and a new black school.

In 1925, Sarasota's black school children marched behind Mrs. Emma E. Booker, their principal, from Knights of Pythias Hall, where school had been held for years, as she led the way to a real school. Built by the Rosenwald Fund next to the railroad tracks at Lemon and Thirteenth (present-day Seventh), the one-story building held four classrooms off a wide central hall and an auditorium. Called Sarasota Grammar School, it was to serve for three decades in three locations before its educating days ended.

Also in keeping with Nolen's plan, Sarasota's downtown high school for white students on Victory Avenue (Main) was removed from the rapidly expanding central city and separated from the old grammar school just behind it on Golf.

With all this building activity, the school district incurred heavy bonded indebtedness in the 1920s. The architectural significance of the schools soon matched the distinctive efforts of the private sector. Under the direction of architect M. Leo Elliot of Tampa and St. Petersburg, billed as "a master in the design of schools," two sets of plans were drawn up for elementary and high schools. A three-story Sarasota High School was designed in the Gothic Revival, or "Collegiate Gothic" style, popularly successful on campuses such as Princeton and Duke universities. The effect of elaborate archways, period motifs, and glazed terra cotta trim culminated in a four-and-a-half-story central tower fronting the new Tamiami Trail south of the brand new courthouse.

Two "immense" elementary schools in the Mediterranean Revival style were built in two-storied stucco at the north and south city limits. Their locations had been calculated to serve the extreme municipal populations, and planner Nolen had named them Indian Beach and Sarasota Heights schools. The school at the north city limits became Bay Haven, while that on the opposite end was named Southside. Scattered communities were graced with new elementary schools of the same style.

Sarasota had become a county entity in 1921 during a period when three consecutive legislative sessions created thirteen new Florida counties and carved five — Charlotte, Glades, Highlands, Hardee, and Sarasota — out of Manatee and De Soto counties. The new Sarasota County created additional facilities to accommodate the pace of its growth. John Nolen had recommended acquisition of a new fairgrounds, freeing the inner city fairgrounds for "a large park." East of the city, the Sarasota County Fair Association opened a new $250,000 plant on Fruitville Road which was to include a mile-long race track and where the New York Giants baseball team prepared to do their spring training in 1926.

Sarasota High School in the 1920s.

Little Ethel Reid with her mother, Eddie Coleman Reid. Ethel earned a good report at Sarasota Grammer School from Emma E. Booker, the principal in whose honor Booker School was named.

The Sarasota High School football team, circa 1928.

Sports was Sarasota's passion. The 1927 Sarasota High School baseball team posed in the open field behind their brand new school on the Tamiami Trail.

Subdivisions and more subdivisions

Stretching north from the Ringling complex on the bay was another large-scale development. Initiated by Adair Realty and Trust of Atlanta, Whitfield Estates subdivision, golf course and country club was constructed upon a 600-plus acre tract fronting on the bay. Although the land lay partly in Manatee County, the tract's social and political orientation was to Sarasota. Whitfield's developers opened offices in the Mira Mar and appealed to Sarasota citizens for utilities and services.

South of Whitfield lay Newtown, a subdivision developed in 1914 for Sarasota's black residents. One of its original parcels lay on the east side of Orange Avenue with side streets Washington, Lee, Douglass, Dunbar, and Hig (present-day 21st through 25th streets). During the boom, the subdivision expanded a few streets south and then eas to Washington Boulevard (then eventually north along bo sides of present-day U.S. 301).

Merle Evans' band played in McAnsh Park in front of the Mira Mar Hotel in 1925. Evans stands center back.

John Ringling's causeway remained a favorite community fishing spot for decades.

Members of Entre Nous, a teachers' club, during a dinner dance they sponsored in the 1930s to buy school supplies.

One Newtown resident, Jane Clark, remembered turn-of-the-century Sarasota when only ten families lived in the vicinity. The black population swelled as laborers and skilled workmen were hired by special agents who went through the rural areas of Georgia and the Carolinas recruiting workers to fill the demand in Florida's boom cities. Willie McKenzie, who arrived in 1925 with a Savannah construction firm, worked on Charles Ringling's ten-story hotel as well as on John Ringling's causeway. As families like McKenzie's followed the work to Sarasota, the city became home for generations of blacks.

As the downtown grew, the black community edged northward and Newtown replaced the original municipal residential area that once included Black Bottom. Later known as Overtown, it had been bounded roughly on the north and south by Tenth and Fifth streets and on the west and east by U.S. 41 and Orange Avenue. Overtown had constituted a complete community with small shops, social facilities, and religious centers such as its first house of worship — Bethlehem Baptist Church.

South of the city, on bayfront land once owned by Charles Abbe, McClellan Park subdivision was ten years old by the time of the boom. It was designed by Katherine McClellan in honor of her father. Miss McClellan, an independent woman of forward vision, was a commercial portrait photographer in Northampton, vice president of the Northampton Equal Suffrage League, and official photographer for Smith College, from which she had graduated in 1882. Her approach to subdivision design presaged an approach typically utilized decades later. McClellan Park incorporated artful Florida themes around environmentally sensitive natural features, including shell streets named for Indians, a tennis court, a yacht basin, and a bayfront yacht club. Constructed in pecky cypress, the community center (present-day McClellan Park School) was built next to the central site feature — an apparent Indian mound.

Just south of McClellan Park, Cherokee Park subdivision was laid out along the bay by J.C. Brown, a silk importer. Nearby Sarasota Heights, of the same vintage as McClellan Park, and originally incorporated as a separate municipality, was incorporated into the city during the boom.

As development reached its peak at the height of the Roaring Twenties, growth extended broadly among Sarasota County's scattered communities. Englewood boasted a golf course, hotel, newspaper, and park, and looked forward to construction of a $5 million university for the children of veterans. Nokomis had a hotel and golf course, newspaper, bank, tarpon tournament, and moving picture house. Sarasota's advertised communities of the period reflected historic as well as glamorous new names and included Indian Beach, Sapphire Shores, Vamo, Osprey, Laurel, Woodmere, Fruitville, Myakka, and Bee Ridge.

Bee Ridge was described as "The center of Sarasota County's citrus industry... a likeable little community only 7 miles by asphalt road from Sarasota."

Don't fence me in

*I*nland, some historic cattle country sections were surveyed, platted, and offered for sale as small farms. Drainage of the Myakka basin had introduced much inland wetlands to agriculture. The "new town of Myakka City," midway between Bradenton and Arcadia, had been developed since 1915 as a trade center for farmers and growers.

Honoré and Potter Palmer Jr. had helped form the Sarasota-Fruitville drainage district, removing water from the giant, historic slough and dredging a straightened drainage canal through the snaking creekbed of Phillippi Creek. In its entirety, the project encompassed more than 40 square miles and included a network of 50 linear miles of canals. Smack in the middle of the wetlands sector was the Palmer acreage platted as Palmer Farms and constituting hundreds of small and several experimental farms, including the Palmer brothers' 1,600-acre Hyde Park Citrus Grove.

According to the Sarasota Chamber of Commerce, the massive project had resulted in 26,000 acres of drained, fertile soil for farming. The Chamber predicted that the great newly exposed beds of muck soil would provide new opportunities for incoming small truck farmers, whose numbers were expected to reach 10,000 by 1927.

A great increase in operations countywide was predicted for dairy cattle, while in the poultry industry Sarasota was expected to become "the Petaluma of the Gulf Coast." Predictions of up to 100,000 acres under cultivation were based upon plans for new inland roads and additional drainage.

Traditional cattlemen found the once-open ranges inflating in value. Even as progress transformed the cattle industry through modern transportation and eradication of tick fever, it carried with it increased real estate interest in inland agricultural areas. Along with transportation and roads had come accessibility; along with dipping and purebreds had come private fences. Forward-thinking

cattlemen realized it was now necessary to buy land rather than count upon the age-old tradition of open ranges.

The merits of each subdivision and inland agricultural development were hyped by the Sarasota *Herald,* the newspaper established in 1925 by George D. Lindsay, Edward Naugle, Linday's son David, and Paul Poynter, who had purchased the St. Petersburg *Times* thirteen years earlier.

The new paper entered the market to compete with an aging superstar, the Sarasota *Times,* published since 1899 by C.V.S. Wilson. Local readers were also served by the cosmopolitan *This Week in Sarasota* published by Moore and Dooley Inc.

The incoming news publishers resembled other investors of the '20s, reinvesting northern capital in the suddenly booming South. Poynter, an Indiana native, and Lindsay, native Pennsylvanian and a former Presbyterian minister, had come to Florida as experienced newspaper owners to invest in the dynamic and profitable prospects of Florida news and advertising.

Bridging the bay

The boom tamed Sarasota Bay, finally connecting the mainland and the keys to overland traffic. Ringling's glorious causeway linked the city to Bird Key and St. Armands, while a 1927 bond issue had underwritten the bridging of New Pass between Lido and Longboat.

South of Ringling Isles, bridge building continued along the bay as the old 1915 bridge to Siesta Key was replaced with a concrete version in 1927, improving traffic access to former Little Sarasota Key and Siesta subdivision. The sandspurred island had come into the twentieth century with a bang when Sarasota's mover and shaker, Harry Higel, had joined with long-time island resident Captain Louis Roberts (whose Roberts' Hotel brought traffic to the island even before bridges) and E.M. Arbogast to organize Siesta Land Company. Siesta Developments dredged bayous and canals, laid sidewalks, built docks, bungalows, and one hotel, and advertised widely. In 1912, a revised plat by Gulf Bay Land Company had involved principals in the Higel, Edmondson, and Roberts families as well as Mrs. Morrill, G.W. Franklin of the Sarasota Yacht Club,

Siesta Key's Crescent Beach.

nd J.H. Faubel. Higel family names dotted the plat — ayou Louise, Higel Avenue, Genevieve Street, and dmondson Road — along with Roberts family names — ayou Hanson, Roberts Road. Even a Morrill Avenue and Faubel Street completed the owners' imprints.

Further canals and hotel areas were reserved. On the orth end of the island (former site of a fishery, even uring the Indian wars), Higel operated a dockside U.S. ost office and eventually built a two-storied, white-framed, olumn-fronted hotel — the Higel Hurst — along the ushing waters of Big Pass. Higel, who had been brutally nurdered on the island in 1921, was memorialized with the aming of the new bridge in his memory.

Stickney Point Bridge crossed the bay at an historically narrow spot, the homesite of "Uncle Ben" Stickney, a native Missourian who had once managed the old Belle Haven Hotel at the foot of Main Street. Stickney established himself on the island to homestead what he categorized as "ordinary agricultural land." Sarasotans regarded his fractional quarter-section as special, where one might tie up at the dock, fish offshore, drink from the concrete-rimmed well flowing in Stickney's lawn, or view the bay through a hammock of grand old oaks.

Nearly ten miles below Stickney Point, a bridge reached Casey Key (called for a time Treasure Island) in 1923.

The boom years were mind-boggling — so many people spent so much money to create so many things. They dredged and filled, surveyed and platted, cleared and graded, drained and planted. They left their imprint everywhere, from Gulf shores to inland pastures. Socially, physically, economically, and culturally, they laid the foundation that would distinguish twentieth-century Sarasota. The creative forces loosed during those years permanently imprinted the look of Florida, especially her coastal cities — at Palm Beach with Addison Mizner, in Miami with George Merrick, in Tampa with "Doc" Davis, in Sarasota with Bertha Palmer, John Ringling, and their contemporary high-rollers. Investors had engineered deal after deal, had speculated over and over. When the nation's cash stopped flowing, they were caught, becalmed in an even tide.

ANATEE COUNTY HISTORICAL SOCIETY

Bay Island Hotel, Siesta Key, during the boom years.

T.F. Arnold postcard series extolled Sarasota's virtues as an agricultural and recreation center in the early 1920s.

A sportsman's paradise.

The Palmer corporate interests had cleared and drained thousands of acres for citrus groves and vegetable truck farms.

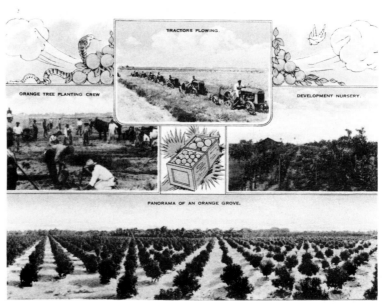

The cattle industry played an important role in advertising the investment portfolio of Sarasota.

10. Circus Town By The Gulf

PHOTO BY STEINMETZ

A favorite of the photographer's, titled "Keep a Stiff Upper Lip."

Aftermath of the 1921 hurricane. The gale pounded ashore wreckage and washed high waters well up Main Street.

Boy Scouts To The Rescue

The hurricane of 1928 struck Florida the night of September 16 with winds gusting up to 130 miles an hour. Coming ashore at Palm Beach, it moved inland, banking water against the shores of Lake Okeechobee, overflowing a dike, and washing out levees to flood communities in the areas of Pelican Bay, Pahokee, Canal Point, Belle Glade, and South Bay. The storm killed an estimated 2,000, many of whom were Bahamian blacks brought to the agricultural region for a season's labor.

Across Sarasota County, the oncoming storm winds mowed down a path of pines across the land, uniformly snapped trunks and layed them down, always pointed west. In Sarasota, the American Legion answered a call for disaster assistance from South Bay with a group of Sarasota Boy Scouts. For one gruelling day, working in receding waters filled with grisly death and snake-infested floating debris, the boys retrieved and disposed of victims, some dead as much as ten days. The waters were dangerously slimy and greenish, and several adult Legionnaires ultimately died from sickness.

Some weeks afterward, the Sarasota Scouts received mementoes of appreciation from the governor and the American Legion.

The boom that transformed the face of Florida's coastal cities began to measurably die down in 1925. The causes were variously ascribed to real estate fraud, housing shortages, transportation service breakdowns, and concern over income taxes. But these did not complete the list of Florida's traumas. In September 1926 and 1928, killer hurricanes struck the coasts of Florida, home to many new residents completely unfamiliar with tropical storms. Hundreds died, thousands incurred injuries and families by the thousands suffered devastating material losses.

The 1926 hurricane hit the Gulf coast early in the afternoon on Saturday, September 18. It struck the islands first. Bashing waves dramatically altered the fragile barrier island of Siesta. Great deposits of sand sealed from the Gulf the final segment of the three-mile-long pioneer pass which formerly wound south from Point of Rock dividing Casey Key and Siesta. The powerful storm filled in the old pass from Turtle Beach to the section of the pass later renamed Heron Lagoon.

In Sarasota, precautions had been taken. Boats had been rushed into Hudson Bayou. Children and mothers had been taken in nightclothes to high floors in downtown hotels, where the children watched wide-eyed as bay waters were sucked out into the Gulf, then later rushed back in a tidal wave. Winds reached 80 miles an hour. A crowd holed up at Lord's Arcade while upstairs in offices, men who had come to work as usual watched with alarm as rising winds reached such strength that Model T's parked along Main Street below Five Points were shoved into the center of the street.

Nearby stores and theatres suffered heavy damage, trees were uprooted, buildings went down. The storm hit equally hard at Nokomis, Venice, and other booming development communities of coastal Sarasota. Power and phone lines were down everywhere. The Sarasota Herald was unable to get out its Sunday issue.

The longest-lasting storm to blow through Sarasota County, however, was to remain in force for years. Sarasota, in company with all her Florida sister cities, was in the direct path of a slower but equally devastating economic storm. She was already observing firsthand an ominous calm descending over the scene of the frenzied wild winds of real estate transactions.

A development gone bust

In 1926, the collapse began in earnest. Although the timing varied, all across Florida property values declined, public debts grew, and banking resources plummeted. Over four years, assessed value of real estate statewide fell 40 percent. Reported net income spiraled downward from a 1925 total of $815 million to $84 million five years later. As purchasers of land and businesses increasingly were unable to make payments on bank loans and mortgages, revenues of financial institutions dropped until the very institutions themselves — and their assets — were threatened. Although 1926 showed some gain in the total number of national and state banks, more than 40 had actually closed. The state government, constitutionally prohibited from bonded indebtedness, ceased capital expenditures, while the debt of local governments statewide, which had reached $600 million by 1929, reflected the situation in widespread failure to meet bond payments.

The railroads and banks that had created and fed Florida's prosperity reeled in the economic storm. In 1931, the Seaboard Air Line Railroad went into receivership. Forty-five national banks and 171 state banks were to close in the nine-year period following 1925.

In July 1929, Tampa's Citizens Bank and Trust Company failed to open, and four other out-of-town banks also closed — including First Bank and Trust Company at Five Points in Sarasota. American National Bank had folded in May of the previous year. Bank of Sarasota, across the street from First Bank and Trust, held on until summer

First National Bank at Five Points, circa 1922, in the building Gillespie built. John F. Burket, attorney and one time owner of the Belle Haven, practiced upstairs; the all-important Badgers Pharmacy operated on the street level.

When at last the big moment arrived, 1920s automobiles stood poised to parade down the phenomenal highway across the 'Glades to Miami.

1932. The following spring, Charles and Edith Ringling's Ringling Bank and Trust Co. voluntarily liquidated, although none of the depositors lost their money as Edith reportedly repaid each in full from personal funds.

Florida's agricultural sector also received a devastating blow. Only six months before the stock market crash of 1929, a dreaded pest was discovered in a citrus grove in the Orlando region — the Mediterranean fruit fly. Further inspections revealed widespread distribution of the insect. To halt further spread, embargoes were placed upon fruit shipments from infected groves, and the governor called out the National Guard to prevent the transporting of fruit from one place to another. Furthermore, all infected groves were ordered burned during a quarantine that lasted until the end of November of the following year. Fruit production fell to nearly half its pre-epidemic total, and the resultant drop in all related industries added significantly to the already depressed statewide economy.

The new Sarasota County, not even a decade old when Sarasota's real estate bubble burst, slumped into economic depression along with the rest of the country. Her citizens' elegant parties slowed down and stopped altogether in many circles. Her beautiful new buildings mutely and daily testified to the grand era that had passed so quickly. The hopes and dreams of Sarasota's developers tumbled into an abyss of unpaid notes and mortgages.

Although some had sources of income safe from the sudden perils, others suffered instantly and tangibly. For more than a decade, Sarasota's breadwinners took any kind of job to feed their families. Former millionaires drove delivery cars. Businessmen parked cars for hotels. Tradesmen drove vegetable trucks across the newly drained muck fields of Palmer Farms. Engineers peddled radios and refrigerators. Accountants pumped gas. Any kind of honest job found grateful takers.

Outside the law, moonshine stills cropped up across Sarasota. The high-profit enterprises operated on wood or gas for fuel, producing 'shine in homemade outfits hidden within deeply secreted bayheads and hammocks. Moonshine was a popular sales commodity in certain backrooms of filling stations and at local juke joints. Local bootleggers smuggled rum and whiskey from Cuba and Canada and distributed their product as far as Tampa in souped up cars with reinforced springs.

Gambling became a popular Sarasota diversion, seen in high stakes games played in a back room of a prime social center, the Plaza Restaurant. In the black subdivisons, gambling took the form of skin games, a sort of poker in which the object was to win, or skin, opponents.

In a development gone bust, the children of Newtown attended school in a deserted office and horsebarn on Orange Avenue (site of present-day Amaryllis Park School complete with the original stall dividers. The black school came to be called Booker in the '30s after the death of Emma E. Booker, the Tuskegee-educated principal of the '20s.

Even though funding and staffing were sadly inadequate for the disastrous depression at hand, Florida created a State Board of Public Welfare in 1927. Within a few years 26 percent of Floridians would be receiving some form of public assistance, but when the bubble burst, the hope of federal relief programs was but a distant vision.

Ringling to the rescue

Sarasota rode into the chasm of the bust along with the rest of Florida, but she had something special to take up some of the economic slack. And that something brought with it a little festivity and merriment and was to further distinguish Sarasota from her neighboring coastal entities.

In the winter of 1926-27, John Ringling summoned Fred Bradna, general equestrian director who ran the circus "like a Prussian drillmaster," according to another Ringling family member. Arriving from winter quarters in Bridgeport, Connecticut, Bradna learned to his complete astonishment that John had decided to move the huge circus's winter headquarters to Sarasota. "I am going to make Sarasota one of the sights of the South," he told Bradna. "I'll lay out the quarters like a zoo, and thousands of visitors will pay to see it. I'll build an open-air arena exactly the size of Madison Square Garden, and on Sundays the acts can practice before an audience. . . Sarasota will become one of the most beautiful cities in Florida."

Bradna carried the heavy news back to Bridgeport, knowing that the loss of the circus would constitute a heavy blow for that city and some circus folk who had made it home for years. When Bradna returned to Sarasota, Ringling gave a stag dinner for 72 at Ca'D'Zan to celebrate purchase of the fairgrounds for the new winter quarters. The festive menu consisted of roast pheasant, wild rice, and special dishes. Center ring was reserved for the appetizer, a soup concocted by Sophie, the Ringlings' cook, featuring the meat of terrapin kept in the terrapin pool on the grounds of Ca'D'Zan.

The sanctity of the Everglades was invaded by dredges and blasting rigs as modern man triumphed over Florida's traditionally indomitable mystery, later dubbed "River of Grass" by Marjorie Douglas.

Next day Ringling and Bradna drove to the fairgrounds. "I have never seen a man more enthusiastic," Bradna observed. Ringling diagramed the entire layout with Bradna, who said afterward that the ultimate design was virtually the same as the one planned on the spot that day.

The layout was complete with horse barns, cat barns, and an elephant house. Mess halls, performing areas, a railroad shop, and barracks rose up to join administration facilities. The old fairgrounds bleachers built by the city were soon walled in and roofed to form part of the large cat house."

The circus train rolled into town the first week of November after a final season performance at Tampa. Loaded with stakes, tents, poles, props, cages, horses, and wagons, the cars came across the Sarasota tracks for the first time — some 100 railroad cars and three advance cars, totaling around 1,400 people during the season, but down to a skeleton crew for winter season.

Car after car deposited its contents, which were unloaded with the precision born of rigorous practice in city after city for nearly ten years. In the 1927 season alone, the circus had set up and struck the show in nearly 150 locations across the country. Into Sarasota with the circus came elephants, gorillas, tigers, lions, bareback riders, clowns, midgets, aerialists, daredevils, acrobats, a few roustabouts, administrators, food preparers, accountants, grooms, musicians, choreographers, and composers.

The circus was to participate each spring in the traditional Sarasota pageant, which featured a community/circus parade. The event improved year after year and became an unqualified success and symbolic of Sarasota's Ringling imprint. Even in the midst of the Depression, visitors flocked to Sarasota and locals arrived early to get a spot along the route to see the beautiful circus wagons, the performers in their spectacular gowns and headdresses, the clowns, and Sarasota's community participants. The circus was to participate in the pageant for three decades, once again underlining Sarasota's distinctive character.

John and Mable Ringling Museum of Art under construction. Raising the statue *David* into place.

A 1963 event featured a circus bandwagon jammed with musicians to commemorate the good old days of the circus parade.

The long road to recovery

Away from the universal fantasy associated with circus, and away from the life John Ringling had breathed anew into his Sarasota, there was the Depression. National recovery measures were finally apparent in Sarasota in the '30s.

The Civilian Conservation Corps (CCC) was the first agency of President Roosevelt's New Deal to operate in Florida. Beginning in August 1933, the CCC provided income for families by creating jobs for their young men, aged 18 to 25, who were hired to build roads, reforest, cut firebreaks, and construct cabins in state, national, and private forests and state parks.

In honor of their mother, in 1934 Potter and Honore Palmer had donated nearly 2,000 acres of Bertha Palmer's Meadow Sweet Pastures ranch for a state park. Lying on both sides of Sugar Bowl Road where it crossed the valley between the Upper and Lower Myakka lakes, the historic area contained prime natural grazing land and a section known by long-time residents as "the old picnic grounds." The gift formed the core of Myakka State Park.

As a result of a CCC project, Myakka Park received several hundred enrollees along with administrators, supervisors, and a young Georgia doctor named Matthews. During the CCC efforts, roads were constructed and improved from the Sugar Bowl Road (State Route 72) entrance to the upper lake, park cabins were constructed of palmetto cabbage logs, and a pavilion, picnic grounds, and outdoor fireplaces were built to grace the new state park, as well as a barn to house trucks and equipment (present-day exhibits facility).

The Federal Economic Recovery Act reached into the lives of Americans everywhere and made a difference. In Sarasota, relief was finally available to individual families, residential mortgages through Homeowners loans, and Works Progress Administration (WPA) projects. Under the National Youth Administration, Chet Ihrig's local athletic teams worked in masonry and carpentry to build the clubhouse at Ihrig Field. A new Osprey Avenue bridge across Hudson Bayou was constructed by the short-lived Civil Works Administration in 1934.

In 1938, the WPA built Sarasota's municipal auditorium, a hangar shaped structure of steel and reinforced concrete to seat 3,200. WPA and city funds combined to build 40 shuffleboard courts, nine tennis courts, and two grass bowling greens, including lighting for night use. The entire 37-acre bayfront park was acquired by the city for taxes, and its unique location on Sarasota Bay was considered a great boon for generations to come. Numerous civic groups pitched in to beautify the grounds, and local men worked to put together financial underwriting for the WPA grant for the auditorium and park. A public library in the park was underwritten by John Tuttle Chidsey, a retired businessman from Connecticut. Other WPA projects employed hundreds of men and women and resulted in improvements to the Osprey Avenue bridge, city sidewalks and development of Luke Wood Park. Another WPA project, construction of Lido Beach Pavilion, moved ahead with labor from local crews and clerks.

Sarasota's downtown bayfront in 1935, from the roof of the Orange Blossom Hotel. At the foot of Strawberry Avenue (now Ringling Boulevard) is the railroad dock where John Ringling once parked his private railroad car.

In the mid-'30s, only three skyscrapers graced downtown Sarasota. On the islands lay the visible effects of the depression, streets and curbings defined empty subdivisions waiting for the market to come to life again.

The municipal complex, circa 1940, before dredging and filling for the sites of present-day Selby Library and Van Wezel Hall. The new hangar-shaped, WPA-built municipal auditorium dominated the bayfront. To the left is Payne Terminal, while out from the bay spread the Newtown area and the surrounding piney woods.

John Ringling North, president of the Greatest Show on Earth.

Henry "Buddy" Ringling North and his son, John Ringling North II, circa 1940.

Posing with their mother, Ida Ringling North, Buddy and John Ringling North prepare to depart winter quarters for New York's Madison Square Garden to open the season.

Ca' D' Zan, the mansion John and Mable Ringling built at Sarasota Bay, was desinged by New York architect Dwight Baum to combine the facade of Palazzo Ducale in Venice with the tower of New York's old Madison Square Garden, where the circus traditionally opened each season.

Interior of Ringling Museum of Art, 1950.

(top row)

Tentmakers in 1942 fashioned the enormous canvas Big Top by hand, as well as the satellite tents that had to be ready to go out each spring for a season of trouping.

The circus chugged through pinelands and palmetto scrub in the 1940s as it headed for New York and season's opening.

The cookhouse, where 1,400 people on tour were fed three meals daily.

The Doll family, Daisy, Tiny, Gracie and Harry, in their train berth, enjoy a friendly poker game.

(second row)

"Alice from Dallas" in her berth aboard the circus train.

Circus bandmaster Merle Evans conducts in "Mrs. Charles Ringling's favorite uniform" — braided and tooled and trimmed in white and gold leather.

John Murray Anderson instructed the circus performers in earnest as rehearsals became increasingly intense.

The tattooed lady.

Pretty equestrian Bobby Steele clears the rail on her high-jumping horse, Tip Top, circa 1949.

(right)

In the blacksmith shop, equestrian stars prepared for the act.

(far right)

Circus chimp and pretty friend.

A Fine Line Between Pathos and Eros

In each face is seen the traditional paradox of the clown, that artistic character who inspires joy and underlines sorrow, who treads in oversized shoes the fine line between *pathos* and *Eros*. The sentimental path of the clown is well-worn and old, but in twentieth century America, the path of the clown frequently led south to Sarasota.

Over the years, Sarasota County has been home base for some of the nation's best-known clowns — men and women whose stylized antics included the likes of the famed Emmett Kelly along with the great "tramp clown" Otto Griebling, the "august clown" Lou Jacobs, and the great "white face clowns" Charlie Bell and Felix Adler, who was called "King of Clowns."

Ten years after the circus transferred winter quarters to Venice in 1959, notable clown Danny Chapman with Mel Miller, former curator of the Museum of the Circus, helped establish the first Ringling Brothers Barnum & Bailey "Clown College." The training program, which opened in fall 1968, operates several months prior to the annual circus season and has produced a class of clown "graduates" each year.

Weary Willie, the famous tramp clown Emmett Kelly. (Steinmetz's favorite photo, entitled "Down in the Dumps.")

Famous Ringling white-face clown Harry Dann poses with a ducky partner.

White-face clown Paul Jerome.

Famous clowns clowning at winter quarters: *(left to right)* "King of Clowns" Felix Adler, tramp clown Emmett Kelly and Paul Jerome pose for white face clown Harry Dann and his ever-present duck as they operate Steinmetz's camera.

The Circus Train

"The departure of the circus train was a great event in Sarasota. . . .

"It seemed that all the people of Sarasota and the hinterland were there to say good-by. They lined the tracks from Winter Quarters to far out on the main line. Mother came down to see her two sons off. With the wind whipping his priestly robes, Father Elslander, assisted by two acolytes swinging censers, blessed the train in sonorous Latin and sprinkled them with holy water. . . .

"Our big engine huffed and puffed and the long line of cars painted in glistening silver and 'Ringling red' began to move. . . . We slid along between the cheering crowds, with every performer leaning out of windows or crowded on platforms. . . . John and I, on the rear platform, were more excited than any of them."

—Henry Ringling North
The Circus Kings, Our Ringling Family Story

Raising the Big Top

After Sarasota became winter home for the circus, the Greatest Show sometimes closed its season with a one-day stand in town, setting up on Ringling Boulevard in open fields near the site of present-day Ringling Shopping Center.

Elephants and roustabouts labored mightily to raise the Big Top while at the summit of the center poles, six pennants, flanked by American flags, fluttered the message "Ringling Brothers Barnum & Bailey Circus."

Season's end generally concluded an epic journey of some thousand employees over nearly 20,000 miles in railroad cars, and raising the Big Top in just over 100 cities and towns.

When the circus folk reached Sarasota, it was around Thanksgiving, and they were home.

A sad journey home

Far from home at Hartford, Connecticut, fourteen months before war's end, Sarasota's own Ringling Circus suffered a tragic defeat when the huge new Big Top designed to seat 12,000 people burst into flames during a wartime tour matinee performance. The ensuing inferno killed 168 and badly injured another 467 of the 7,000 customers present at the performance — mostly women and children. The circus management had been headed by John and Henry Ringling North until January 1943, when it passed to Charles and Edith's son, Robert, as president, and Sarasota accountant James A. Haley (who had married Aubrey Ringling in 1943) as first vice president and assistant to the president. Haley was the highest ranking circus officer present and was therefore among the group arrested and charged with involuntary manslaughter. (Haley ultimately served a year and a day in jail. The Florida legislature unanimously voted to reinstate his citizenship and he was afterward elected to the U.S. House of Representatives, where he served more than twenty years.) John Ringling North received the staggering news in New York, while Henry read it in *Stars and Stripes* in Europe where he was serving with the Officers Strategic Services. After nine days in Hartford, the circus limped back home to winter quarters, carting the rubble of the fire — massive charred tent poles and bleachers, smashed acrobatic rigging, and the blistered animal chute that had trapped most of the victims inside the inferno. The circus train made its customary entry into town, dropping off passengers at Lemon Street downtown, then turning east toward Winter Quarters. But along the familiar route stood concerned Sarasotans, who felt badly for *their* circus. To raise revenue to pay off damage claims and get back to work, the circus went out on the rails after only a few weeks, heading for Akron, Ohio, in early August to perform in public stadiums and arenas — without its Big Top, rigging, or bleachers.

Loading the menagerie, 1940s.

Roustabouts en route on circus train, a time to read and sleep between towns.

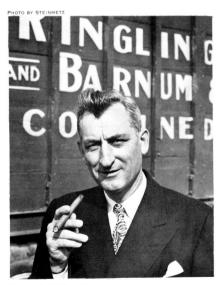

James A. Haley, Sarasota accountant, became vice president of the circus and later was elected to the U.S. House of Representatives.

The Baby Parade of the Sara de Soto Pageant proceeded down Main Street at Five Points in 1946. The event drew a large crowd dotted with servicemen.

Aerial view of Sarasota bayfront, circa 1945, from rear of Ringling Hotel.

The Federal Building, constructed during the midst of the Depression, became the city's post office in 1934.

Clem Pearson, Sarasota's sheriff from 1932-39, in the days when the sheriff of each county was required to commence execution in capital punishment cases.

War and prosperity

Although the 1941 attack by Japanese forces on Pearl Harbor signaled the beginning of an awesome conflict for the United States, it also ended the economic depression that had gripped the country for more than a decade. Millions of dollars were suddenly pumped into the economy, gearing up for a conflict the country and its allied forces could not afford to lose.

At home, coastal residents participated in routine community blackouts. Wide-eyed children vacationing on the beaches helped their mothers pull down shades and turn out lights at eight p.m.

Rumors of German submarines offshore and saboteurs let loose in Florida kept fears real and regular. In 1942, German submarines struck down a number of vessels in Florida waters — the *Pan Massachussetts* went down off the coast of Cape Canaveral; 24 ships between the Cape and the Bahamas; a tanker off Miami; another off the Florida Keys; and in midsummer, yet another off the Apalachicola coast.

The Civil Air Patrol organized that spring to help guard home coasts. The planes flew out of Florida bases, including Sarasota. Additionally, the Coastal Picket Patrol used civilian craft to cope with offshore submarine activity. (In at least one recorded instance, saboteurs did, in fact, come ashore from a sub at Ponte Vedra Beach and made it as far as New York and Chicago before they were apprehended.) Some Sarasota men were pressed into service on patrol craft in local waters, and until the Navy assembled its own craft, their vessels often were employed at Miami and other Florida coastal zones.

A few (John Birdsall, Charlie Walpole, Bob Luzier) joined the Coast Guard and served at Egmont Key, where men from the patrol craft boarded incoming and outgoing vessels to check destination papers and cargo consignments.

Kentucky Military Institute Color Guard, at Venice during World War II.

The gate to the Venice airfield stood near U.S. 41 on the southeast corner of Rialto and San Marco.

The Venice airfield baseball team, the Venice Aerials, posed before their base dugout complete with grins and one bat boy.

Sarasota's wartime benefits included World War II training fields, one in Sarasota, the other in Venice. In the background lies the private field built earlier at Venice by Dr. Albee and others.

Florida, with her good year-round climate and open, uninhabited flat terrain, became an expansive training school and airfield for the military. Entering the war with six training bases and flying schools, by the close of the war, Florida had 40, two of them in Sarasota County.

Late in the '30s, a WPA project had addressed the needs of Manatee and Sarasota citizenry for a modern airport to replace the one built in 1929 on Fruitville Road. The two counties had formed a Sarasota-Manatee Joint Airport Authority and had acquired acreage near the bay, close to Whitfield and the Ringling estates. Using WPA grants, Civil Aeronautics monies, and county funds, the work went forward. The airport authority had eventually leased a bayfront tract of land from Powell Crosley Jr., whose boom-period house had been constructed in the 1920s.

The U.S. Army was occupying the site as a base by 1942, installing hangars, barracks, signal towers, signal systems, and eventually supporting the activities of several thousand personnel. Farther south at Venice, a field was established in 1942 which eventually based some 6,000 men. (Both bases were deactivated in 1945-46 and became civilian fields, accommodating local populations rapidly swelled by the wartime activity.)

Local citizens became accustomed to the sight of the flight training craft and the sound of firing from the practice ranges. Sarasota resident James A. Haley looked up from mowing his grass one day to see two planes collide in midair. After one such collision the debris of two planes crashed to the ground on the Palmer estate, The Oaks. The fuselages were recovered by military equipment, but for generations Sarasotans discovered an occasional bomb or shell casing sunken in bay waters or forgotten in piney woods.

According to newspaperman Karl Grismer in his book published at the end of the war, more than 2,000 Sarasota men and women enlisted in the military services, many to serve far from home. Sarasota Bay Post No. 30 of the American Legion sponsored a chapter in the book entitled "Lest We Forget," incorporating pictures and biographies of nearly 70 Sarasotans who died in the war.

Just as military training had transformed the face of Florida's population, so had the resultant population increase transformed the economy of the Depression. Sarasota's subdivisions, hotels, apartments, tourist camps, and beaches all benefitted. Lagging housing spaces were suddenly filled to capacity — and beyond. As in all Florida, Sarasota's facilities became part of the war effort — restaurants became mess halls, bayfront estates like Powell Crosley's were leased to the military for officers quarters. And after the war, Sarasota continued to boom. During the ten years following 1940, Florida's population was to increase 46 percent, while Sarasota's population rose nearly 85 percent.

PHOTO BY STEINMETZ

Wartime shortages hit everyone, even circus performers. Trapeze stars Antoinette and Art Concello repaired their safety nets in 1942 with American cotton staple rope in lieu of the Egyptian variety.

11. The Prosperous Years

A 1947 party at Sarasota's new exhibition hall, occasioned by the Sara de Soto pageant.

Two stars: Emmett Kelly clowns with Antoinette Concello, famed Ringling flyer.

Many of the interior details of the Ringling Museum were imported from Europe during the heydays of the circus king.

"Twin Hemisphere" bandwagon on display at Sarasota's Circus Hall of Fame.

The great august clown, Lou Jacobs, with circus performers.

By 1950, Sarasota looked back upon a decade of dramatic change. Gone was the Depression. In its place stood a postwar building boom and a population that had jumped dramatically. The county had recorded construction in late 1949 of nearly five hundred homes, five churches, thirty-five stores, ten apartment houses, seven motels, two fire stations, and a new radio station.

Siesta Key idyll, fishing from the front lawn.

A whiskey still and five-gallon jugs of 'shine were confiscated in the mid-'40s in a bay head off Clark Road by Sheriff Pearson, Deputy Sweeting, and beverage agents.

The fortunes of war

The city of Sarasota had a population of 19,000 people, nearly doubled from 1945, while the City of Venice had just under 1,000. Venice also had blossomed with completion of a quarter million dollar government project, the City of Venice Trailer Park. Sarasota's legislative delegation instigated efforts to gain long term projects such as the routing of U.S. 41 around the bay and creation of a bayfront park. Ultimately, funding was also designated for replacement of John Ringling's deteriorating original wooden causeway and a modern public hospital, Sarasota Memorial, was targeted for planning and construction.

Sarasota County had assembled a small air force to advance against a long-time enemy — the mosquito. The "Sarasota Mosquito Squadron," a Piper Cub and three Stearman biplanes, sprayed DDT, one of the experimental products tested in wartime research and found to have wide practical application in insect control. (The potential side effects of DDT were not known until later.)

By 1947, Jerry Collins, new owner of Sarasota Kennel Club, held the powerful post of Rules Chairman in the Florida House of Representatives. The legislature adopted a junior college program and increased facilities for higher education in institutions suddenly bulging with postwar students. To cope with the pressing postwar municipal needs, the Sarasota delegation successfully introduced a measure that provided a city manager form of government for Sarasota, a change passed nearly three to one by local referendum and which was to result in some four decades of continuity under City Manager Kenneth Thompson. Legislative action also addressed the citrus and cattle industries, modifying the existing citrus code to block industrial practices of shipping unripe fruit.

Even Florida's peacetime industries had been transformed during the war. Requisitioned by the government, the state's canned and processed fruits had gone for military and lend lease programs, and the combined efforts of the Florida Citrus Commission and the University of Florida's Agricultural Experiment Station had developed a frozen concentrate process which was of great value to the government as well as to the commercial industry after the war.

Cattlemen crashed head on into modern pressures when the legislature overrode their opposition to closing the open ranges. In 1949, at the urging of Governor Fuller Warren, the legislature barred cattle from all state roads. (During the two preceding years, cattle on the highways had caused nearly 1,000 accidents, killed 24 people, and injured more than 200.) The face of Sarasota's historic inland ranchlands was forever changed, the open range a thing of the past.

Randy Bundy, bandleader and circus treasurer, poses among the palms in 1947.

Ted Williams, champion batter of the Boston Red Sox and a Sarasota celebrity during the Red Sox' spring training season, 1949.

Sarasota artist Thornton Utz in his Palm Island studio in the 1960s.

Sarasota's prominent gathered at Colony Beach in 1960 to be photographed for *Dodge News*. Left to right: inventor Guy Paschal; cartoonist V.T. Hamlin, creator of "Alley Oop"; Stu Rae, Chicago art director; author MacKinlay Kantor; John D. MacDonald, author and creator of Travis McGee; Colony Beach host Herb Fields; and artists Gil Elvgren and Ben Stahl.

The year was 1955, Elvis Presley was king of rock and roll, and the volleyball games at Lido Beach pavilion were a favorite place for the high school crowd.

Even a staged tarpon catch in 1955 could be exciting in Sarasota Bay where the annual tarpon tournament remained a popular event.

A great leap forward

*I*n early 1951, Cecil B. De Mille arrived in Sarasota to film *The Greatest Show on Earth*. Scenes were shot at winter quarters, as well as along Main Street where the circus parade turned out record crowds. Sarasota school children were let out of school to take part in audience scenes for the filming.

In 1952, Sarasota built the first modern school in Newtown, the black community. Situated on Orange Avenue across from wooden buildings that had served as schools for years, Booker High School contained five buildings housing homemaking and industrial arts, a cafeteria, a gymnasium, an auditorium, twelve classrooms, and for the first time, indoor bathroom facilities.

In 1957, plans were drawn for Booker Elementary School (present-day Booker Middle School), to be constructed across the street from Booker High. In 1959, two wings of six classrooms each were constructed as Amaryllis Park Primary School (present-day Booker East). Five years later, Roland W. Rogers, who had been principal of Booker for twenty years of progress and change, was appointed to the administrative staff of the county schools.

As 1959 turned to 1960, Sarasota pointed with pride to a new health department, a Siesta Beach pavilion, remodeling of the courthouse, reconstruction of U.S. 41 from Bee Ridge to Stickney Point Road, acceptance of a county planning program, and adoption of an air pollution control code. Roads were a major theme — final plans to route U.S. 41 along the downtown bayfront had been approved in 1957. Soon dredges were depositing spoil along the bayfront to build up a wide new median and roadbed and to create a new bayfront Island Park and marina. The chairman of the County Commission lobbied for a good roads program, a sewer system for lower Phillippi Creek, federal flood control aid, expansion of county office space, and increased recreation facilities.

Monumental changes had transformed Sarasota's circus as well. Ringling Brothers Barnum & Bailey's Big Top had been struck for the last time in Philadelphia on July 16, 1956. Crippled by union demands, the circus had been halted and, once again, limped home. When "The Greatest Show on Earth" reopened, it was to perform forever after inside buildings. And in 1959, winter quarters moved to Venice, where a new building — a sort of permanent Big Top — had been equipped with bleachers and newly designed riggings.

Also in the decade, the Arvida Realty Co. of Miami had acquired an important sector of John Ringling's own development projects. Though the years had passed quickly, the changes had been so slight that John Ringling's dredge still lay where it had been left along the shoreline of Ringling Isles, and the ghostly form of the Ritz-Carlton stood tall above the treeline along the shore of New Pass. Purchasing lots on Lido along with the downtown John Ringling Hotel, Arthur Vining Davis had corporately gained the Ringling Isles holdings on Bird and Otter keys and the large parcel of southern Longboat Key which was to be developed in a deliberate, single-concept plan that would distinguish it from many multiparceled barrier island entities.

Residential construction continued unabated, even in high-water areas. In September 1962, a thirteen-inch rain produced floodwaters which rose into homes along Phillippi creek. A tract in the Palmer family's old Hyde Park Citrus area had become South Gate subdivision. As the bulldozers cleared the land, advertisements billed it: "South Gate, where you live among the orange blossoms."

South Gate was followed by Forest Lakes Country Club Estates, then by Gulf Gate. Built on property which once featured the Siesta Drive In, Gulf Gate proclaimed itself a "total community," with thousands of residences, hundreds of businesses, several churches, a golf club, fire stations, and a branch library.

Twenty miles south and east of Gulf Gate, the largest development complex planned in Sarasota had begun in 1954 when Arthur C. Frizzell sold massive tracts in Sarasota and Charlotte counties to Florida West Coast Land Development Company of Miami. The land package comprised two complete townships encompassing nearly 72 square miles in Sarasota County alone. Oil and mineral rights previously had been vested from Frizzell to various oil companies. The area, through which both the Myakka River and Big Slough flowed, became known as North Port.

Manatee and Sarasota counties acquired a junior college in 1957 named Manatee Junior College in Bradenton. The facility provided tuition-free education to residents of the two counties.

In June 1961, the news heralded the creation of a liberal arts college for Sarasota, to be called New College, and to be built on a seventeen-acre tract acquired from the airport plus additional acreage from the state, as well as a portion of the Charles Ringling bayfront estate. The Charles and Edith Ringling house had been saved from the auction block, and the preserved estate ultimately became the bayfront sector of New College. The Board of Trustees of the new institution gave generously. In 1963, the college's selection committee announced the designation of famed architect and planner Icoh Ming Pei to design the campus. The charter class matriculated in fall 1964, and completion of construction was planned for September 1966.

Even as progress paraded through the prosperous years, Florida's history remained her present. Hurricane Donna struck in September 1960, felling trees, flooding low areas, and causing power outages that resulted in a holiday for Sarasota's public school students. On a heavier note, the storm caused significant property damage and the National Guard was called out in the Florida Keys at Marathon.

PHOTO BY STEINMETZ

Perched high above Main Street on a lift over the camera truck, Cecil B. De Mille directed the parade scene for *The Greatest Show on Earth*. Released the following year, in 1952, the film won an Academy Award for best picture.

PHOTO BY CHUCK KENNEDY

Lido Beach was honored with a Hobie cat regatta in 1977.

erial view of St. Armands Key.

The Field Club, one of the most historic private clubs in town, is much in demand.

The Riverview High School Kilties Marching Band passes the reviewing stand at President and Mrs. Ronald Reagan's Inaugural Parade at Disney World in Orlando.

Even as late as 1950, Booker High School's senior class numbered about two dozen, while the football team, the Tornadoes, coached by Carl C. Williams, dressed out that year for the photographer at about the same total.

Booker High School's first band in 1950, flanked by Principal Roland Rogers, left, and band conductor Valentine, right.

Sarasota bayfront in 1968 after filling for U.S. 41 and bayfront park. Gulfstream Avenue at far right was once the bayfront edge.

Bradenton-Sarasota airport terminal appeared newly completed and ready for postcard photos in summer 1959.

The staff of Sarasota's traditional downtown meeting place, The Plaza on First Street, posed in 1951 for posterity.

Lido Beach pavilion in the 1940s. Designed in art deco by Ralph Twitchell, the pavilion formed a nucleus of activity for Sarasotans by day and night. Notice the nearly pristine state of Bird Key in the background.

Stickney Point Bridge in 1945 before construction of the intracoastal waterway — a quieter traffic era when a man-and-wife team turned a hand crank and the span pivoted laterally to open.

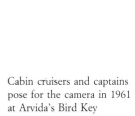

Cabin cruisers and captains pose for the camera in 1961 at Arvida's Bird Key development yacht club.

Construction of Van Wezel Performing Arts Hall in 1969. The entrance foyer and fountain had taken shape.

Fascia and vertical roofing detail, a design by Frank Lloyd Wright Associates, has become a Sarasota hallmark.

Van Wezel Performing Arts Hall.

A local attraction, the increasingly rare flamingo.

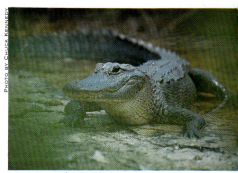

Florida wetlands are home to the alligator, as well as a great variety of dramatically beautiful wading birds.

The cattle egret, a native of Africa, appeared in Florida via South America in the 1950s, blown ashore during a hurricane.

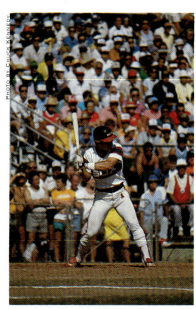

The Chicago White Sox at Payne Park. Batter up.

A show and sale at the Sarasota Art Association during Sarasota's annual pageant week in 1949, when art was booming all over Florida.

The annual sailboat races at the foot of Main Street on Labor Day weekend, 1952, captured by Steinmetz from the roof of the Orange Blossom Hotel.

The inland passage

Transportation retained its traditional priority in Florida during the postwar period. One such project rivaled the Tamiami Trail in complexity and struggle — an inland navigation route along Florida's west coast from Tarpon Springs south to Punta Rassa. Since the days of De Soto, the difficulty of navigating the shallow lower bays and inlets had plagued the Sarasota coastal areas. The project initiated in Congress had received approval (without appropriations) in 1941.

Taken from a back burner after the war, the state legislature had created WCIND — West Coast Inland Navigation District — to raise local funds for the project. Routes had been proposed prior to 1953-54, the most controversial of which were in southern Sarasota bays; finally, a route through Venice was selected (called Route C1). From 1955 through 1961, condemnation suits proceeded to obtain rights-of-way along the route. Construction finally began in 1961 and proceeded from both ends — Fort Myers and Tarpon Springs — toward the middle. In 1967, the waterway was opened ceremonially at the cut in Venice opposite the new Ringling Brothers' circus grounds. There, near the circus which was so definitive a part of Sarasota, another historic entity was born, the inland passage.

Culture comes of age

In 1968, construction began on a big item for cultural Sarasota — a performing arts hall. Designed by chief architect William Wesley Peters, the 1,800-seat, purple-hued Van Wezel building opened in January 1970. It became a prominent component of Sarasota's centers for the performing arts, which included the Players Theatre and the Asolo State Theatre. Imported from Italy for John Ringling's Museum and purchased in 1950 by the state of Florida, the reconstructed Asolo Theater opened in February 1952. It would ultimately house Florida State University's master of fine arts degree program for practicing theatre artists. In 1983, the Asolo Opera Association, which had operated in the little theater for more than twenty years, moved to the renovated Edwards Theater at Pineapple Avenue and First.

After nearly a century of familial circus enterprise and nearly half a century of ownership of the combined shows, Ringling Brothers Barnum & Bailey Circus left family ownership. In the Coliseum in Rome, scene of the gory forerunner of the twentieth century circus, the North brothers publicly conveyed the family's stock to Judge Hofheinz of Houston and Irving Feld for $9 million. Henry Ringling North, the younger of the two brothers and former vice president of the circus, agreed to appear for some years at the annual openings in Madison Square Garden.

Siesta Key's Palm Island development in 1951 was mostly new fill, punctuated by clusters of palmettoes and graced by the new curving road.

The 18th century Asolo theatre was added to the Ringling Museum of Art fourteen years after John Ringling's death. Inspired by a 15th century art patron, Caterina Cornaro, queen of Cyprus, the Italian construction and design prominently feature Caterina's portrait at the balcony center, facing all who play the stage.

State of Florida officials accept the John and Mable Ringling Museum of Art from executors of the estate in 1946. Left to right: John Ringling North, Governor Millard F. Caldwell, Secretary of State R.A. Gray, Superintendent of Public Instruction Colin English, and Comptroller J.M. Lee.

The Ringling Museum storage room, circa 1950s, contained an array of finds — carved panels, ornate columns, furniture, and a harpsichord that eventually found its way to the display rooms.

Steinmetz's familiar photo of David silhouetted by early evening shadows against the Ringling Museum courtyard.

A retrospective on accomplishment

On New Year's Day 1970, Sarasota County publicly reflected on her accomplishments. Even as man had, for the first time, walked on the moon, Sarasota's population had reached and surpassed 100,000. Urbanization had stretched continually southward, and the County Commission had authorized, for the first time, new ordinances under home rule provisions of Florida's new constitution. The county was moving ahead with plans for a new jetport to serve the west coast of Florida; Sarasota Memorial Hospital had been permitted to authorize revenue bonds without a referendum; the county had been the scene of the biggest haul of marijuana ever uncovered in Florida; by referendum, voters had defeated plans for a $2.7 million beach acquisition; and Sarasota's blacks had boycotted integration plans.

On the front page of the Sarasota *Herald Tribune*, President Nixon announced his intention to fight integration delays. In Sarasota, the desegregation of student bodies, required by September 1970, had produced a plan which would close the black community's Booker High School, Booker Elementary School, and Amaryllis Park Primary School.

In closing the Sarasota schools, long a focal point of the community, the integration plan called for busing all black students out of the black community. They were to be integrated into the white schools to achieve acceptable federally established percentages (sixteen percent for Sarasota) rather than across-the-county mixing which would allow Booker to continue. Sarasota blacks first had boycotted, then they had rioted in Newtown. Police arrested scores for "failure to disburse and violation of curfew," and one police officer was shot by a sniper. In the southern part of the county, Laurel's black population supplied integration quotas for Venice and Nokomis. (Eventually, the Booker and Bay Haven complexes were to house special programs with voluntary enrollment.)

Adding to the local pressures, the growth of Sarasota had been drastically affected by the "trinity" of modern times — drainage/mosquito control, air conditioning, and Supreme Court ruling that broadened interpretation of homestead exemption to apply to condominium units. The three elements promoted a density and growth heretofore unknown.

Sarasota's Sun-Debs learned to model and pose at Lido Beach pavilion.

Local youth string orchestra performs on stage at Van Wezel Hall.

Ralph Twitchell's design for the Lido Beach pavilion included art deco seahorses.

Riverview High School.

The New College Campus of the University of South Florida.

Waterfront drive along Sarasota Bay.

Roland Rogers became principal of Booker High School when the school was still unaccredited and housed in a 30-year-old wooden building moved to the campus from a former site. Booker High School became a source of pride and a focal point for the entire community.

Fredd Atkins became, in the centennial year 1985, the first black citizen elected to the City of Sarasota Board of Commissioners.

In 1971, a referendum had approved a charter for a new county government. Drafted by a thirteen-member body, the charter would delegate to the county the kind of independent authority historically reserved for municipalities. No longer an extension of the state legislative powers, under "home rule" the county might govern and tax and formulate governmental structure. Initially proposed to eliminate the constitutional offices of sheriff, appraiser, elections, clerk, and tax collector, the charter was modified to show no change in those offices before the public could accept it. The resultant charter established a county administrator form of government in which an administrator selected by the commissioners would hold direct authority over all county departments. Within fourteen years, the new charter (which was adopted by only six Florida counties) created fifteen departments under an administrator and a total of 900 employees. In ten years, the annual budget went from $12 million to $50 million as government expanded to include countywide administration of entities formerly handled by cities, including a judicial system, buses, tax assessor and collector, libraries, and animal control.

The county pointed with pride to accomplishments of the 1980s and to its role as a national leader in growth planning — measures such as impact fees, transfer of development rights, water supply, and open space safeguards through purchase of the 16,000-acre MacArthur tract (part of the former Ringling tract). To set density limits across the county, a land use plan labeled "Apoxsee" was adopted in 1981; a new Municipal Services Taxing Unit ordinance was designed to pay annually for road improvements and public park construction. A natural resources management department would address the needs of wetlands, beaches, forestation, mosquito control, etc., and a total of fifteen departments were designed to carry forth the responsibilities of home rule.

The size of Sarasota's government had long outgrown the glorious building Dwight Baum designed in the 1920s. Its original one wing for the judiciary and one for government and jail had now been added to several times — new courtrooms and offices on the south, a new jail on the east side. The county purchased Charles and Edith Ringling's old hotel next door and rehabilitated it as the county administration complex. Just as the Ringlings had planned it in their Courthouse Subdivision, the hotel took on a new function, ironically suited to its heritage in a way that the Ringlings could not have foreseen.

Amid all the growth and change, the inland cattle and agricultural industries struggled for critical Green Belt protection. Much of Sarasota's ranch lands remained in the hands of a relatively small number of families, some now third and fourth generations of ownership. The Sarasota whose American period had begun with a handful of fishing families in seasonal settlements now hosted families by the thousands. Across the county stood 125 churches, three synagogues, five libraries, five professional theaters, three major hospitals, approximately 100 banks and savings and loan institutions, and nearly a dozen nursing homes. The kind of appeal the first land speculators had always envisioned had finally taken hold — some 140 years later. But it arrived in spades.

By 1980, Sarasota had nearly doubled her totals of the previous federal census, reaching just over 200,000. Municipal Venice had grown to 12,000, Northport to 6,000, and Longboat to nearly 2,400. Sarasota, the city that had been a hub and constituted 70 percent of the total county population in 1930, now represented only 25 percent. As the sprawl of population growth took hold, the municipalities were dwarfed by the unincorporated areas and the balance of power shifted accordingly.

As Sarasotans entered the '80s, the times were fraught with change at home and conflict far away. In New York, the General Assembly of the United Nations debated the provisions of the most recent SALT agreement. While Soviet troops were invading Afghanistan, the City of Sarasota still agonized over the perpetual challenge of development of its waterfront Florida Power & Light parcel, and municipal citizens worried over the new issue of dual taxation. Early in the 1980s, Sarasota's Jewish worship centers added a third synagogue, on Longboat, to join two others, Temple Emmanuel, and Temple Beth Sholom. In 1982, the three-generation Lindsay family ownership of the Sarasota *Herald Tribune* ended with sale to the New York Times Company. In Newtown two years later, citizen sentiment grew to challenge in court a system of representation that had historically precluded the election of a black Sarasotan to the city commission.

Church of the Redeemer, Episcopal sanctuary on historic Gulf Stream Avenue.

Cataclysm and prospectus, 1985

In summer 1984, a citrus canker was found in Florida. Carried on trees from infected nurseries, the disease was rampant in a wide distribution of mature groves. To halt the spread of the mysterious disease, many groves were burned, and an embargo prohibited the transporting and sale of fruit except by certified processors. Governor Bob Graham and Secretary of Agriculture Doyle Conner joined the clamor of growers who called for reimbursement for their awesome and industry-threatening losses.

In January 1985, while orange plastic canker warnings still dotted the perimeter of Florida groves, and sports fans riveted their eyes upon the Super Bowl, a killer freeze struck. For the second time in as many years, central Florida's rolling hills took the brunt. Within days, final bits of green foliage were gone from the panoramic landscape, tree bark hung black and split on bared trunks, and oranges lay rotting on the ground. At Sarasota, the groves had been saved by a cloud cover which rolled in off the Gulf and hovered over inland groves, holding in radiant heat from the earth.

On St. Patrick's Day, two tornadoes followed a violent rain from the Gulf onto the mainland at Venice. Striking Venice Beach at 4:50 a.m., the roaring twisters traveled three miles across the inland in a path several thousand feet wide. In a matter of minutes, the funnels tossed cars and trucks, sucked roofs off houses, hurled walls, doors, and laminated beams and air conditionerrs through the air. Two died, 50 were injured, more than 100 homes disintegrated. That many more were damaged, while at least a dozen major modern stores received violent damage. Hours after the tornadoes touched Sarasota, Governor Graham declared it a disaster area and arrived on the scene the next afternoon.

The cataclysmic events of the first few months of 1985 resemble in microcosm the force of events that catapulted Sarasota into her post-World War II form. The population growth predicted by pioneers had come at last. But with it came American technology and shortsightedness which laid a heavy hand upon the delicate environment.

Bulldozers, backloaders, and cranes filled the air with their noise and the skyline with their shapes. Stands of trees that had grown for lifetimes were leveled in a week. Residential neighborhoods were sacrificed to automobile throughways. Inland, the first multilaned limited-access highway in the history of the Gulf coast was completed in the '80s, causing great and sudden growth change patterns in the formerly rural sector.

A measure to "revitalize" the city historic allowed greatly increased density for the original nineteenth century Town of Sarasota and paved the way for rampant destruction of historic sites. High-profit construction of high rises blocked the bay and created pockets of slum housing.

Dredges dug deep ditches where shallow, living shorelines once stretched. Miles of seawalls were constructed, the landside filled with untold tons of dredged bay bottom. Mangroves and sand flats were strangled by freshwater runoff and pollutants ditched into the bay. High-density construction sprang up on fragile barrier islands. Expensive subdivisions were platted and nestled along "lagoons," actually old passes whose history predicted that storms might again change their relationship to the Gulf.

The age of fantastic growth had come. Florida's 1985 legislative session found itself preoccupied with growth management, addressed in major bills offered by legislative leaders as well as by Governor Graham. Following her 66 percent population increase between 1970 and 1980, *U.S. News & World Report* assessed Sarasota as the fourth fastest growing metropolitan area in the nation.

Ever since the coast was strung with Indian mounds, hardwood hammocks, and flamingoes in rows, so have the treasures and breathtaking beauties of the past taken on poignant added significance *after* they have slipped away. Sarasotans, like other responsible Floridians, have come to relize that today's concerns direct tomorrow's growth. Sensitivity to environmental, social, architectural, spiritual, political, and industrial history has become more acute.

Slowly the light has dawned. Gradually, the actions of a concerned populace reflect an informed awareness and address the challenge ahead. Modern technology can be used to enhance, rather than destroy, the quality of life destinctive to Sarasota. With knowledge and planning, Sarasotans should be able to meet their future armed with the implications of Sarasota's yesterdays.

Governor Bob Graham cuts the ribbon in 1981 to officially open interstate highway I-75 at County Line Road.

Hurricane Elena, Labor Day weekend 1985, blows rolling surf across lawns of waterfront residences.

Working cattle in the pens, a traditional structure found across the modern Florida inland.

A hundred years ago, in 1885, the *Glasgow Herald* advertised the organization of a colonial emigration to "accessible, healthy, and fertile lands at Sarasota, abutting the Gulf of Mexico." Circulars proclaimed Sarasota Bay to be "a Sportsman's Paradise" and predicted that a community there would take the foremost place as an "American Sanatorium." While buyers read with interest, sellers planned the town that was to be. On a surveyor's worktable somewhere, a grid of streets and avenues was applied to Florida's Township 36 South, Range 18 East. The whole was labeled "Town of Sarasota." Thus in a bit of coastal wilderness, along a sparsely inhabited bay front, a modern city was born.

The new town once heralded in Glasgow is today the hub of what has been viewed as the fourth fastest growing metropolitan area in the United States. Retirement pensions and social security benefits have brought to many Americans some final decades of leisure, while the comfort of air conditioning and the streamlining of modern transportation routes have propelled many of them south. Growing pains associated with rampant post-World War II growth have taught hard lessons all across the Sun Belt, especially in coastal south Florida and visibly in Sarasota County. But the same modern technology that made it all happen holds the keys to solving the resultant dilemmas. Sarasotans are facing the predicted growth of tomorrow, armed with plans and safeguards born of the lessons of a hundred years of yesterdays.

Janet Snyder Matthews
1985

PHOTO BY SUSAN HENRY

Modern mobile home park residents represent a sizeable percentage of Sarasota County's population. Country Club Estates, developed on the original City of Venice country club and golf course along the Intracoastal Waterway, contrasts markedly with the quaint trailer camp lifestyle crafted by Steinmetz during the '50s.

Steinmetz captures the idyllic lifestyle of the '50s in a winter tourist trailer park, complete with hanging bananas, a parrot cage and a plastic flamingo.

PHOTO BY STEINMETZ

Joseph Janney Steinmetz, a native Pennsylvanian and Princetonian (Class of '27), arrived in Sarasota early in the 1940s to photograph the circus for *Life* Magazine. Within a few years, he had set up a commercial studio and made it home.

His work was overlaid with his personal sensitivity to the invisible inner human dimension, something he had been capturing since his early beginnings when he invented the candid wedding album for a friend, an original idea which launched his commercial career. Steinmetz's work portrays Sarasota's social history along with her industry and environment.

His work has been described as "an awesome piece of history," but he characteristically downplayed the hype with, "All I want to do is make people laugh."

Steinmetz snapped some 140,000 photographs during his career. When he was not away on assignment for *Life* or *Time* or *Saturday Evening Post,* he was at home, pursuing with rare sensitivity the life style and variety of a Sarasota captured in the glitter of circus, the glare of pristine beaches, the cultural appeal of a thriving colony of authors and artists, and the seasonal retreats hidden along stretches of barrier islands largely undeveloped.

Steinmetz's style has been called "brilliant," "exciting," and has been praised for its "artistic perfection." His participation in personal selection of his photographs for this centennial history was completed only ten weeks before his death, in fall 1985.

EPILOGUE

In the dozen years since the first edition of *Sarasota: Journey to Centennial* was published, the growth of Sarasota County that made it the fourth fastest growing metropolitan area in the nation continued unchecked. The growth industry survived an attempted moratorium, fueled repeated unsuccessful attempts to thrust urban development east of the Interstate-75 corridor and turned the southern area of the county into a lusty political force. The pressures of growth compelled the county to search beyond its borders for water and forced its citizens to look inward to shape the form the county should assume as it enters the 21st century.

As a consequence of growing from a population of 257,667 in 1988 to an estimated population in 1997 of 311,403, the county grappled with stormwater management, solid waste disposal, central wastewater treatment service and transportation needs that growth only exacerbated. As a result, old ways of doing things and reaching political decisions were challenged as new citizens made new demands on government services. Sarasota County, like most of coastal Florida, was dragged from its comfortable status as a haven for artists and writers, a tourist destination and a retirement home into the Internet age and the financial, cultural and social complexities of a modern metropolitan area.

Shocked by hindsight and seeking foresight, progress has been hesitant, sometimes seeming to take two paces backward for each step forward. But neither an inch of snow on Christmas Eve 1989 or an 18-month episode of red tide in 1995 and 1996 - not even impact fees imposed on growth to help pay for roads, parks and other infrastructure - stemmed the tide of new homes flowing over former pastures and groves or the avalanche of new residents.

The county in 1981 adopted a comprehensive plan called *Apoxsee* to shape growth and development. Compliance with 1985 and 1986 state mandates forced a nearly continuous process of revision and updating that since then, has produced new elements addressing new demands. For instance, in 1989, in response to widespread public fears that growth was demolishing history, the County Commission adopted an Historic Preservation element initiating formal review for historic and archaeological significance of all development projects from roads to new subdivisions.

In that same year, a Stormwater Environmental Utility was begun, funded by user fees, to counteract flooding. Within two years, work began on the first two basins - Hudson Bayou and Phillippi Creek - to improve drainage while reducing runoff and improving the quality of water discharged into the bays. A June 1992 storm which dumped as much as 14 inches of water in 24 hours, flooding homes throughout Colonial Gables and nearby subdivisions, sparked an immediate outcry for relief. As a result, construction of the Celery Fields Regional Stormwater Project was accelerated to store 1,000 acre-feet of water in a massive detention pond excavated in the Fruitville farming area in the headwaters of Phillippi Creek.

Also in 1989, two separate activities with far-reaching consequences occurred - the start of a 5-year, $6-million scientific study and management plan called the Sarasota Bay National Estuary Program - and approval by the voters of a one percent infrastructure sales tax to pay for roads, libraries, public safety, schools, and parks and recreation facilities.

Directed by Mark Alderson and sponsored by local, state and federal entities, the Sarasota Bay NEP studied Sarasota Bay from Anna Maria Sound to the Venice Inlet. A 1990 *State of the Bay Report* summarized existing knowledge and outlined the anticipated scope of work. *Sarasota Bay: 1992 Framework for Action,* documented losses of mangroves and submerged marine grassbeds and identified fecal bacteria, nitrogen pollution and heavy metal contaminants as factors in the bay's decline. *The Bay Repair Kit,* a homeowner's manual, promoted practical strategies citizens could use to reduce impacts on the bay. The final publication, a *Comprehensive Conservation & Management Plan,* guides strategies to improve estuarine habitats and water quality.

The election in 1994 of Rep. Lisa Carlton to the Florida House of Representatives and Sen. Katherine Harris to the Florida Senate gave Sarasota County, with Rep. Shirley Brown, its first all-female legislative delegation, and restored the first Republican majority to the Senate since Reconstruction.

A controversial issue deliberately sidestepped by the NEP because of its potential to disrupt the program was the final disposition of the former Midnight Pass, closed under an emergency county permit in 1983 by two Siesta Key homeowners protecting their homes from its northward migration. As a result of recommendations made by a series of facilitated workshops, the County Commission in 1997 agreed to help fund a scientific study of Little Sarasota Bay to determine whether closing the pass had degraded the bay.

In 1990, the Tampa Bay NEP was established and in 1995, the Charlotte Harbor NEP was authorized. They promised unparalleled potential for truly significant improvements to two of Florida's largest estuaries - benefits from which could only flow to Sarasota Bay.

Coincidentally, 72 percent of Florida's voters in November 1994 approved a constitutional amendment banning entanglement (gill) nets from state waters extending 9 miles offshore. After a record volunteer petition drive by the Florida Conservation Association, the voters eliminated the lucrative but destructive practice of netting mullet for their roe, exported as an Oriental delicacy. By 1997, *Sarasota Herald-Tribune* fishing editor Steve Gibson reported sport fishermen in Sarasota Bay routinely releasing redfish that surpassed the legal length (27 inches), many exceeding 40 inches in length.

While it is unlikely either the NEP or the net ban will restore to local bays the sounds reported by pioneers of mullet "roaring through the passes," the ban devastated the colorful and historic commercial fishing industry and reflected the power of growth to overwhelm established tradition. Few voters in the 1990s could relate to the plight of commercial fishermen such as those who colonized Cortez Village, a National Register District on Anna Maria Sound, where generations of fishermen created an industry and a tradition.

1989 approval by Sarasota County voters of a one-percent infrastructure sales tax produced funding that tapped spending by visitors and residents to build roads and sidewalks throughout the county; add or expand public libraries for North Port, the Woodmere community, Gulf Gate and Englewood; renourish public beaches on Longboat Key and at Venice; build or improve schools; add or improve parks ranging from Little Five Points Park in Sarasota to the 136-acre Englewood Sports Complex; improve emergency management, fire, police and other public agency communications; renovate the Sarasota Municipal Auditorium and restore Hazzard Fountain to the site; and perform myriad other community improvements without borrowing money or raising ad valorem taxes.

Despite the public benefits of that tax, county voters defeated a referendum in 1994 to extend its termination past 1999 and, as this book goes to press, the success of a second referendum for extension remains problematic. 1989 also witnessed the tragic death in June of County Commissioner T. Mabry Carlton Jr., a seventh-generation native Floridian whose passionate promotion of public acquisition of the John T. and Catherine MacArthur property as a public preserve and source of potable water became his landmark public legacy. Carlton was killed when his light plane crashed while he was coordinating a cattle drive on his sprawling ranch. In 1994, the water plant at the T. Mabry Carlton Jr. Memorial Reserve was dedicated and water pumped from its 11 wells began flowing to county utility customers.

In 1990, a water supply shortage widely perceived by environmental groups galvanized by the Growth-restraint and Environmental Organization triggered a November referendum seeking a two-year moratorium on building and development. Although soundly defeated, the campaign triggered a search for additional sources of potable water which culminated in a three-part strategy that included extending water supply contracts with Manatee County; continuing development of the Carlton Reserve supplies; and building a pipeline to link the Carlton Reserve plant to the Peace River/Manasota Regional Water Supply Authority at Fort Ogden - a project called the Peace River Option. It remained publicly controversial in Charlotte County in 1997, sparking criticism as an ill-disguised scheme to risk the environmental health of Charlotte Harbor to accommodate Sarasota County's growth.

Also in 1990, voters amended the County Charter to require comprehensive, mandatory recycling which expanded existing newspaper and yard waste recycling programs to include raw cardboard, plastics and glass. In 1986, the county, anticipating a 1970 state mandate to close the Bee Ridge landfill, purchased for $8.6 million the 6,000-acre Walton Tract lying between the Myakka River and Cow Pen Slough three miles east of I-75. Following a protracted legal challenge on environmental grounds by Sarasota resident Maynard Hiss, the county in 1993 renamed the property the Pinelands Reserve and began its $86 million program to install a sanitary landfill and recycling/composting center on 550 acres, reserving the remaining property for buffer and conservation areas.

Sarasota voters' sense of environmental stewardship continued unabated as the combination of a $20 million 1986 bond referendum and an Environmentally Sensitive Lands

A 1910 photograph of fishing boats and fish houses on the Cortez waterfront evokes a traditional way of life all but erased by a 1994 constitutional referendum banning gill netting for mullet.

acquisition program supported by the one-percent infrastructure sales tax bracketed the county with irreplaceable public preserves ranging from the Lemon Bay Park/France property in Englewood to the Phillippi Plantation in Sarasota.

In 1992, the County Commission acquired 303 acres adjoining the State Road 681/I-75 corridor as the state Preservation 2000 acquisition program added 914 acres to the Oscar Scherer State Recreational Area, elevating it to full park status. The county's acquisition became controversial when it designated that slender triangle of land as right-of-way for an extended Honore Avenue, planned as an arterial link between Sarasota and Venice.

Four years after a citizens assembly for wastewater management demanded action, the County Commission in 1990 adopted its Vision 20/20 plan to develop a county owned central sewer utility system. Endorsed by Argus, the League of Women Voters, the Taxpayers Association of Sarasota County and environmental groups, the plan will replace over 100 package treatment plants, consolidate privately owned utilities and install a reclaimed water reuse system to irrigate public and private lands, restore wetlands and augment surface and ground water systems. Despite the posting of Phillippi Creek by the county Health Department banning swimming or other contact due to fecal bacterial contamination, and a subsequent survey which revealed viral contamination, South Gate area homeowners in 1996 and 1997 challenged studies contending their septic tank drainfields required replacement by sewers.

Expansion of the Sarasota-Bradenton Airport in the late 1980s culminated with the dedication in 1990 of a $56 million, three-story terminal and concourse building greeting travelers with lavish artistic and interior landscaping appointments. While struggling to expand its appeal to business travelers and compete with Tampa International Airport, the airport acquired a U.S. Customs base which in 1993, facilitated renaming it the Sarasota-Bradenton International Airport to reflect its appeal as a destination for Canadian and European travelers.

Downtown Sarasota in 1992 and 1993 renovated lower Main Street using Tax Increment Fund financing to dress up storefronts, adding sidewalk benches, landscaping and brick-paved pedestrian crosswalks. Probably the most dramatic alteration extended Main Street to Bayfront Drive/U.S. 41, reconnecting the city to its waterfront via Bayfront Park for the first time in a generation. Following design principles advanced in 1983 by the Regional/Urban Design Assistance Team (R/UDAT) exercise coordinated by the Florida Gulf Coast chapter of the American Institute of Architects, a 1986 Downtown Master Plan guided improvements in residential and commercial neighborhoods on Central, Osprey, Orange and other avenues. The emphasis on neighborhoods as sponsors of change swept not only through the city, but also sparked county planning incentives that focussed on Englewood's Dearborn Street, the Nokomis and Laurel areas and Osprey.

A nationally accorded Venice Main Street program celebrated its tenth anniversary in 1997 as public acquisition of the abandoned Venice Railway Station owned by Seminole-Gulf Railway came closer to reality with funding commitments by both the city and the county. Availability of the 13-mile track owned by CSX Railroad from Venice to Sarasota as a public linear park became a shared goal after the Ringling Brothers and Barnum & Bailey Circus closed its Venice winter quarters in 1992.

In 1995, frustration felt by all participants as the county Planning Commission neared the inconclusive end of a two-year deliberation on RU-27, the revised and updated future land use element of the comprehensive plan, triggered the formation of a unique new force in county planning - a self-appointed, self-directed citizens task force to study the future of rural areas east of I-75. Called the Multi-Stakeholders Group (MSG), it relied on respect, consensus and mandatory participation to foster education and understanding between advocates and opponents of extending the Urban Service Area boundaries east of the interstate.

The elevation of social and political influence of the county's black populations reached a popular zenith in

"Buck" O'Neil's high school "graduation". John Jordan, "Buck" O'Neil, Jr., accepts accolades at his "graduation" March 10, 1995 from Sarasota High School during "Buck O'Neil Day" celebration.

PHOTOS COURTESY SARASOTA COUNTY HISTORICAL RESOURCES

1995 as John Jordan "Buck" O'Neil Jr., a professional baseball scout and former star of the Negro League's Kansas City Monarchs, returned to Sarasota to receive the Sarasota High School diploma that school segregation policies had denied him 69 years earlier. O'Neil, who emerged as a popular hero following narration of his experiences in Ken Burns' 1994 PBS documentary *Baseball*, shared with Burns the dedication at Twin Lakes Park of the "Buck O'Neil Baseball Complex."

On the political front, following the sudden death of Dolores Dry, who in 1994 succeeded Fredd Atkins as a black Sarasota city commissioner, Rev. Jerome Dupree was elected the third African American to serve in that position.

Inevitably, however, the jurisdictional geography of private and public land ownership in the county focussed most of the new growth on south Sarasota County. Rural areas east of the Interstate-75 corridor held the Myakka River State Park, the Carlton Memorial Reserve and the Pinelands Reserve - all exempt from development pressures. In addition, large, private ranches such as the Carlton, Walton, Longino and Hawkins ranches and the Hi Hat Ranch - all of which resisted development - squeezed growth further south.

Two notable exceptions were the Palmer Ranches, owned by real estate tycoon Hugh Culverhouse, owner of the Tampa Bay Buccaneers football team, and the Taylor (nee Berry) Ranch. In 1984, Sarasota County and the Florida Department of Community Affairs approved the Palmer Ranch incremental Development of Regional Impact, setting in motion the phased development of 10,500 acres in central Sarasota County stretching from Clark Road south to Venice. In 1997, a development subsidiary of the Taylor Ranch rezoned 322 acres for up to 600 homes in South Venice, nibbling further development from a 16,000-acre holding that already had contributed the south campus of Manatee Community College, an elementary school and a Wal-Mart superstore to the growing south county area.

The pressures of growth, however, galvanized new political strength in south Sarasota County which in 1997, forced concessions on private and public developments that elevated Not In My Backyard (NIMBY) concerns to new power. In the Woodmere community, South Venice 2010 forced recognition of flaws in county traffic planning policies and shaped the design of both Home Depot and Wal-Mart stores. In the Laurel area, homeowners turned out en masse to force rejection by the Planning Commission of the siting of a minimum security jail on the county's new central landfill site on the Pinelands Reserve. Their combined influence - reinforced by the sale of Venice Hospital to Bon Secours and the subsequent formation of the not-for-profit Venice Foundation as a source of charitable community influence - served indelible notice that south Sarasota County would assume new prominence and influence in the continued growth of Sarasota County as it crossed the Millennium threshold.

A 1953 night-lit photograph of the Hazzard Fountain and Sarasota Municipal Auditorium illustrates an image restored in 1996 to Sarasota's gateway streetscape.

By Janet Snyder Matthews, Ph.D. and Allan H. Horton
September 12, 1997

EPILOGUE (cont'd from 1997)

Despite widespread predictions by computer experts and other prognosticators of widespread disaster and havoc attending the Millennium passage, 2000 arrived relatively quietly with few apparent glitches in computer-driven functions ranging from contractual deadlines to international flight schedules. Sarasota celebrated the occasion with fireworks and a downtown street fair at Main and Lemon that was remarkable for its restraint.

But the decade elapsed since publication in 1997 of the second edition of *Sarasota: Journey to Centennial* witnessed continuing and implacable change from climate to local communities and personalities.

John J. "Buck" O'Neil, lauded in the 1997 Revised Edition for his stellar achievements as a Negro League baseball player, manager, major league scout and baseball ambassador, in October 2006 received posthumous honors one week after his death at 94. O'Neil, along with former state Senator Ed H. Price, Jr., was inducted into the Grassroots Leadership Initiative Hall of Fame, a new, local program encouraging community leadership.

At the induction ceremony held at Lakewood Ranch, Price, a graduate of Sarasota High School like O'Neil, lauded his fellow inductee's achievements, glossing over his own enviable record as a Tropicana executive, humanitarian and two-term state senator.

In 2007, the local reputation for excellence in sports enjoyed locally since Price graduated from high school as all-state in three sports, continued. Sarasota High School won the 2007 Class 6A baseball title; Venice High School took the 5A baseball title; and Bradenton Prep won both the boys' and girl's 2007 golf titles. Meanwhile, no fewer than Manatee High School, Bradenton Christian, Sarasota's Cardinal Mooney and Manatee's Southeast High School won regional competitions in football or volleyball.

Sarasota County's growth advanced undeterred by hurricanes, escalating impact fees and environmental constraints as its official population in 2005 reached 359,783, an increase of nearly 50,000 persons – adding the equivalent of another city of Sarasota – in eight years.

Despite that growth, treasures of the past continued to beckon new residents and visitors to Sarasota's past. In 2007, Historic Spanish Point, the 30-acre pioneer homestead preserved in Osprey, marked its 25th or Silver Anniversary – which this Second Revised Edition celebrates – as the community's first National Register-designated site. In those 25 years, Historic Spanish Point had attracted 500,000 visitors to its site interpreting 5,000 years of human history on Little Sarasota Bay. Since 2000, with the launching by volunteers of its reconstructed Cedar Key sailing sharpie, *Lizzie G*, its lessons from the past have sallied forth into the marine environment, resurrecting a time when the waterways provided recreation, sustenance and trade.

Growth in south Sarasota County's two largest communities - North Port and Venice – triggered aggressive and politically controversial municipal annexation policies as each city attempted to accommodate development pressures free of county constraints.

In 2007, a new, cooperative planning agreement between the county and the cities of Venice and North Port got off to a rocky start as North Port, miffed at what it considered unfavorable terms, withdrew. At the time of the second edition's publication, that impasse remained unresolved. Meanwhile, as relentless demand for housing continued to prove compelling, familiar landmarks countywide were replaced by larger, more imposing structures and former pastures grew residential subdivisions.

Possibly no development was more transforming than Lakewood Ranch, the sprawling community mixing recre-

The sharpie schooner "Lizzie G" sails at the inaugural Great Florida Gulf Coast Small Craft Festival held in Cortez on Anna Maria Sound in 2006. Her crew (from left) are Jack Branson, John Calhoun and Nick Pocock, all of whom are Historic Spanish Point-certified captains.

ational, residential, commercial and institutional development across 8,500 acres of the 31,000-acre Schroeder-Manatee Ranch. Straddling the Manatee-Sarasota County line east of the Interstate-75 corridor, Lakewood Ranch installed such amenities as cricket and polo clubs, championship golf courses and acres of lakes created from shell and fill borrow pits. By 2007, it boasted 12,000 residents, offered two jobs for every rooftop and still grazed 1,500 beef cattle, maintained 1,300 acres in citrus groves and 3,500 acres of vegetable, timber and sod farms.

Meanwhile in Sarasota, the Ringling Causeway bridge, opened in 2003 after a decade of fractious debate at a cost of more than $1 million per foot of vertical clearance - $68 million and 54 feet high over the Intracoastal Waterway – transfigured the city's waterfront. A reader of the Second Edition returning to Sarasota in 2007 might fail to recognize the 21st Century city – particularly if approaching over that bridge from Bird Key.

What had been a relatively low-rise city with few rooftops protruding above the mainland tree canopy no longer resembles the sleepy fishing village-artist colony once touted as its dominant ambiance. From the expanded and renovated "Purple People Eater" – the fond moniker bestowed by bemused locals on the Van Wezel Performing Arts Hall's purple façade – to the relatively untouched shoreline of the Selby Botanical Garden – the city of Sarasota skyline in 2007 bristled with 10- to 15-story high-rise condominiums. Towering over them all was the Sarasota Ritz-Carlton hotel/condominium, erected in 1998 on the site of the historic John Ringling Towers hotel.

Prognosticators who predicted that the advent of a Ritz-Carlton in Sarasota would attract development capital unlike any the community had seen to date were vindicated as condos began popping up like out-sized toadstools. From gold-hued, Near Eastern-style domes to red-tile-roofed Mediterranean Revival facades, their architectural styles promoted new eras of growth and development that overwhelmed the low-rise designs spawned by architects Ralph Twitchell, Paul Rudolph and others who gave Sarasota global renown with their Sarasota School of Architecture movement. In neighborhood after neighborhood and particularly along their waterfronts, Sarasotans watched aghast as Med Rev "starter castles" erected for baby-boomer retirees replaced or towered above single-story homes.

the downtown area's growing stature. On lower Main Street and Palm, permitting by city officials of the erection of the 1350 Main condominium tower shaded sidewalks and streets with overhanging "leasable space" that confiscated public air rights and triggered angry criticism.

At the Main Street/Lemon Avenue intersection, the Pineapple Square development was approved in 2006. It proposed to install 130,000 square feet of retail shopping, 210 residential units and a 600-space parking garage in a mammoth mixed-use development wrapping the city in a pedestrian "mall" extending from First Street to State Street and up Lemon Avenue to Main Street.

Meanwhile, not even the relatively remote twin terrors of Hurricane Charley, which in 2004 devastated nearby Charlotte Harbor and Charlotte and DeSoto counties – and Hurricane Katrina, which devastated New Orleans in 2005 – appeared to deter a real estate boom of fantastic proportions. As the Sarasota County Commission in 2004 adopted its 2050 comprehensive plan amendment to protect the bucolic ambiance of rural lands east of Interstate-75, real estate speculators in neighboring Manatee County bid farm and ranch lands to giddy $30,000-per-acre sales.

As median home prices in the Bradenton-Sarasota area jumped from $161,500 in 2002 to $343,600 by 2005, the terms "affordable" and "workforce" housing became buzz words as minimum-wage workers moved farther from Sarasota to find housing. The Laurel Civic Association, long before the issue had gained social cachet, quietly expanded its affordable housing program to erect five modern homes for low-income families, capitalizing on grants secured from The Venice Foundation and the U. S. Department of Housing and Urban Development.

Even in Charlotte County, however, and despite many local residents living in travel trailers after Hurricane Charley's devastation, median home prices jumped 115 percent to $236,900 over the same period.

Not until 2006 did the burgeoning "bubble" in escalating real estate markets wilt as speculator Neil Mohamed Husani fled after cashing in the considerable chips he had acquired through superheated leveraging of over-priced properties. Exploiting suspect property appraisals and serial title transfers, Husani from 2004 to 2006 paid $49 million for 2,000 acres of undeveloped lands in Manatee and Sarasota counties. He immediately sold those properties to his "partners" for $131 million after securing $93 million in loans

A modern, fiberglass cruiser transits the historic Blackburn Point Bridge connecting North Casey Key to the mainland. The bridge is the last swing bridge operating in Florida on the Intracoastal Waterway system.

Construction in 2003 of the 11-story Whole Foods Center, sited one block distant from the new 10-story Plaza at Five Points tower and the 73,000-square-foot Selby Public Library, dedicated in 1998, further flaunted

The former Bertha Palmer pavillion at the Oaks Estate on Little Sarasota Bay, visible today from the intercoastal waterway. Painting by Sarasota artist, Robert Chase for *Ford Times*, 1962.

from several banking institutions deluded by apparently unlimited market prospects. There was, however, a price to pay, and as this 2007 *Journey* edition went to press, several foreclosures of loans held by those "partners" were under way. Husani, of course, reportedly lived like a sultan – albeit a fugitive sultan.

Meanwhile, whether or not linked to the climatic phenomenon of global warming, dramatic weather events increasingly dominated local and national headlines during the decade.

In February 1998, just one month into Gov. Jeb Bush's first term in office and as John Glenn, 66, orbited Earth to study aging in space 36 years after his initial orbit, Florida's deadliest tornadoes killed 38 and injured 250 Floridians, destroying over 3,000 homes from Dade to Orange counties.

Later that summer, record drought sparked 2,300 wildfires that incinerated 500,000 acres in Central Florida, torching 300 homes and causing $400 million in property losses. Hard on the heels of that drought which cost North Florida farmers $100 million in parched pasture and crop losses, flooding cost Dade County farmers $150 million while back-to-back hurricanes Earl and Georges dumped two feet of rain on the Panhandle's already beleaguered farmers. All in all, in 1998 the FEMA declared six federal-disaster emergencies for seven weather-related events in Florida, causing old-timers to shake their heads in dismay while Sarasota continued to live a charmed life.

Defying all development precedents, in August 1998, the J.P. Igloo Ice and Inline Sports Center opened in Ellenton, bringing to sultry Southwest Florida the region's first ice rink at a cost of $16 million. Throughout local subdivisions, skateboards gathered dust as excited kids played street hockey on inline skates, polishing skills that could serve on ice.

Sarasota County had continued its tradition, established in 1994, of embracing women as strong political leaders by electing Rep. Lisa Carlton to the Florida Senate in 1998. Carlton subsequently was selected by her colleagues as Senate President Pro Tempore in 2006 as she continued to serve as chair of the Senate Appropriations Committee – the first senator to serve successive terms in that important position.

In addition, Nancy Detert also was elected in 1998 to the House District 70 seat vacated by Carlton, serving with distinction until 2006 when her bid for Congress ended in a Republican primary defeat. As this Second Revised Edition of the Epilogue went to press, Detert was an announced candidate for the Florida Senate.

Also in November 1998, former state Senator Katherine Harris, a Longboat Key resident, became the first woman and the second Republican elected to the Florida Cabinet as the state's final elected Secretary of State, the office having become appointive by a Constitutional revision which reduced the elected Cabinet to three members – a Secretary of Agriculture, Chief Financial Officer and Attorney General. Just two years later, she gained fame and notoriety when, as the state's chief elections officer, she certified George W. Bush as the winner of the presidential election over Democrat Al Gore following a contested Florida election re-count which placed "hanging chads" in the popular lexicon as election referees tried to determine a voter's intention as they surveyed imperfectly cast paper ballots.

In 2002, Harris won election to the U. S. House of Representatives from District 13, assuming the seat vacated by retiring Rep. Dan Miller of Bradenton and was re-elected in 2004. In 2006, running without the support of the state or national Republican Party leaderships, Harris lost her election bid to replace Democratic U.S. Sen. Bill Nelson. But the subsequent race for the District 13 seat she relinquished fostered extended conflict and controversy that focused unwelcome attention again on Florida's - and Sarasota County's - voting processes.

The 2006 election between Republican Vern Buchanan and Democrat Christine Jennings was conducted with touch-screen voting machines that – while devoid of the "hanging chad" issue - failed to register 18,000 votes on ballots cast in Sarasota County for the District 13 race. When no cause for the undervote could be determined, Jennings mounted a challenge that by mid-2007, had triggered an ongoing investigation by Congress through the Committee on House Administration that had not reached a finding by publication of this Epilogue.

Meanwhile, Buchanan, the winner of the District 13 seat by a slim 369-vote margin, served District 13 as its Congressman.

The massive undervote did, however, spark political reform at both local and state levels as Sarasota County and the state decreed that future balloting must, by 2008, leave a "paper trail" capable of reliable audit.

Meanwhile, the dynamics of Sarasota's municipal growth gathered headlines as renowned urban planner Andres Duany journeyed from Dade County in 2000 to oversee revision of the City of Sarasota's master urban plan, advocating a "walkable" city which would tame traffic, link the Island Park waterfront to the urban core and guide the city's "maturation" as a thriving business and financial center. His return visit in 2006 found little to reassure him the city had faithfully enacted his plan.

North Port broke ground in May 1999 on the first high school erected in 40 years in Sarasota County, bringing hometown pride of place – at a cost of $42 million - to the county's largest municipality in total incorporated area. Two years later when the new school opened, it enrolled 1,800 students in grades 6 through 10. By 2007, the city registered 6,758 students in five schools, including four elementary, one middle and high school – achieving by far the greatest growth in school population in Sarasota County and cementing North Port's reputation for welcoming young families.

Meanwhile, although a $46 million financial shortfall severely strained the Sarasota School District, a bond referendum deemed essential failed to secure voter approval. Facing another $14 million deficit, the School Board trimmed $17 million from its budget, eliminated 100 teaching positions and ultimately, relied upon popular Superintendent Wilma Hamilton and a citizens advisory committee to mount a proactive and successful campaign. Hamilton and her cohorts secured voter approval in a second referendum in 2002, raising $200 million with a 1-mill ad valorem tax to provide a solid financial foundation for education in Sarasota County. In 2006, under the leadership of Superintendent Gary Norris, and a proactive School Board, a subsequent voter-approved referendum extended the tax, pledging $250 million in additional funds over four years.

As the state's population soared in 2001 to 16 million, it gained two new seats in Congress, adding political impetus to a bill mandating the largest public works program in the world – the re-plumbing of the Florida Everglades drainage system to restore, at an estimated cost of $8 billion, sheet flow of fresh water across the "River of Grass" to its estuarine outfalls into the Gulf of Mexico. As the costs of engineering its complexities soared, by 2006 the estimated cost of the project had reached $10.5 billion.

Terrorism – both domestic and international – riveted attention to national headlines and newscasts in 2001. On June 11, Timothy McVeigh, the unrepentant Gulf

From the new Ringling Causeway Bridge to the Ritz-Carlton Tower hotel and condominiums (illuminated turrets at right), development has dramatically changed the Sarasota waterfront in the past decade.

War-decorated veteran, who in 1995 bombed the Alfred P. Murrah Building in Oklahoma City, killing 168 persons, was executed.

Just three months later, on 9/11/2001, terrorist hijackers flew jetliners into the World Trade Center towers, the Pentagon and a farm field in Pennsylvania, killing the 19 hijackers and 2,973 innocent persons. Coincidentally, advisors told President George W. Bush of the disaster as he read to first graders at Emma E. Booker Elementary School in Sarasota during a "photo-op" promoting his education bill.

Subsequent investigations revealed that three of the hijackers, all Middle Eastern citizens, had lived in Nokomis and received flight training at Huffman Aviation, located at the Venice Municipal Airport. The unwelcome notoriety focused media and thus, public, attention on Venice temporarily, but consequential and lasting changes in American life and society continue to be felt in heightened security strategies imposed from passport controls to airline flight precautions.

There was, of course, good news, in 2001.

In Venice, the $68 million project to 4-lane and resurface Business 41 through the central business district proceeded with remarkable alacrity and minimal disruption due to an aggressive and unusual public relations campaign shared between the City of Venice and the state Department of Transportation. Even the replacement of two Business 41 bridges over the Intracoastal Waterway caused minimal disruption to traffic flow.

Meanwhile, the city purchased the Venice Area Chamber of Commerce headquarters on the Intracoastal Waterway, making the property available as a trailhead for the Venetian Waterway Park being developed by Venice Area Beautification, Inc. Nearly complete at this writing, the park will offer hiking and biking trails flanking both sides of the Intracoastal Waterway from the restored Venice Depot to Caspersen Beach and, ultimately, link to Sarasota via 13-miles of the Southern Gulf/CSX rail line acquired by Sarasota County as a "rails-to-trails" recreational amenity.

In May 2007, the man almost solely responsible for the county's purchase and renovation of the Venice Depot, retired railroadman Rollins Coakley, 85, died at his home in Utah, where he had moved in 2002 to be closer to family. Known as the "pit bull of historic preservation," Coakley was relentless in his pursuit of the $2.1 million project.

In Sarasota, demolition began in May 2007 of the towering Sarasota Quay adjacent to the Hyatt Hotel. Once demolished, the site will be redeveloped by the Irish-American Corp., in a billion-dollar project building shops, condominiums, offices, restaurants, hotel rooms and other amenities evocative of the "mixed-use" development promoted by the Duany-inspired downtown development plan.

Remarkably, throughout all the growth-related change and development, Sarasota County and the state continue their aggressive environmental land acquisition programs, inspired by bond referenda that repeatedly garner overwhelming voter approval. In 2006, Gov. Jeb Bush signed the Babcock Preservation Act, inking the state's largest land acquisition deal to preserve 74,000 (of 91,000) acres of grazing and swamp land straddling Lee and Charlotte counties. At a total cost of $350 million, the contract pledged funds from the 10-year, $3 billion Florida Forever program established in 1999 plus tapping local contributions, including $40 million from Lee County's coffers. The deal with owner/developer Syd Kitson allowed urban development of 17,000 acres, but preserved an expanse of native lands that environmentalists lauded as providing essential refuge from Lake Okeechobee to the Caloosahatchee River for such endangered species as the Florida panther and black bear.

Locally, Sarasota County had, by 2007, acquired more than 16,000 acres of publicly owned or easement-protected lands through its Environmentally Sensitive Lands Protection Program which was funded by a 0.25 mill ad valorem tax approved by referendum in 1999. As the program approached its $53 million bonding cap in 2005, the county floated a follow-up bond referendum that garnered 80 percent approval from voters to extend the program 10 years until 2029, and committed an additional $250 million to the protection of rapidly vanishing upland and lowland habitats.

Relying on contracting solely with willing sellers, the county's protected lands inventory by 2007 stretched from its Eastern Ranch Lands parcels west to Ainger Creek, adjoining the Myakka State Forest; and south from the Gum Slough parcel protected through conservation easements acquired from the Schroeder-Manatee Ranch to its Lemon Bay Preserve, where at publication of this updated Epilogue, negotiations with private owners continued to expand the 42 acres acquired of the 429-acre site.

Whether the Manatee-Sarasota area can maintain its unique appeal as a cultural center that enjoys unparalleled environmental assets without allowing growth to exhaust such vital resources as air quality and water supplies remains to be seen. As this Silver Anniversary edition of the *Sarasota: Journey to Centennial* goes to press, however, this extended Epilogue closes on a note made hopeful by the generally positive history it relates – that strong leadership evincing sound economic, environmental and social principles can, and has, produced an enviable record in a sterling community.

By Allan H. Horton
June 2007

From the Ritz-Carlton (far right) to Golden Gate Point and Bird Key (left background), the Sarasota waterfront has undergone massive change and growth in the past decade.

Partners in Progress

Historic Spanish Point
Archaeological Consultants, Inc.
A.G. Edwards & Sons, Inc.
The ADP Group, Inc.
Ball Construction, Inc.
Beall's, Inc.
Cyrus Bispham & Family
Boone, Boone, Boone, Koda & Frook
Center for Sight
City of Sarasota
City of Venice
Clyde Butcher Gallery
Community Foundation of Sarasota County
Kevin Daves
Diocese of Venice in Florida
Education Foundation of Sarasota County, Inc.
    Sponsored by Jim and Shirley Ritchey
The Episcopal Church of the Redeemer
FCCI Insurance Group
First Baptist Church of Sarasota
First Presbyterian Church
    Sponsored by Charlie and Dee Stottlemyer
Frederick Derr & Company, Inc.
The Glasser/Schoenbaum Human Services Center
Gulf Coast Community Foundation of Venice
Herald-Tribune Media Group
Hi Hat Ranch
Icard, Merrill, Cullis, Timm, Furen & Ginsburg, P.A.
The Jelks Family Foundation
    Sponsored by the family of Katharine Nau
Kerkering, Barberio & Co.
Longino Ranch, Inc.
The Mabry Carlton Ranch
Matthews, Eastmoore, Hardy, Crauwels & Garcia, P.A.
Manatee Community College
    Sponsored by Walter Serwatka and Constance Holcomb
Michael Saunders & Company

Mote Marine Laboratory
    Sponsored by Frederick Derr & Company, Inc.
Myakka Valley Ranch
The Pat Neal Family
Northbrook Cattle Company
Northern Trust
The Out-of-Door Academy
    Sponsored by Stanley Meuser and Veronica Meuser
The Perlman Music Program
    Sponsored by Jan and Lamar Matthews, Jr.
Pines of Sarasota
    Sponsored by Dr. Robert E. and Lelia Windom
    Arthur M. and Viola L. Goldberg
    John W. and Pamela Overton
Professional Benefits Inc.
Purmort & Martin Insurance Agency, LLC
The John and Mable Ringling Museum of Art
    Sponsored by John Ringling North, II
    and Shirley Ringling North
Ringling College of Art and Design
Piero Rivolta
The Ritz-Carlton, Sarasota
Sarasota Conservation Foundation
Sarasota Family YMCA
Sarasota Memorial Healthcare Foundation, Inc.
    Sponsored by Northern Trust
Schroeder-Manatee Ranch, Inc.
Seibert Architects, P.A.
SunTrust Bank, Southwest Florida
Syprett, Meshad, Resnick, Lieb, Dumbaugh & Jones
Toale Brothers
United Way of Sarasota County, Inc.
The Urology Treatment Center
Wendel Kent & Company, Gator Asphalt Company
    & Quality Aggregates Incorporated
Wilson Jaffer, P.A.

HISTORIC SPANISH POINT

Silver Anniversary 1982-2007

A short drive south of Sarasota takes residents and visitors to a special, unspoiled place, Historic Spanish Point. This 30-acre environmental, archaeological and historic site, the first property in Sarasota County to be listed in the National Register of Historic Places, is preserved by the Gulf Coast Heritage Association, Inc.

For thousands of years this site was home to some of Florida's first inhabitants. As early as 3,000 B.C., prehistoric people fished and hunted here, making tools from shell, bone and wood, building homes, and surviving off a bay teeming with fish. Over centuries they created large shell middens, or garbage dumps, that now provide important evidence to archaeologists of how they lived. At Historic Spanish Point, visitors actually can go inside the 15-foot-high shell ridge midden to see an audio-visual program and exhibits describing the layers of debris which are the chapters of the history book for Florida's earliest people. An exhibit kiosk interprets the nearby burial mound that is also preserved.

Centuries later, the large point of land extending into Little Sarasota Bay attracted new settlers. John and Eliza Webb and their five children traveled to Florida from New York in 1867 in search of a homestead. An old Spanish trader in Key West told them about this site and upon their arrival, the Webbs named their new home Spanish Point. Over the next forty years, the Webbs became involved in industries that are part of our state's heritage: citrus, boat building and tourism. Today's visitors can pack fruit in the citrus packing house, tour the 1901 Guptill House built by Webb daughter Lizzie and her husband Frank, watch volunteers in the Guptill Boat Yard build and maintain traditional wooden boats, and spend a few minutes in Mary's Chapel, with its beautiful stained glass windows, which has been authentically reconstructed adjacent to the pioneer cemetery.

In 1910, a new visionary arrived at Spanish Point. Bertha Matilde Honore Palmer, the widow of Chicago entrepreneur Potter Palmer, discovered Florida and selected the Webb homestead and neighboring lands for her own winter estate, Osprey Point. Over the next few years, Mrs. Palmer and her sons purchased thousands of acres in Sarasota County for citrus production, cattle ranching and real estate development. Today at Historic Spanish Point, visitors can enjoy three beautiful Palmer gardens – the Sunken Garden with its majestic pergola, the Duchene Lawn, and the Jungle Walk which features a miniature aqueduct with water splashing down a shell cascade.

Connecting the gardens and historic buildings are nature trails which meander through native Florida vegetation. Outdoor interpretive exhibits describe mangrove and hammock habitats, native freshwater wetlands, butterfly gardening and traditional wooden boat building. Cock's Footbridge takes visitors over Webb's Cove, where the *Lizzie G*, a 23-foot-long sailing sharpie launched in 2000 by volunteer boat builders, offers visitors sailing trips on Little Sarasota Bay that interpret the site's maritime heritage. In addition, the *Magic*, a replica of the motor boat launched by volunteers in 2006, takes visitors for rides on the bay much as its predecessor did in the early 1900s.

After Mrs. Palmer's death in 1918, what is now Historic Spanish Point remained in the family until 1980, when the 30-acre National Register site was donated to Gulf Coast Heritage Association, Inc. The Association is a not-for-profit, membership organization that everyone is invited to join. Its mission is to connect people of today with 5,000 years of human history in southwest coastal Florida by preserving and interpreting objects and traditions significant to our region's past. Following the best of professional standards, Historic Spanish Point was accredited by the American Association of Museums in 2002.

Part of the museum complex is the Historic Spanish Point Visitors Center at Osprey School, an adjacent National Register property located on U. S. 41. It provides convenient and accessible space for programs, exhibitions and meetings. Historic Spanish Point is open to the public Monday-Saturday from 9:00 to 5:00, and on Sunday from noon to 5:00. Guided tours are offered daily and special programs and activities are featured throughout the year. For information about membership, volunteers or programs, please call 941-966-5214 or visit our website at www.historicspanishpoint.org.

Frank and Lizzie Guptill's house reveals life in pioneer Florida.

Mrs. Palmer's Sunken Garden and Pergola overlook Little Sarasota Bay.

ARCHAEOLOGICAL CONSULTANTS, INC.

A 30 Year Success Story

Archaeological Consultants, Inc. (ACI), Florida's first choice in cultural resource management, was established in 1976 by native Sarasotan, Marion Marable Almy. Two years later she was joined by Joan Deming as corporate Vice President. Almy and Deming met in graduate school, the first two graduates of a new Public Archaeology program pioneered by the University of South Florida (USF) in Tampa. The two archaeologists entered the specialized field of cultural resource management, which was emerging to meet the demands of new federal and state legislation.

During the first decade, ACI grew slowly. To help the company off the ground, its owners dug into their own pockets for capital. Their kitchen tables served as offices, and they depended on family cars for field work.

Finally, ACI received its big break. The company was awarded a contract by the Florida Department of Transportation (FDOT) which began using consultants for the first time. A year later, with the large state contract under its belt, ACI rented its first office, 750 square feet on U.S. 41, and bought a used four-wheel drive Jeep. A second FDOT contract followed – this time, a multi-year, multi-service agreement. To meet the Department's needs, another full-time archaeologist, two part-time architectural historians, and a consulting historian were added.

Registering ACI as a women-owned business with local, state, and federal governments boosted visibility, and the volume of work climbed steadily. The next large contract came from an unlikely source, the National Aeronautics and Space Administration (NASA). Beginning with a multi-year contract in 1990, ACI conducted an archaeological survey of the 140,000-acre Kennedy Space Center (KSC). Today, ACI continues to work for this federal agency. Building on the successful evaluation of the significant Apollo-era facilities at the KSC, ACI has embarked on a multi-year contract to evaluate historic properties associated with the U.S. Space Shuttle Program at Kennedy Space Center and other centers across the United States.

ACI's commitment to professionalism and a quality product has resulted in national and state recognition. ACI's business acumen was recognized in *Your Company* magazine, published by American Express, which featured ACI principals Almy and Deming as a cover story describing their bare-bones management style. Not long after, the U.S. Small Business Administration presented ACI with the Administrator's Award for Excellence in recognition of outstanding contributions and service for work on behalf of the National Aeronautics and Space Administration at the Kennedy Space Center; the Florida Trust for Historic Preservation recognized ACI for "significant achievements in the preservation of Florida's rich heritage" for A Window to the Past, a unique archaeological exhibition, located inside a 2,000-year-old shell midden at Historic Spanish Point; and, in 2006, the *Maddux Business Report* featured ACI as their cover story in conjunction with ACI's 30th Anniversary.

Growing confidence and an expanding marketplace led Archaeological Consultants, Inc. to larger facilities and staff. ACI's Sarasota office, located in the International Office Park, with a research library, laboratory and computerized data base archives, became the corporate headquarters as satellite offices were added in the Tallahassee and Tampa Bay areas, and in the City of St. Augustine.

In addition to building and managing a successful business and enjoying an active family life centered around husbands and children, Joan and Marion serve the communities that have contributed to their success. Both have been elected President of the state-wide Florida Anthropological Society, served as officers for the Florida Archaeological Council, helped found local archaeological societies, and have been honored as Distinguished Alumnae by the USF Department of Anthropology. Serving on local, regional and state committees, Joan and Marion continue to provide a critical link between historic preservation and Florida's future development.

ACI principals, Joan Deming and Marion Almy (photo from the *Maddux Business Report*, April 2006).

ACI has worked with NASA since 1990 to document historically-significant resources.

Archaeologists and Architectural Historians prepare for project initiation.

A.G. EDWARDS & SONS, INC.

Sharing in southern Florida history for more than 40 years. Caring for nest eggs for more than 120.

Since its birth in 1887 as a brokerage firm in St. Louis' financial district, A.G. Edwards has steadily evolved to meet the needs of the investing public. Now a major force in the financial services industry, A.G. Edwards and its affiliates encompass more than 6,500 financial consultants and a network of more than 700 offices nationwide and in Europe. Through the years, A.G. Edwards has become a firm with one focus — its clients.

1880

General Albert Gallatin Edwards retires from the post of assistant secretary of the Treasury for the Sub-Treasury bank in St. Louis and founds A.G. Edwards and Son in 1887 with his eldest son, Benjamin Franklin Edwards I.

1900
The first A.G. Edwards office outside St. Louis opens in the heart of American capitalism — One Wall Street in New York City.

1920
With World War I over, the American economy grows rapidly. Ben's son, Presley Edwards, joins the brokerage in 1925 and becomes a partner in 1928. During the massive stock market crash in 1929, A.G. Edwards' conservative margin lending policy and diligent client service is believed to have minimized the fallout for the firm and clients.

1940
World War II ends the Great Depression, investors return to the stock market, and the firm resumes branch expansion plans delayed by war. In 1949 the firm becomes one of the first American brokerage firms to install a computer. The modern branch system also originates during this period.

1960
Benjamin F. Edwards III, great-grandson of the firm's founder, assumes leadership of the firm and introduces more efficient processes and greater branch autonomy.

A.G. Edwards opens its Venice, FL, branch office in 1964. The Sarasota, FL, branch opens two years later in 1966.

In October 1967 the firm incorporates to limit the partners' liability and enable the firm to pursue long-term branch expansion and technology investment plans.

1980
The 1980s usher in a period of economic expansion and market volatility. With the advent of mutual funds and 401(k) retirement accounts, investors gain new options to create and preserve wealth. The firm's Investment Banking Division opens regional offices starting in 1986, and the firm begins offering trust services, through an affiliate, in 1987.

2000

The booming economy of the 1990s begins to weaken after the Sept. 11, 2001, terrorist attacks — but A.G. Edwards continues to look forward to a bright future. In March 2001 Bob Bagby, a 39-year veteran of the securities industry, becomes chairman and chief executive officer. In 2003 Bob oversees the launching of a new branding initiative to help more investors learn about the firm's unmatched client service.

7100 S. Beneva Road
Sarasota, FL 34238
(941) 922-4400

400 Madison Drive
St. Armands Key
Sarasota, FL 34236
(941) 388-5075

4242 S. Tamiami Trail
Venice, FL 34293
(941) 408-8797

700 N. U.S. 41 Bypass
Venice, FL 34285
(941) 488-6751

CARING FOR NEST EGGS. THAT'S WHAT WE DO.

2007 A.G. Edwards & Sons, Inc. • Member SIPC

THE ADP GROUP, INC.

Creating Value Through Design Excellence

*I*n 1984 when the ADP Group was formed, Sarasota, particularly as a downtown core, was in the doldrums. Storefronts were vacant, no new construction was in the offing, and after dark, there were few amenities to draw newcomers to the area. What had traditionally been the heart of the community lacked the vibrancy that characterized previous eras. When the banks, offices and retail merchants closed their doors at 5 o'clock, downtown was mostly deserted.

It seemed an unlikely time to form a company that specialized in architecture, design and planning. But Bruce Franklin, who moved to Sarasota in 1979 with a dual degree in architecture and urban planning, AIA architects Robert M. Town III and Javier Suarez, and a few years later, Peter Houk, were visionary enough to see in Sarasota the potential to become one of the most attractive destinations on Florida's Gulf Coast, and their company would help to lead the way.

The ADP Group is the result of the merger of Land Resource Strategies, Inc., a land planning and permitting firm, with ADP Associates, Inc., an architecture and interior design firm. Joined together, the partners offered a service company which, according to Franklin, gives "total management control from a single point of communication."

The firm assists investors, developers, corporations and institutions in planning and developing real estate. It provides services in land acquisition and development feasibility analysis, evaluation of marketing and environmental opportunities, land planning, zoning and permitting.

The ADP Group provides architectural, design and planning services within a client's budget and schedule requirements, supported by concise, accurate documentation. Over the years, it has gained extensive and diverse experience in fields ranging from office, commercial, institutional and residential to historic preservation projects.

In 1990, the Group expanded its interior design capability to complement its expanding club design services. The ADP Group has developed an extensive club portfolio and is now the largest clubhouse design firm in Florida.

Growing in tandem with Sarasota, the ADP Group has developed strong community ties and forged positive working relationships throughout the county. As Franklin put it, "We're not here just to build buildings, we're here to help build the community."

In 1991, the firm completed its two-story office building at 149 Cocoanut Avenue in the heart of the then-fledgling Theatre/Arts District. At the time, it was far from the thriving area it has become, but the Group's foresight has been borne out. The building, designed by Suarez and Town, won a 1991 City Beautification Award.

In 1993, the ADP Group won the Frank Berlin Sr. Small Business of the Year Award presented by the Greater Sarasota Chamber of Commerce. At the awards ceremony, Franklin's assertion of strong community involvement was echoed by Chamber chairman Bill Curtis, who said: "I am impressed by their entrepreneurial spirit and their commitment to our community." In 2003, the Economic Development Corporation of Sarasota County awarded their prestigious Service Company of the Year Award to the firm.

By the time of the real estate boom of the early 2000s, the ADP Group, which had grown to a professional staff of 42, was poised to design some of the most significant buildings in the "new" Sarasota. Working with a client list that includes Michael Saunders & Company, Irish American Management Services, Redquartz Development, Ersa Grae Corporation, Arvida Corporation, John D. and Catherine T. MacArthur Foundation, Citibank International, Equity Properties and

Principals pictured left to right: Bruce Franklin, Javier Suarez, AIA, Robert Town, AIA, Peter Houk

Plaza Five Points Mixed-Use Project

Development Co., Bird Key Yacht Club, JRT Development Corporation, Maas Brothers, Jordan Marsh, First Communities, Ringling Brothers and Barnum & Bailey Circus, approximately $1.24 billion in projects were either completed or in the works. Among them were such signature buildings as the Greater Sarasota Chamber of Commerce headquarters, Plaza at Five Points, the Frances Carlton Arms, Sarasota High School, North Port High School and Performing Arts Hall and Rivo at Ringling.

The ADP Group is committed to continuing its mission of creating value for clients through design excellence in diverse markets. Yet, it is Sarasota which will remain the focus of the firm's principals in their commitment to the community.

BALL CONSTRUCTION

30 Years of Craftsmanship and Preservation

Often a successful business venture is built on the vision of one man, and Ball Construction, Inc. is built on the vision of its founder and president, Daniel Patrick "Pat" Ball.

When Pat incorporated his company in 1974, he created a corporate culture committed to skilled craftsmanship and attention to detail. He and his wife Judy knew this would be the only way to produce the highest quality workmanship—a must for the competitive custom home market. According to Pat, who was joined in the business by son, Jeff, "word of mouth advertising" quickly became a key component in their successful family business. "Satisfied clients, from Sarasota to Boca Grande, recommended us to their friends and colleagues." As a result, a business which began at home has grown into a multi-million-dollar enterprise housed in its own restored building offices.

In 1987, Gulf Coast Heritage Association selected Ball Construction as the general contractor for the restoration of the kitchen of the 1901 Guptill House at Historic Spanish Point. Working closely with Herschel Shepard AIA, a nationally recognized preservation architect, Pat "received a good grounding in the preservation ethic," and as Pat's work proved to have the highest quality workmanship and attention to detail, other Historic Spanish Point projects followed: reconstruction of the Webb Citrus Packing House, renovation of the White Cottage, and construction of Cock's Footbridge, plus the exhibit building for the unique archaeological exhibition, *A Window to the Past*. The latter garnered an award for Ball Construction, Inc. and its partners from the Florida Trust for Historic Preservation in 1990.

With growing experience and enthusiasm for historic preservation, Pat and Judy became involved with other conservation/historical organizations, including the Historical Society of Sarasota County, the Alliance for Historic Preservation, and the Crowley Museum and Nature Center. Both Judy and Pat have served on the Board of Directors of Gulf Coast Heritage Association, and in 1995, Pat chaired the oversight committee when the Association renovated the 1927 Osprey School, today's Historic Spanish Point Visitors Center. Shortly thereafter, Sarasota County presented Pat and Judy with the 1999 Community Environmental Service Award in recognition of their leadership role "in promoting resource conservation." The Crowley Museum and Nature Center also benefited from the Ball's expertise and philosophy of volunteerism— over "a month of Sundays" they led other weekend volunteers who lovingly restored the 19th century Tatum House which had been moved to Crowley.

As Cà d'Zan, the mansion John and Mabel Ringling built, underwent extensive restoration in the late 1990s, Ball Construction teamed with other firms to play a key role in the restoration of the steel windows and the marble elements. The wood work restoration followed and focused on John Ringling's bar and bar room, as well as the replication of several doors and the repair of the unique, beautifully coffered wood ceilings.

By 1995, Pat and Judy Ball restored the historic 1920s Payne Chapel (original AME Church) at the corner of 5th Street and Central Avenue. Restoration of the adjacent Hood Furniture building and three small frame houses moved to the area from a turpentine camp followed. The Ball's commitment to restoring Sarasota's early business district has led to the revitalization of the Rosemary Historic District, once an economically depressed area. Ball Construction continues to support its commitment to the area with offices on the second floor of the historic church building.

In 2000, the Ringling Museum called upon Ball Construction to disassemble the interior of the 18th century Asolo Theater, design and build custom storage containers, and help develop a unique labeling system so each artifact could be restored in the museum's curatorial laboratory. When the multi-year conservation process was completed, Ball's team worked hand-in-hand with the curators to reinstall the beautifully restored historic theater in the new reception center on the Ringling campus.

Pat standing on one of the most unusual "restoration" projects in Historic Spanish Point - the reconstruction of Cock's Footbridge across Webb's Cove in 1990. The original bridge dated to the late 1880s and connected the homestead cottages and early boarding homes.

Ball Construction employee working on the Asolo Theater Restoration Project.

AME Church prior to restoration.

Restored AME Church building.

BEALL'S, INC.

Beall's, Inc., a pioneering retail chain, has its early roots right here in Sarasota-Bradenton. Beginning with the founding store in 1915 on Main Street in Bradenton and a store in the Five Points area of Sarasota in the early Twenties, later closed because of the Depression, Beall's has been a retailing presence in Sarasota and Bradenton for more than 80 years. Today, Beall's Department Stores and Beall's Outlet Stores operate over 500 retail stores in 14 states with Sarasota County home to eleven outlet and five department stores.

In 1914, Robert M. Beall, Sr. moved to Palmetto and bought a dry good store. It wasn't long before Robert realized the region had enormous potential for economic growth and moved the store across the river to Bradenton.

He spent $2,500 to invest in merchandise and used overturned wooden crates as display fixtures. He sold fabrics, clothing and a few household items. The store was named the Dollar Limit, since nothing cost more than one dollar. Shortly thereafter, due to inflation following World War I, the store name changed to The V (Five) Dollar Limit.

In the 1940s, Robert Beall's son, E.R., joined the family business following his graduation from the University of Florida and service in the Army Air Corps. By 1946, the store name changed to Beall's Department Store. It was E. R. Beall's vision that began the company's expansion into shopping centers with the opening of Beall's second store in Bradenton's Westgate Shopping Center.

In 1961, Venice became the site of the third Beall's Department Store. Located in the Venice Shopping Center, where a Beall's Outlet Store stands today, the store flourished. Beall's continued to open its department stores over the next thirty years and today, Beall's Department Stores total nearly 90 locations throughout Florida.

In 1970, E.R.'s son, Robert M. Beall, II (Bob) joined the family business afte completing his military duty, earning an MBA at New York University, and working for Bloomingdale's in New York City. During the 1970s, all three generations of the Beall family were active in the company.

In 1987, Beall's tested a discount store concept in Florida to address the trend towards deep discount, bargain shopping, which became Beall's Outlet. Since 1987, Beall's has invested heavily in its Outlet division, growing the concept to a chain of over 470 stores with 275 in Florida and the remainder located in 13 Sun Belt states from California to North Carolina.

Following a successful pilot in 1998, Beall's Department Stores launched an initiative to double the size of its prototype store. The larger 70,000-plus square foot store enabled the company to broaden its appeal to families, younger customers and the wave of baby boomers that began migrating to Florida at the turn of the century. Despite intense competition in the department store sector, Beall's has succeeded by offering its customers an assortment tailored to the Florida lifestyle, a feat that national chains have struggled to achieve.

In 2006, Steve Knopik was named CEO of Beall's, Inc., marking the first time in its history that a non-family member was charged with the responsibility of leading the company. Bob Beall continues to be active as the Executive Chairman and Chairman of the company's Board of Directors.

Beall's is also a committed citizen of the communities in which it operates and to the state of Florida as a whole. Through its Robert M. Beall, Sr. Charitable Foundation, it has generously given to many whose lives have been disrupted by hurricanes and to children who need financial assistance in order to afford a college education.

Today, with an experienced, dedicated management group, a team of more than 11,000 exceptional employees and sales approaching $1.3 billion, Beall's is poised to continue growing with Florida and Sarasota well into the next Sesquicentennial.

1915 - The Dollar Limit on Main Street, Bradenton, on the ground floor of the St. James Hotel.

Early 1970's - E.R., Robert M. II, and Robert M. Beall, Sr. working together.

CYRUS BISPHAM & FAMILY

From Dairyman to Developer

Cyrus Bispham and his family have been part of Sarasota history for many decades. His father, Jack, was born in Manatee and moved to Longboat Key in 1910. A few years later, he married Catherine Graves, who moved to the area from Fitzgerald, Georgia. Two daughters were born, Dona and Ruth, and the Bisphams kept livestock and grew vegetables. A hurricane in 1921 brought waves crashing over Longboat Key, washing chickens and hogs into the bay. After that, the Bisphams moved to Sarasota, purchasing land where The Landings development is today, and started Bayside Dairy. Cy Bispham, his brother, Jack, and sister, Evie, were born on the new property.

Cy and Jack began milking cows when they were still young children. "We'd get up at 3 a.m. to milk the cows, then deliver milk before school started," Cy recalls. Bayside Dairy grew to 60 cows that were milked every morning and night. The Bisphams hired several men for $1 a day plus room and board to help with the milking. Mrs. Bispham did all the cooking and housekeeping for the hired help as well as for her own family.

In addition to milking cows, the dairy business of the 1920s and 1930s included collecting firewood for the steam-powered bottle washer which had a protruding brush that rotated to clean the bottles. Next the bottles were placed inside a steam chest for sterilization. Milk was sold in quart and pint bottles delivered to schools and restaurants. The dairy's first pasteurizer held about 30 gallons and was also heated by steam. The first milking machines were purchased during World War II, when labor was scarce.

Another aspect of the dairy business was delivery. The Bisphams sold three kinds of milk: "raw milk," pasteurized milk and homogenized milk. They also sold light cream, heavy cream, buttermilk and chocolate milk. The bottles were packed in ice in the milk crates to keep them cool during delivery. The delivery routes also included selling half-pint bottles of chocolate milk, orangeade, grapeade, grapefruit juice and pineapple juice to area filling stations. During World War II, the Bisphams started delivering milk every other day with routes north of Main Street on one day, and south of Main Street the next. Afternoon routes would alternate between Longboat and Lido keys and Siesta Key.

After graduating from Sarasota High School, where he excelled in football, track and boxing, Cy Bispham joined the paratroopers in 1944. Following service in the Philippines and Japan, he returned to Sarasota. In 1948, Cy married Doris Wagner and together, they have raised four children: Cy Jr., Jack, Lori and Lisa.

Jack Bispham had given each of his sons one-fourth interest in Bayside Dairy when they finished high school. The boys stayed on to help relocate the family business to the Gulf Gate area in 1950, where they built a new, larger dairy which gradually grew to milking 200 cows. Doris also was active in the business as the dairy's bookkeeper. They started buying milk from other dairies for delivery. Times were changing, however, and soon Sealtest milk from Tampa began delivering milk to Sarasota in paper cartons. The cost of converting their machinery to paper cartons would have cost $25,000, so the Bisphams sold all their milk routes to Hood's Dairy in 1955.

For five generations, the Bispham family has been involved in agriculture in the Sarasota area.

In 1949, Cy Bispham posed for this snapshot in a new Bayside Dairy barn, now Gulf Gate Clubhouse.

Two years later, the Gulf Gate property was sold. Cy bought 1,150 acres east of town to continue Bayside Dairy while his brother and father each bought farms in Live Oak, Florida. Soon the Bayside Dairy grew to 850 Holstein cows. Bayside Dairy continued in operation until 1987.

Cy Bispham was active with local, state and national dairy boards and served 25 years on the Sarasota County Fair Board, and ten years on the Florida State Fair Board. As a member of the Sarasota County Charter Commission, he helped craft the County Charter. He also served on the Sarasota County Planning Commission, two terms on the Sarasota Chamber of Commerce Board, and is a past president of the Sarasota Bay Rotary Club. Doris Bispham has been active in area garden clubs and church work. Both Doris and Cy are charter members of Pine Shores Presbyterian Church, where Doris has been a deacon and Cy an elder.

Today, Cy Bispham is focusing his energy on a beautiful real estate development called Serenoa, so named for the many saw palmettos on the land. *Serenoa repens* is the botanical name of the saw palmetto.

"My children have grown up on the land, and now my grandchildren," said Cy. "It pleases me to see our land turned into an upscale residential community." Residents enjoy seeing the deer, ducks and other wildlife plus the wide open spaces of the golf course and 83 acres of stocked lakes. Cy and his family are proud of their Sarasota heritage and are working together to ensure future generations can enjoy this area and its nature as well.

BOONE, BOONE, BOONE, KODA & FROOK

E.G. (Dan) Boone, with his wife Freda, opened his law office in Venice in 1956, when the population in south Sarasota County was 4,000. In 2006, the firm of Boone, Boone, Boone, Koda & Frook, the oldest law firm in Venice, celebrated 50 years of practice in an area which has grown to about 180,000 residents. After 17 years in downtown Venice offices, first in the Venice-Nokomis Bank building and then the Florida Power & Light Co. building, the office moved to Avenida Del Circo.

While growing his law practice, Dan Boone helped Venice obtain various needed services. Boone, with a group of local business owners, formed the Civic Action Association to elect city council members supportive of a bond issue to fund sanitary sewers, city water and paved streets. He prepared and filed an application for the First National Bank of Venice (now SunTrust Bank) and was instrumental in securing a new post office at the corner of West Venice Avenue and Harbor Drive.

Boone applied for and obtained state permission for the first cemetery between Sarasota and Punta Gorda, located on SR 776 between Venice and Englewood. He obtained the land and was a founder of Grace Methodist Church which has grown to a membership of 1,200. He has held numerous church offices over the years and served as president of the Venice-Nokomis Rotary Club. After purchase by Publix erased the only golf course between Sarasota and Fort Myers, Boone obtained permission from the FAA to use 354 acres of land on the Venice Airport to build the 27-hole Lake Venice Golf Course.

Boone has supported Venice High School activities, funding the construction of the VHS baseball field and raising money for the football stadium in 1957, and the new stands, press box and lighting 20 years later. Dan and Freda Boone, in charge of the football season tickets for 27 years, were inducted into the Venice Sports Hall of Fame in 2003.

Boone's most lasting contribution to the Venice area was obtaining the deed from the US government of the land between the Venice Airport and the Gulf of Mexico, preserving in perpetuity as public property land that would have been developed.

Jeff and Steve Boone joined the firm in the early 1980's and continued the tradition of community service. Jeff Boone served on the Venice Planning Commission for 10 years, including as chairman; chaired the Venice Zoning Board and the Blue Ribbon Venice Charter Review Board; has held numerous church offices; was president of the Venice Area Chamber of Commerce and president of the Venice-Nokomis Rotary Club; and was an assistant coach of the Venice High School football team.

Steve Boone has been president of the Venice Area Chamber of Commerce; a board member and president of the Gulf Coast Community Foundation of Venice; a member of the Manatee Community College Board of Trustees; a board member of the Boys & Girls Club; and was appointed to the Florida Bar Grievance Committee. He served as the first president of the Venice-Englewood-North Port Bar Association.

The firm consists of the three Boones and partners John Koda and Peggy Frook. All five attorneys are graduates of the University of Florida College of Law. Dan Boone has served on the Board of Trustees of the University of Florida Law School for 20 years and has

At a Venice City Council Meeting in 1957, Dan Boone stands alongside court reporter Don Bell

The Boone Law Firm Building on the Island of Venice

been a member of the University of Florida President's Council for over 30 years. John Koda first joined the firm in 1989 and specializes in litigation. Peggy Frook, who first worked at the law firm as a legal assistant, concentrates on real property practice, wills, trusts and estates. Both Mr. Koda and Ms. Frook are involved in Big Brothers Big Sisters, Habitat for Humanity, and the Venice Symphony.

The firm conducts a general law practice in all courts with specialties in wills, trusts, estate and probate law; real estate practice; hospital and nursing home regulatory work; business and corporate practice; and is engaged in all phases of land use law including purchase and sale, planning, re-zoning, platting, annexation and development approval. The firm does not handle any criminal or family law.

The hiring of a lawyer is an important decision that should not be based solely on advertisements. Please ask us to send you free written information about our qualifications and experience.

CENTER FOR SIGHT

Bringing Clear Vision to Life

Established in 1986 by David W. Shoemaker, MD, one of the nation's leading eye surgeons, Center For Sight has earned a reputation for excellence built on two decades of service to this community. Dr. Shoemaker has been performing cataract surgery since the early 1980s, and is recognized nationwide for his pioneering work in advancing the field. He was a principal investigator for the foldable intraocular lens, the implantable contact lens and a number of other advances in cataract surgery. In addition, he is one of a select group of physicians nationwide who serve on an FDA panel that evaluates new ophthalmic devices.

"This practice initially focused on cataract surgery," recalls Dr. Shoemaker. "Over the years we've expanded our facilities, our staff and our services to meet the changing needs of this growing community," he noted. "But even as we grow, we remain committed to treating all patients with the personal attention and respect they deserve."

Today, Center For Sight provides care to more than 65,000 people annually, at central offices in Sarasota and Venice and at regional offices that serve North Port, Englewood and Sarasota-Osprey Avenue. Surgery is performed in the comfort of the fully accredited Center For Sight surgery center located in the main Sarasota office. The Center's team includes seven board-certified physicians, eight optometric physicians, a specialist in hair transplantation, a licensed master aesthetician, optical experts and a dedicated support staff of nurses, technicians and other eye care professionals. Together, they offer a range of services designed to provide comprehensive care to people of all ages.

Those services include cataract and lens replacement surgery; LASIK laser vision correction; cosmetic facial plastic surgery; treatment of glaucoma, macular degeneration and other eye disorders; skin care services; eye exams and corrective lens prescriptions; an on-site optical department that features the latest designer frames and lens options, and even a hearing center.

As director of Cataract and Lens Replacement Surgery, Dr. Shoemaker is an acknowledged leader in advancing the techniques of this procedure. "Cataract surgery has changed dramatically over the past two decades," he said. "Now it's a pain-free, five-minute procedure that restores sight immediately and allows people to enjoy their lives again, often without the need for glasses."

LASIK and other laser vision correction procedures are another area where Center For Sight excels. William J. Lahners, MD, a board-certified eye surgeon with fellowship training in LASIK, heads the Center's Laser Vision Services. Dr. Lahners was the first surgeon in the region to perform IntraLase LASIK, the breakthrough all-laser approach that is completely bladeless. The procedure uses the Allegretto Wave laser - the most precise LASIK technology available - for enhanced outcomes and safety. In the skilled hands of Dr. Lahners, IntraLase LASIK delivers vision outcomes unmatched by any other technology in use today, allowing more patients to enjoy 20/20 vision than ever before.

The one constant among all the varied services at Center For Sight is personal attention. "We strive to make every visit a rewarding one for our patients," Dr. Shoemaker stated. This commitment is reflected in the special touches that set Center For Sight apart: fresh coffee and cookies in the waiting area; courtesy transportation for surgery patients; observation rooms where family members can be close by while patients have surgery; even a hand to hold during the procedure. Everything is focused on making you feel comfortable and welcome.

In addition, Dr. Shoemaker and his staff are dedicated to improving the quality of life in this community for everyone. Center For Sight supports Lighthouse for the Blind, a national organization that provides education and services to people with visual impairment. Over the years, Center For Sight surgeons have volunteered for Mission Cataract USA, providing free cataract surgery and follow-up to patients who cannot afford care. Dr. Shoemaker also shares his passion for sculling with the youth of the community, serving as director of the Sarasota Scullers Youth Rowing Program.

Whatever your vision care needs, from advanced cataract surgery with the new premium lenses, to state-of-the-art LASIK that can eliminate your need for glasses, to the latest treatments for glaucoma and other eye disorders, you'll always receive unsurpassed care at Center for Sight, Southwest Florida's premier vision care center.

Commitment to quality of care and quality of life is the hallmark of Center For Sight; the distinction that makes it such a vital part of this community. To learn more about the many services available at Center For Sight call 941-925-2020 or visit centerforsight.net.

HISTORY OF SARASOTA

A History of the Mayors

*I*t probably was a balmy day on October 20, 1902, when Colonel J. Hamilton Gillespie hosted at his home the first meeting of the Town Council of the newly incorporated town of Sarasota, and took office as the town's first mayor, an office he held for five years. It's unfortunate that today's audio and video recordings of meetings were not available, for certainly it would be of great interest to hear and see those pioneer leaders in action. Not the least of that pleasure would have been hearing Col. Gillespie's strong Scottish accent. He came to Sarasota in 1886 as one of the early Scottish settlers who gave Sarasota much of its heritage. He was one of the smaller numbers who stayed to develop the area, and his contributions to the community until his death in 1923 were many. It has been said that he "dominated Sarasota for many years, partly because of his vibrant personality and partly because the company he represented owned practically all the original town site."[1]

After the Town of Sarasota became a city effective January 1, 1914, A.B. Edwards, a Realtor, served as the city's first mayor for three years, and would serve a second term two years later from 1919 to 1921. E.J. Bacon was mayor of the city from 1921 to 1931, and E.A. Smith served two terms, 1931-1937 and 1939-1945.[2]

During those first four decades, the town and city of Sarasota was governed by the mayor and town council, with the mayor empowered with the authority of what has become known as the strong-mayor form of municipal government. In 1946, it had become apparent that the complexities of running this growing city in those post-war years required special knowledge and experience in municipal management, and Sarasota changed to the city manager form of government. Occasionally, members of the general public suggest returning to the strong mayor form of governance as a possible way to have more direct citizen control, but that move has not received serious consideration, arguably because of the quality of the city managers that have served since 1946.

Colonel Ross E. Windom, a former city manager of the cities of Westerville and Portsmouth, Ohio was appointed Sarasota's first city manager on January 19, 1946 and began his duties on February 1 of that year.[3] He served until 1948, and after a brief interim management, Kenneth Thompson, an engineer and city administrator in Miami, was hired in 1950 and would hold that office until his retirement in 1988. It is believed that Thompson's length of service is a national record. The people of Sarasota - past and present - believe that even this record of service was surpassed by the quality of Thompson's leadership. His administrative and engineering skills and foresight during those decades of greatest expansion assured that the required services and infrastructure were in place.

In his honor, shortly after his retirement, the City Commission named the city's largest park, formerly known as City Island, Ken Thompson Park. In 1987, David Sollenberger, selected after a nationwide search, became city manager and served a transition period with Mr. Thompson. Under Mr. Sollenberger's administration, the tradition of excellence continued, with leadership that met the complexities of the 1990s and the public's demand for greater involvement in government.

In 2001, Michael A. McNees was appointed City Manager, helping steer the city through a period of unprecedented growth. In 2006, V. Peter Schneider, who plans to retire in 2008, was appointed as interim City Manager and the city embarked on a national search to select an individual with the necessary leadership ability and administrative skills to lead the city into the next decade. On June 18, 2007, Robert Bartolotta, former City Manager of Jupiter, Florida, was appointed City Manager.

With the change to the city manager system, the role of the mayor also changed, and since that time, the mayor has been elected by the council, since called the City Commission. Since 1981, the commission has followed a tradition of rotating the position each year among the commissioners. In this form of governing the city, the mayor has no greater authority than the other commissioners. The mayor acts in an official capacity to sign all documents, chair meetings, and act as the ceremonial representative of the city.

Throughout the history of the town and city, mayors have come from almost as many businesses and professions as their numbers. Colonel Gillespie had studied law in Scotland and had a military career in that country. In Sarasota, he was a land developer. He has been followed by several who also were in the development, real estate or construction business. Many of the mayors owned their own businesses. Several were retired when they became mayor. Commissioners have been attorneys, former or active educators, a journalist, a banker and also a homemaker.

In 1982, Rita J. Roehr became Sarasota's first woman commissioner and mayor. In 1985 the city changed from an at-large system for selecting commissioners to a "mixed" system of electing two commissioners from the city at-large and one commissioner from each of three geographic voting districts. With this change, in 1985, Fredd "Glossie" Atkins became the first African-American commissioner in Sarasota and was selected as the first African-American mayor by his fellow commissioners in 1987.

The old minute books of the city show that even in the early years, as in recent times, every mayor was careful to avoid any conflict of interest if his business or profession was in any way related to an action of the council. The earliest indication of these ethical standards was the careful and detailed manner in which Col. Gillespie's loan of $200 to the town for constructing the first "calaboose" (as they called it) was documented.[4] That generosity to lend what was then a significant sum (albeit at 8% interest) certainly was surpassed on February 11, 1903 when the Council formally accepted the Colonel's gift to the city of the Rosemary Cemetery. It is today the resting place of Col. Gillespie and members of his family and is a peaceful sanctuary that keeps in our memories the

Exhibit case of photographs of Mayors. City Hall. Sarasota, Florida.

men and women who were the founders of the town and who drafted the first governmental rules of procedure.

There are significant influences in the city's current charter and operating procedures apparent from those first rules drafted by the Town Council on October 27, 1902[5]. Although some of that era's formality would seem foreign today, including the requirement that a member of the council should rise to request permission from the chair to speak. Notably, the in-the-sunshine conduct of city business that now is the law and the public's right to full participation were not the norm a century ago.

One of those early procedures was started by Col. Gillespie at the end of his term as mayor on November 5, 1907, when he addressed the Council reviewing his five years as mayor and "laying before you what I esteem to be the most essential needs of the town."[6]

In 1996, a Charter Review Committee recommended that each mayor shall, at the end of the term, give a state-of-the-city address, reviewing and reporting the accomplishments of the year. That procedure had been used earlier, but was left to the discretion of each outgoing mayor. It is not known if the Charter Review Committee was aware that Col. Gillespie had set an example years earlier.

Sarasota's history is depicted in the City Hall lobby in an exhibit case with the pictures of the mayors with their dates of service, starting with a picture of J. Hamilton Gillespie standing in his colonel's uniform. It cannot be doubted that, as every mayor and commissioner passes by those pictures, he or she is reminded of the debt owed to those who started the town and city, and of the responsibility to build upon that legacy.

City of Sarasota, Florida
June, 2007

[1] Karl H. Grismer, *The Story of Sarasota* (Tampa, The Florida Grower Press), 304.
[2] City of Sarasota, Florida, Records of the City Auditor and Clerk.
[3] Grismer, op.cit., 251.
[4] Town of Sarasota, Minutes of the Town Council, Book No.1, 6.
[5] Ibid., 1-5.
[6] Ibid., 198.

CITY OF VENICE

How Venice Became What it is Today

Several key events over the past 50 years made Venice, the "City on the Gulf," what it is today. The following is a time line of turning points for the city:

1926: At the request of the Brotherhood of Locomotive Engineers, city planner John Nolen created a city with Northern Italian Renaissance architectural ambiance. It drew people from across the country to experience its beauty, Gulf of Mexico views and warm winters. The extension of the railroad and "Velvet Highway" (Tamiami Trail) made their arrival possible. The BLE owned 80 square miles (compared to the 16.158 of today's city limits), of which a portion was incorporated in 1927.

1929: The bust of the 1920s building boom left Venice with a declining population.

1932: More people arrived with the cadets of Kentucky Military Institute, which set up winter headquarters along Tampa Avenue. The current Venice Little Theatre, Venice Centre Mall and Summerville Retirement residences were once part of the KMI campus, where the Lyndon, Kentucky students spent the winter. Many students returned later in life to live in Venice.

1933: Dr. Fred Albee, a New York orthopedic surgeon, established the Florida Medical Center, where northerners could seek treatment away from the snow and freezing rain.

1942: The Venice Army Air Base was established and the airport built to train fighter pilots for World War II. Immediately the population jumped by 1,000 people, many of whom returned to live in Venice after the war or in retirement. At the end of the war, the airport was deeded to the city with the stipulation that it be used for aviation or fall back to the ownership of the federal government. Today, it is owned and managed by the city, and functions under Federal Air Regulations. When the army base dismantled, the city's population decreased accordingly. In 1957, about 1,000 people lived in Venice.

1960s: Ringling Bros. and Barnum & Bailey Circus moved its winter headquarters from Sarasota, bringing entertainers and business associates to Venice. The circus also attracted visitors who could get a first look at the new show before it went on the road in the spring. Around the same time, the U.S. 41 Bypass and Intracoastal Waterway were constructed. In 1960, the population was an estimated 3,444.

1970s: The building boom was on again in Southwest Florida during the 1970s and 1980s. The population of Venice was 6,648 in 1970 and 11,973 in 1990. The popularity of the state during these decades is often attributed to the development of central air conditioning, mosquito control, mild hurricane seasons and pleasant winters.

From 1995, when the city's population was 17,216, until 2005, the number of people living in the Venice city limits increased by 3,584 or less than an average of 360 people per year.

The south bridge over the Intracoastal Waterway was rebuilt and named Circus Bridge in 2004. Ringling Bros. and Barnum & Bailey Circus had its winter headquarters in Venice from 1960 to 1991.

The Venice Little Theatre once housed the Orange Blossom Garage and the Kentucky Military Institute gymnasium, before it was renovated for use as a nationally award-winning community theater.

The Venetian Golf and River Club, built around 2003, was part of the expansion of the "North Venice" area, which took place between 2000 - 2005. It demonstrates the commitment of the city to its adopted architectural standard of Northern Italian Renaissance.

Between 1995 - 2005, the city of Venice annexed several thousand acres to the northeast of town. The annexation of Henry Ranch, a parcel of 1,100 acres along the Myakka River realized John Nolen's dream of creating a city from the Gulf of Mexico to the Myakka River. WCI Properties developed almost 1,600 homes known as Venetian Golf and River Club. It was the first development along the East Laurel Road corridor in the city limits.

Throughout the first decade of the 21st Century, the area has been going through the city's developmental approval processes to create mixed-use housing and commercial areas, as well as affordable housing.

To accommodate the needs of the United States Post Office and the local emergency response, the area was named North Venice.

- Pam Johnson, Public Information Officer, City of Venice, 2006

CLYDE BUTCHER GALLERY

By Clyde Butcher

The drive from California to Florida towing a 9,000-pound sailboat earned us the road name of "Asphalt Sailor." My wife, Niki, and our children, Jackie and Ted, were excited about reaching Florida. We launched our boat in St. Petersburg and headed south for a three-month sailing trip to the Dry Tortugas and the Keys. Our second evening in paradise brought us to a calm anchorage off the Venice Yacht Club.

The following morning, our 12-year-old daughter, Jackie, was watching the children from the Yacht Club as they raced their sailboats. I asked her what she was so intent about and she replied, "It looks like so much fun. I'm guessing which boat is going to win the race." Never in our wildest imagination did we think that her future husband was one of the 12-year-old boys racing that day. Neal says that more than likely he was racing because his family was deeply involved with the Venice Yacht Club.

In 1980 we made Florida our home, settling in Ft. Myers along the Caloosahatchee River. As we began learning about the state we now called home, I noticed that many people photographed the birds and alligators in Florida, but no one seemed to photograph the landscape. With the tremendous development in South Florida, I was concerned that our environment was going to disappear and there would be no record of it. I didn't know if I could make a living photographing swamps, but I knew it was important to do for the historical record. I also hoped that by showing people what the natural landscape of Florida looked like that perhaps more of it could be saved from destruction. At that time, I was photographing Florida with color film.

In 1986 our son, Ted, was killed by a drunk driver. Our family grieved in our own separate ways. I went into the Everglades and photographed in black and white. Black and white photography was my heart's desire, and Ted's death brought to me the reality that life is short - shorter for some - and I needed to take my time on this earth and do what my heart desired. The images of Florida in black and white seemed to touch people in a more expressive way than my color images. I am thankful for that appreciation.

As my artistic reputation grew, we moved into the Big Cypress National Preserve and started Big Cypress Gallery located on the Tamiami Trail in the middle of over a million acres of wilderness in South Florida. The sizes of my images range from 8 x 10 inches to 5 x 9 feet. The large sizes meant I needed a bigger darkroom than the one I had in our gallery.

Fifteen years after Jackie sat on the stern of our sailboat watching the children race at the Venice Yacht Club, she sat on the beach watching windsurfers. As she sat under a palm tree in the company of a dog tied to the tree, she was attracted to a handsome windsurfer walking toward her with a big smile on his face. Jackie met the owner of the dog, Neal Obendorf. They married two years later and moved to Venice. Jackie and Neal love Venice because it is truly a community that cares about the people who live there.

At about that same time I was looking for a larger space for my darkroom. Jackie became interested in my business and approached me, asking, "If I sold my own business, could I help you run your business?" Her stipulation was that she didn't want to leave Venice. We were very excited about having her become involved in our life and what made it even nicer was that Neal was interested in helping me in the darkroom. We purchased a building that had enough space for a gallery and a large darkroom and, in 2000, began the Venice Gallery and Studio. We now have two galleries, one in Venice and one in Big Cypress National Preserve.

As I write this short story I am sitting on my porch overlooking the bay where we dropped anchor in Venice in 1979. My grandchildren, Kayla and Robbie, are having a great time sailing near the dock and I marvel at the twists and turns of life.

HISTORY OF THE COMMUNITY FOUNDATION OF SARASOTA COUNTY

*I*n 1979, visionary leaders of the South West Florida Estate Planning Council collaborated in forming an organization to bring together philanthropic clients and nonprofit service agencies throughout the area. They created the Community Foundation of Sarasota County, a public charity with roots that stretch back to 1914, when the first community foundation began in Cleveland, Ohio. Today's more than 700 locally controlled community foundations across the nation are united by a single mission: improving the quality of life in a community through the establishment of permanent charitable funds, well invested, that generate millions of dollars each year in grants and scholarships supporting education, the environment, animal welfare, health and human services.

From its modest beginnings with just a single volunteer, a telephone and a confident board of directors, the Community Foundation of Sarasota County has grown to more than 580 charitable funds and $157 million in assets, awarding over $6 million in grants and scholarships each year. In addition, the Nonprofit Resource Center supports thousands of charitable organizations in fulfilling their missions through workshops, training, consulting and staffing resources, and peer-to-peer learning experiences.

The Community Foundation is a valuable community resource that responds to all kinds of community needs. In hurricanes Charley and Katrina, the **Disaster Relief Fund** provided a vehicle for direct donations to organizations on the ground in the affected areas. With a grant from this fund, the Red Cross was able to open an office in Arcadia and service a needy population. With the **Season of Sharing Fund**, a six-year collaboration of the Community Foundation and the Tribune-Media Group, hundreds of families and individuals on the brink of homelessness have received emergency grants for rent, car repairs, utility bills, and medical expenses. Throughout the year, the **Helping Hands Fund** also addresses critical human needs as identified by social service caseworkers. The Community Foundation thus provides leadership in addressing the kinds of human service gaps that no single funding source can tackle alone.

The Community Foundation also partners with other organizations as a neutral convener and catalyst for change. With Children First and Sarasota Memorial Hospital, for example, the Connecting Fathers & Families Initiative jump-started parenting education programs that continue to strengthen families years later. In cooperation with the Senior Friendship Centers, a nationally recognized Falls Prevention Program now offers balance classes to seniors that teach them how to avoid dangerous falls that often lead to permanent injury and loss of independence. The Education Partnership among the Community Foundation, the William G. and Marie Selby Foundation and the Gulf Coast Community Foundation of Venice awarded the Sarasota County School District extensive funding to provide administrators, staff and teachers with meaningful professional training, expert advisors and best-practice tools to establish small learning communities in the schools, helping pave the way for technical and 21st century learning.

Individual donors often leave legacies of everlasting impact through the Community Foundation. One such woman was Jo Bowen Nobbe,

Each year, Roland Abraham gives hundreds of students a boost with their college education through his scholarship fund with the Community Foundation of Sarasota County.

The Community Foundation headquarters on Fruitville Road in Sarasota is a community resource to all non-profit organizations, volunteers and supporters.

Since Stewart W. Stearns joined the Community Foundation of Sarasota County as president and CEO in 1988, assets have increased from $300,000 to over $157 million.

who first gifted her home to fund scholarship opportunities for high school graduates and ultimately left a $17 million bequest in her estate. The income earned from Mrs. Nobbe's gift underwrites a variety of educational programs, including a creative college loan payback award to Sarasota County teachers; summer enrichment for underprivileged children; and an innovative dropout prevention program implemented in all Sarasota County high schools.

Similarly, the gift of one longtime Community Foundation board member and supporter has had a huge impact on the community at large. When Leila Gompertz donated two million dollars for the purchase of the former Elk's Club property on Fruitville Road in Sarasota, the Community Foundation had the opportunity to construct its first headquarters. Through the sale of a piece of the unused land for the development of Foundation Park, a structure was erected for the Community Foundation staff with state-of-the-art meeting rooms on the first floor. Little did one donor realize, however, that the Leila & Michael Gompertz Center would become a destination resource for more than 12,000 people in the nonprofit world annually, a venue for workshops, seminars, board retreats, special presentations and events at no charge. In more than 28 years of operation, the Community Foundation as an entity and as a physical presence in the community has truly demonstrated its motto: **For good. For ever.**®

KEVIN DAVES

Kevin Daves is a Kansan by birth and a Sarasotan by choice. Born, raised and educated in "The Sunflower State," he graduated from the University of Kansas in 1976 with a degree in Architecture and began a career that took him throughout the United States. As part of his involvement in a wide range of commercial, residential and hospitality projects, Kevin developed expertise in historical renovations.

In 1993, Kevin was invited to Sarasota to assess the feasibility of renovating the John Ringling Hotel. He became enamored with the beauty, charm and vitality of the Florida West Coast in general and the Sarasota area in particular. Although the Ringling Hotel was beyond saving, Kevin saw an opportunity for a premier project on the 11-acre bayside site in downtown Sarasota.

Just prior to The Great Depression, John Ringling planned to bring a Ritz-Carlton Hotel to Sarasota. It was intended to be the first Ritz-Carlton other than the flagship property in Boston. The original plan was to build the hotel on property Ringling owned on Longboat Key. The stock market crash of 1929 scrapped those plans and Ringling instead built a hotel under his own signature on the downtown site.

Fast forward 60-plus years and in an ironic historic twist, Kevin approaches the Ritz-Carlton corporation to finally realize John Ringling's dream to bring a Ritz-Carlton to Sarasota.

Although told time and time again that it couldn't be done, Kevin assembled a development team designed to bring this five-star resort hotel to Sarasota. His perseverance and vision drove the project through eight long years culminating with the opening of The Ritz-Carlton Hotel and Condominiums in November 2001.

It marked the first time a Ritz-Carlton hotel opened on schedule and was the first project to combine luxury condominium units with a hotel, providing the added value of hotel services and amenities to the condominium residents. Another innovation was incorporating beach, spa and golf facilities in a separate private club open to members and hotel guests.

From the beginning, the hotel garnered numerous awards as one of the world's outstanding resorts. The hotel's Vernona restaurant is recognized as one of Florida's Top 25 restaurants and one of the state's Top 5 Luxury Resort Restaurants. In 2007, the resort was again named to *Condé Nast Traveler's* Gold List for The World's Best Places to Stay; *Travel & Leisure's* 500 Greatest Hotels in the World, the U.S. *Zagat Survey's* Top 50 U.S. Resorts and received the AAA Five Diamond Lodging Award.

When Kevin announced his next local project would be a luxury golf community built around a Jack Nicklaus-designed golf course, Sarasota resident and golf legend Tony Jacklin called and offered a photo for the golf clubhouse. The photo, depicting that famous moment at the 1969 Ryder Cup when Jack conceded a par putt to Tony - resulting in the first tie in the history of the Ryder Cup - provided the inspiration for the project.

Daves named the 1,200-acre parcel of land east of Lakewood Ranch on the border of Manatee and Sarasota counties "The Concession," after that historic Ryder Cup moment.

When Jack Nicklaus was briefed on the concept, he invited Tony to join him as co-designer. And, just as they had shared the top honors at the 1969 Ryder Cup, they again shared top golfing honors with The Concessions' Jack Nicklaus Signature Golf Course being named "Best New Private Course In America" for 2006 by *Golf Digest* magazine.

At the clubhouse groundbreaking in January of 2007, Michael Saunders, Sarasota's preeminent Realtor, recalled her initial shock at Dave's proposal to build this extraordinary community in "the middle of nowhere."

Ignoring the odds once more, Daves persevered. Today, families have begun moving into their homes at The Concession Golf Club & Residences. Along with the *Golf Digest* "Best New Private Course" award, *Travel and Leisure Golf* magazine has named The Concession to its list of "Top 100 Golf Course Communities."

Kevin remains bullish on the future of Sarasota. He and his wife, Lynda, together with their four children, divide their time between Sarasota and a home in Wichita. Daves' other investments in the community include the Chart House Center on Longboat Key and a luxury condominium site on Lido Key. Kevin is also involved in the community, serving on various boards and committees including the Ringling School of Art.

DIOCESE OF VENICE IN FLORIDA

The Roman Catholic Diocese of Venice was founded October 25, 1984. Spurred by the unstinted growth of the Catholic population in south Florida and in order to better meet their spiritual needs, Pope John Paul II announced on July 17, 1984, the establishment of two new Florida Dioceses: Palm Beach and Venice.

Bishop John J. Nevins, an auxiliary bishop of the Archdiocese of Miami, was named the first bishop of the new Diocese of Venice. He was installed as bishop on October 25, 1984. At the same time, Epiphany Church in Venice was consecrated as the Cathedral, the official church and See of the Diocese of Venice in Florida.

The Diocese of Venice includes the counties of Manatee, Sarasota, Charlotte, Lee, DeSoto and Hardee, formerly in the Diocese of St. Petersburg; Highlands County, formerly in the Diocese of Orlando; and Collier, Hendry and Glades counties, formerly in the Archdiocese of Miami. It is a 9,035-square-mile area of southwest Florida, approximately 140 miles long (north to south) and an average 70 miles wide (east to west). At the time it was created, the Diocese had a general population of 809,400 with approximately 116,000 Catholics in 39 parishes.

Bishop Nevins Academy – the Diocese of Venice broke ground on Bishop Nevins Academy in 2000. The academy, located on the southwest corner of Fruitville and McIntosh Roads in Sarasota, houses St. Martha School and Dreams Are Free, the Diocese's special needs school.

St. Martha Church circa 1912 – St. Martha Church was the first Catholic Church in Sarasota County.

Bishops Dewane and Nevins – Bishop John J. Nevins, right, was the first Bishop of the Diocese of Venice. Bishop Frank J. Dewane became ordinary of the Diocese when Bishop Nevins retired in January 2007.

The Catholic faith was introduced into the Gulf Coast of Florida during the exploration of the coast by Hernando DeSoto in the early part of the 16th century. In 1567, Jesuit Father Juan Rogel began a mission to the Caloosa Indians in the Charlotte Harbor/Fort Myers area, dedicated to St. Anthony of Padua. In the 19th century, missionaries from Savannah, St. Augustine and then from Tampa visited the area; a Catholic church was built in 1888 in Manatee County. In 1889, the care of the area fell under the jurisdiction of the Jesuit Fathers from Tampa who made regular visits to Bradenton, Fort Myers and later to Arcadia and adjacent missions.

In 1927, Bishop Patrick Barry established both St. Martha Parish in Sarasota and St. Joseph Parish in Bradenton and appointed Father Charles Elslander as the first pastor of both parishes. Within the current boundaries of the Venice Diocese, only St. Francis Xavier Parish, Fort Myers, established in 1920, is older.

For many years, these two parishes served all the Catholics in Sarasota and Manatee counties. Over time, other churches rose up around the two counties and the diocesan boundaries eventually changed, putting the parishes first in the St. Petersburg Diocese and, later, the Venice Diocese.

For 23 years, the Diocese of Venice has cared for the spiritual needs of the Catholic population in southwest Florida. The Diocese has grown not only in people and parishes, but also in the services provided so as to meet the increasing needs that come with a burgeoning population. From the establishment ranging from Catholic Charities to the foundation of two new schools for students with special learning needs, the Diocese continues to care for its ever-changing flock.

The Catholic Center, built in 1987, is the administrative headquarters of the Diocese of Venice in Florida located in the city of the same name. It houses the various departments, offices and staff who assist the bishop in his responsibilities to serve the pastoral needs of the faithful in southwest Florida.

In April 2006, Pope Benedict XVI appointed Most Reverend Frank J. Dewane as coadjutor bishop of the Diocese of Venice. He first arrived on April 24th at Sarasota-Bradenton International Airport to be introduced to the Diocese of Venice. At the same time of this initial visit, Bishop Dewane visited St. Martha School, Dreams Are Free and Cardinal Mooney High School, three of the Catholic Education institutions in Sarasota. Bishop Frank J. Dewane was ordained on July 25, 2006 in Epiphany Cathedral, Venice. This event was televised in the ten-counties of the Diocese, including Sarasota and Manatee. As coadjutor, Bishop Dewane assisted Bishop Nevins in the administration of the Diocese.

Bishop Nevins retired as ordinary of the Venice Diocese on January 19, 2007. At that time, Bishop Dewane became the second bishop of the Diocese of Venice in Florida. Bishop Dewane has been warmly received by the communities and resides in Sarasota.

EDUCATION FOUNDATION OF SARASOTA COUNTY, INC.

Sarasota County Public Schools' Proud Partner

The Education Foundation of Sarasota County, Inc. provides the Extra Edge of Excellence for the children in Sarasota County Public Schools.

Dedicated to quality education for all children, the Education Foundation of Sarasota County is an independent, not-for-profit organization that works in partnership with the community and Sarasota County public schools. Through the generosity of our caring community, the Education Foundation funds worthwhile initiatives such as classroom grants, academic and fine arts programs, cutting edge technology, and leadership development.

Sarasota County has always been committed to excellence in education, from the days of the one room school house to today's modern school system. Parents and concerned citizens have always worked together to support and improve our community's schools. Today, Sarasota County Schools benefit greatly from the caring organization known as the Education Foundation of Sarasota County.

The organization that would become the Education Foundation began in late 1988, when a task force of Sarasota citizens - Arthur Wood, Jr., Dee Stottlemyer, Shirley Ritchey, Jim Henry, and Dr. Henry Huesner, along with Superintendent Dr. Charles W. Fowler and Dr. Robert E. Perkins of the Selby Foundation - met to discuss issues surrounding public education and the viability of forming a foundation in support of public schools. Dr. Perkins led the organization until businessman James Tollerton was elected the first chairman of the board. 501 (c) (3) tax exempt status was obtained, and on November 21, 1988, a newly elected 17-member Foundation Board of Directors with representation from throughout our community established their mission to support our public schools.

Since the Foundation is concerned with all public schools in the county, the legal name was amended to Sarasota County Public Schools Foundation, Inc. in 1990. That same year, in order to provide the best quality service to the schools system, a full time executive director was hired with support from a William G. Selby and Marie Selby Foundation grant. In 1994, the organization was renamed Education Foundation of Sarasota County, Inc.

Many community members have served on the Education Foundation Board of Directors. Several community leaders have served as Chairman, including Don Smally, Kimball Bobbitt, Shirley A. Ritchey, John Berteau, Stuart Barger, Beverly Koski, Guy A. Azar, Walter G. Mills, Pam Daniel, Javier Suarez, Kathy Schersten, Pam Truitt, Pete Biegel, Jon F. Swift, and R. Scott Collins.

Since its inception, the Education Foundation has provided direct fiscal support of nearly $7 million dollars to Sarasota County public schools. The group has secured the support of major businesses and many individual donors as sponsors and underwriters of many district-wide programs. Savvy business people and donors realize that their investment in the public school children of Sarasota County impacts the quality of life in the community. Through their generosity, the Education Foundation has developed and supported a wide array of important programs. These include such long-standing programs as Edge of Excellence Classroom Grants, Evening of Excellence Student Art Program, Building Blocks for Success Grants, Academic Olympics, Regional Science Engineering and Technology Fair, and Teacher of the Year. In recent years, in response to district needs, the Education Foundation has established a number of new programs that encourage student achievement. Among them are the Roads to Reading and Love to Learn literacy programs, TeXcellence Home Computer Program, the Center for Leadership, and Beyond the School Day Tutorials. The Named Tribute Program has been created so that significant monetary contributions to the Education Foundation that benefit our schools can be appropriately commemorated. With school board approval, a school board facility can be named in perpetuity – as a tribute to the generosity of an individual, organization or business.

With the support and hard work of the Education Foundation, the Sarasota County public school district will continue to be enriched and its students encouraged to pursue academic excellence. The future of the Education Foundation and our community schools is vested with the citizens, businesses and friends of public education.

For more information about the Education Foundation of Sarasota County and the Extra Edge of Excellence it provides to our local schools, visit EdFoundation.net or call (941) 927-0965.

This smiling student loves school. The Education Foundation provides books and tutorials.

Two young Science Fair winners proudly display their ribbons.
(Photo credit: Kristin McGuigin, Bryn-Alan)

These Education Foundation scholarship winners worked hard to earn their prizes.

This history made possible through a gift from
Jim and Shirley Ritchey

THE EPISCOPAL CHURCH OF THE REDEEMER

The Episcopal Church in Sarasota began in 1885 in the home of Colonel and Mrs. A.B. Coachman, who, with Colonel and Mrs. E.W. Morrill, prayed together from the *Book of Common Prayer*. As more Episcopalians moved into the frontier community, they worshipped in a boarding house, a common room of the Belle Haven Inn, the Grable Building, the Methodist Church, and the parlor/dining room of Col. John Hamilton Gillespie on Palm Avenue.

Gillespie, a Scottish Presbyterian, joined the small group of Episcopalians in 1886. Confirmed in 1888, he was licensed as a lay reader and became the *de facto* leader of the Sarasota Episcopalians. He was ordained a Deacon in 1922. Meanwhile, he had been busy founding the town, becoming its premier civic and cultural leader. He was Sarasota's first mayor, its earliest philanthropist, founder of its library and school, its first golfer and founder of its first golf links, among the earliest in Florida.

The first church building, with various expansions, housed the congregation from 1904 to 1950. Built as a Guild Hall largely through contributions from Sarasota women, it was located in the back yard of Gillespie's house. It was appropriated as a church building, meeting a canonical requirement for becoming a missionary parish of the Diocese in 1904.

Twenty-Six Communicants signed the application for Mission status. The early parish lists comprise an impressive roster of men and women who were civic, business and professional leaders in Sarasota. Many are buried in the town's first cemetery, Rosemary, on land given by Gillespie. Several surnames survive as street names and public places.

The parish, named Church of the Redeemer, after Mrs. Morrill's home church in Biloxi, Mississippi, grew with the community. Lay leadership dominated its first decade with occasional archdiaconal visits from clergy of Christ Church, Bradentown, along with annual episcopal visits. From its beginning, retired clergy, sometimes winter residents, presided at Eucharistic services. One retired clergyman, Dr. Francis Burdette Nash, became the first full-time priest-in-charge of the small parish in 1915. He led the congregation with the assistance of Gillespie, Dr. Jack Halton and other lay persons, supervising a significant expansion of the Guild Hall that eventually landed on the corner of Orange Avenue and Morrill Street. The first rectory, on Morrill Street, was built for Nash and his family in 1923.

Capable clergymen followed Dr. Nash, sometimes in quick succession, to be shepherds of the faithful and to lead growth, paralleling the growth of the city, even in the depression years of 1926-27. A parish house was built to join the Church on its Southeast corner, reflecting the increasing need for Christian education and a meeting place for fellowship. The music of the parish, according to several contemporary accounts in the *Sarasota Times*, was extraordinary, attracting music lovers not only to the church but also to community concerts. That tradition continues today, under the long-term leadership of Dr. Ann Stevenson-Moe, and the Composer-in-Residence, Dr. Daniel Moe. A new Nichols and Simpson organ, completed during centennial celebrations, has enriched the musical heritage of the parish.

The new church, designed by the studios of Cramm and Ferguson, was completed in 1950 on spacious bayfront lots donated in part by a gracious Jewish landowner, Mrs. Ida Klein. Funding for the building came from the parish, community members, the proceeds of the sale of the old church building; and the significant gift of a benefit performance by the Ringling Circus.

Distinguished clergy, including Fathers Lillycrop, Soper, Moses, Reeves, Fitzgerald, Iker and the current Rector, Fr. Fredrick Robinson, have left deep imprints on the parish and community. Laity have provided outstanding leadership, both in women's and men's ministries; and in educational and mission outreach. As the "mother church" of Sarasota, Redeemer has enabled several new missions in the town and county that would become parishes. Community institutions have originated from the Redeemer; overseas missions have benefited from the presence of youth and adult missioners from the parish.

Laity and clergy alike have, through service and monetary gifts, contributed to the beautification and utility of the church building and grounds, including extraordinary needlepoint, stained glass and furnishings. Centennial celebrations in 2004 saw the renovation and naming of Gillespie Hall, the addition of a veranda, a new pipe organ, new stained glass windows on the west end, and a tiled depiction of the Compass Rose, a symbol of the Anglican Communion, under the Hope Tower.

All point to the Glory of God through the continuing mission of the Church of the Redeemer, equipping the People of God for the work of ministry.

FCCI INSURANCE GROUP

Protecting Business, Property and People

In 1959, a group of local Sarasota business owners in the construction industry decided they needed to find a way to save money on the cost of workmen's compensation insurance. The result? On April 1, the not for profit Florida Contractors and Construction Industries Self Insurers Fund was born. The first year there were a total of 28 members in the FCCI Fund and $52,079 in total premium.

Despite the small growth rate stemming from a decision to stay local so the Board of Trustees would know members personally, by 1968, the FCCI Fund more than doubled its premium to $120,000 and increased its membership to 46. Over the next ten years, the FCCI Fund would grow to 100 times its size due to the building boom in the 1970s. Additionally, FCCI would open up its membership statewide and change its name to Florida Construction, Commerce & Industry Self Insurers Fund to reflect the expansion of members beyond the construction industry. During this same time, workmen's compensation would become known as workers' compensation, signifying other changes taking place in the American workforce.

The FCCI Fund was not only growing, it was leading the way in setting industry standards. The cornerstone of FCCI, a 10-step safety program, set the stage for FCCI safety engineers to travel throughout the state inspecting worksites and counseling employers in ways to reduce accidents and improve loss ratios. When Florida passed a law requiring insurers to provide loss control programs, FCCI's program had already been in place for one year and was the first program to meet state guidelines.

Also during this time, medical costs were skyrocketing, and as a result, insurance companies were increasingly withdrawing from providing workers' compensation coverage in Florida. In an approval letter for a dividend refund for FCCI members, the chief of the Florida Bureau of Workmen's Compensation commented, "It is interesting to note that while the insurance industry was suffering huge underwriting losses during 1976, this fund developed a surplus."

In addition to prudent underwriting guidelines, the FCCI Fund was recognized nationwide for its successful rehabilitation of workers representing 25% of all FCCI industrial claims involving lost time. This was eight times better than the national average! In the early 1980s, a national task force, aware of FCCI's success, studied the operations of the FCCI Fund to help develop model legislation for the self-insurance industry.

Locally, FCCI kept outgrowing its facilities and moved from 12 South Pineapple to 21 North Lemon, to a converted house at 2540 South Tamiami Trail, to a three-story building at 1751 Mound Street, then to a five-story building at 2601 Cattlemen Road, and finally, in 2001, to a 260,000-square foot, state of the art facility at 6300 University Parkway in Lakewood Ranch.

Over the years, FCCI has expanded its product line to include all lines of commercial property and casualty insurance. The biggest change to date, however, may have occurred in 1994 when the FCCI Fund converted to FCCI Mutual Insurance Company, thereby ensuring that its members would never be assessed for additional premium due to the inadequacies of other self-insured policyholders in or out of the FCCI Fund. With this conversion, FCCI also expanded across the Florida state line into the nearby southeastern states of Georgia, Mississippi, and Alabama. As of 2006, FCCI writes business in 13 contiguous states and has plans to expand even further.

In summary, FCCI has grown with the community - from a handful of employees in 1959 to more than 670 today; from $52,000 in premium to more than $551 million; from 28 member insureds to over 15,000. As a leader in the commercial property and casualty industry, FCCI is proud of its Sarasota heritage and proud to be, for so many businesses throughout the Southeast and Midwest, the First Choice in Commercial Insurance.

SUMMARY HISTORY OF FIRST BAPTIST CHURCH OF SARASOTA, FLORIDA

Reverend William H. Hild, Jr., Pastor

As wise men of old have said, a great journey begins with a single step. The earliest beginnings of First Baptist Church of Sarasota literally began with such a single step. On March 23, 1902, Isaac Redd, sixty-seven years old at the time, took a two-hour walk from the Bee Ridge area of Southwest Florida to the tiny hamlet called Sarasota to meet with five individuals that helped lay the foundation for a new Baptist church. Those early visionaries were the Rev. Henry Messer, his wife Keziah, James Bates, Nathan Hayman, and Patsy Dancy; that church would become the First Baptist Church of Sarasota, with the Rev. P.O. Miller as its first pastor.

First Baptist Church, December 1962.

First Baptist Church, 1924, currently Church Chapel.

The local Methodist church kindly offered to allow the fledgling Baptist congregation to meet on Sunday afternoons in their church building. Three years later, the first building of the new congregation was completed on the south side of present-day Second Street (then Eighth Street) near Central Avenue. Major encouragement came from member William Worth who owned Worth Grocery and joined the church in 1903.

The first church was a one-room white frame building. It had a bell tower, with a genuine bell that called the members of the church to worship since they all lived within easy walking distance. Sunday School enrollment rose to forty, and soon the Ladies' Aid Society was organized. This group raised the money to purchase the first Bible pulpit. In 1914, a pastorium was added next door to the church. It welcomed the ninth pastor of the church, Rev. J.R. Henry. The living room also served as a Sunday School classroom for the junior girls' Bible study class.

Dedication Sunday, 1962.

First Baptist Church Parsonage, 1914.

By 1919 the one-room building had become too small for the growing congregation. With the arrival of pastor Dr. A.J. Beck, the congregation decided in 1920 to purchase a building site at Main Street and Adelia for the grand total of $2,500, just in time, as the population of Sarasota grew from 3,000 to 25,000 during the next six years! First Baptist built a new sanctuary employing Neoclassical Revival Style on the property purchased at that location. Today this structure is called The Chapel. The church dedicated the new sanctuary, along with a $30,000 pipe organ and beautiful stained glass windows on December 14, 1924. The first church building was donated to the Bethlehem Baptist Church on Central Avenue, Sarasota's first African-American Baptist Church.

Under the able tutelage of Dr. W.R. Hamilton, the leadership of First Baptist Church saw the need for the addition of its present sanctuary. A Sanctuary building committee was commissioned in 1958 with a formal building committee named in 1959. They recommended that architects Kannenberg and Hanebuth draw up plans for the new sanctuary. Contractor William A. Berbusse, Jr. won the construction bid of $635,000. On May 29, 1962, the cornerstone of the new Georgian Colonial Style sanctuary was laid with the first worship service being held on the Sunday before Christmas, 1962. The formal dedication was held on February 3, 1963. The addition of a Family Life Center and a Children's Educational wing occurred in 1980. First Baptist Church purchased its first property on the south side of Main Street in 2001 when it bought the two-story office building at 1670 Main Street. This facility was totally remodeled in 2004 and serves as the ministries offices and main hall for receptions and additional Bible study rooms.

First Baptist has been instrumental in the founding of many of the Baptist Churches that minister to the greater Sarasota area. Bay Haven Baptist (originally Second Baptist Church), Southside Baptist Church, Mt. Calvary Baptist Church, Kensington Park Baptist Church, Gulf Gate Baptist Church (today Gulfgate Church), as well as several language congregations that have been birthed by the First Baptist Church of Sarasota.

In January of 2006, under the leadership of the Reverend William H. Hild, Jr., Senior Pastor for the past ten years, First Baptist purchased an additional piece of property located immediately east of the church on Main Street. This purchase, the largest in the history of First Baptist Church, further cemented its 105-year history of ministry, evangelism, and worship to the greater Sarasota community. It finds its ministry blessed by God in amazing ways with an ever growing sense of enthusiasm to proclaim the "...riches of Christ" to the hundreds of thousands who call Sarasota home.

FIRST PRESBYTERIAN CHURCH

When the Presbyterian residents of Sarasota met to form a church in 1906, theirs was a small community. The town had incorporated in 1903, but there were yet to be any paved roads, water or sewer lines, or seawalls. Livestock roamed freely through town, leaving homeowners to fence their yards to prevent damage to trees and gardens. After a week-long meeting, the Presbyterian Church was organized on February 16.

With an initial membership of eleven, the church lacked pastoral oversight until September 1907. Soon thereafter, the congregation voted to raise money for a building and met for worship during the intervening months in the homes of Mrs. Prime and Mr. and Mrs. Hebb. The members purchased land at the corner of Orange and Fifth (now Ringling Boulevard) and laid the cornerstone in late 1908 for their first building. At that point the work ceased, for there was not enough money to continue. A loan, obtained the following year, enabled them to erect the outer walls and roof.

First services were held in the new building in March 1910 even though burlap covered the window openings and neighbors provided some of the chairs. In spite of an incomplete facility, the church soon organized a Sunday School with C.V.S. Wilson, publisher of the *Sarasota Times*, as the superintendent.

With financial help from denominational offices, the Presbyterians were able to call their first pastor in 1911. The following year they paid off their loan and finished work on the building. Help from sister churches came in the forms of an organ from Pennsylvania and hymnals from Iowa. The congregation dedicated the building in February 1913, more than four years after breaking ground.

During the building and population boom of the 1920s, the church members sold the Orange Avenue property and purchased a lot at the east end of Oak Street. Initial plans for a much-needed larger structure failed to materialize and for three years the congregation worshiped in a variety of community buildings. The Presbyterians finally moved into their new Mediterranean Revival style home in 1928.

The number of Presbyterians grew as Sarasota did after World War II. The Presbyterian Church responded in two ways under the leadership of the pastor, Dr. B. Lowry Bowman. Construction of a new sanctuary in 1949 and additional classrooms in 1954 met some of the growth needs. A physically more far-reaching effect was achieved, however, when the congregation initiated and supported the development of additional churches. Whitfield Estates, Pine Shores, and Northminster Presbyterian Churches grew out of Sunday School programs established by First Presbyterian. In each of these situations, and in the development of Siesta Key Chapel, members of First Presbyterian Church became part of the new congregations, at least for a few years, to help them become established.

From the time of its Reformation Era beginning, the Presbyterian denomination has valued education. Within that tradition and as a service to the community, Sarasota's Presbyterian Church opened a kindergarten in 1947 under the direction of Nell Horton and later added classes for three and four-year-olds. The kindergarten component of the program closed two decades later, no longer in demand after kindergartens opened in the public schools. The preschool continued, however, and since 1985 has offered programs for children from age two-and-a-half through pre-kindergarten. In 1995 the preschool earned accreditation from the National Association for the Education of Young Children.

Members of First Presbyterian Church have taken inspiration from the visual arts pieces at the church. The earliest of these is a small round stained glass window which depicts Jesus praying in the Garden of Gethsemane. One of the first windows in the Orange Avenue church, it was moved to Oak Street and is now located in the chapel. In front of the church complex, the William Shannon memorial sculpture has framed an entrance way since 1978. Sarasota artist Thornton Utz created the sculpture, "The Way of the Cross." In 1996, Utz designed for the chapel the Eve Perkins memorial windows, which portray Utz's reflections on heaven and earth. In 2006, as part of the church's 100th anniversary celebration, an outdoor Chartres Cathedral design labyrinth was constructed using historic bricks from a vacated portion of adjacent Bowman Court. This prayer and meditation setting is a lasting gift to the Sarasota community.

First Presbyterian Church remains a downtown church. On the cusp of the 21st Century, the members broke with tradition and called their first woman pastor, Dr. Susan Forester DeWyngaert. Together they are challenged to find ways to communicate the Gospel for a new time in a changing world.

The Presbyterian Church on Orange Avenue, about 1912 (Photo courtesy of Sarasota County Historical Resources Department.)

Stained glass window of Jesus in the Garden of Gethsemane.

First Presbyterian Church at the eastern end of Oak Street, one of the few remaining red brick roadways that once crisscrossed the City of Sarasota, 2007.

This history made possible through a gift by Charlie and Dee Stottlemyer

FREDERICK DERR & COMPANY, INC.

Building Sarasota's Infrastructure

*F*rederick Derr & Company, best known for building major highway projects such as University Parkway, Lakewood Ranch Boulevard, Lockwood Ridge Road, Tallevast Road, and Winchester Boulevard, has also earned a superb reputation for applying innovative and creative ideas to projects.

One such example is a soil cement step revetment for beach protection. The company pioneered the design and construction of the first structure of this kind on the coastline of Florida, completed in January 1989. The purpose of the revetment was to protect a section of beach road on North Casey Key from storm damage. For many years, this road was either seriously damaged or destroyed by major storms causing the isolation of North Casey Key residents. This successful project has resulted in protection of beachfront homes, significant maintenance cost savings to the County, and a stabilized beach providing enhanced nesting areas for Loggerhead Sea Turtles.

Board of Directors, Seated: Keith Ravazzoli, Frederick M. Derr, William Tarolli. Standing: Roland Carter, William Bartlett, Elton Kirkland, Thomas Ruth.

Soil Cement Step Revetment, 300 block N. Casey Key.

Frederick Derr & Company has received many awards. In 1989, the Myakka Chapter of the Florida Engineering Society honored Frederick M. Derr as the Engineer of the Year. In the 1990's, the company received the "Excellence in Civil Construction" award and an Outstanding Technical Achievement award for its coastal protection structures from the Florida Gulf Coast Chapter of Associated Builders and Contractors and from the Myakka Chapter of the Florida Engineering Society respectively.

Tallevast Road Improvements.

Stockholders, Thomas Donovan, Thomas Ruth, William Tarolli, Keith Ravazzoli, Roland Carter, Raymond Rogers, Gemma Fulton, Robert Tennant, Frederick M. Derr, Elton Kirkland, Russell Bonynge, and William Bartlett.

Frederick Derr & Company has had a long history of successful site development projects. A partial list includes Bollettieri Academy, Town Center at Schroeder-Manatee Ranch, Longwood Run, University Park, Bay Oaks, Misty Creek, Three Oaks, Stoneybrook, Bayfront Park for the City of Sarasota, Pomello Ranches, Harborage, Rosedale Highlands, Pinetree, Ventura Village, and Lakewood Ranch Corporate Park.

The Frederick Derr & Company team is proud of the part they have played in constructing golf courses at Venice Golf & Country Club, Waterlefe Country Club, Venetian Golf & River Club, Lakewood Ranch Golf & Country Club, and University Park Country Club Golf Course (holes 19-27).

Founded in 1961 by Wendel F. Kent, the company was originally known as Wendel Kent & Company. In October 1967, Frederick M. Derr returned home to Sarasota and joined the company after serving ten years in the U. S. Navy Civil Engineer Corps. He had been appointed to the U. S. Naval Academy in 1953 by Congressman James A. Haley. During the course of his military service, Derr earned three engineering degrees and became a Registered Engineer in New York, Louisiana, and Florida. Soon after Derr arrived, the company began to grow and several other enterprises were founded which eventually became separate companies.

The first was General Asphalt Company which produced and placed hot mix asphaltic concrete. This company eventually became an autonomous corporation known as Gator Asphalt Company and was subsequently sold in 1999.

In 1975, Kent & Derr, Inc. was formed to install underground cable for General Telephone (GTE). After ten successful years, the demand for this service subsided and the company employees and capital assets were absorbed by the other related companies.

By 1976, a need was seen to produce road construction materials, and Quality Aggregates came into being. Quality Aggregates was sold to Schroeder-Manatee Ranch in 1999.

On February 28, 1986, Derr acquired the majority interest in Wendel Kent & Company, and became its President and CEO. On March 1, 1991, the name of the company was changed to Frederick Derr & Company, Inc. In 2005, Keith Ravazzoli was elected President and COO, and Frederick Derr became the Chairman of the Board and CEO.

Under Derr's leadership, the company achieved an enviable reputation for providing benefits to its employees. It was one of the first construction companies in Sarasota to establish a drug-free work environment policy. The company has also been an industry leader in providing health insurance, a 401(k) retirement plan, an incentive bonus, payroll reviews, life insurance, disability insurance, safety bonus, paid holidays, and vacation pay.

The company has definitely left its mark in Sarasota and Manatee Counties over the years. Although it began as a small road building operation, it is known today for its expertise in heavy highway construction, site development, utility installation, coastal protection structures, and golf courses.

Over the years, the company earned a reputation for quality work at fair prices with on time completion of their projects, giving the company its motto. In the same vein, its Mission Statement cites a corporate philosophy that stresses the highest level of service to customers and maximum opportunity for employees.

THE GLASSER/SCHOENBAUM HUMAN SERVICES CENTER

The Glasser/Schoenbaum Human Services Center (recognized nationally in 2000 as a unique Management Service Organization) was established to improve the human services delivery system of Sarasota. It accomplishes its goal by making affordable services accessible to the disadvantaged members of the community and by reducing the operational expenses of the service providers to release more dollars for services.

The Center is named for its founder, Dr. Kay Glasser, and its first major contributors, Betty and Alex Schoenbaum, who contributed $450,000. Dr. Glasser's volunteer efforts brought private and public philanthropy together with a consortium of seven financial institutions for a 2.5 million dollar mortgage to construct the facility.

It took five years before the Center was opened in March, 1990. This 501(c) 3 facility consists of 13 office buildings and 17 co-located, non-profit human services agencies providing preventive and treatment services to individuals and families with child, spouse and/or substance abuse, mental, developmental, and health problems. In addition, literacy instruction, consumer credit counseling, legal assistance, volunteer opportunities and job training and job placement are available. The overriding goal of the Center and its agencies is to help low-income, disadvantaged people achieve self-sustaining, productive lives so they may become participating members of the community.

The Center has benefited the disadvantaged at-risk members of the community, the service providers, and the community as a whole.

The disadvantaged have benefited in several ways. Bus service at the entrance of the Center has made a range of low-cost services accessible to people with problems. Individuals and families who apply for financial assistance to the Department of Children and Families (located across the street from the Center) are referred to appropriate treatment services to help them become self-sustaining. Clients also benefit from an improvement in the quality of services because the physical proximity of the agencies enhances interaction and intercommunication between agencies and between agencies and their clients.

The Center has provided several benefits to the agencies. Since November 1993, when the mortgage was eliminated, the agencies have occupied their offices rent-free and pay minimal maintenance and utilities costs. The resultant savings of almost six million dollars have been made available for more services to an ever growing population. In addition, the agencies enjoy adequate free parking, meeting rooms in the conference building and an attractive campus.

Since November 2005, a Partnership for Service, Scholarship and Research with the University of South Florida Sarasota-Manatee has enhanced further the benefits the agencies have. The Center has become a teaching/learning/laboratory for Masters degree social work students who serve as interns providing clinical services to clients and who will conduct research, a function which the agencies have not had time to pursue. They will collect, organize, analyze and write up the findings detailing both the scope of human need and the benefits that each agency delivers to the community.

Sarasota as a whole has benefited because its quality of life depends upon the quality of life of its individuals, children and families. The availability and increased utilization of affordable and accessible services has contributed to that quality of life by rehabilitating and maintaining people as well-functioning, self-sustaining citizens who are able to contribute to the vitality of the community.

Dr. Kay E. Glasser, Mr. Alex Schoenbaum, Mrs. Betty Schoenbaum. May, 1995 at the Fifth Birthday Celebration of the opening of the Schoenbaum Human Services Center.

1997. The Center's Conference Center.

In order to ensure the future of the Center which is on City-owned land leased for a dollar a year for 99 years, Dr. Glasser's efforts since 1991 have been and are being dedicated to "growing" the Dr. Glasser Endowment Fund for the Human Services Center in the Community Foundation of Sarasota County. The income from this fund will avoid assessing the agencies to meet future capital needs of the buildings and permit them to continue to maximize their resources for the benefit of those who need their services.

GULF COAST COMMUNITY FOUNDATION OF VENICE

Leadership, Partnership, and Endowed Philanthropy

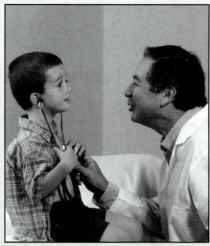

Gulf Coast Community Foundation of Venice builds strong communities through leadership, partnership, and endowed philanthropy. A public charity committed to improving quality of life in the communities it serves, it is the largest community foundation in Florida and among the 50 largest in the United States.

The Foundation began in 1995 with $85 million derived from the sale of Venice Hospital to Bon Secours Health System, Inc. Since then, the Foundation has grown to $226 million in assets as of June 2006, and in that time has awarded more than $62 million in grants in the areas of health and human services, arts and culture, education, civic affairs, and the environment.

The Foundation has evolved into a community leader and catalyst for positive change, able to forge partnerships across the public, private, and independent sectors to most effectively address emerging regional needs. As it keeps growing along with the needs of the community, the Foundation continues to make a remarkable impact throughout the Gulf Coast region.

Making a Difference

Befitting its origin, the Foundation has invested significantly in health and human services providers that have made lasting improvements in our community's health and well-being. The Foundation created and funded the original partnership with area hospitals that became the Community Health Improvement Partnership, or CHIP, a model community-based health initiative that empowers citizens to identify and address their community's health needs.

Education is another focus of the Foundation, with initiatives and grants designed to improve preschools through graduate institutions in our area. Through its Strategic Grantmaking in Education initiative, the Foundation has invested millions of dollars in Sarasota and Charlotte county schools to improve teaching and enhance student achievement. The Foundation helped establish and fund the Gold Seal project, which dramatically improved the quality of early childhood education in southern Sarasota County, while a partnership with Manatee Community College and the University of South Florida brought a four-year-degree program to Venice. Each year the Foundation awards more than $350,000 in scholarships to deserving local students who are pursuing higher education.

Preserving our region's unique landscape and environmental character has gained critical urgency in recent years, so the Foundation's Board of Directors added the environment to its grant-making focus areas in 2004. From pocket parks and recreational trails along the Intracoastal Waterway in Venice to a new preserve in Osprey with public access to Little Sarasota Bay, the Foundation partnered with organizations like Venice Area Beautification, Inc. and Sarasota Conservation Foundation to protect and enhance our community's coastal resources.

Other Foundation initiatives and grants have encouraged civic involvement. A partnership with Venice MainStreet and the City of Venice, for example, established the Children's Interactive Fountain in downtown Venice—a favored gathering place for residents and visitors of all ages. Foundation investments in area art centers, Historic Spanish Point, the Ringling Museum, and other local institutions have enriched the lives of citizens through the arts and cultural experiences.

Volunteers form the heart of the Foundation, with volunteer committees carefully reviewing grant proposals and scholarship applications and making recommendations to the volunteer Board of Directors. The Board consists of dedicated citizens who represent a broad range of interests and skills throughout the communities served by the Foundation.

Community Change Agent

Beyond awarding grants, the Foundation has become a community change agent. When a challenging real estate market priced homes out of reach of working families and individuals in the region, the Foundation purchased land in central Sarasota County to develop The Bridges, a community built on the principles of economic, social, and environmental sustainability.

To strengthen its nonprofit partners for the long term, the Foundation created Building Better Boards, a multiyear initiative that provides resources and training to improve board governance. More than 800 local board members have participated in the program, and several local consultants were trained and certified to continue educating the nonprofit community on good board governance. The Foundation also introduced new "green" grant guidelines in 2006 to empower its nonprofit partners to construct healthier, more sustainable buildings.

To ensure that resources keep pace with ever-increasing community needs, the Foundation promotes endowed philanthropy along the Gulf Coast. Working with generous donors and their professional advisors, the Foundation facilitates tax-advantaged gifts designed to achieve donors' charitable, financial, and family goals. Our community will continue to grow and change, but the Foundation will be here forever, ensuring that every gift has a lasting impact on the community.

HERALD-TRIBUNE MEDIA GROUP

Like the communities it serves, the Sarasota Herald-Tribune has grown and diversified in ways that seemed unimaginable in 1925, when its first editions rolled off the presses. What began as a small, morning daily has grown into the largest news operation in Southwest Florida. Multiple newsrooms contribute to six zoned editions each day, a 24-hour television channel, a Web site, a magazine group and other news and advertising ventures.

Anchoring the Herald-Tribune Media Group is its sleek, new headquarters on Sarasota's Main Street – just blocks from its original newsroom. The news organization's expansion reflects a marketplace that has changed dramatically since the paper's founder, David B. Lindsay, reached out to Sarasota County's 8,200 residents more than 80 years ago.

Lindsay first glimpsed Sarasota in 1918 from the cockpit of a World War I biplane. The young Army Air Corps lieutenant, based at a training field in Arcadia, was looking for a site for an auxiliary landing strip for training missions. He found one not far from the present Sarasota County Courthouse.

The Herald-Tribune Media Group's new headquarters blends Sarasota's architectural history with state-of-the-art technology.

After the war, Lindsay and his younger brother, Dick, second-generation newspapermen from Marion, Ind., saw an opportunity to launch a newspaper in Sarasota and published the first edition of the Sarasota Herald on Oct. 5, 1925, in what is now the Woman's Exchange consignment shop on Orange Avenue in downtown Sarasota. It became an afternoon publication in 1929. When the Lindsays acquired the competing publication, the Sarasota Tribune, in 1938, the Sarasota Herald became the Sarasota Herald-Tribune. The Herald-Tribune returned to morning publication in 1952, when the Lindsays introduced a new afternoon daily, the Sarasota Journal, which was published until 1982. That was the same year The New York Times Co. purchased the successful, family-owned newspaper from the paper's second publisher, David B. Lindsay Jr.

Soon thereafter, its new owners moved the Herald-Tribune's printing operations to a plant on University Parkway that would accommodate new high-speed color presses. They also began laying the groundwork for other innovations.

In 1995, the Herald-Tribune was one of the first newspapers in the country to launch a 24-hour television operation. Sarasota News Now (now SNN News 6) was created in partnership with Comcast Cable. The Web site was introduced in 1997.

The Herald-Tribune Media Group continues to grow with the region. In 2006, it vacated the cramped and retrofitted headquarters it had occupied for nearly 50 years on U.S. 41 and moved into its new, $27 million headquarters that blends Sarasota's architectural history with state-of-the-art technology.

In addition to the 850,000 people who live in Sarasota, Manatee, Charlotte and DeSoto counties, the Herald-Tribune Media Group's

SNN News 6, Southwest Florida's first 24-hour local news channel is fully integrated with the Herald-Tribune's print and online operations.

newspaper and television operations reach a worldwide audience through its award-winning Web site, heraldtribune.com.

Newsrooms in Bradenton, Lakewood Ranch, Sarasota, Venice, North Port, Englewood, Port Charlotte and Tallahassee regularly provide updates on news developments throughout the day to the company's multimedia offerings of local, national and international news, business, sports, features, entertainment listings and editorials.

The news organization's print, television and Internet operations also provide multiple platforms for advertisers to reach Southwest Florida's residents and visitors.

Technological advancements and the public's changing appetite for how and when it wants the latest headlines and community news will continue to bring about changes at the Herald-Tribune Media Group, but its mission to inform the communities it serves remains unchanged.

HI HAT RANCH

Cattle have played an important part in Sarasota's history. Pioneers let cattle roam the unfenced range and the cow hands were known as cow "hunters". As the county grew, so did the cattle industry. One of the largest ranches developed was the Hi Hat Ranch, begun in 1937 by Ross Beason, a New York businessman who acquired approximately 42 square miles and began many improvements. He erected 600 miles of barbed wire fence, 147 miles of roads and strung over 40 miles of telephone lines, including a private line into Sarasota. He dug 27 lakes and began a private airfield. Beason was said to have purchased the property largely for his son, Lt. Ross Beason, Jr., an Air Force pilot. However, after the death of his son during World War II, Ross, Sr. lost interest and sold the ranch to Herman E. Turner, a Bradenton construction engineer who had worked for Beason.

Herman Turner was the son of D.W. Turner of Bradenton and a Manatee County native. With his father, he was an operator of the Curry-Turner Construction Company and later formed his own business, H.E. Turner Construction Company, which built Army camps and airfields, among which was the Army Air Base in Venice.

Herman Turner bought the Hi Hat Ranch in a series of three transactions between 1943 and 1945, assuming total control of the ranch's 26,200 acres on April 1, 1945. The final 10,000 acres he purchased included a log ranch house, homes for workers, loading pens, dipping vats, 94 miles of roads and the unfinished airfield. Turner completed the airfield with a runway one-half mile long and over 200 feet in width. That last parcel also included over 3,400 acres of improved pasture and 4,000 acres of undeveloped land.

Dubbed "one of the most remarkable pieces of property in the state," the ranch was purchased exclusive of cattle, Beason already having disposed of his herd. Turner engaged Clyde Bailey, of Bailey and Sons from Oxford, Florida, to help restock the ranch. Turner also established a horse-breeding farm and took over the pine nursery that Beason had begun, planting over 1,500,000 pine seedlings.

Although Herman Turner's main focus was cattle, he participated in many community and business affairs. He was president of the local Cattlemen's Association and 1967 recipient of the Florida Cattlemen's Association Award for Faithful Service to the Cattle Industry of Florida. He helped found the Manatee County Community Chest, predecessor of United Way, and served two terms as president. Turner served as president of the Sarasota Livestock Association, first chairman of the Board of Supervisors of the Sarasota Soil Conservation District, president of the Florida State Quarterhorse Association, and was a developer of the Cowpen Slough Drainage District.

Governor Leroy Collins appointed Turner interim sheriff of Manatee County in 1960. He was a founding trustee of New College,

The distinctive Hi Hat brand graces the ranch office building. Photo by Allan Horton.

Herman Turner with champion quarterhorse "King Kleberg" purchased as a yearling from the King Ranch, Texas, about 1946.

a Presidential Counselor of Stetson University, and a member of the Vice Chancellors and Trustees Society of the University of the South. He chaired the Board of Island Bank, and served as director of Manatee National Bank, Westside National Bank and Barnett Bank of Manatee.

After running the ranch for nearly 15 years, Turner turned over daily management of the ranch to his older son, Latimer H. Turner, in the late 1950s. The ranch prospered under Lat Turner's direction. Due to the cyclical nature of the cattle business, Turner diversified by planting a 300-acre orange and grapefruit grove, harvesting timber, leasing parcels for sod and vegetable farming, and selling acreage for residential development.

In 1980, the City of Sarasota purchased 2,500 acres for a spray irrigation system for treating wastewater effluent from its sewage treatment plant, reducing the discharge of treated effluent into Sarasota Bay. A contract stipulation lets the ranch lease the spray field and use reclaimed water to irrigate improved pasture and citrus groves, saving millions of gallons of well water from aquifer withdrawal. About 500 acres of the leased spray irrigation parcel grows Floritam sod for residential yards under a sub-lease to Florida Premier Turf, Inc.

In 2003, Mote Marine Laboratory purchased 200 acres to establish an aquaculture park breeding and raising commercially valuable fish, including sturgeon for caviar.

Following Lat Turner's death in 1990, Herman Turner's grandsons, Chuck and Rick Turner, assumed management, with oversight from other family members, of the 10,000-plus-acre ranch. Today, Hi Hat Ranch continues to be a successful, diversified enterprise.

Fat cows, part of the large commercial beef cow herd at the Hi Hat Ranch, graze a lush ranch pasture. Photo by Allan Horton.

ICARD, MERRILL, CULLIS, TIMM, FUREN & GINSBURG, P.A.

For More Than Fifty Years, A Firm Commitment To You

In the summer of 1953, a young lawyer named Tom Icard was building a new solo law practice in a tiny downtown office in sleepy Sarasota, Florida. Tom's commitment to his clients, his high standards of integrity and proficiency and the growing needs of businesses and individuals in the area helped establish what is now one of the preeminent law practices in Southwest Florida.

Soon after opening his practice, Tom realized he would need a partner to assist with the quickly growing client base. It took just one meeting with Bill Merrill Sr. for both to realize they shared a passion for the law and common ideals that they could build upon for many years to come. Bill had just completed a stint in the Air Force as a judge advocate and was considering returning to his native Minnesota to practice law. But their meeting changed all those plans, and Icard's sole practice quickly blossomed into Icard & Merrill, housed in their own building at 2045 Main Street.

By 1958, a long-running period of expansion was under way. In order to meet the demands of a fast-growing client base, the firm asked James W. "Woody" Cullis, a former classmate of Mr. Icard practicing personal injury law in Miami, to join the firm. Within a few months, the firm expanded further when Curtis J. Timm joined the firm. A former classmate of Mr. Merrill's at the University of Minnesota, Mr. Timm had moved to Sarasota from Minneapolis. He was instantly recognizable in the Sarasota area because he wore a suit and tie, even in the warm and humid Florida weather. Over the next 20 years the firm continued to expand with the addition of Michael J. Furen, who added his expertise and reputation in real property law. Soon after, three new partners, Michael L. Foreman, Stephen D. Rees, and James E. Aker also joined the firm.

In the mid-1980s, the firm faced challenges on technological and economic fronts. Icard Merrill had already become the first law practice in Sarasota to utilize new computer technology to facilitate more efficient client services and firm administration. With all four founding partners having passed, partners Troy H. Myers Jr., F. Thomas Hopkins III, and Charles J. Bartlett were elected as shareholders. The firm sold its office building and instead leased space at 2033 Main Street, where the firm's downtown offices remain today.

With new leadership and operational systems in place, the firm sustained significant growth through the 80's and 90's. Joining as partners were highly regarded family lawyers Arthur D. Ginsburg and C. Eugene Jones and real estate attorneys J. Geoffrey Pflugner, Steven R. Greenberg and Paul D. Beitlich. Partner William W. Merrill III became the first son of a founding partner to join, and along with partner David M. Levin, gave the firm depth in the areas of land use, administrative and environmental law.

Contributing expertise in banking and commercial transactions, Robert E. Messick joined the firm, and Robert G. Lyons became a partner, bringing additional personal injury and insurance claims support. Thomas F. Icard Jr., the second son of a founding partner to join the firm, brought his construction law practice from Tampa. More recently, Partners John J. Waskom and Richard S. Webb joined the firm, practicing in real estate, mobile home park law and probate litigation. Jaime L. Wallace became the firm's first woman partner, integrating her successful family law practice.

Over the past 50 years, Icard Merrill has experienced steady and continued growth. The stability and cohesiveness of its founding members who practiced law together for more than 25 years, and the firm's dedication to increasing its depth and expertise in the varied disciplines of law have served the firm well in maintaining its preeminence in the Sarasota legal community. Currently, the firm employs more than 100 attorneys and staff and is one of the largest law firms in Southwest Florida, with offices in Sarasota, Manatee and Charlotte Counties.

Through it all, and in all aspects of the practice and community leadership, the lawyers of Icard Merrill have been committed to integrity and excellence. In the words of the firm's founding partner, Thomas F. Icard, the goal of Icard, Merrill, Cullis, Timm, Furen and Ginsburg, P.A., has always been—and continues to be—"to conduct a sophisticated law practice with an outstanding reputation for honesty and integrity as well as legal capability."

Main Street Office, Sarasota – 2007.

New Manatee County Office at Lakewood Ranch – 2007.

Former offices on Main Street in Sarasota, circa 1960's.

DOCTORS MARY AND ALLEN JELKS AND THE JELKS FAMILY FOUNDATION

Mary Irene Larson was born in Galva, Illinois, on May 23, 1929, near Altona, a small, Swedish farming town. Following elementary education in a one-room schoolhouse, she graduated from high school in Altona with a class of 16. After one year at Western Illinois University, Mary transferred to the University of Nebraska, where she earned pre-medical and medical degrees cum laude.

Allen Nathaniel Jelks Sr. was born August 2, 1930, in Macon, Georgia, the birthplace of his parents. He attended public schools in Ft. Lauderdale, where his parents and grandfather were Gold Coast pioneers. Allen received pre-medical training at Emory University in Atlanta and in 1955, graduated as valedictorian from Duke University School of Medicine.

Mary and Allen met in 1955 as pediatric interns at Johns Hopkins Hospital in Baltimore. From 1956 to 1958, Allen was the pediatrician at the U.S. Naval Submarine base in New London, Connecticut. Mary and Allen were married June 16, 1957, and completed their pediatric training at Johns Hopkins in 1959. They moved to Florida to join the faculty at Shands Teaching Hospital at the University of Florida.

Mary and Allen located their private pediatric practice in Sarasota because of its diverse cultural and recreational amenities. They maintained their practice from 1960 until their retirement in 1985, serving as staff members at Sarasota Memorial Hospital and members of the Sarasota County Medical Association.

During her 25 years in practice, Mary became a Board Certified Allergist. She continues to collect pollens and molds daily from her rooftop monitoring station, identifying samples and reporting her findings to local media and national allergy groups. Mary has authored two allergy books and in 1997, she was honored as Allergist of the Year by the Florida Allergy and Immunology Society, where she is affectionately known as "Florida Queen of the Pollens." Mary also received the 2006 Outstanding Volunteer Clinical Faculty Award by the American Academy of Allergy, Asthma, and Immunology.

Since the 1960s, Allen has been a leader in the Rotary Club of Sarasota Bay, where he received the Distinguished Service Award. Allen is a fervent believer that railroads are a superior transportation option and works to maintain railroad connectivity to southwest Florida. He is active in the National Railway Historical Society, United Way, YMCA, and the American Heart Association. Both Mary and Allen are members of the First United Methodist Church in Sarasota.

Mary and Allen are devoted to environmental conservation, particularly in Sarasota County. In 2003 they were awarded the Community Environmental Service Award; the Environmentalist of the Year Award by Sarasota County; and named the Environmental Heroes of the Year by the Growth-Restraint and Environmental Organization.

Mary and Allen are proud of their four children, who grew up in Sarasota.

Helen Jelks King and her husband, Chris, are optometrists in Englewood. The King's older son, Benjamin, is a music theory and political science major at Florida State University; Bryan is a government education major at the University of North Florida.

Allen, Jr., is an attorney in Panama City, where he and his wife Debbie (Stephens) have a private law practice.

Howard Jelks is a federal fish biologist in Gainesville. His wife Lisa (Spinella), also from Sarasota, edits academic journals at the University of Florida.

Alice Jelks Lezcano, her husband Edgar, and son Daniel, operate a wholesale plant nursery near Pensacola.

In 1994, the family formed the Jelks Family Foundation, Inc. to help preserve Florida's unique and natural spaces. Because the Myakka River has been an important recreational resource to the Jelks family, the Foundation helped Sarasota County acquire 615 acres, known as The Jelks Preserve, protecting 1 1/2 miles along this wild and scenic river.

The Jelks family members each support the diverse communities in which they reside, and are focused on conserving natural resources in a state that is experiencing rapid environmental change. Mary and Allen Jelks believe "Sarasota is a view of Paradise" and work diligently to give back to the community.

Dr. Allen N. Jelks, Sr. and Dr. Mary L. Jelks

Allen, Jr. and Debbie Jelks

Howard and Lisa Jelks

Alice, Daniel and Edgar Lezcano

Chris, Helen, Benjamin and Bryan King

This history made possible through a gift by the family of Katharine Nau

KERKERING BARBERIO, Established 1972

"Celebrating 35 Years of Excellence"

Kerkering, Barberio & Co., Certified Public Accountants, was founded in 1972 by Dick Kerkering and Allan Barberio. At the time, the small office located on St. Armand's Circle was comprised of three staff members – Kerkering, Barberio and one receptionist/secretary.

After many years on Ringling Boulevard, Kerkering Barberio moved to its current location, the Courthouse Centre building at 1990 Main Street, Sarasota, Florida, in 2005. Occupying the entire eighth floor, the transition entailed bringing a total of 120 employees together into 30,000 square feet of space with additional staff members working at the Northern Trust Bank building located at 6320 Venture Drive in Lakewood Ranch.

Throughout the years, Kerkering, Barberio & Co. expanded its services from its humble beginnings in tax and accounting services to a multifaceted business and financial organization. As the largest full-service, independent accounting firm on the southwest coast of Florida, its wide array of services now include audit, business valuation, employee retirement planning, estate and trust planning, financial planning, financial advisory services, healthcare advisory services, litigation support services, real estate support services, and technology solutions. Moreover, with its international taxation expertise, the firm attracts clients from all over the world.

Kerkering Barberio has the expertise to provide financial and technological solutions for a wide range of industries. Clients range from small non-profit organizations to multimillion-dollar manufacturing entities. With a dedicated team of professionals possessing industry-specific knowledge, they can quickly respond to client needs with staff who know their clients' business.

Today, Kerkering, Barberio & Co., Certified Public Accountants, has three sister companies to house all combined services under one roof known as "your one-stop resource for financial, consulting and information services." These companies are Kerkering Barberio Financial Services, Inc.; KB Pension Services, Inc.; and SouthTech Solutions. In short, as a group of several companies, they are simply referred to as *Kerkering Barberio*.

Assured of the opportunity to continue to flourish in the future by satisfying the needs of individuals and businesses alike, Kerkering Barberio is recognized for providing the highest quality of services and products. Equally important is their commitment to the community with many shareholders and members of management serving various non-profit organizations as well as maintaining strong involvement in the local Chambers of Commerce.

Now retired, Dick Kerkering and Allan Barberio, the founding fathers, built the firm with "excellence." Kerkering Barberio still believes today that successful relationships are built on trust and excellent service, a tradition that has held constant over the past 35 years. For that reason, the firm keeps its focus on its ties to the community and the people who have helped it grow.

Kerkering Barberio's mission is to meet the business and financial needs of its clients. They value client relationships and the community in which they live and grow and are constantly striving to enhance client service and their presence on the west coast of Florida. Kerkering Barberio is proud to be a part of Sarasota's significant history and looks to another successful quarter century ahead.

To learn more about Kerkering Barberio and its market, visit them at www.kbgrp.com or see them in person at their offices in the Courthouse Centre.

LONGINO RANCH, INC.

From Turpentine & Rosin to Cattle, Timber & Citrus

Our story starts with John Green Lewis, a long time turpentine operator, financier and banker who migrated to Florida from North Carolina in the early 1880s. Lewis had considerable knowledge of lands and timber in Florida and in 1934, during the depths of the Great Depression, he financed his son-in-law, Berryman T. Longino, in the establishment of a turpentine operation in Sarasota County. Together they purchased 12,000 acres in the eastern part of the county which contained one of the few remaining stands of virgin slash pine in south Florida. An existing railroad through the property further enhanced the purchase of this land. When the Tampa Southern Railroad built a connector from Sarasota to Fort Ogden in DeSoto County, the company built several section houses and a siding near Sugar Bowl Road (now SR 72). It was called Sidell after a railroad town in Illinois.

In 1934, Longino established a corporation named Sidell, Inc. and constructed a turpentine camp consisting of turpentine still, thirty or more homes for camp labor, a church, a schoolhouse and a commissary. He imported laborers from throughout Florida and Georgia to operate the plant. The products, turpentine and rosin, called naval stores, were shipped to Jacksonville and Savannah to be sold on the world market. Some turpentine was sold locally to paint and hardware stores. In the late 1930s, Longino opened a second operation near the community of Bee Ridge in partnership with L. F. Grubbs. Workers from the Bee Ridge camp tapped pine trees leased from the Palmer family, stretching from the communities of Fruitville to Osprey. After World War II, the naval stores industry declined due to cheaper synthetics developed during the war, increased labor costs and a shortage of productive pine timber. By 1952, the turpentine operations ceased.

Buster Longino at the groves peeling grapefruit for two of his grandsons, Forrest and William St. Pierre.

Sidell, Inc. was eventually inherited by the Longino children – Mary Lucille Purvis, Jesse Elizabeth Curry, Shirley Minton and B. T. "Buster" Longino. In 1950, Buster Longino, a U.S. Navy veteran and a graduate of the University of Florida with a degree in forestry, began to raise cattle on the family land. In 1951, Buster married Martha Jane Mulhollen of St. Petersburg and settled in the Pine Shores area of Sarasota. Buster and Jane had three children, Sarah Jane, Jack and Rebecca, all of whom graduated from local schools. In 1960, Sidell, Inc. acquired Buster's cattle operation, elected him president of the company and changed the corporate name to Longino Ranch, Inc. in honor of B. T. Longino, Sr. Soon after formation of the Longino Ranch, the corporation sold one third of its land and developed the remaining lands into improved grasses, timberland and native pastures.

Over the years, the cattle herd increased and the stock improved, grazing upon upgraded pastures. A 40-year program of pine timber management produced saw logs, plywood, poles and pulpwood in a sustainable rotation of harvesting and natural re-seeding. Through successful game management practices, abundant wildlife inhabits the ranch.

In 1986, the ranch joined Shirley Longino Minton's in purchasing an 800-acre citrus grove in St. Lucie County. The partnership, Treasure Coast Groves, in 1991 developed 300 acres of citrus at the Longino Ranch in Sarasota.

In 2002, family members realized that environmentally sensitive lands surrounding the ranch were disappearing at an alarming rate.

The structure of the mitigation bank looking west.

In order to preserve some of these lands for future generations, the extended Longino family joined Sarasota County and the Southwest Florida Water Management District in placing a conservation easement on approximately half of the Longino Ranch. The purpose of this easement is to prohibit development of this property in perpetuity.

The conservation easement was followed, in 2005, by the establishment at Longino Ranch of the first mitigation bank in the Myakka River watershed. A mitigation bank provides a state and federally regulated vehicle in which developers are able to reduce the environmental impact of their projects by purchasing credits to restore and conserve sensitive lands within their local watershed. This melding of environmental preservation and economic benefits for ranch/farm lands serves as a model for providing viable options for the maintenance of family agricultural holdings in Florida.

Converting 8,000 acres of raw flatwoods lands into a productive, sustainable, environmentally friendly ranch has been a lifelong quest of Buster Longino with the aid and inspiration of his wife, Jane, their children and the rest of the family. It is his desire that this land will remain in agribusiness with large areas of native habitat preserved for future generations to enjoy.

In honor of his lifelong contributions to conservation and agriculture in the State of Florida, Buster Longino was inducted into the Florida Agriculture Hall of Fame in February 2007.

THE MABRY CARLTON RANCH

The Mabry Carlton Ranch Inc. embodies one pioneer Florida family's history. History is a family tradition, dating back to 1066 when the Carltons came to England with William the Conqueror. The Carltons emigrated to America and Massachusetts in 1636, and Thomas Carlton fought in the Revolutionary War. Moving south, the local branch of the far-flung family settled in Florida eight generations ago and since then has farmed and raised cattle and citrus throughout the state. Carltons fought in the third Seminole War and during the Civil War.

T. Mabry Carlton Jr. headed the ranch until his death in an airplane accident in 1989. At that time, his widow Barbara and their two daughters, Lisa Carlton Robinson and Kim Carlton Bonner, assumed the reins. They run the day-to-day operation of the ranch and all three live on the ranch. Lisa and her husband, attorney Rob Robinson, have two daughters, Carlton and Savell, and a son, Mabry. Kim and her husband, firefighter/paramedic Tom Bonner, have a daughter, Katie. The 17,000-acre ranch in eastern Sarasota County covers over 25 square miles of cattle and citrus country through which Big Slough runs. Its cattle are branded with the wineglass, a brand used by three generations.

Like other pioneers, the Carltons raised cattle on open ranges - native pasturage along river valleys and interior flatwoods. Carlton family "cow camps" were scattered at Micco Bluffs on the Kissimmee, Sidell, the Big Slough camp, and Hickory Ford between the Peace and Myakka rivers. During the era of cattle drives north to Brandon and south to the Pine Island port of Punta Rassa, open ranges prevailed in Florida. Even in the mid-20th century, traffic was routinely interrupted by grazing cattle.

Although the Carlton family enjoyed traditional cattle drives, Mabry's grandfather, Thomas N. Carlton, foresaw the day when Florida's ranges would no longer be open. He was among the first cattlemen to purchase land, trucks, and barbed wire. Mandatory fencing closed the range in the late 1940s. When Mabry was 13, he helped remove State Road 72 stopgaps, replacing them with miles of barbed-wire fence - a measure not required by state law until a year later. In another innovative venture, the family ranch became one of the first Sarasota operations to develop groves in flatwood areas previously considered unsuitable for citrus.

As the family enterprises increasingly confronted contemporary demands, the Carltons adopted new approaches to traditional agribusiness. Thomas N. Carlton bought one of the first portable electric generators to drive electric cutters for sheep shearing. After Mabry graduated from Stetson University and pursued postgraduate study in citrus at Florida Southern College, education became a key influence in the Carlton family with both Lisa and Kim becoming Stetson graduates. Kim holds a Master of Arts degree in History from the University of West Florida and both daughters earned law degrees.

Today, the family continues to stress modern agribusiness techniques begun by Mabry. The ranching operations have diversified into other areas such as timber harvesting and sod production. Through an aggressive fence-building program in conjunction with an ecologically balanced land management operation, the cattle roundup time has been cut in half.

Barbara Carlton was awarded the "Farmer of the Year Award" by the Sarasota County Soil and Water District and was named "Woman of the Year in Agriculture" by the State of Florida in 2001. The family also has maintained its commitment to preserving the environment by entering into a conservation easement with the Southwest Florida Water Management District to ensure that vast portions of native rangelands will remain pristine in perpetuity.

In addition to operating his ranch, Mabry stressed the importance of community service. He was actively involved in numerous state and local government positions and served as a Sarasota County Commissioner from 1980 until his death in 1989, where his contributions included public acquisition of the Ringling-MacArthur tract, now renamed the T. Mabry Carlton Jr. Memorial Reserve. Lisa served two terms in the Florida House of Representatives and nine years in the State Senate. Kim serves as a Sarasota County Judge.

The Carlton family continues to operate the ranch in one of the nation's fastest growing counties. Through continued community and political involvement, the family hopes to instill in the next generation a dedication to the land and an ecological sensitivity to the needs of the ever-growing urban population. By combining these goals, they hope the next generation will engage modern practices so that Florida's historic agribusiness industry will remain a viable force.

MATTHEWS, EASTMOORE, HARDY, CRAUWELS & GARCIA

The lawyers and staff of Matthews, Eastmoore, Hardy, Crauwels & Garcia are pleased to join this celebration of Sarasota history and look forward to being an important part of Sarasota County's bright future.

Combining more than one hundred years of legal experience in Sarasota, attorneys A. Lamar Matthews, Jr., Theodore C. Eastmoore, Arthur S. Hardy, and Martin Garcia founded Matthews Eastmoore in 1991 to continue and enhance their work as trial and governmental lawyers. By limiting their practice to civil litigation and public body law, the lawyers of Matthews Eastmoore are able to provide their clients with the highest quality legal representation before state and federal courts throughout Florida. The firm has had the privilege of representing many of the area's law firms and lawyers who find themselves involved personally in litigation.

The roots of Matthews Eastmoore run deep in the Sarasota community. Senior partner Lamar Matthews is a native Sarasotan who has earned his reputation as one of the area's preeminent trial lawyers through over forty years of successful work in Sarasota and Manatee County courtrooms. Mr. Matthews is actively involved in all aspects of the firm's litigation practice and has served as general counsel to the School Board of Sarasota County for twenty years.

Martin Garcia concentrates primarily on commercial law issues. Mr. Garcia regularly prosecutes and defends claims involving business disputes, contract, real estate, and construction matters. Mr. Garcia regularly practices in both state and federal court and before the American Arbitration Association.

Ted Eastmoore, Pat Crauwels, Keith DuBose, and Marjorie Henry center their practices on prosecuting and defending claims of negligence, wrongful death, and professional malpractice. Representing both plaintiffs and defendants gives the firm's lawyers the advantage of having broad and diverse experience allowing them to better represent individual clients.

Art Hardy takes primary responsibility for the firm's governmental practice. Mr. Hardy provides the daily legal services needed by the county's largest employer, the School Board of Sarasota County. Alan Roddy also concentrates his practice on governmental law, representing clients appearing before public boards on a variety of land use issues and litigating issues relating to local government. Additionally, the firm has represented numerous public bodies over the past several years including Sarasota County, the Sarasota Sheriff's Department, the Office of the County Attorney, Sarasota's County Administrator, the Sarasota-Manatee Airport Authority, the Palm Beach Airport Authority, the City of North Port, and the City of Gainesville.

Although proud of their accomplishments in the courtroom, the lawyers of Matthews Eastmoore recognize that the practice of law involves a public service and trust which does not end at the courthouse door. The firm, therefore, has encouraged its members to take an active role in community and Bar activities. The firm has produced two presidents of The Florida Bar Young Lawyers' Division, four members of that Division's Board of Governors, a president of the Sarasota County Bar, three presidents of the Sarasota County Bar Association Young Lawyers' Division, a chair of the Florida Bar's General Practice Section, a president of the Judge John M. Scheb American Inn of Court, a president of the Sarasota/Bradenton Chapter of the American Board of Trial Advocates, and several members and chairs of both the Judicial Nominating Commissions for the Second District Court of Appeal and the Twelfth Judicial Circuit Court. Members of the firm have also served on the Board of Trustees of Manatee Community College, and the Sarasota Housing Authority as well as numerous charitable foundations. Mr. Matthews was also privileged to serve as general counsel to Governor Bob Graham in 1980, and Mr. Hardy was similarly honored to serve as counsel to Senator Bob Graham in Washington in 1999.

Since its inception, Matthews Eastmoore has protected the legal rights of thousands of individuals, businesses, and governmental institutions in state and federal courts throughout our state. The firm remains committed to continuing to serve its clients and the Sarasota community.

The hiring of a lawyer is an important decision that should not be based solely on advertisements. Please ask us to send you free written information about our qualifications and experience.

MANATEE COMMUNITY COLLEGE

Celebrating 50 Years — and Just Beginning

Manatee Community College (MCC) is celebrating its 50th anniversary along with all those who contribute to and benefit from this important community asset.

Over five decades, as Manatee and Sarasota counties have developed, the College has kept pace, even while remaining committed to its original purpose—providing accessible, quality education. Staying focused has led to success: MCC is the first choice of more than half of the area's high school graduates for higher education.

MCC's academic performance attracted Dr. Sarah H. Pappas, who became the College's fourth president in 1997.

"The main reason I came to MCC was its reputation for quality," Pappas said. "We are known for our graduates' success, and our faculty members deserve the credit."

The MCC story began in the mid-1950s when civic leaders and educators in Manatee and Sarasota counties saw an opportunity to bring higher education to local residents. On Sept. 17, 1957, the Florida Legislature established Manatee Junior College as the area's first public institution of higher education. The College was charged with three missions: To offer a university-parallel curriculum, to provide vocational-professional courses to meet the needs of the community, and to provide a program of continuing education for adults.

Dr. Samuel R. Neel Jr., a dean at Florida State University, was named MJC's first president and immediately met a challenge. Legislators had approved MJC but did not plan to meet again for two years to enact funding. The delay was not acceptable to MJC supporters. State Sen. Ed Price and Neel went to Tallahassee to appeal for a prompt solution. Their strategy worked, and the new College was launched.

MCC's open-door policy makes a college education possible for many students who otherwise would be left out. From the first busy registration, it was clear that MJC met a vital need. The number of students expected for fall term 1958 was 250, but 502 enrolled. A scramble for borrowed space ensued, and the first classes were held in an aging high school in downtown Bradenton.

In September of 1959, excited students and faculty moved to the present 100-acre campus in southwest Bradenton. That same year, 270 senior citizens attended a lecture at the Palmetto Trailer Park, thus beginning the Center for Corporate and Community Development, the College's flourishing noncredit division that serves more than 30,000 people annually in workforce, professional development, personal enrichment and traffic safety classes.

The College remains in the vanguard in state and national arenas. MJC was Florida's first community college to receive national accreditation for its Nursing Program and was a model for other colleges, including Purdue University. Ours remains one of the nation's most respected nursing programs. In response to a current critical shortage of nurses, the Nursing Program was expanded with the help of area hospitals and state grants.

Nursing graduates are joined by radiography, physical therapist assistant, occupational therapy assistant and dental hygiene graduates who excel on required state and national examinations. Programs respond to local needs.

MCC President Dr. Sarah H. Pappas with students.

One example: A group of dentists from Sarasota and Manatee counties partnered with Pappas to persuade legislators to fund a local dental hygienist program. Today, dental hygienists train in a state-of-the-art facility at MCC Bradenton that also houses a Dental Hygiene Clinic where the community obtains low-cost oral hygiene treatments.

In another progressive step, MJC welcomed its first African-American students in 1962—well before the passage of the Civil Rights Act of 1964 and the Voting Rights Act of 1965. Dr. Charles Jackson, a Palmetto resident and one of the first students to integrate MJC, later described the greeting by students, faculty and administrators as "a heartwarming experience."

The College's ongoing commitment to diversity is evident at the Family Heritage House Museum, a resource center for the preservation and study of African-American achievements and the only museum of its kind at a community college.

At rapid pace, the new College established more "firsts." The Florida Community College Activities Association was born at a meeting of community college presidents, called by MJC, to standardize competitive team sports. The Lancers baseball program, started in 1959, has gone on to enjoy national ranking with many student-athletes advancing to university and professional teams. In addition to men's baseball, competitive teams today include men's basketball and women's volleyball and softball.

In a community known for embracing the arts, a local arts enthusiast some 40 years ago donated seed money for the Samuel R. Neel Auditorium (later named the Neel Performing Arts Center). The 837-seat center is a favorite venue for College and community concerts and productions.

Today's fine and performing arts disciplines include art, film, humanities, mass communication, music and theatre. A fine art gallery draws thousands of visitors, and a high-profile film program recently was named among "the world's best film schools" in the two-year college category by *MovieMaker* magazine.

Expanding its reach, the College adapts to new learning styles and changing economic climates. College presidents Dr. Wilson F. Wetzler and Dr. Stephen Korcheck, who followed Neel, oversaw additions of buildings, academic programs and student activities.

In 1985, Manatee Junior College was renamed Manatee Community College, a reflection of its growing role in workforce training and community outreach. The same year, Gov. Bob Graham dedicated MCC's 100-acre campus in south Venice. College classes had been taught in the Venice area since 1973, and the establishment of a permanent campus near the Venice-North Port-Englewood junction signaled MCC's commitment to the emerging area.

MCC opened its third location, the Center for Innovation and Technology, in fast-growing Lakewood Ranch, east of I-75, in 2003. The Center features a high-tech auditorium, computer classrooms, meeting rooms, videoconferencing capability, a spacious catering facility and a mobile laptop lab.

During Pappas' tenure, MCC properties have been renovated and recognized for their functional design and aesthetic appeal. Students and faculty members give the improved campus settings high marks for being conducive to learning.

The Foundation for Manatee Community College Inc., formed 25 years ago, has grown to an endowment of more than $40 million and oversees nearly 400 scholarship funds.

Credit and noncredit students take classes at all three campuses and locations throughout the communities. While traditional classrooms remain popular, online learners are increasing. Students can log on to register for and take classes, get grades, get tutored, check out books, pay bills and take care of virtually all College-related business—on their own schedule.

"Innovation" is a key concept propelling today's College leaders. Faculty members took the lead in infusing 21st century skills throughout the curriculum.

Creative thinking was required when the state asked community colleges for solutions to a critical shortage of qualified teachers. MCC responded quickly, offering a year-long alternative certification program for teacher preparation designed for adults with a minimum of a bachelor's degree outside the field of education.

Fifty years ago, three objectives for the College were stated: Full community support, an outstanding faculty and outstanding students.

Today, there is abundant evidence that all three goals were achieved. The communities served by the College provide outstanding support for its programs and budgetary needs. More than 9,000 students are enrolled in credit courses, and faculty and students earn top honors in academics, athletics, civic and professional endeavors.

Thirty-one thousand students have graduated from MCC. Many with A.A. degrees advance to the University of South Florida to pursue their baccalaureate degree. MCC graduates continue at other state universities in Florida and at prestigious establishments including Harvard University, University of Miami, Emory University and University of Pennsylvania.

1997: MCC's four presidents - left to right: Dr. Wilson Wetzler, Dr. Samuel Neel Jr., Dr. Sarah H. Pappas and Dr. Stephen Korcheck.

1958: Touring the future site of Manatee Junior College.

Fall 2004: MCC graduates.

Students interested in quickly entering the workforce have a choice of more than 20 associate in applied science (A.A.S.) and associate in science (A.S.) degree programs. Career degree graduates have an outstanding placement rate in jobs related to their degrees.

MCC alumni include teachers, doctors, publishers, attorneys, reporters, actors and professionals satisfying the workforce needs of local businesses and enterprises in far-flung locales.

Pappas offers a prediction: "As long as MCC holds true to its core values, and keeps its inspired and innovative faculty and staff and a culture of teamwork, the next 50 years will be even more amazing at Manatee Community College."

This history made possible through a gift by Walter Serwatka and Constance Holcomb

MICHAEL SAUNDERS

Cementing Her Family's Legacy of Excellence, Committment and Success

Of a young Michael Saunders, her late father, Frank Mayers, once said: "Michael can throw a cast net better than she can dance." Mayers was referring to his eldest offspring's considerable talents as a fisherman, gleaned from idyllic summers spent growing up at the water's edge on north Longboat Key. He could just as easily have been forecasting her future as a business entrepreneur. Few have cast a wider net - or wielded more influence - over Southwest Florida real estate than Michael Saunders.

If a fisherman needs a little luck and a lot of skill, the same could be said about Saunders' success in piloting Michael Saunders & Company from a single office on St. Armands Circle to a regional network of 18 full-service real estate offices. Luck had everything to do with inheriting her father's sales ability and people skills; her mother's values, grace and sense of style; and living in a place she loves. The rest involved skill and a passionate determination to build a successful enterprise by adhering to her vision, values and sharply intuitive business sense.

Michael Saunders.

Michael Saunders, seated left, and Drayton Saunders.

Thanks to a lifetime spent in the community and the 30-plus years running her company, Saunders has sat squarely at the epicenter of one of Florida's fastest growing and most affluent regions. No change in the Sunshine State has come at a more dizzying pace than the growth of Southwest Florida over the past ten years. A barometer of that growth is the parallel expansion of Michael Saunders & Company. In 1995, the company had an annual sales volume of just over $274 million. Ten years later volume had exploded 11-fold, rocketing upward to the tune of $3.07 billion.

Nothing about her company's phenomenal growth has been accidental. It was never about luck, or being in the right place at the right time - although Saunders' native-born understanding of the market didn't hurt. Growing up along the coast helped her identify a major gap in the real estate market—a niche that was being woefully underserved at the time. She set out to bridge that gap by focusing mainly on selling upscale waterfront properties. At the same time, she provided buyers and sellers something they didn't automatically expect from a real estate company—outstanding customer service, uncompromising integrity and cutting-edge marketing. Saunders also created an office environment that reflected the image and quality of the upper-end waterfront homes she intended to sell.

John Savarese's 100-foot steamer, "*The Mistletoe*." Photo by Felix Pinard courtesy, Florida State Archives.

Saunders, who appreciates a good adage, would approve of being called "a chip off the old block." Her model of a career woman was an aunt who sold advertising and wrote for the former *Evening Independent* in St. Petersburg. But it was her father and a great-uncle, John Savarese, who invested her - she strongly believes - with drive, entrepreneurial spirit and a passion for sales and marketing.

In 1872, Savarese, a native of Naples, Italy, came to America as a

John Savarese on Longboat Key about 1925.

10-year-old. He joined his brother, Louis, in the fish business in Savannah, Georgia before eventually moving to Tampa, where he established a wholesale fish business in 1885.

Successful from the outset, Savarese employed up to 550 men after only 10 years in business. His fleet consisted of 15 sailing vessels, 150 small craft and a large steamer, the *Mistletoe* - which provided the first reliable scheduled transportation between Tampa and Sarasota in the late 1800's. Savarese was one of the first industrial leaders of Tampa and highly influential in the economy and social progress of the city. The list of his professional and civic affiliations included many years as Italian consul at Tampa; two terms on the Tampa City Council; member of the Tampa Board of Trade; director of the Citizens Bank and Trust Company; and president of the Florida Fish Dealers Association. Savarese also was a co-founder of the prestigious Tampa Yacht Club.

Saunders, too, has seen years of hard work rewarded with equivalent success. Entering her fourth decade as the dynamic force behind a real estate enterprise that employs more than 500 sales associates and an administrative staff of over 200, Saunders is poised to propel the company toward a new level of international distinction. Already well-known worldwide for representing the finest properties on the Gulf Coast, Saunders recently cast her net beyond Southwest Florida to represent luxury properties Punta Cana in the Dominican Republic and Eleuthera in the Bahamas.

After receiving twin degrees in history and psychology from Florida State University, Saunders became a history teacher at Manatee High School before joining the Manatee County Court system as a juvenile court counselor. Then, as a single mother, she sought a career change that would provide greater independence and financial security. Real estate seemed the perfect solution. The rest, as they say, is history.

Saunders' longstanding involvement in the Southwest Florida community recalls the civic legacy of John Savarese. Her groundbreaking achievements in real estate notwithstanding, Saunders never lost her love for teaching or let business diminish her strongly held conviction that one person can make the difference in the life and welfare of a child. Her philanthropic activities largely involve underwriting programs that protect, educate or otherwise enhance the quality of life for children and young adults. Her causes include Boys & Girls Clubs of Sarasota, Child Protection Center, Florida Studio Theater's Children Write-A-Play Program, the Education Foundation of Sarasota County, the Florida State University Foundation, Junior Achievement, the Manatee County Schools Foundation, the University of South Florida Foundation and the Foundation for Manatee Community College.

Her commitment to the environment - plus her love of fishing, the sea and the natural beauty of the native Florida landscape - has led Saunders to serve as honorary board member Mote Marine Laboratory, and as chairman of the Board at the the Marie Selby Botanical Garden.

Whether Michael Saunders ultimately decides to trade-in her real estate hat for a fly-fishing visor remains to be seen. If she does, she won't have to cast her net any further than her own family tree to christen a successor. Son Drayton has come of age, learned the business from the ground up and someday will assume the mantle of leadership.

Drayton, now 34, flexed his own entrepreneurial muscle shortly after finishing his formal education. While studying at Colgate University, he refined a passion for Latin America culture that had begun in high school. His altruistic nature had prompted him to roll up his sleeves and go to work with Amigos de las Americas, a non-denominational, non-profit group that focuses on solving basic problems in poor rural communities. He helped build homes for teachers in Costa Rica and worked in conjunction with CARE International to improve basic sanitation, health and hygiene practices in the highlands of Ecuador.

Prior to joining Michael Saunders & Company, Drayton spent eight years in Santiago, Chile, where he opened the country's first bagel and coffee shop. After selling the business in 2003, he returned to Sarasota and assumed the position of president of the title and mortgage divisions of Michael Saunders & Company. Since then, he has grown the combined divisions from 6 to a total of 23 full-time professionals. At the same time he has re-vamped different elements of the company's core services, focusing on technology, marketing and training.

Like his mother, Saunders pursues a plethora of community commitments in spite of escalating corporate responsibilities. He is involved in the Downtown Partnership, the Sarasota Chamber of Commerce, The Dyslexia Foundation, and the Community Foundation of Sarasota County, serving on the boards of each. He is also one of five founding members - and the current chairman - of the Young Professional's Group, an organizational offshoot of the Greater Sarasota Chamber of Commerce. The YPG's mission is to help its members establish professional relationships, become politically and philanthropically active, and contribute to the economic development of the region. Thanks to the efforts of Saunders and other founders, the YPG claims more than 800 active constituents.

The ties that bind Drayton to Michael and Michael to the generations before her are more than just a few strands of shared DNA. Common values, the pursuit of excellence in their chosen careers and an abiding sense of giving back to the community are the real bonds that unite the family's past with its future. To Michael Saunders, "values" means building relationships based on trust, communication and integrity; "excellence" means leading the industry with forward-thinking initiatives and leaving it better off; and "giving back" means making Southwest Florida better for everyone in exchange for the wonderful life it has bestowed on her and her family.

MOTE MARINE LABORATORY

Sarasota's Window to the Sea

Mote Marine Laboratory is renowned for excellence in marine science research and education. More than 200 professional staff members participate in more than 250 funded research projects locally and around the world.

In 1955, Dr. Eugenie Clark was wooed to quiet, sparsely populated Charlotte County by William H. Vanderbilt and his wife, Anne, who wanted to start a marine laboratory. The Lab, first known as the Cape Haze Marine Laboratory, began with a small, wooden building, a dock and a shark pen with Dr. Clark as director. Dr. Clark later became a renowned shark expert nicknamed "the Shark lady" for her studies of sharks at the Cape Haze lab.

By 1960, growth mandated expansion of the Cape Haze Lab. Meanwhile, Sarasota county, city and Chamber of Commerce officials had mounted a campaign to attract a research facility to Sarasota which resulted in the Cape Haze Marine Laboratory moving eventually to Siesta Key near Midnight Pass. With the move to Siesta Key completed, visiting scientists from prestigious institutions traveled to Sarasota to take advantage of the lab's facilities and collaborate with its scientists.

In 1965, Dr. Clark left the lab and was succeeded by two interim directors, Dr. Sylvia Earle and Dr. Charles Breder.

At this juncture, William R. Mote stepped forward. Bill Mote was a Tampa native and a successful transportation industry executive who wanted in his lifetime to do something worthwhile connected with the sea. When he learned of the lab, he turned his drive and vision to making Cape Haze Marine Laboratory thrive.

Bill Mote recruited Dr. Perry Gilbert, renowned professor of zoology at Cornell University, to transform the lab from a field station to a major research center. A citizens committee helped map the lab's future and in 1967, the lab's name was changed to Mote Marine Laboratory in honor of its major benefactor.

By 1975, it was clear that Mote Marine Laboratory had to move from its Siesta Key location. Initial plans called for relocation to Charlotte County, but as word spread that Sarasota was going to lose the research facility, community leaders rallied to find a suitable waterfront location for Mote.

Property was identified on City Island and Sarasota City Manager Ken Thompson worked closely with then-State Representative Bob Johnson, Bill Mote and Perry Gilbert to make the new site a reality. In May 1977, the Lab moved to City Island. Work later started on a marine science education center, now known as Mote Aquarium.

With the lab settled in its new home, Dr. Perry Gilbert retired in 1978 and Dr. William Taft became Mote's new director. He inaugurated a new emphasis on environmental assessment projects, many of which focused on Sarasota issues. Dr. Kumar Mahadevan, a benthic ecologist, joined the laboratory in 1978 to lead those projects, followed by coastal ecologist Dr. Ernest Estevez, in 1979, and organic chemist Dr. Richard Pierce, in 1981.

Dr. Taft left Mote in 1983 and, after two interim leadership changes, in 1986, Dr. Kumar Mahadevan was named Executive Director with Dr. Richard Pierce as Research Director. With the lab's leadership, Sarasota Bay was included in the National Estuary Program in 1988; Charlotte Harbor followed in 1995. The lab's Center for Shark Research was designated a National Center by the U.S. Congress in 1991. Marine mammal research flourished and the Ann and Alfred Goldstein Marine Mammal Center opened in 1994. Today, Mote's Sarasota Dolphin Research Program is the longest-running study of wild dolphins in history. Mote also has taken a lead role in aquaculture research at Mote Aquaculture Park. In 2006, Mote signed a historic partnership agreement with the University of South Florida to operate a joint Center of Excellence in Marine Science to focus increased resources on coastal monitoring systems.

As Mote's research endeavors expanded, so did its educational outreach, led by popular aquarium and summer camp programs. Mote's education programs have touched thousands of Sarasota County students, and programs have used video-conferencing technology with Sea Trek programs to broadcast from the Keating Marine Education Center extending Mote's scientific expertise to students in other states and countries.

Mote's cadre of 1,500 dedicated volunteers embody the sense of spirit displayed by the Lab's professional staff and have helped sustain its success through all its changes and expansions. Dr. Kumar Mahadevan said, "It has been 20 years since I took the helm of Mote Marine Laboratory. My excitement has not waned for the sea, our last frontier, and its exciting inhabitants. I just hope that Mote will always exist as a place where those in Sarasota and beyond can learn about the sea."

William R. Mote and his sister, Elizabeth Mote Rose, standing in front of the Laboratory on Siesta Key.

Cape Haze Marine Laboratory in 1955.

The July 1997 ground breaking ceremonies for the new Mote Marine Laboratory connector building. Pictured from left to right: Dr. Alfred Goldstein, Chairman, Board of Trustees; Dr. Kumar Mahadevan, Executive Director; Dr. Perry Gilbert, Director Emeritus; Hon. Bob Johnson, Chairman Emeritus, and City of Sarasota Vice Mayor Jerome Dupree.

Mote Marine Laboratory on Siesta Key with the distinctive shark tanks in 1970.

This history made possible through a gift by **Frederick Derr & Company, Inc.**

MYAKKA VALLEY RANCH

Myakka Valley Ranch began in 1958 with the purchase of 2,400 acres in southeastern Manatee County from cattleman Murray Harrison of Palmetto. Structured as a simple family partnership involving civil engineer Freeman H. Horton, his wife, Mabel, and son, Allan, the ranch was native land with a single barbed wire fence around it. Its neighbor to the south and west was the Myakka River State Park.

At purchase, the ranch supported a small herd of feral horses and grade beef cattle under a grazing lease contracted with cattleman Thurmond Smith of Palmetto. It also boasted flowing streams that drained westerly to Clay Gully and the Myakka River.

In the nearly 50 years since, federal estate tax obligations following the deaths of both Mabel and Freeman Horton, in 1974 and 1978 respectively, plus satisfaction of a mortgage balloon note, reduced the ranch to 1,215 acres. Of that expanse, about three-fourths remains mixed native habitats that support a diverse variety of wildlife, including sandhill cranes, Sherman's fox squirrels, gopher tortoises and, on occasion, Florida panther. The flowing streams have long since dried up.

Allan and Martha Horton, 2007. Photo by Cat Horton.

The first beef cattle that carried the "Running MV" brand of Myakka Valley Ranch were nine purebred Polled Hereford cows and a bull purchased by Allan Horton with savings earned as a merchant seaman aboard the USS *Hydrographer*, a converted Liberty ship engaged in North Atlantic geodesy for the US Coast & Geodetic Survey. Subsequent purchases of grade beef cows from the Longino Ranch and others formed the foundation of the crossbred (Braford/Brangus) cow herd that now grazes the land. Among the attributes used to select replacement heifers and registered bulls is dark pigment around the eyes, an inheritable trait that protects cows from cancer eye. Mabel Horton's favorite cows were the brindles, whose black and brown stripes provide effective camouflage when they hide in shady thickets.

With enlistment in the U.S. Army in 1960, subsequent employment activities and post graduate studies following graduation in 1969 with a BS Agriculture degree in animal science from the University of Florida, Allan didn't resume ranching fulltime until 1973, when he and his wife, Martha, moved from Gainesville to the ranch. Two years later, after the birth of their son, Will, they moved to Sarasota, where their daughter, Catherine, was born in 1976. Their absentee management of the ranch began while Martha, a registered Landscape Architect, pursued private practice and Allan worked as a reporter for the *Sarasota Herald-Tribune*. In 1977, Johnny Kersey joined the ranch as resident manager.

Improvements to the ranch have included fencing and cross-fencing to enhance cattle management and movement; improved selection of replacement heifers and purebred bulls for weight gain and ease of calving; expansion of native and improved Bahiagrass and Pangola grass pasturage to boost nutrition and winter shelter; excavation of additional watering holes; rotational grazing and control burning practices to restore and maintain forage improvements; and the expansion of pasture renovation and hay harvesting activities to offer contract services to neighboring ranches.

Throughout its history, management of the Myakka Valley Ranch has emphasized the value of retaining as much native habitat as practicable to combine cow-calf production with protection of wildlife. After early, unfortunate experiences with leased hunting, all hunting rights on Myakka Valley Ranch lands have been reserved for the owners' and manager's immediate families.

As nearby ranching properties have succumbed to the alluring and explosive development of residential "ranchettes" and hobby farming operations, the mantra established at the Myakka Valley Ranch states "the asphalt stops at our fence." Accordingly, the Horton family has actively pursued legal strategies that would preserve in perpetuity the open-space, wildlife habitat and productive agricultural assets of Myakka Valley Ranch.

They believe that long-term goal best contradicts the growing urban trends expressed in the lament written by Allan Horton, a published cowboy poet, titled *"Where Meadowlarks Once Flew."*

"So, now on the highway there's a new sign erected,
A sign of the times we should have expected.
'For sale,'" it says, "'prime growth opportunity,'"
As another ranch is erased by a new Florida community."

The owners and managers of the Myakka Valley Ranch intend its rich pastures and shady hammocks will never become "a new Florida community."

THE PAT NEAL FAMILY

The Tradition of the Neal Family Embraces Southwest Florida

Neal Communities is changing the way homes are built in southwest Florida. And there are no signs of slowing down. Not now, not anytime soon. Their rock-solid reputation stands out from the crowd, creating award-winning lifestyle communities that exist in harmony with Florida's natural habitats.

It all started almost fifty years ago. In the late 1960s, Paul Neal left Des Moines, Iowa, where he was an attorney and a successful developer of Holiday Inns, and moved to quiet and relatively undeveloped Manatee County. Here he began his real estate ventures with a condominium project and shopping plaza on north Longboat Key. "I remember my father saying 'I need you here to help me,'" laughed his son, Pat Neal, president of Neal Communities. "And that's basically how I got started in this business."

John, Pat and Charlene Neal

Pat's first visit to Florida's west coast was in 1965. After graduation from the prestigious Wharton School of Finance and Commerce at the University of Pennsylvania, he settled in Manatee County. In the summer of 1969, history was made when Paul and his son, Pat, started their first project together - the Whitney Beach condominiums. Prices started at $18,900.

"My dad was a great salesman," stated Pat. "He understood people and how to effectively communicate with them. But he was also extremely creative. Because I was more financially minded and focused on the details and the organizational aspects, we made a great team."

The experience Pat gained while working with his father fueled a newfound passion for land development and refueled an existing one – politics. Never one to rest on his laurels, Pat ran for the state Legislature in 1974 and was elected. A pair of two-year terms in the House was followed by a pair of four-year terms as state Senator, chairing the Senate Natural Resources and the Senate Appropriations committees. Among his many accomplishments, Pat wrote the first state wetlands protection law and was honored with every top environmental award given by the state Legislature during his tenure. He returned to Manatee County with the experience and determination to establish a building and development company like never before, one that truly respects the fragile relationship between the natural environment and the built environment.

After Paul retired - for the third time - in 1980, Pat Neal's new developments were created on his own or with other partners but always with the environment in mind. "As I begin to create a neighborhood, I always feel a commitment to the land and look for opportunities to plan around nature," he says. "The beauty of the Florida landscape presents unique challenges. I believe we have been extraordinarily successful integrating residents and wildlife to coexist beautifully."

In 2004, Pat's son John joined the family business. He initially served as head of Geographic Information, managing the development and implementation of Geographic Information System (GIS), a program that modernized Neal Communities' tracking, design, and commitment to building a better community.

But, in the beginning, John wasn't particularly interested in a real estate career. "When you're young and trying to do something on your own, entering the family business can be intimidating at the very least. But I don't regret my decision one bit," he stated.

It was Pat Neal who did the persuading. In addition to carrying on the business, Pat saw the tremendous value John could bring to the company. Despite the abundant land and real estate experience already within the halls of Neal Communities, John's fresh approach, technical acumen, and business expertise has been a tremendous asset to the company. The successful momentum he gathered through his other business experiences has propelled him toward a powerful career in the family business.

John Neal as a developer is currently working on two very successful projects which have opened recently and on a third which opened in early 2007. It is easy to see from the emerging neighborhoods that John has listened and has taken every opportunity to learn from his father's outstanding record with the inclusion of lush landscape, amenities and the meticulous attention to detail that buyers have come to expect from Neal Communities; and, if you look, you'll also notice John's own influence in these neighborhoods.

Charlene Neal also plays an integral role in the family business. To match the vision of Neal's exceptional homes, Charlene was instrumental in creating the 6,500-square-foot Neal Design Gallery in Lakewood Ranch, a one-of-a-kind in creative concept, size, and convenience. Vice president of design, Charlene, has been in the building and design business for over 29 years, creating more than 50 models for Neal Communities, starting with the Players Club on Longboat Key. The Players Club with its classic Mediterranean architecture, as with all Neal Communities' neighborhoods, has stood the test of time. Even though the community was completed in 1983, it is just as fresh and architecturally interesting today as it was then.

After building more than 7,000 homes, Pat Neal sees his core market clearly. A baby-boomer himself, he recognizes the need to provide high quality homes, loaded with luxury features and amenities, at a reasonable price.

"Our homes are for the third move-up and the first move-down buyers. The third move-up buyers are around 45 years old with children and typically are looking for their third home. Their income has grown and they know what they want. The first move-down buyers are empty-nesters in their fifties. They want amenities and luxury but are also extremely value conscious," Pat says. "These two markets don't squander money. They demand quality in workmanship, strong customer service, and effective warranties."

In addition to quality construction, Neal Communities has earned a reputation for delivering outstanding customer service throughout the entire process of buying and building a new home. Because of this, Neal Communities enjoy one of the highest referral ratings in the home building industry.

People who buy Neal homes come from all over the world and include regional, national, and international buyers. They tend to buy more than one Neal home during their lifetime and, because of this, Neal Communities is continuing to build in Wisteria Park, Forest Creek, River's Reach, The Harborage, Lakewood Ranch, and University Park Country Club, a landmark community on University Parkway in southern Manatee County. They will soon be breaking ground for a new neighborhood on the Braden River called River Sound.

The Neal family has contributed their talents to developing some of the area's finest communities. John states, "We're a local company that creates local jobs for local workers. Because of the family connection, we've always been responsive to our neighbors and their needs." As with all of its current and past communities, the Neal philosophy is to utilize dazzling landscapes and award-winning homes to add long-term value to both the development and the surrounding neighborhood.

Pat Neal has experienced extraordinary success in negotiating complex environmental permitting requirements and has a thorough knowledge of Florida's sensitive natural landscape, crucial to responsible land planning and development. No other Florida developer has earned the stellar reputation for environmental stewardship more than Pat Neal. Under his leadership, Neal's companies work hard to protect the natural environment, even improving it whenever possible.

Pat Neal is recognized nationwide as a trendsetting builder and a visionary thinker. Pat feels strongly that a good developer gives back to the community. Those beliefs are reflected in the many children's educational programs and arts organizations that Pat and Charlene support, in his partnerships with schools and churches, and his numerous affiliations with civic and community organizations.

Responsible land development, environmental sensitivity to the preservation of natural habitats, innovative home building, and a commitment to customer service have earned Neal 35 prestigious Aurora awards, five Best in American Living awards for architectural excellence, seven Fame awards, and hundreds of local and regional industry awards. Today, Neal Communities is one of the largest privately-owned building and development companies in Southwest Florida.

Neal believes the legacy of a home builder is the properties he has built. "The homes that Neal Communities creates are the reflection of what I am and my goal is to be able to be proud of what I have done. It is the legacy, aside from my family, that I leave for my life." With accomplishments as long and impressive as Pat Neal's and the vision he builds into every neighborhood, it is apparent he will be building for a very long time.

NORTHBROOK CATTLE COMPANY, GALWAY, IRELAND

A Florida Cracker in the West of Ireland

*I*n 1953, my father, Henry Ringling North, and uncle, John Ringling North, decided to go to Scotland for a week to fish for salmon. As neither of them knew anything at all about salmon fishing, I don't know what prompted them to do so.

When they arrived at their hotel at 9 pm, the dining room was closed and the only thing the hotel could provide for dinner was sandwiches. This was not my uncle's idea of dinner, so he decided they should leave the next morning. He told my father at breakfast he had just remembered that an assistant manager at the Ritz in Paris was now managing a hotel in Dublin, Ireland, and he was sure the food would not only be great, but that it would be available after 9 pm.

A short flight took them to Dublin where my father decided he would like to find the farm that their grandfather had left at the time of the Irish Famine. With some effort they did find it in County Galway.

Over the next few years, with even more difficulty, they managed to buy the 550-acre property. In 1960, my father asked me if I would like to go to Ireland and set up a cattle operation on the property. Since I had never been out of the U.S. except for two days at Niagara Falls in Canada, I was delighted at the prospect. When I finished military service in October 1962, I went to Ireland.

On arrival in Ballinasloe, County Galway, I was amazed to see that most of Northbrook, as the property was named, was more like a swamp than a cattle ranch. A large-scale drainage scheme took up most of the first few years. Also a large fencing job, as even boundary fences were more or less nonexistent.

After these two jobs were finished, we were ready to get some cattle. The Ringling Bros. and Barnum & Bailey Circus had at one time owned a farm in Peru, Indiana, where my father had become very interested in Angus cattle, an interest he had all his life. Angus cattle were not very plentiful in County Galway, so we purchased our first few cows in County Sligo. For the next few years, we ran a cow/calf operation, but there seemed to be more money in finishing steers. In 1966, my father built a feed lot; it was a copy of one belonging to a friend of his in Millbrook, New York. This has been in use ever since, mainly for feeding other people's cattle on contract over the winter months. At about the time the cattle yard was built, I saw a movie named *The Culpepper Cattle Company* and Northbrook became the Northbrook Cattle Company.

My father always had a great interest in Northbrook; my uncle, generally, had none. One time my father was leaving a day before my uncle was scheduled to visit; he told me he wanted my uncle to become more interested, and that I was to show him around the fields, cattle, forestry and anything else I could think of. On his arrival, I told my uncle what my father had said. He looked decidedly uninterested and quickly changed the subject. Two days

Northern Ireland, 2006. Sorcha North, 18, competing in the Young Rider Irish National Competitions on 7-year-old Callaighstown Cruiser."

later, to my amazement he came into the cattle yard at 2 in the afternoon. He generally never got out of bed before 5. As usual, he was dressed in a blue suit, blue shirt and blue tie. "I'm ready for the grand tour, Johnny; let's go." For the next three hours we bounced around the ranch in a Toyota jeep, Uncle John asking questions about every part of our cattle operation. When we were finally finished, he said: "Thank God – the things I do to please my little brother." The only other time he asked about our business was in 1978. We had our own cows, but were grazing steers on contract. He asked if we could make more grazing our own steers. I said we would. So, he said why not do it. When I told him it would cost $100,000 that we didn't have, he didn't say anything. He left the next day and a week later a check for $100,000 arrived.

At present, we have 30 Angus and shorthorn cows which we breed to a Canadian Angus bull. We sell all our weanlings each fall. Over the summer, we graze on contract about 250 steers and 20 to 50 of our own, depending on the market. We sell them all in the fall as finished beef. They finish on grass alone with no meals (grains). Hormones are illegal in all European Union countries, so our beef is a totally natural food. In the winter, we feed 320 cattle in our feedlot on contract. Some years, we finish out our own cattle over the winter, but usually it is more profitable to do it on contract.

In addition to the cattle, we have 100 acres of commercial timber, most of it planted by my father. We use horses to work the cattle and also breed a few horses to sell.

We are considered by the Angus Producers Association as one of the top commercial Angus operations in Ireland. *All because you can't get dinner after 9 pm in Scotland.*

—John Ringling North II

NORTHERN TRUST

Northern Trust, one of the nation's largest and most respected private banking, trust and investment companies, opened its Sarasota operation on April 1, 1977. That marks Northern Trust as the oldest ongoing financial services organization in Sarasota. Throughout its history in the Sarasota and Manatee counties region, Northern Trust has had a very positive impact, not only with the individual, corporate and nonprofit clients that it serves, but also with the community at large. Northern has provided very consistent and generous support of the arts, education, health and social services organizations that have made our community great. This commitment to both client and community is the key aspect of Northern's distinctive legacy in this region.

Turning to its history in Sarasota, Northern Trust did not establish roots in this community in the conventional manner. Most banks enter new markets by acquiring an existing banking operation. But the Northern Trust private banking model is unique with its focus on the integration of private banking, trust/fiduciary, and investment management solutions. Therefore, the business was established on a completely de novo basis. In 1977, a team of eight financial services professionals was assembled. They had strong motivation, great ideas and first-rate skills; the only missing ingredient at the time was their first client, as they were starting from a fresh sheet of paper!

The new Sarasota office enjoyed great early success. The team was very ably led by Barry G. Hastings, a young trust professional out of the Miami office (Barry would retire some 25 years later as the President & Chief Operating Officer of Northern Trust Corporation in Chicago). By cultivating strong professional ties with the lead lawyers and accountants in the area, Northern Trust was able to build a major portfolio of strong client relationships that paved the way for a significant investment in this community. Initially, Northern Trust operated out of leased space in an existing office building on Main Street, and then a street level location on South Lemon Street. But in 1980, a 2-acre tract of land was purchased at Ringling Boulevard and Orange Avenue in downtown Sarasota. Construction was immediately undertaken on the Northern Trust Plaza Building, an 11-story, 110,000 sq. ft. office building that is the hub of its Sarasota/Manatee operation.

Of interest in this "history of Northern Trust" is the story of the original roots of the company. Northern Trust was established in Chicago in 1889 with a business strategy that still holds true today: to work with individuals, families, businesses and foundations on strategies to build and retain wealth. Northern Trust was founded by Byron Laflin Smith, a respected banker, and his initial shareholders included storied business leaders such as Marshall Field, Philip Armour and Martin Ryerson. As was the case with the Sarasota operation, the business enjoyed great early growth which paved the way for a true signature building: an architectural and engineering wonder that was opened at the corner of LaSalle and Monroe in 1906. That building still serves as the worldwide headquarters for Northern Trust. With its focus on safety and soundness, Northern Trust's most rapid period of growth was during the Depression era (1929-1935), this at a time when bank failures were much more of the norm.

Northern Trust Bank Sarasota Office.

Fast forwarding to the current time, Northern Trust is proud that its culture still holds many of the important tenets from its 1889 charter. Highly-personalized service, conservatism, business ethics and integrity, and community partnership are all part of today's corporate mission. Northern has also displayed the ability to anticipate and implement state-of-the-art technology, financial planning approaches, and new investment solutions to continue to best serve its clients. And the effectiveness of this business approach is born out by client feedback and by the growth that Northern has enjoyed over the years. Here in the Sarasota/Manatee region, Northern serves clients out of offices in Longboat Key, Venice, Lakewood Ranch, and Bradenton, in addition to the downtown Sarasota office.

THE CLASS OF 2007 PRESENTS THE HISTORY OF THE OUT-OF-DOOR ACADEMY

Our school has a rich and unique history, founded in 1924 by two entrepreneurs, Fanneal Harrison and Catherine Gavin. While in Europe during World War I, participating in the relief effort, they worked under the leadership of Dr. Ovide Decroly – a renowned physician, educator, and philosopher from Brussels. In 1922, while on vacation at the Harrison winter home on Siesta Key, they laid the foundation for a progressive school in the sunshine where children studied outdoors. They followed Dr. Decroly's principles of education, which taught that instead of teacher-imposed discipline, curiosity, freedom, and self-discipline would motivate learning.

The Out-of-Door School, as it was originally named, opened in 1924 with ten students and five teachers. Classes "for healthy minds, bodies, and spirits" included not only the academics, music, art, horseback riding, swimming and dancing, but also practical skills like carpentry. After Sarasota architect Ralph Twitchell, founder of the movement known as the Sarasota School of Architecture, designed their library, the students built it, shingled its roof, and even made the door hinges. This building is still in use today as the office of our lower-school division head.

Distinguished visitors such as Eleanor Roosevelt, Jane Addams, and Thomas Edison visited the school regularly during those early years. In 1930, the National Geographic even carried its picture in one of their publications. Fourteen years after founding the school, Harrison retired, and the ownership of the school passed through several members of her family. Then, in 1977 the parents of the school children pooled their assets, purchased the school and incorporated it as a 501(c)(3) non-profit organization. It was at this time that the name of the school was changed to The Out-of-Door Academy.

Over the years The Out-of-Door Academy has transformed into a vibrant, two-campus, college preparatory school with a well-balanced curriculum focused on strong academics, the arts and athletics. In 1997, The Out-of-Door Academy, being one of Florida's oldest independent schools, opened a second campus at Lakewood Ranch expanding its educational offerings to high school students.

The Out-of-Door Academy now serves over 600 students in grades PreK through 12, and is a Cum Laude Society School, a member of the National Association of Independent Schools and the Florida Council of Independent Schools. The School offers students an innovative educational program in a caring and supportive community. The college preparatory curriculum is both challenging and rich with course offerings including the arts, modern language, honors and AP courses. Our dedicated and experienced faculty is made up of expert teachers who are committed to the personal growth of each individual student, both in and outside the classroom. Small class sizes foster relationships between faculty and students that last for a lifetime. A strong partnership also exists with our families, who volunteer their time and resources to enhance the educational environment and strengthen our community.

For more than 80 years, The Out-of-Door Academy has remained dedicated to its long-standing commitment to the pursuit of knowledge and the development of self-confident, responsible young people.

This history made possible through a gift by
Stanley Meuser
and
Veronica Meuser

Please contact us for more information, or to arrange a personal tour.
Phone: 349-3223
Admissions: 554-3400
PreK - Grade 6 – Siesta Key
444 Reid St. – Sarasota
Grades 7 -12 – Lakewood Ranch
5950 Deer Dr. – Sarasota
www.oda.edu

THE PERLMAN MUSIC PROGRAM (PMP)

When Toby Perlman started the Perlman Music Program in 1993, she dreamed it would one day become a year-round network of programs providing exceptionally talented string students an unrivaled educational experience. Remarkably, in the short time since then, the program has accomplished just that. At the same time, the city of Sarasota has established an international reputation as a model for the role arts and culture should play in a community. In 2004, these two entities joined forces, establishing a unique and powerful partnership that has allowed both to enhance their respective cultural goals.

History of the PMP

When Toby Perlman was a 19-year-old violin student at Juilliard, she began to dream of a new kind of musical institution dedicated to training the next generation of classical music leaders. She dreamed of a program devoted to a supportive and nurturing learning environment, one capable of adapting to the needs of each individual student, and one that counteracts the immense pressures often placed on students of extraordinary talent.

Since its inception in 1993, PMP has become a sophisticated series of programs, including two sessions held each summer on Shelter Island, New York; the six-week *Summer Music School @ PMP*, and the two-and-a-half week Chamber Music Workshop @ PMP. Additionally, PMP's mission is sustained during the winter months with its *NYC Yearlong Mentorship Program @ PMP*. Over the years, these programs have been enhanced by the occasional international tour to places such as Israel and China.

At the heart of PMP's guiding philosophy is a belief in personalized and intimate learning experiences for students. Boasting a remarkable student to faculty/staff ratio of better than 2:1, PMP's faculty, led by Itzhak Perlman, includes some of the most highly respected and sought-after pedagogues in the world. This environment provides the valuable resources necessary to nurture remarkable talent, while at the same time promoting both leadership and real-life social skills. PMP takes great pride in noting that virtually all of its young graduates continue their studies at leading conservatories and distinguished colleges – and most of them cite PMP as one of the most formative elements in their musical and personal development.

Sarasota Winter Residency @ PMP

A few months after the PMP's acclaimed international residency in Shanghai, China, David Klein asked Toby if she had ever considered Sarasota for a PMP winter residency. Excited by the idea, Toby saw such a residency as an opportunity for a mid-year renewal of the Program's educational objectives. As a well-respected classical music advocate, a Sarasota resident, and the husband of PMP's own viola faculty member, Heidi Castleman, David was the perfect person to bring such an idea to fruition.

Thanks to David Klein's and Heidi Castleman's tireless efforts, this idea became reality. On December 19, 2004, thirty-two young musicians, along with faculty, staff and fellows, checked into the Hyatt Hotel for the first of many trips to Sarasota. During these two week residencies, PMP students enjoy a busy schedule that includes daily practice, private lessons, chamber music coaching and rehearsals, orchestra and chorus rehearsals, multiple performance opportunities, beach outings, and festive holiday celebrations hosted by generous Sarasota donors.

Primary sponsorship was provided the first year by The Florida West Coast Symphony, and was assumed in 2005 by the Van Wezel Performing Arts Center and its affiliated Van Wezel Foundation. These sponsors, along with countless other Sarasota donors and volunteers, provide essential support including marketing and publicity; transportation; hotel rooms; meals; practice and performance space; and even nightly snacks for PMP students.

The combined efforts of everyone involved results in a dynamic two-week residency that energizes and inspires the local community. Nearly daily events that are free for the public include open orchestra rehearsals conducted by Itzhak Perlman; open chorus rehearsals conducted by Patrick Romano; masterclasses by PMP faculty members; *Works in Progress* concerts held at local churches including Temple Sinai, Church of the Palms, Kirkwood Presbyterian, and St. Thomas More Catholic Church, and a very special family concert. Each year, more than 10,000 people attend rehearsals and *Works in Progress* concerts, while the family concert is presented to a packed house of children and their families, all learning about music from PMP's talented students and faculty. In addition, there is a Celebration Concert and Dinner held annually at the Van Wezel Hall.

The Perlman Music Program is eternally grateful for its strong partnership with the City of Sarasota, and all the generous sponsors who make the *Sarasota Winter Residency @ PMP* possible. Thanks to the efforts of Sarasota's civic leaders, and the enthusiasm and involvement of its citizens, PMP has a truly special place to call its winter home-away-from-home.

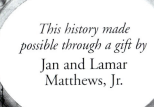

This history made possible through a gift by
Jan and Lamar Matthews, Jr.

PINES OF SARASOTA STORY

Care, Compassion, Community

We've come a long way since 1948!

It is hard to imagine what our community would do without Pines of Sarasota. Some of Sarasota's most influential and compassionate citizens played active roles in the growth and development of this charitable, not-for-profit senior care community. Nearly sixty years have come and gone and Pines stands as a "crown jewel," providing outstanding health care and services to citizens who have outlived what they considered a carefully planned retirement. Throughout the years, our mission has remained constant – and our 17-acre campus has grown to include not only long term care, but also comprehensive rehabilitation services, assisted living, an Alzheimer's specialty unit, respite care, a child daycare and learning center and a Thrift Shop.

Clearly, for our community there is no substitute for Pines.

One could say that Pines of Sarasota and the City of Sarasota grew up together. By the early 1940's, it had become apparent that Sarasota was in desperate need of a home to care for elderly citizens in poor health with limited incomes. The Kiwanis Club of Sarasota recognized that need and by March of 1948, Kiwanis members had raised approximately $40,000 to open the first buildings on the current site, giving Pines the distinction of being the oldest long-term care community in Sarasota and quite possibly the oldest in the entire state of Florida.

The Kiwanis Club felt that a representative group of responsible citizens from Sarasota County could best govern the operation. The name Sarasota "Welfare" Home was adopted to signify a home built for the benefit and well being of the community elders. Original members of the board included Mrs. Charles Ringling, Mrs. J.M. Tuttle, J.T. Blaylock, Benton Powell and Judge Forrest Chapman. Al Shogren, Sibley L. White, W.A. Wynn and Arthur E. Esthus were also initial members. It was during that same organizational meeting that John Bloomer, Mrs. L.G. Palmer, Mrs. Dudley Palmer, Mrs. Athol Marcus and Father C.L. Elslander were voted in as additional directors of the board.

At that initial meeting, Sibley White was elected President and acted as administrator the first year of operation. In 1949, Alfred E. Shogren assumed that position and served until 1967. Al Shogren's assistant, G. Norwood Cullers, served as President and Administrator until his retirement in 1992. His assistant, Bruce Colby, followed in the presidency until the late 1990's. John W. Overton assumed the leadership of the campus in June of 2001, and remains in that same capacity today.

Board of Directors Vice Chairman, J.R. Wells Purmort

Board of Directors Secretary, Mary Alice Jackson, Esq.

Board of Directors Treasurer, O. Howard Davidsmeyer

Board of Directors Chairman, Arthur M. Goldberg

This history made possible through a gift by Dr. Robert E. and Lelia Windom, Arthur M. and Viola L. Goldberg, and John W. and Pamela Overton

The early history is fascinating, especially considering that the introduction of Medicare and Medicaid was still eighteen years away. A letter written by the corporate secretary in October 1949 revealed that "The SWH, Inc. is obligated to take care of elderly people who are receiving old age pensions from the state of Florida, and who are residents of the state of Florida; however, we have been taking other people who are able to pay a reasonable amount with the understanding if and when the space is needed they must give up their accommodations to make room for the old age pensioners." At that time there were seventeen 'guests' in the home with a capacity of twenty-four. The cost per meal per guest was about 25 cents, according to board minutes on April 27th of that year.

The initial rules and regulations for the home indicated "for the purpose of residing in the Home each resident will be required to pay monthly in advance the amount of at least $42.50 and reasonably higher rates will be charged to those whose financial circumstances permit." The rules went on to state "all applicants must submit a report of their financial status, listing all property owned both real and personal, and giving amounts and sources of all income."

After the first three buildings were constructed there was a remaining balance of $3,700, $400 in cash and receivables and pledges totaling $1,700. Opening day was Nov. 16th, 1948 with the facility having been built primarily by volunteers to solve a community need.

In 1948, there was an initial staff of three with a $15,000 annual budget. By 1960, eighty-four residents were cared for with a staff of thirty-four. The campus was comprised of seven buildings including a home for the resident superintendent. A grant from the William G. and Marie Selby Foundation paid for the Al Shogren building addition in 1963, the same year that the Thrift Shop was established. The Thrift Shop is still operated by volunteers and offers a variety of donated merchandise for sale to campus visitors. Proceeds from these sales are used to further the well-being of our residents.

By 1974, the campus expanded to seventeen buildings with the final nursing home addition of 24 beds at a cost of $107,000. In 1976, we were privileged to receive a visit from President and Mrs. Gerald R. Ford during their brief stay in Sarasota. To our knowledge, this is the only facility of its kind ever to have received a presidential visit.

It was during Norwood Culler's tenure that the campus was renamed Pines of Sarasota, and expansive growth continued. The assisted living facility opened in 1990, while Sarasota native and well-known attorney Robert A. Kimbrough served as chairman of the Pines' board of directors. Mr. Kimbrough devoted twenty-eight years of outstanding service to Pines before retiring at the end of 2006. The Evalyn Sadlier Jones Child Care and Learning Center opened in 1992 to provide a center for children of Pines' staff to receive pre-school education. The Pines of Sarasota Foundation was organized with the sole mission of raising community support and financial assistance for the Pines organization. Arthur M. Goldberg served as President of the foundation until his retirement in 2000. Mr. Goldberg would later serve as Chairman of the corporate board, a position he holds today.

Today, Pines has a capacity of 204 skilled nursing home residents, seventy-two assisted living residences, respite care, a nationally recognized childcare center and our ever-important Thrift Shop on its 17-acre campus. Pines has developed a number of collaborative relationships with other not-for-profits in this community that advance the recreational, cultural and learning opportunities for the residents.

Just as in the early history of Pines, spirited community leaders over the years have continued to give to this campus in volunteering their time and extensive talents. Today's board members exemplify that same vision, compassion and diversity. Corporate board officers include: Arthur M. Goldberg (Chairman), J.R. Wells Purmort (Vice Chairman), Mary Alice Jackson, Esq. (Secretary) and O. Howard Davidsmeyer (Treasurer). Other board members include Foundation President Estelle Crawford, Dr. Robert E. Windom, Dr. David A. Giordano, attorney Robert A. Kimbrough, Rev. Jerome Dupree, accountants Susan B. Grundy and Carl Smith, bankers Richard H. Mott, and Shawn Byrd, insurance executive James B. Tollerton, Brig. General (Ret.) Roswell E. Round, former Sarasota Fire Chief Harold Stinchcomb, rancher Berryman T. Longino, retired businessman George Manser, businessman John B. Davidson, John and Vivian Browning, Florence Brown, Catherine Boyer, Jack A. Smith, Bruce Glazener, Alvin Wilhelm and professional musician and entertainer Lillette Jenkins-Wisner.

The Future of Pines – Prudent Stewardship

The future need for Pines of Sarasota is obvious given the significant number of seniors who may require care and services, while at the same time confronting declining governmental reimbursements. Today Pines is engaged in a capital campaign to replace the nursing home and Alzheimer/dementia unit. Much of the current nursing home physical plant is now antiquated; replacement will significantly improve the environment for our nursing home residents and also increase staff efficiency. A particularly exciting aspect is opening our Rehabilitation Therapy Center. This new, larger Center expands service beyond residents to members of the community for their outpatient rehabilitation needs. The total two-phase project cost is $20 million.

Remarkably, Pines has been debt-free for nearly half a century and has not sought community support for capital improvements since 1988. This is a generous community and our contributors can take pride in knowing that they are giving to a cause so vital to the welfare of our seniors.

PROFESSIONAL BENEFITS INC.

Since 1970, Professional Benefits Inc. (PBI) has become one of Sarasota's largest and most successful independent insurance agencies. Founded by Jim Tollerton, PBI specializes in insurance coverage for professionals with an emphasis on disability insurance, professional liability, workers' compensation, health insurance and retirement plans.

PBI President Jim Tollerton attended Southside Elementary School and Brookside Junior High School and was president of the Class of 1964 at Sarasota High School. He graduated from Florida State University in 1968, where he was a class officer and member of Sigma Chi.

After a brief stint as a trust officer, Jim joined a large insurance company as an agent in 1970. He soon earned his Chartered Life Underwriter (CLU) degree. Later he earned the Chartered Financial Consultant (ChFC) designation and Registered Health Underwriter (RHU).

Jim became an independent agent in 1977, joining Bill Hollister at his Sarasota agency. "We merged our agencies with Bill in 1978, and were fortunate to retain him as my friend and advisor for over 25 years," Jim says. "His wise counsel until his death in November 2004 (a week before his 90th birthday), was invaluable in PBI's growth."

Jim's expertise, particularly in disability insurance, was recognized by his peers when he was designated chair of the Life, Health & Disability Section of the American Society of Financial Service Professionals in 2004.

Jim has devoted countless hours to the Sarasota community. He was elected (as a Republican) to the Sarasota Memorial Public Hospital Board in 1974 at the age of 28, eventually serving three terms. In 1986 he established the EXCEL program at Sarasota Memorial to honor outstanding employees. He still funds the program today, and over 150 employees have been recognized as key to maintaining Sarasota Memorial's reputation as the best community hospital in the country.

In addition to the hospital, Jim has served in various board and officer positions for the Sarasota and Florida Chambers of Commerce, SCOPE, YMCA, The Education Foundation (founding Chairman), FSU Alumni Association, Sarasota Seminole Boosters, Sarasota Association of Life Underwriters, Church of the Redeemer Vestry, SunTrust Bank, Estate Planning & Planned Giving Councils, among others.

"I believe in putting some sugar back in the bowl," Jim explains.

Jim brings that same spirit to the PBI offices. He is quick to recognize the talents of his PBI staff and the large role they play in the company's success. Over the years, that loyalty has become an admirable two-way street. Pam Buckles joined PBI in 1986 and is the company's longest-serving employee.

Another long-time employee, Suzi Regulski-Shirey, has made significant contributions to the benefits operation of PBI since joining PBI in 1993.

Elizabeth "Liza" Battaglia joined PBI in 1998. "Liza's background in workers' compensation and running a physician's office was a natural entrée to working with PBI's medical clients," Jim says. He credits her expertise with building an impressive workers' compensation and professional liability service for over 400 medical practices. Liza is recognized as a regional leader in these services, handling programs for the Sarasota County Medical Society as well as in Manatee, Charlotte, Lee and Collier counties.

Front Row (left to right): Liza Battaglia, Jim Tollerton, Fritz Sprenger.
Back Row (left to right): Debbie Haney, Angela Acha, Marci Townsend, Maryann Pickering, Taylor Tollerton, Pam Buckles, Suzi Shirey.

Jim Tollerton and Bill Hollister.

Another key player at PBI is Franz "Fritz" Sprenger. Fritz joined PBI in 1996 upon his retirement from Sarasota Memorial as VP of Human Resources. "I knew Fritz well from my work at the hospital, and his reputation for honesty, industry and affability is unsurpassed," Jim says. Fritz's primary responsibilities at PBI are to advise and counsel the agency's over 3,000 retirement plan participants.

In 1982, PBI earned the endorsement of the Sarasota County Medical Society for individual disability insurance. Karen Beachy partnered with Jim to write over 100 physicians the first year of the program. She later left PBI to earn her BA at Florida State, but subsequently returned as an independent accounting consultant.

Continuing the family tradition, Jim's daughter Taylor joined the firm in January 2007 after graduating with honors from FSU College of Business with a major in Risk & Insurance.

The 21st century has been especially productive for PBI. In 2005, it reached a milestone when it surpassed $1,000,000 in revenues. In 2006, PBI earned the statewide endorsement of the Florida Institute of CPAs as its designated disability insurance agent-of-record.

"I credit our success to the work ethic of our employees and our continuous focus on treating customers to the best products and services available," Jim says. "That makes an unbeatable combination, and allows me to come to work each day with pride. We live in a great city, work in a great business, and have a great staff. What could be better?"

PURMORT & MARTIN

In 1876, when the insurance industry was still in its infancy on this continent, Minor LaDoyt Purmort, a founding secretary of what is now the The Central Companies in Van Wert, Ohio, began a five-generation insurance tradition. That company grew and prospered into the 20th Century as each new generation advanced its position of responsibility and leadership.

In 1957, Paul Walworth Purmort Sr., third generation in the business, retired as secretary of the company and brought his family to Sarasota. He quickly tired of retirement and in 1958 formed, with two of his sons, what is now Purmort & Martin Insurance Agency.

Richard A. A. Martin II, a long-time Sarasota resident who was active in the life insurance business, and whose father was the first President of the Siesta Key Association, joined the firm and became part owner in 1959. In 1994, the Sarasota Insurance Center merged with the agency and its owner, Paul H. Mercier, became a principal. He subsequently retired in 1997.

The original 1958 office consisted of one desk and a typewriter and was located in the rear of a small real estate office at 2805 North Tamiami Trail, immediately across form the Ringling School of Art. The following year the agency purchased a small home at 3000 South Tamiami Trail and converted it into offices when South Gate was brand new and virtually at the edge of town.

The agency grew and prospered. In 1967, it purchased the John T. Land Insurance Agency and office building at 2940 South Trail, at first occupying two offices in the building, but within ten years, occupying the entire structure.

In 1978, the agency sold the office building after purchasing its present location at 2301 Ringling Boulevard and constructing modem office facilities. On September 1, 2004, Wells Purmort sold his portion of the agency and a new entity, Purmort & Martin Insurance Agency, LLC was formed and purchased the agency. The four equal owners were Richard A. A. Martin, Jr. Matthew J. Stepulla, Russell H. Bobbitt and James R.W. Purmort II. Wells Purmort was employed by the agency as Manager and insurance agent.

The readers of the *Sarasota Herald-Tribune* have consistently selected the agency as "The Best Insurance Agency." The employees of the firm do not take this honor lightly, but continuously strive to maintain this reputation by living up to their mission, goal and commitment. That mission is "to provide independent business owners and individuals with professional advice on insurance products which meet their special needs." Their goal is "to build a long term relationship with our clients, based on mutual understanding, integrity, and trust." Their commitment is "to provide fast, accurate response to requests, with the same high level of personal service we would expect if we were the clients."

Throughout history, the insurance industry, by quickly responding to natural disaster, has become an integral part of this country's economy. Likewise, the owners and employees of Purmort & Martin have been an active and integral part of the insurance industry nationally and locally. Local organizations they have supported through board leadership or major financial support include: the Child Development Center, the Siesta Key and Sarasota chambers of Commerce, Sarasota Historical Society, the Sarasota Committee of 100, Sahib Temple, Crimestoppers, the Argus Foundation, the Sarasota Family YMCA, Sarasota Boys and Girls Club, the Downtown Association of Sarasota, and many other groups.

Boards and committees they have represented in the insurance industry are: the Florida Association of Independent Agents, Professional Insurance Agents of Florida, Sarasota Independent Insurance Agents Association, Cincinnati Insurance Company Presidents Club, CNA National Pacer, Encompass Insurance National Northstar, Central Mutual Inner Circle, and Sarasota Insurance Women's Association.

Agency founder Paul Purmort's son, J. R. Wells Purmort, now serves as manager. Paul's grandson James R.W. Purmort II, who joined the agency after serving six years in the United States Marine Corps, continues the family tradition. Additionally in September 2003 to June 2004 his marine reserve unit was called to active duty and he served in Iraq during the Iraqi Freedom, garnering the Silver Star with a V for his service.

The owners recognize their most important assets are the tremendously dedicated employees who make up the family that is Purmort & Martin Insurance Agency, LLC. The agency is proud of its reputation as a leader in both the industry and the community. They do not take lightly this privilege and responsibility, but are committed to continue to support and nurture the many groups and organizations which combine to make Sarasota the cultural capital of Florida and a beautiful and wonderful place to live.

The mural which adorns the firm's reception area reflects the insurance industries' origination and continued close association with fire departments.

Standing left to right: Matt Stepulla, Jamie Purmort, Russ Bobbitt. Seated: Rick Martin, Wells Purmort

THE JOHN AND MABLE RINGLING MUSEUM OF ART

A Must See in Sarasota

The John and Mable Ringling Museum of Art is the remarkable legacy of circus entrepreneur, art collector and financier John Ringling, and his wife, Mable.

The 66-acre estate includes the Museum of Art; Ringling's winter residence, the Venetian-Gothic Cà d'Zan mansion; historic grounds and gardens; and the Circus Museum including the world's largest miniature circus at the Tibbals Learning Center.

A Legacy

Blessed with entrepreneurial genius, John Ringling (1866-1936) with his brothers produced The Greatest Show on Earth while, with his beloved wife, Mable (1875-1929), he created their greatest legacy, The John and Mable Ringling Museum of Art.

Upon his death in 1936, John Ringling left his art collection and estate to the people of Florida. In 2000, the State of Florida transferred stewardship of the Ringling Museum to Florida State University, establishing the Ringling estate as one of the nation's largest museum/university complexes.

A Passion for Art

As European travel kindled the Ringlings' passion for art, John Ringling purchased masterpieces by Rubens, van Dyck, Titian, Velázquez, El Greco, Gainsborough and Reynolds, and a collection of Cypriot antiquities purchased from the Metropolitan Museum of Art, among other works. He dreamed of building a museum to make Sarasota a cultural destination.

In 1925, Ringling engaged architect John H. Phillips to design a museum that emulated Florence's Uffizi Gallery, echoing its graceful colonnades that open onto an Italianate garden. In October 1931, "The John and Mable Ringling Museum of Art" was dedicated and opened to the public.

Today, the Museum of Art displays European, American and Asian works. The Old Master paintings, among the rarest and most celebrated in the United States, are the most important of the Museum's holdings.

The Museum's collection continues to grow. In 2002, it received the Koger Collection of Chinese ceramics, which features beautifully proportioned and elegantly formed utilitarian and decorative pieces. In 2006, Dr. Helga Wall-Apelt, noted art collector and philanthropist, pledged funds to support the future Dr. Helga Wall-Apelt Asia Art Gallery featuring her collection of magnificent jades, stone figures and bronzes.

A design approved by John Ringling himself inspired the Ulla R. and Arthur F. Searing Wing for traveling exhibitions to house major traveling exhibitions and display portions of the permanent collection.

A Lasting Love Letter

Having traveled often to Europe, John and Mable Ringling appreciated the culture and treasures of the continent's architecture. They fell in love with Venice, and determined that their home on Sarasota Bay would emulate the grandeur of the Doge's Palace, combined with the gothic grace of the Cà d'Oro. The mansion, completed in 1926, soon became the epicenter of cultural life on Florida's west coast, attracting such luminaries as New York Mayor Jimmy Walker, entertainer Flo Ziegfeld, comedian Will Rogers, and many others. Lavish parties were held with orchestras serenading guests from the Ringling yacht, moored off the marble terrace. Their dream home, known through Venetian dialect as the "House of John," became what one writer called John's "love letter to Mable."

A Wonderful Delight

In 1948, the Ringling Museum of the American Circus became the first museum to document the rich history of the circus. With many circus people living nearby, the collection grew quickly. Today, the Ringling Museum collection includes rare handbills and art prints, circus papers, business records, wardrobe, props, and all types of circus equipment, including beautifully carved parade wagons.

The Howard Bros. Circus model is an authentic replica of the Ringling Bros. and Barnum & Bailey Circus, when the tented circus was in its heyday (circa 1919-1938). Complete with eight main tents, 152 wagons, 1,300 circus performers and workers, more than 800 animals and a 57-car train, the model is a 3/4-inch-to-the-foot scale replica that occupies 3,800 square feet in the Circus Museum's Tibbals Learning Center. The "largest miniature circus in the world" was created by master model builder and philanthropist Howard Tibbals of Tennessee and Florida.

A Jewel Box of a Theater

The Historic Asolo Theater is thought to be the only 18th-century theater in America. It was built in 1798 by architect Antonio Locateli, who designed the theater in the Castle of Caterina Cornaro, in the Italian town of Asolo, near Venice.

The theater was purchased by the Ringling Museum's first director, A. Everett Austin, Jr., and installed on Museum property in the 1950's where theater, opera and music performances helped establish Sarasota as a cultural center. In 2004, the theater was dismantled and in 2006, it was cleaned and prepped for its new home in the Museum's Visitors Pavilion where today, it again offers theater, dance, music and film.

Cà d'Zan, from Sarasota Bay.

Museum of Art Gallery 21.

Historic Asolo Theater.

John and Mable Ringling at the circus.

Circus Museum's Howard Bros. Circus model main entrance.

This history made possible through a gift by **John Ringling North, II and Shirley Ringling North**

RINGLING COLLEGE OF ART AND DESIGN

For more than 75 years, Ringling College of Art and Design has cultivated the creative spirit in students from around the globe ... changing the way the world sees art and design. Founded in 1931 by noted art collector, real estate magnate, and circus impresario John Ringling, the private, not-for-profit college is fully accredited by the National Association of Schools of Art and Design (NASAD) and the Southern Association of Colleges and Schools (SACS) to confer the Bachelor of Fine Arts (BFA) and the Bachelor of Arts degrees (BA).

Located in Sarasota, Florida, the campus includes more than 100 buildings and enrolls 1200 students from around the world – more than sixty percent of whom live on-campus. Its faculty members are all professional artists, designers, and scholars who actively pursue their own work outside the classroom.

In recent years, Ringling College has evolved into one of the most prestigious institutions of its kind in the U.S., alongside Rhode Island School of Design, Pratt Institute, Parsons School of Design, and the Art Institute of Chicago. With a better than 1:2 computer to student ratio, it is also recognized as a leader in the use of technology in the arts. In 2006, *BusinessWeek* magazine named the College one of the top 60 design schools in the world, and one of only 10 in the entire United States. In 2007, Ringling's Computer Animation program was rated #1 in North America by the acclaimed *3D World* magazine.

The College's rigorous curriculum engages innovation and tradition through a strong, well-rounded, first-year program and a deep focus on the liberal arts. Students study one of 13 disciplines leading to a BFA degree: Advertising Design, Broadcast Design/Motion Graphics, Computer Animation, Digital Film, Fine Arts, Game Art & Design, Graphic & Interactive Communication, Illustration, Interior Design, Painting, Printmaking, Photography & Digital Imaging and Sculpture; or they may pursue a BA degree in the Business of Art & Design.

Ringling College students and alumni are heavily recruited throughout the country by a wide variety of outstanding companies like Hallmark Cards, CNN, Sony Pictures Imageworks, Pixar Animation Studios, DreamWorks, Disney, Electronic Arts (EA), American Greetings, and even the Central Intelligence Agency. Its students and alumni receive many accolades for their superior art and design talents in art and design competitions on the local, regional and national levels.

The College prepares each graduate to be both successful in their chosen career, as well as socially responsible artist-citizens. A comprehensive residence life and student life program complements the classroom academic focus by teaching students leadership skills via student clubs and organizations and providing an opportunity for a wide variety of social interaction, recreational and career-oriented activities. Students donate hours upon hours of their personal time to volunteering on a variety of local community public service projects. Their desire to offer of themselves to support those in need is one of the most significant signs of their belief in personal involvement and social responsibility.

Aside from the degree program, Ringling College provides students and the community access to its noted **Selby Gallery** – "Sarasota's premier gallery for contemporary art" – to view the works of nationally and internationally known artists, illustrators, photographers, sculptors, and designers. When complete, the College's **Sarasota Museum of Art (SMOA),** Sarasota's newest museum, will provide students and the entire Sarasota community access to the latest in modern contemporary art, while at the same time, preserving the historic Sarasota High School in a creative re-adaptation to house the museum as well as Ringling College art studios and classrooms.

For those who want to explore personal creative pursuits, the College's **Continuing Studies and Special Programs** and **Longboat Key Center for the Arts** divisions foster lifelong learning, personal development, and cultural enrichment through community art classes, workshops, exhbitions, and special events. And, the independent, not-for-profit, **Ringling College Library Association (RCLA),** established in 1975, fosters the educational growth of students, faculty, and community through the ongoing development of the college's on-campus Verman Kimbrough Memorial Library. In its 30-plus-year history, the 2,000-member, all-volunteer Library Association has donated more than $3-million toward the purchase of books, research materials, on-line services and many other resources for the library through its highly acclaimed Town Hall lecture series.

For more information, contact us via email at info@ringling.edu, or visit us online: www.ringling.edu.

PIERO RIVOLTA

The Artist Entrepreneur

Piero Rivolta has pursued his love of adventure in his native Italy and, since 1980, in Sarasota.

When he moved to Sarasota, Rivolta brought with him his enthusiasm for creating a good life for himself and others by applying his boundless energy and creativity to a wide range of projects, from commercial and residential buildings to marine design and boat building; from automotive and public transport design to the arts, including chamber music, opera and literature.

Piero Attilio Rivolta began his professional career near Milan, Italy, when he assumed direction of the family sports car business, Iso Rivolta, upon the untimely death of his father, Renzo Rivolta. Piero, a graduate engineer, thus became the youngest chief executive in the automobile industry and led the company in the development of legendary and technologically advanced cars, including the Iso Rivolta Grifo, now a treasured collector's item worldwide. Somehow, he managed to do all this while continuing to indulge his love of sailing, skiing and equestrian competition.

Before moving to Florida, at a time when Italian industry was struggling in the face of European economic uncertainty, Piero developed commercial and residential projects around Milan; built a textile factory in Brazil; and developed a shopping center in Santo Domingo. Before making the move permanent, Piero had tested the local waters by building a condominium of 14 large units in Bradenton Beach, working with Tivoli Homes, a company organized for that purpose and still a key player in the Rivolta Group. A series of development projects followed, including: Longwood Run, a project of approximately 550 residential units and a tennis club; completion of Cedar Creek, which had been in receivership; acquisition, completion, management and sale of Center Pointe in downtown Sarasota; acquisition, completion, management and sale of The Oaks Club; acquisition, renovation and sale of 3 acres in downtown Sarasota, now the site of the Sarasota Herald-Tribune building. Most recently, the Rivolta Group has completed Rivo at Ringling, a new condominium in Sarasota's downtown. The site also houses an office center, including the Rivolta Group headquarters, a bank and a retail complex.

His son, named Renzo after his illustrious grandfather, in addition to providing architectural concepts for the real estate projects, also heads up Renzo Line at Rivolta Yachts, a designer and producer of high quality and high-tech boats, manufactured in Sarasota and sold around the world. The industrial design facilities at Rivolta Yachts and those managed by Piero's daughter, Marella, in Milan have attracted international attention for their advanced technologies and imaginative concepts. During all of this, Piero has somehow found time to continue his writing, publishing a book of poetry and his newest novel, "Sunset in Sarasota." He continues to guide the festival he founded more than 20 years ago, La Musica International Chamber Music Festival, whose April concert series has garnered acclaim both in the United States and Europe. Is this artist entrepreneur a Renaissance Man? You bet he is!

SARASOTA'S RITZ-CARLTON LEGACY

*I*n 1926, Sarasota's most famous founding father Circus Magnate John Ringling began construction of a Ritz-Carlton Hotel on the southern end of Longboat Key. Ringling had dreams of making Sarasota an upscale destination – attracting the "ultra exclusive… the best, the richest people of the nation" and had agreed to pay his good friend and business associate Mr. Albert Keller of The New York Ritz-Carlton a sum of $5,000 per year in order to use the prestigious Ritz-Carlton name.

With great fanfare and in true Roaring Twenties style, construction began on the luxurious building. Ground was broken mid-March while Ringling was still trying to raise money from Sarasota investors by selling shares of The Sarasota Ritz-Carlton Hotel Company stocks. It is not known exactly how much Ringling lavished on his hotel, but the sum of $400,000 is frequently mentioned. When hopes were still high for the hotel, people played golf on a course built on the grounds. Mable Ringling entertained a group for lunch on the unfinished terrace. Before its doors were even opened, it was Sarasota's hottest spot.

Construction was abruptly halted in November 1926 by the onset of the Florida Land Bust as well as the Great Depression. He resumed construction, but eventually was forced to shut down the project permanently. The partially constructed, ornate building, known by locals as the "ghost hotel," sat abandoned for more than 40 years until it was demolished to make way for new development in the late 1960s.

75 years later, Ringling's dream of a Ritz-Carlton Hotel in Sarasota was realized as The Ritz-Carlton, Sarasota opened its doors on November 16, 2001.

Today, the splendor and opulence of The Ritz-Carlton, Sarasota celebrates Sarasota's heritage. 2400 of the original brown-rose bricks from the unfinished Ritz-Carlton on Longboat Key have been laid in the courtyard of The Ritz-Carlton, Sarasota surrounded by a rose garden, the favorite flower of Mable Ringling, John's wife. Meeting rooms and dining venues have been named for hotels and buildings built during the community's boom years of growth and development from the 1880s to 1920s including The Belle Haven, The Mira Mar, The Palms, St. Armands, The Bay Island, Cà d'Zan and The Bay View. The resort's signature restaurant, Vernona, is named for the El Vernona Hotel, built in 1926 by developer Owen Burns. The Ritz-Carlton, Sarasota stands on the same property that Ringling acquired around 1931 after Burns lost the El Vernona to a mortgage company. The original building, designed by noted architect Dwight James Baum was finally known as the John Ringling Towers.

A Picture Perfect Setting for Luxury

Since the opening of The Ritz-Carlton, Sarasota, the utmost importance has been placed on the traditionally high standard of luxury. As a result, the resort has received a majority of the foremost awards that the hospitality industry and leading consumer organizations can bestow including AAA's prestigious Five Diamond Award.

Conveniently located on the sparkling waters of Sarasota Bay near the city center, the resort offers 266 guest rooms featuring indulgent amenities, spacious balconies and sweeping views of the Bay, the marina or the city skyline. For the most discriminating traveler, The Ritz-Carlton Club Level features its own private lounge and dedicated concierge team and is reachable only by keyed elevator access.

The Ritz-Carlton Members Spa Club at The Ritz-Carlton, Sarasota is a full-service wellness destination spa with more than 100 wellness and anti-aging treatments using the beneficial properties of ocean minerals, natural elixirs and pure-organic essential oils. Guests of the resort are also invited to enjoy the privileges of The Ritz-Carlton Members Beach Club, an exclusive tropical retreat on beautiful Lido Key offering a private beach, gulf-front pools, elegant changing facilities, several dining options, banquet venues, a beachfront tiki bar and more. And golfers can take advantage of The Ritz-Carlton Members Golf Club, featuring an 18-hole USGA championship course designed by renowned golf course architect Tom Fazio.

The Ritz-Carlton, Sarasota affords a sophisticated blend of casual Gulf Coast lifestyle and cosmopolitan excitement. Whether exploring the city's fine dining, historical and shopping attractions or just lounging in the Florida sun, visitors will find it the perfect place to soak it all in.

Actual postcard from the 1920s - Artist's rendering of John Ringling's never completed Ritz-Carlton Hotel on the southern tip of Longboat Key.

15 Tee at The Ritz-Carlton Members Golf Club.

Hotel pool overlooking beautiful Sarasota Bay.

SARASOTA CONSERVATION FOUNDATION

Protecting Sarasota County's Bays, Beaches and Barrier Islands

Sarasota Conservation Foundation envisions an Emerald Necklace of places on the bays, beaches and barrier islands that recall Sarasota County's historic character and heritage. Anyone who has watched dolphins play in the surf, walked a deserted beach after a tropical storm or watched pelicans and osprey nesting on a mangrove island knows how uplifting and reassuring those experiences are. Appreciating these moments underscores that every acre conserved is a meaningful victory.

Bay Preserve at Osprey. (Photo by Clyde Butcher)

Sarasota Conservation Foundation is a local non-profit land trust founded in 2003 to protect the character and natural integrity of Sarasota County. The Foundation accomplishes its mission to protect the environment, character and biodiversity of Sarasota County's bays, beaches and barrier islands by: holding conservation easements and owning nature preserves; collaborating with individuals, organizations and communities; and advocating responsible stewardship.

Albert Joerger, PhD., the founder of the Sarasota Conservation Foundation, has extensive expertise in intelligent conservation. His passion for the Gulf Coast is based in part on having family ties with Sarasota County as a fifth generation winter resident. Over the years, Dr. Joerger saw many beautiful waterfront areas slipping away. Realizing that time was running out to preserve the community from the environmental impact of over development, Dr. Joerger relocated his family to Sarasota and established the Sarasota Conservation Foundation.

The pressures and challenges placed on our natural areas and parklands drive the Foundation's work. The Foundation has created parks, preserved rare natural habitats, and collaborated with public, private, and independent entities to receive grant funding and build membership support. The Foundation's interaction with local landowners, policy makers, and other non-profit organizations provides it with unique insights into Sarasota County's exceptional historical, social, and biological landscape. The community need for an active local conservation organization has become increasingly apparent as the Foundation continues to receive landowners' inquiries about its acquisition program.

The Foundation's first land acquisition was Michael Biehl Park, located at 100 West Tampa Avenue in Venice. The park is a gateway and trailhead to the Venice Waterway Park and the County's Rails to Trails project. Michael Biehl Park provides access to the waterway trail developed along the Intracoastal Waterway as it meanders through Venice. The property utilizes native plant landscaping and serves as a tribute to the days when Venice and its surrounding Gulf Coast communities were founded. This property was purchased by Sarasota Conservation Foundation with grant funding from Gulf Coast Community Foundation of Venice. Sarasota Conservation Foundation's relationship with the City of Venice has resulted in the City developing the property into a public park. This collaborative approach has allowed multiple parties to participate in expanding public water access.

Sarasota Conservation Foundation was awarded a $6.6 million grant from the State's Florida Communities Trust the largest ever awarded by the Trust to a non-profit organization. The funds were used to purchase four-plus acres of bay front property in Osprey that is called Bay Preserve at Osprey, and is a center for the arts, education and the environment.

Bay Preserve at Osprey provides visitors public water access to Little Sarasota Bay. The park is immediately south of 273 acres of protected lands including Palmer Point Park's beach access, Jim Neville Preserve's rare habitat, and the estuary located at the mouth of North Creek. On-site services will include a natural history center, the Foundation's offices, environmental programs and classes, native plant information, and a wildlife viewing platform overlooking Little Sarasota Bay.

The Foundation also holds conservation easements in Sarasota County. From a beachfront property located on Casey Key to a conservation easement on a portion of the Manasota Beach Club, the Foundation assures these areas will be permanently protected for both wildlife and future generations. A conservation easement or land protection agreement is a permanent, binding agreement between a landowner and a land trust that can provide significant tax benefits while restricting the amount and type of future development on the property and enabling the owner to own, sell and pass the property on to their heirs. The Foundation's partnership and collaboration with local landowners has proven to be an invaluable tool in furthering successful conservation efforts in Sarasota County.

Sarasota Conservation Foundation will continue to build upon its goals of preserving natural habitat, increasing biodiversity and increasing awareness of land conservation to ensure future generations will have access to Florida's most compelling places. To join us in our mission or for more information about the Sarasota Conservation Foundation, please visit our website at http://www.sarasota-conservation.org or call 941 918-2100.

SARASOTA FAMILY YMCA

Embracing Values and Building Leaders

The Sarasota Family Young Men's Christian Association, Inc. (YMCA) is a charitable nonprofit organization, qualifying under Section 501(c)(3) of the US Tax Code. The Sarasota Family YMCA was founded in 1945 and currently has a budget exceeding $90 million and over 1,000 employees. The mission statement of the YMCA is: "We build strong kids, strong families, strong communities."

Carl Weinrich, president and CEO of the Sarasota Family YMCA for more than 30 years, is a true visionary and collaborator. About 15 years ago, Weinrich began non-traditional social service programs to help children and families. The Y's approach recognizes a community problem, concern, or void and identifies community resources, talent, and expertise that can repair or positively affect the issue. Finally, a partnership of collaborative members focuses on the same mission and commits to the project. This makes the Sarasota Family YMCA unique!

Historic Highlights:

1945   Frank G. Berlin, Sr., president of the Sarasota Chamber of Commerce, founded the Sarasota Family YMCA to provide activities and programs promoting family life. The first YMCA office was located at 310 South Orange Avenue.

1960   The Frank G. Berlin, Sr. Branch was established for health enhancement and youth sports and activities, giving Sarasota County its first indoor swimming pool.

1981   The YMCA Foundation of Sarasota, Inc. organized to support the activities of the Sarasota Family YMCA. Under the leadership of President Karin Gustafson, the Foundation has helped enable many community programs and projects.

1983   The Berlin Branch added the Sudakoff Gymnastic Center, an 8,000-square-foot specialized gymnastic facility.

1990   The second branch was added to the City Center building, relocating in 1998 to Main Plaza. In 2003, it was dedicated as the Babe Weiller YMCA Branch in honor of a member of the YMCA Foundation Board of Trustees.

1991   The YMCA Youth Shelter, a 20-bed residential facility for runaways, truants, and ungovernable youth, ages ten through 17, opened in 1991.

1992   The YMCA introduced the HIPPY program (Home Instruction for Parents of Preschool Youngsters), a home-based program for the educational enrichment of preschool children and to promote increased awareness by parents of their potential as home educators.

1993   The Sarasota Family YMCA and a committee of volunteers opened the Hardee County Family YMCA.

1994   The YMCA added the Transitional Living Program, which serves older, homeless youth ages 16-21 by providing shelter, life skills training, and support services.

The fourth branch, through collaboration with Sarasota County Parks and Recreation, opened in Palmer Ranch and was named the Evalyn Sadlier Jones Branch.

The YMCA became the lead agency of a coalition in the privatization of Child Welfare/Foster Care and related services, making Sarasota County the first county to implement and set the standard by which all 67 counties within Florida handle foster care. The program provides comprehensive services to children and families needing foster care or at risk of needing foster care. The services provided include foster parent recruitment, training and licensure; adoptions; foster care; protective supervision; and voluntary family services. In 1999, foster care expanded into Manatee County, in 2001 into DeSoto County and in 2004 into Pasco and Pinellas counties. Known as the Safe Children Coalition, it serves more than 6,000 abused, neglected or abandoned children daily.

1997   The YMCA opened Kalish House, a group home for male foster care adolescents up to the age of 18 with twelve boys.

Renaissance Ranch opened to serve girls in foster care. In 2005, construction expanded the facility to accommodate 20 girls and it was renamed Bowman Ranch after Paul Bowman, chair of the YMCA Foundation Board.

2000   The Selby Aquatics Center opened its 50-meter pool, diving arena and Water Park at the C. J. Lofino Family Complex in Palmer Ranch. This complex includes the Evalyn Sadlier Jones Branch.

The administrative offices and the YMCA Foundation moved to the newly constructed Kane Plaza.

The Frank G. Berlin, Sr. Branch opened its new 80,000-square-foot facility.

The Bari Brooks Center opened to provide a safe environment for teens and families at the Berlin Branch.

2005   The Josephine Lofino Splash Pool, an addition to the C. J. Lofino Family Complex, opened.

2006   Y Reads, an after-school mentoring and literacy program for first and second grades, was introduced to students from Fruitville and Emma Booker elementary schools.

The Welch Family Teen Center, at the Evalyn Sadlier Jones Branch, opened.

Operation Graduation provided a comprehensive academic after-school enrichment program for students in Newtown.

What is next for the Sarasota Family YMCA? Visit our website at www.sarasota-ymca.org for more information.

SARASOTA MEMORIAL HEALTHCARE FOUNDATION, INC.

Healthcare Foundation Marks Three Decades of Advancing Healthcare Through Philanthropy

The founding of Sarasota Memorial Healthcare Foundation, Inc. - originally Sarasota Memorial Hospital Foundation, Inc.- more than three decades ago demonstrates what can happen when dedicated individuals harness private efforts for the public good.

As Sarasota's population expanded and Sarasota Memorial Hospital struggled to keep pace with rapid developments in medical technology, the need for a separate organization to solicit the support of Sarasota citizens became apparent. Thus, Sarasota Memorial Hospital Foundation, Inc., was established on February 25, 1976, as an independent not-for-profit charitable corporation.

The charter of the Foundation is broad; it may receive gifts, grants and bequests for unrestricted or restricted purposes. Any qualified not-for-profit healthcare organization in the county may be aided by the Foundation and it may expend funds for equipment, clinical studies, research, staff training, education and capital projects.

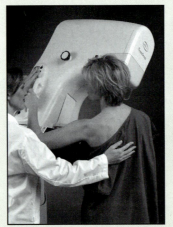
Digital Mammography

The robotically assisted da Vinci S™ Surgical System®

SARASOTA MEMORIAL
HEALTHCARE FOUNDATION
INCORPORATED
1976
1515 S. OSPREY AVENUE, SUITE B-4, SARASOTA, FL 34239
(941) 917-1286   SMHF.ORG

Making an Impact

The first major gift of the Foundation was the contribution in 1980 of $180,000 towards a CAT body scanner. April 1983 saw the opening of the Open Heart Surgery Center, funded by a $500,000 gift to the Foundation by Sarasota philanthropist and Foundation trustee Harry Sudakoff.

In 1985, Henry Cape, Jr.'s bequest of $3,700,000 resulted in construction of the Cape Ambulatory Surgery Center. A $2,800,000 bequest in 1987 from the estate of Harry O. and Alwena H. Mayer enabled the Foundation to purchase the first Magnetic Resonance Imager (MRI) in Sarasota.

Since the reorganization of the Foundation in 1994, the net assets have grown from $7.2 million to $37 million in 2007. Accomplishments in its second and third decades included gifts of $1 million to build and endow the Jo Mills Reis Care Center; $1 million for the creation of the Meckler Admission Center; $1.2 million to establish the first endowed chair in nursing at the University of South Florida (USF) College of Nursing in Nursing Infomatics; and $150,000 to establish an endowed professorship in Oncology at the College of Nursing at USF.

Foundation grants of nearly $1 million also have resulted in the purchase of specialized brain-surgery equipment and a research affiliation with Harvard Medical School to study Parkinson's disease and other neurodegenerative diseases.

Most recently, Foundation efforts have taken on even more significance with the funding of $7 million towards development of a new Emergency Care Center (ECC); $1,431,172 for digital mammography equipment; $298,839 for a maternal-neonatal intensive care transport unit; $678,538 for a surgical 'navigation' system for knee and hip replacements; $400,000 towards the robotic surgical system for urological surgery, gynecologic oncology and mitral valve replacement; and $465,000 for the patient safety lab - to name just a few.

Furthering the Mission

That Sarasota Memorial Hospital has evolved into one of the premiere public healthcare centers in Florida speaks volumes about the early founders and subsequent leaders. This is made possible, to a significant degree, by contributions to the Foundation from individuals, foundations and corporations. Few community-owned hospitals offer the range of sophisticated services, technology and equipment as does Sarasota Memorial Health Care System (SMHCS).

Meeting the Need

Alexandra (Alex) Quarles, CFRE, President and CEO of Sarasota Memorial Healthcare Foundation, Inc., noted, "As a premier not-for-profit organization, we have been most fortunate for the wisdom of our trustees and the financial support of our community to further our mission."

Supporting superior healthcare presents the Healthcare Foundation with many opportunities and challenges as SMHCS strives to continue providing nationally recognized healthcare services in the face of increased competition and declining reimbursements.

The Sum of its People

Since its establishment in 1976, the Foundation has provided grants of more than $32 million and stands ready to assure the community that the SMHCS will continue to be one of the best healthcare centers in the country.

The Foundation is the sum of its people - of the individuals who have gone before and those who continue to believe in the concept of quality healthcare for all members of our community. It has been a remarkable story of caring individuals who have humanized a county hospital through their private philanthropy - an extraordinary journey of Voluntary Action for the Public Good - and we are just getting started.

This history made possible by
Northern Trust

SCHROEDER-MANATEE RANCH, INC.

All the comforts of home, with the past and future at your doorstep…

A short drive east on University Parkway will bring you to the entrance to Lakewood Ranch. Drive further and you will experience the vibrant Schroeder-Manatee Ranch, Inc. This beautiful acreage straddling Sarasota and Manatee counties is best known for the award-winning, master-planned community of Lakewood Ranch, which comprises just 8,500 acres of the total land area. But if you look a little closer you'll find much more; Schroeder-Manatee Ranch (SMR) is a 100-year-old working ranch and agricultural enterprise.

In 1905, settler John Schroeder purchased this timber acreage to support a furniture manufacturing endeavor and until 1915, the land was largely a timber operation. In 1922, the Uihlein family (pronounced "EE-Line"), founders of the famed Schlitz Brewery in Milwaukee, acquired the ranch from John Schroeder. Land cleared by the timber operation was cultivated to grow vegetable crops and pasture cattle. The Uihlein family continued to expand and diversify over the decades and today, the Ranch features 1,500 head of cattle; some 1,300 acres of citrus groves; 3,500 acres of tomato, vegetable, tree and turf farming; and a shell aggregate mining operation.

The various operations at Schroeder-Manatee Ranch all work together. For example, the shell mining operation, SMR Aggregates, provides necessary road and construction materials for Lakewood Ranch and the surrounding area. The empty mining pits then become attractive lakes for fish habitats as well as recreation. Much of the turf for new homes and golf courses is grown on the property. Since drought is a problem in Florida, SMR Farms works with state universities to evaluate and grow improved turf and drought-tolerant grasses that will thrive in Lakewood Ranch.

The commercial real estate efforts have created the largest corporate park in Sarasota County. A diverse group of businesses - including higher education, light manufacturing, engineering, financial services and construction - make their homes in the Ranch. Two jobs (non-construction) are created for every rooftop, meaning many people work close to where they live.

Schroeder-Manatee Ranch and Lakewood Ranch are not only great places to live and work; they are also great places to play. The property is home to the Sarasota Polo Club and the Sarasota Cricket Club. The Sarasota Polo Club was established in 1991 and is now the second largest in the country, with nine beautifully manicured fields. The Club had the prestigious honor of hosting the first stop of the Triple Crown of Polo Championship Series in March 2006. This game was broadcast nationally on ESPN 2 and was the first polo event to be broadcast all over the world. It is now an annual event.

Rex Jensen, President and CEO.

As developers of Lakewood Ranch, LWR Communities, LLC respects the SMR heritage and continues the tradition of making development fit the land, not the land fit development. All sensitive habitats are mapped before any plans are drawn. The

Lakewood Ranch Golf and Country Club.

company then designs around them and maintains adequate buffers of native vegetation for habitat protection. The company worked with Sarasota County to preserve nearly 2,000 acres of environmentally sensitive land. LWR Communities then assumed responsibility for maintaining and managing the protected property in perpetuity.

Understanding that many creatures also call the Ranch home, acreage has been set aside for open green space, wildlife sanctuary and connected, safe corridors for animals. There are deer as well as river otters, eagles, gopher tortoises, Florida sandhill cranes and many more species. More than 12,000 people – some 6,000 households – call Lakewood Ranch their new home town. These residents enjoy safe walks and bike rides along the more than 100 miles of interconnected trails, sidewalks and paths at the Ranch. There is also a 110-acre nature preserve, a restored 451-acre wetland preserve and more than 400 acres of man-made lakes.

Charolais Bulls in SMR Pastures.

Every aspect of SMR and Lakewood Ranch takes environmental stewardship into consideration. To further the commitment, Lakewood Ranch has earned the Florida Green Building Coalition's "Green" designation. This means Lakewood Ranch meets high standards for land use, community design and location. Lakewood Ranch is proudly leading the way as the largest 'Green' community in the country.

SMR is definitely rich with history. Acquired more than 100 years ago at a time when Florida was being settled and tamed, the company developed a cowboy culture of hard work, few pretenses and honest dealings. It remains today as it was in 1922; a privately held family company with goals that assure sound land stewardship and emphasize the importance of community involvement.

Citrus Trees in SMR Groves.

The first people to blaze a trail in Schroeder-Manatee Ranch left hoof prints. That flavor still remains today as our cowboys, some in boots and some in suits, continue our legacy of agriculture and stewardship…

SEIBERT ARCHITECTS, P.A.

SEIBERT ARCHITECTS, P.A. is a firm with over fifty years of experience in architecture, interiors and planning throughout the southeastern United States and the Caribbean. The firm is well known as a leader in the development of the "Sarasota School", a recognized and much-copied architectural style. The aesthetics of that style provide recognition that the firm has enjoyed on a national and international level.

The firm was founded in 1955 by Edward J. Seibert, FAIA, and today is our area's longest continuing architectural practice. Samuel C. Holladay, AIA, along with associates Michael L. Epstein, AIA, Dale S. Parks, AIA, and Pamela L. Holladay, ASID, carry on the legacy of the firm. Since Edward Seibert's retirement in 1994, Sam Holladay, who has a 35-year association with Seibert Architects, is now the principal and owner of the firm. Michael Epstein has been with the Seibert Architects PA since 1990 and Dale Parks joined the firm in 2000. As project architects, these two lead the firm's design teams. Pamela R. Holladay, ASID, joined the firm in 1975 and is a licensed Interior Designer.

Seibert Architects PA offers complete professional services including architecture; interior and landscape design; construction documents; construction administration; and engineering services in direct response to individual client needs, the site and climate. We continue to take special pride in meeting the challenge of creating work of artistic integrity, which is functionally and technically resolved. An important part of the firm's tradition is our proven ability to implement a project that reflects the desires and aspirations of the client. With a record of successful designs on Florida's Gulf Coast, Seibert Architects PA has the capability to uniquely assist clients with their projects.

Our firm's work is characterized by strong, sculptural designs and structures distinguished by their eloquent simplicity and clarity of form. Our public clients include The School Board of Sarasota County, DeSoto County School District, Sarasota County, The Gulf Coast Heritage Foundation and The Hermitage Artists Retreat Foundation. Projects for our private sector clients include offices, commercial buildings, interior design and custom homes. Below are a few examples of our work.

RESIDENCE: GORSKI HOUSE, BOCA GRANDE, FL

Winner of the AIA Merit Award of Excellence 2005, this house was completed in 2000. The program includes capturing extensive views of the natural environment afforded by the site. Designed as an open pavilion, the house provides expansive views of the neighboring water and mangrove preserve. The house carefully balances openness and clearly defined spaces, using architectural features to define boundaries.

INTERIOR: MASON HOUSE, SARASOTA, FL

The Mason House located in Sarasota, Florida on Siesta Key, an example of an interior renovation project which transformed this house to one with an open space, focusing attention on the waterfront views and a strong connection of inside to outside. A clean, elegant interior with natural materials create a serene space which serves the homeowners' desire for simplicity.

GOVERNMENT: BUS TRANSFER FACILITY, SARASOTA, FL

The design for Sarasota's Bus Transfer Facility, located in the central business district, is intended to convey the structure as a public pavilion. The orientation of the project's site runs perpendicular to the strong east/west walkway of City Hall. Four central columns serve to frame City Hall's axial walkway and the visual terminus of a new public art plinth creating a symbolic gateway to the City Hall complex.

Seibert Architects PA has received numerous awards and honors for innovative design excellence in a variety of work, based on sensitivity to the Florida Gulf Coast environment and concern for its inhabitants. To that end, client participation is facilitated throughout the course of design to arrive at a building that is technically and aesthetically responsive. Our goal is to continue to meet each new project with an effective solution celebrating Florida's natural environment and culture.

SUNTRUST BANK, SOUTHWEST FLORIDA

SunTrust Bank, Southwest Florida is a leader in Sarasota's banking community. The bank was formed as the result of a merger between SunTrust, formerly SunBank, and Coast Bank of Sarasota. These two powerhouses combined to form one of the leading banks in the Southwest Florida region.

It was the purchase of Flagship Banks, Inc. that first brought SunTrust (then SunBank) to Sarasota in 1983. As a leader in the industry, and well known by businesses and individuals throughout Florida, SunBank was not a stranger to Sarasota. SunBank was one of the first banks to install drive–in teller windows and opened the first statewide automatic teller machine network in Florida.

SunTrust embraces the philosophy of active community involvement and continues to build on their tradition of supporting local organizations and encouraging employees and officers to volunteer in cultural and civic arenas. Linton Allen, a founding father of SunBank, believed that if a bank were to be profitable, it had to be strong enough to serve its customers adequately. But if a bank was to truly succeed, it needed to concern itself with keeping its employees healthy and happy so they too could contribute their talents to the community. Mr. Allen often said, "Build your community and you build your bank." It is this tradition that has prevailed through the changes and growth to remain the cornerstone of each successive mission statement.

SunTrust Bank, Southwest Florida is honored as one of the area's leaders in community involvement and support which ranges from arts and education to social services and economic development. The Association of Fundraising Professionals recognized SunTrust as a nominee in the "Outstanding Corporate Partner" category in 2006. SunTrust also participates as a consistent leader in the annual Pacesetter Campaign for the United Way.

Today, the location at 1777 Main Street acts as the headquarters for SunTrust Bank, Southwest Florida. SunTrust Bank, Southwest Florida has over 74 full service offices located throughout Manatee, Sarasota, Charlotte, Lee, and Collier counties. Margaret Callihan is chairman of the board, president and chief executive officer for the entire Southwest Florida region; the fourth largest region in SunTrust's Florida network, which today is comprised of over 516 offices from Pensacola to Miami.

SunTrust Banks, Inc., headquartered in Atlanta, is one of the nation's largest banking organizations, serving a broad range of consumer, commercial, corporate and institutional clients. As of December 31, 2006, SunTrust had total assets of $182.2 billion and total deposits of $124.0 billion. The Company operates an extensive branch and ATM network throughout the high-growth Southeast and Mid-Atlantic states and a full array of technology-based, 24-hour delivery channels. The Company also serves customers in selected markets nationally. Its primary businesses include deposit, credit, trust and investment services. Through various subsidiaries the Company provides credit cards, mortgage banking, insurance, brokerage, equipment leasing and capital markets services. SunTrust's internet address is suntrust.com.

SYPRETT, MESHAD, RESNICK, LIEB, DUMBAUGH & JONES

The law firm of Syprett, Meshad, Resnick, Lieb, Dumbaugh & Jones, P.A. has been serving the area since 1968. The Firm has grown with the community and now includes nine lawyers and a support staff of fifteen.

In January of 1968, Jim D. Syprett and John W. Meshad formed the partnership of Syprett & Meshad. Michael L. Resnick joined the firm in June of 1973. M. Joseph Lieb, Jr. joined the firm in November of 1976. In July of 1980, the law firm became Syprett, Meshad, Resnick & Lieb, P.A.

John D. Dumbaugh joined the firm in March of 1983; Teresa D. Jones joined the firm in June of 1986; and Peter J. Krotec joined the firm in May of 1989. In January of 1993, the law firm reorganized and became Syprett, Meshad, Resnick, Lieb, Dumbaugh & Jones, P.A.

As a full service law firm, we have become thoroughly diversified. A law firm of necessity requires a broad spectrum of legal concepts. Accordingly, each attorney is involved in continuing legal education in an effort to maintain a diversity of knowledge with concentrated expertise in specific areas of law. Many of our attorneys are board certified in their field of expertise by the Florida Bar Association.

John Meshad, Teresa Jones, Joseph Lieb, John Dumbaugh, Jim Syprett, Michael Resnick

We offer a full range of legal services, with expertise in personal injury, real estate, criminal, family, commercial and corporate law, as well as will preparation and trust and estate planning. We are noted for having an excellent litigation department, specializing in commercial, constitutional, banking, construction and personal injury law for both plaintiff and defendant. Several of the attorneys are board certified in real property law, with emphasis on land use zoning, planning, development and finance.

While our practice encompasses business transactions throughout the entire southeastern United States, most of our practice deals with the State of Florida, with particular emphasis in the Sarasota metropolitan area. We are active in the community and have a sincere interest in the growth and stability of our community and its residents.

The hiring of a lawyer is an important decision that should not be based solely on advertisements. Please ask us to send you free written information about our qualifications and experience.

TOALE BROTHERS

Funeral Homes, Crematory & Pre-Arrangement Center

Toale Brothers Funeral Home is an institution in the Sarasota/Bradenton area. The firm was established in 1912 by George Thacker and is one of Sarasota's earliest businesses to be continuously operated. F.W. VanGilder later joined Mr. Thacker. As Sarasota grew, the fledgling funeral home grew. Its first location was on Main Street in Sarasota and then moved to Orange Avenue. That location is known today as Toale Brothers Colonial Chapel.

In 1948 the firm was purchased by George E. Toale and John P. (Jack) Toale, Sr., brothers from Bradenton. They were residents of Florida since 1925 and graduated from Bradenton High School and the Cincinnati School of Embalming. Catherine Toale Christian joined her brothers in the business and was the first woman in Florida to become a licensed embalmer.

Just a few years after purchasing the funeral home, Jack and George realized the need for branch funeral homes to serve the growing area. The Gulf Gate Chapel, the Bradenton Chapel and the Crematory were constructed. A Pre-Arrangement Center was also opened to offer families an office setting to discuss pre-arranging a funeral or cremation and to discuss the savings of a Trust 100 pre-financed funeral contract.

George Toale's love of antique collecting is evidenced in the beautiful pieces decorating the funeral homes. The antiques add warmth to the public areas and bring back fond memories for the families served. Remembering and gathering are part of the grieving process.

George and Amorette Toale, together with Jack and Vivienne Toale, raised six sons in Sarasota. Three of their sons operate the business today. David (Jack's son), Curtis and Robert (George's sons) were born and raised in Sarasota.

After completing higher education, David, Curtis and Robert became licensed funeral directors and embalmers. For over 30 years they have managed the company and given countless hours to community and civic organizations. This family owned business is operated with the help and support of family members. David's wife, Kathleen, has 25 years of service in the administrative and pre-need areas of the firm.

Robert's sons, Jason and Jeffrey, have joined the management team. They are second generation Sarasotans. Both are married and active in the community. They have completed their mortuary science education. Jason holds a Bachelor's degree from the University of South Florida and an MBA from Rollins College. Jeffrey is a graduate of the University of South Florida with a Bachelors degree. They are learning our business values, which have been handed down through the generations: Respect, Service and Integrity. David and Kathleen have since retired in December of 2006 after many years of dedicated service.

Our long history of service and dedication to the community is also reflected in our staff. They represent hundreds of years of professional care to the tens of thousands of families we have served over the years.

With a third generation involved in our family business we look forward to the future. We have the wisdom of years of experience and the energy of youthful leaders. We plan to maintain our place as one of the oldest and most respected family run funeral homes in Florida for many years to come.

Locations: Colonial Chapel, 40 North Orange Avenue; Gulf Gate Chapel, 6903 South Tamiami Trail; Bradenton Chapel, 912 53rd Avenue, West and the TRUST 100 Pre-Arrangement Center, 114 North Orange Avenue, Sarasota.

Sarasota's first funeral home constructed in 1925.

1997 - Colonial Chapel - the 1925 structure with many renovations.

UNITED WAY OF SARASOTA COUNTY, INC.

Founded in 1948, United Way of Sarasota County began as the "Community Chest of Sarasota County" and raised $42,044.87 during the annual campaign the first year. The inaugural Board of Directors included such community leaders as Leroy Fenne, Emmet Addy, Frances Filson, Wilfred T. Robarts and Robert C. Stickney. In 1959, we changed our name to United Appeal of Sarasota County. Fifteen years later, in 1974, we adopted our current name, United Way of Sarasota County, Inc., and at a commemorative dinner held at the University Club that same year, local volunteers unveiled the United Way Foundation of Sarasota County. R. Wendell Spragins inspired the formation of the Foundation and Milton L. Fischman's gift of $100,000 helped the Foundation begin to fulfill its mission of supporting United Way's efforts through an endowment program.

Building from the success of the Foundation, we began our own United Way Tocqueville Society in 1987. Founding members included Jane Bancroft-Cook and Alex and Betty Schoenbaum. The Tocqueville Society is a national program designed to deepen the understanding, dedication and support of individuals to United Way and to recognize their commitment. Membership in the Society is granted to individuals who contribute at least $10,000 annually to United Way.

Today, United Way is woven into the fabric of Sarasota. We continue to develop and promote innovative community initiatives and develop new programs like United Way 2-1-1. 2-1-1 is a special abbreviated telephone number reserved in the United States as an easy-to-remember three-digit telephone number meant to provide quick information to health and human services. This important service helps local citizens find the assistance they need with one free, confidential phone call.

United Way of Sarasota County's mission is to help make our community a better place through helping others. We strive to be the most effective United Way in the country, in the most caring community in America. We achieve lasting impact by partnering with health and human service organizations located right here in Sarasota County. These partners provide residents of Sarasota County with the help they need to live better lives.

As we continue to grow with Sarasota, we are constantly looking for ways to better respond to local needs. Gradually, we have responded by evolving from a fundraising and agency-funding organization to an impact organization. In recent years, we have become even more proactive in assessing our community's needs and forming new partnerships to focus on critical issues like building strong children and families, rescuing people in crisis and empowering people to independence.

Just as we did in 1948, we focus on solving these fundamental issues with the help of our many community volunteers. We could not exist without their dedication and generosity. They review the many health and human services programs in our community and make decisions on where United Way funds are invested. Contributing their resources and expertise, they collaborate on critical initiatives to create lasting community impact. They serve on our Board of Directors, our Community Impact Committee and many other committees, donating countless hours to focus on what matters most, making a positive and lasting impact on our community's most critical needs.

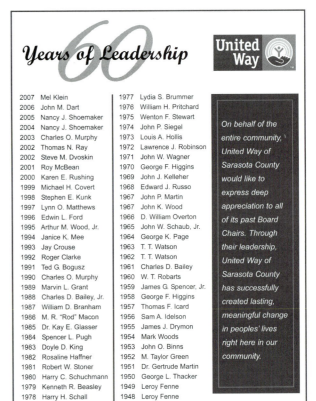

THE UROLOGY TREATMENT CENTER

The Urology Treatment Center has become a world-class clinical practice sustaining distinguished and prestigious medical research. Begun in 1980 by Dr. Winston E. Barzell, it is a five-physician practice employing more than 25 staff members at its office in the Waldemere Medical Plaza.

Dr. Barzell is a graduate of McGill University Medical School. He completed a clinical fellowship in urologic cancer at Memorial Sloan-Kettering Cancer Center in New York, where he became an attending surgeon and an Associate Professor of Surgery at Cornell Medical College-New York Hospital. While there, he met his future partner, Dr. Willet F. Whitmore III, whose father, Dr. Willet F. Witmore Jr., was chief of surgery at Memorial Sloan-Kettering and widely acknowledged as the father of urologic oncology.

Dr. Whitmore joined Dr. Barzell in 1984 after serving as an Assistant Professor of Surgery at Harvard. In 1997 they formed Barzell-Whitmore Maroon Bells Medical Equipment and became a world leader in prostate brachytherapy accessory equipment with 12 patented devices. CIVCO Medical Instruments, now a division of Roper Industries, purchased their company in 2003.

Dr. Barzell pioneered 3D-pathological mapping of the prostate, a technique that allows patients with minimal disease alternatives to traditional prostate cancer treatments. Some patients are spared treatment altogether, whereas other patients may be candidates for focal cryoablation, "the so-called male lumpectomy," a technique enabled by Dr. Barzell's mapping procedure. Dr. Barzell's presentation at the Society of Urologic Oncology in 2006 brought widespread recognition from numerous academic centers and Sarasota became a nationwide destination for patients and physicians seeking advice and care. At the Urology Treatment Center, patients needing whole-gland treatment may choose from the entire spectrum of prostate cancer treatments, including radiation therapy, cryotherapy or robotic-assisted laparoscopic radical prostatectomy, a technique introduced to Sarasota by Dr. Robert Carey.

In 1987, Dr. Alan Treiman joined the practice after completing his urologic training at the Harvard Program at Brigham and Women's Hospital in Boston. Dr. Treiman introduced laser treatment of urinary calculi to Sarasota Memorial Hospital and was a founding member of Man to Man, a nationwide prostate cancer support group initiated in Sarasota which has become the American Cancer Society's national prostate cancer support group.

Dr. Kenneth Bregg was recruited in 1994 for his expertise in urinary incontinence and female urology. Dr. Bregg trained at New York Hospital-Cornell Medical Center and completed a fellowship in female incontinence at the UCLA Medical Center in Los Angeles with Dr. Schlomo Raz.

Dr. Joshua Green joined the group in 2000 and has developed a strong reputation specializing in infertility and vasectomy reversal. He introduced laparoscopic and percutaneous renal surgery to Sarasota Memorial Hospital. Dr. Green is a graduate of Jefferson Medical College in Philadelphia and received his urologic training at the University of Miami School of Medicine.

Dr. Carey ushers in era of robotic surgery to Sarasota

In early 2006, the Urology Treatment Center and Sarasota Memorial Hospital entered the era of robotic surgery by recruiting Robert I. Carey, MD PhD from the University of Miami. With the arrival of a fellowship-trained, experienced laparoscopic and robotic surgeon, the board of trustees for Sarasota Memorial Hospital approved the purchase of Florida's first da Vinci S-model surgical robot. Robotic technology allows the surgeon to visualize structures at 15x magnification with 3D vision. Rather than requiring a large incision, the surgeon passes precise robotic instruments through the skin via 8 mm incisions. The robotic instrument tips allow sub-millimeter cautery-free dissection of the neurovascular bundles and other vital structures around the prostate.

Dr. Carey earned his PhD in chemistry at the Massachusetts Institute of Technology and completed a National Institutes of Health fellowship at Harvard University. He became an Assistant Professor at the University of Lausanne, Switzerland and produced two patents that allowed environmentally safe robotic-assisted synthesis of peptides and proteins. His pharmaceutical company MaxC Pharm holds the patent for a drug delivery system for treating urothelial carcinoma. He received his training in urologic surgery at the University of Miami, Miller School of Medicine. He specializes in laparoscopic and minimally invasive approaches to urologic cancer, reconstruction and urolithiasis.

Shortly after his arrival in Sarasota, Dr. Carey was honored by the Endourological Society at the World Congress of Endourology with a First Prize for his work with direct real-time temperature monitoring for radiofrequency ablation of renal tumors. Within his first year in Sarasota, Dr. Carey continued the tradition of keeping the Urology Treatment Center in the ranks of high profile academia. He gave invited lectures at the American College of Surgeons, the American Urologic Association, and the Endourological Society.

Sarasota has become a recognized center for robotic surgery and for renal tumor ablation.

WENDEL KENT & COMPANY, GATOR ASPHALT COMPANY

Building Sarasota's Streets and Highways for a Generation

Coming as strangers from Illinois in 1959, the Wendel Kent family never dreamed they would become part of Sarasota's history, and that they might become a force in the way the community was to develop. From their chosen home on Siesta Key the Kents eagerly began their life in Sarasota.

In 1960 Wendel began a job as Sarasota Assistant City Engineer. Ken Thompson was the capable and popular City Manager at the time. Wendel has always suspected Ken was a bit of a humorist when he directed Wendel to solve the acute and persistent drainage problems on St. Armand's Circle. During the project it became clear that only so much could be done and that John Ringling long ago should have pumped up three more feet of fill while he was at it.

As pleased as Wendel was to be working for the City of Sarasota, he wanted to own and operate his own roadbuilding company. In March 1961 Wendel Kent and Company began as a small soil cement base and concrete curb and gutter operation. Then in the fall he acquired a small asphalt paving company which became General Asphalt Company. Expansion required more working capital and at this crucial point, Homer Whitman and Benton Powell of The Palmer Bank gave Wendel his first business loan. Then, one after another, these companies won the road building jobs that would become the solid foundation of the business.

Gator Asphalt Company State and National Award Winning Paving Team.

Wendel Kent, Founder & Chairman.

In 1961 they constructed the driveways for the Jamaica Royale complex on Siesta Key. Subsequently in 1962, came the construction of six miles of the Bee Ridge Road extension. In 1963 came Wendel's first Florida Department of Transportation job, rebuilding Old Bradenton Road in north Sarasota from Route 41 to DeSoto Road. Also in 1963, among other work, Wendel won his first contract with the Sarasota-Bradenton Airport Authority. Also important was residential construction work in Bayshore Gardens, similar work for Rolland King and Carl King in South Gate and Gulf Gate, and work for developer Reid Farrell in Phillippi Gardens. (The latter work was high-lighted by one of Sarasota's frequent "100-year" rains — 17 inches in 48 hours.)

Between 1963 and 1967, the companies continued to do more site and street construction in Gulf Gate, South Gate, the City of Sarasota, Manatee County, and a major county road in Hardee County.

In 1967 Frederick Derr came on board at Wendel Kent and Company as second in command. He brought to the company his civil engineering and management skills and rose to become president. The company was sold to Fred in 1986. Wendel continued to own and operate General Asphalt, now Gator Asphalt Company.

In 1976 Thomas Downs joined Gator Asphalt Company. He learned from and succeeded Marshall Alford at Gator. As President of the company he has led it to its position as today's leader in asphalt paving in the Sarasota/Bradenton area.

The two companies always constituted a team effort, and Wendel depended on his employees to build with him and to prosper with him. With the original purchase of the soil-cement operation in 1961, came the men Robert Pressey and Doc Brown. Robert still works for Frederick Derr & Company (formerly Wendel Kent & Company) today. Over the years Harry Drymon, Elton Kirkland, Ralph Swathel, Marshall Alford, Tom Baker, Tom Downs, Kevin Hicks, Michael Novak, Hugh Cannon and others were added to the team that would become Gator Asphalt (the name was changed in 1980 from General Asphalt) and Quality Aggregates. In the office through the years, the invaluable services of Wendel's first secretary, Ann Fredericks, and later his personal assistant, Elizabeth White, as well as the financial acumen of Ken Williams, Norveil Clark and Terry Darr, smoothed the way for the activities of a busy and thriving paving and materials business.

"DOC" Brown Compacting Soil Cement Base circa 1960's.

Robert Pressey with Wendel Kent & Co. from the beginning.

Due to the rapid growth of the Sarasota area and the constant need to transport people to and from their daily tasks in a smooth and efficient manner, the Seventies, Eighties and Nineties brought to the companies the work on Beneva Road, Bee Ridge Road, Fruitville Road, State Road 70, new US-301, Manatee Avenue and more. A particularly challenging project was the reconstruction of deteriorating portions of I-75.

Always in the forefront of technological advances, Gator Asphalt won state and national paving awards on several occasions. In 1980 and 1989 the company won state and national awards for excellence for paving on I-75. Another

& QUALITY AGGREGATES INCORPORATED

proud moment came in 1990 when the company was honored with a national award from the National Asphalt Paving Association for work at the Sarasota-Bradenton Airport. In addition, the company had no penalties on the job, a rare achievement on an FAA project. Gator Asphalt was required to accomplish the work at night, and for the first time made extensive use of new laser technology. During this time, recycling old concrete and asphalt became technologically feasible. Gator Asphalt adopted this new method, almost eliminating the litter of old concrete and asphalt in the dumpyards.

In 1982 Wendel formed Quality Aggregates Incorporated to dig and process sand, shell and fill material on the Schroeder-Manatee Ranch for the construction industry. In 1983 Quality-Aggregates began the processing of pure silica sand for the manufacture of glass containers by Tropicana Products in Bradenton. Glass sand is an important and exacting part of the business to this day, as is sand/shell for the concrete block industry. In 1987 Hugh Cannon, a geologist with many years' experience in the mining industry, brought a real professionalism to the operation and became president of the company.

Thomas Downs, President
Gator Asphalt Co.

Wendel and Evelyn Kent raised their family the old-fashioned way, with Evelyn running a tight ship at home, trying to persuade their three sons to wear socks to school when socks were *not* the "in thing." Years later, Wendel and Evelyn learned that in the morning the socks were draped on the sea grape at the Cedar Park Circle bus stop and put on again in the afternoon when the boys got off the bus. None of the children is active in the family firms today, having chosen the widely diverse businesses of newspapers, computers and home construction.

In the 1970's and 1980's Wendel enthusiastically embraced the sincere efforts of Sarasotans to change the community from a small coastal resort into a modern, thriving and well planned city and county with a viable business core and a stimulating cultural life servicing the ever-growing tourist industry, as well as the year-round residents. Sarasota was on a roll during these years, and Wendel played an active part as President of the Chamber of Commerce, the first President of The Argus Foundation, a member of the administrative committee of The Selby Foundation, a founding director of The Enterprise Bank, a founding member of The Siesta Key Chapel, and a long-time trustee (and now trustee-emeritus) of the Siesta Key Utilities Authority. Other civic activities include serving as Trustee of the Sarasota Memorial Hospital Foundation, member of the Sarasota Bay Rotary Club and director of The Florida Transportation Builders Association. Wendel was named Engineer of the Year by the Sarasota-Manatee Engineering Society and Businessperson of the Year by the Sarasota County Chamber of Commerce.

Hugh Cannon, President
Quality Aggregates Inc.

Gator Asphalt Company's Modern Environmental Award Winning Plant.

Quality Aggregate's Plant producing sand for Tropicana's glass bottles and sand for the construction industry.

Looking back upon all of this, Wendel says, "I believe that after World War II in America, and in Florida in particular, opportunities for the small entrepreneur to compete against the big fellows were as good as they have ever been, certainly since the 20's. I have always been very proud that I could compete locally with larger successful companies which do business on a national scale.

"In the present day I look back fondly upon a varied and satisfying life and feel I have been an active force in the community that is Sarasota today. I enhanced my life (and simplified my finances) by staying married to my college sweetheart and now have assumed the role of senior adviser to my three sons, who still tend, on occasion, to hang their socks on a sea grape 'out there somewhere.' I am the first to admit I didn't do all this alone and that I had lots of firm, friendly, and loving pushes along the way."

WILSON JAFFER, P.A.

In the spring of 1934, Clyde H. Wilson, a new graduate of the University of Florida College of Law, opened a law office in Sarasota. Over the years, the practice grew and changed, and today that firm, Wilson Jaffer, P.A., serves the community while upholding the firm's founding principles of legal excellence, honesty, innovation and plain, hard work.

The Wilson family has been in Florida for seven generations and in the Sarasota area for five. Augustus Wilson, Clyde Wilson's grandfather, moved to the Old Miakka area in 1877. He later served as Indian Agent for the State of Florida and was a tireless advocate and lobbyist for Indian rights. His letters to the federal bureaucracy pleaded for free Florida homesteads and free public education for Florida's Indians, unpopular causes at the time. His most radical position was that south Florida should be given to the Indians.

Augustus Wilson also was Postmaster, county Property Appraiser and a state Senator, during which service he introduced the bill that created Sarasota County, in 1922.

Clyde Wilson's father, Dr. Cullen Wilson, M.D., moved into Sarasota and established his medical practice in 1907. Although a leader in the business, medical and religious communities, he is probably best remembered for bringing the first automobile to Sarasota, in 1909.

During the sixty years that Clyde Wilson practiced law (until a few days before his death in 1994), he served as State Attorney for eight Florida counties between Tampa and Miami; as president of the Sarasota County Bar Association; as chair of the Circuit Grievance Committee; and as a founding trustee of the Attorney's Title Guarantee Fund. He was an outstanding lawyer, church and community leader, and devoted family man.

When Clyde H. Wilson, Jr. joined his father's law practice in 1965, it was a general practice representing mostly local clients. In 1970, Clyde Wilson, Jr. started a software business and developed expertise in this infant industry. Combining this software expertise with his legal skills, he became involved in technology licensing and litigation. After John Jaffer joined the firm in 1977, the firm focused on "computer law" (today called "technology law").

The firm served as a true pioneer in the field of technology law. Clyde Wilson, Jr. was a co-founder of the Computer Law Committee of the Florida Bar and served three terms as Chair. He was also a founder of a similar committee for the Litigation Section of the American Bar Association and another for the Association of Trial Lawyers of America.

Assisted by other lawyers in the firm, Clyde Wilson, Jr. authored a book titled *Winning Techniques for Computer and High Tech Litigation*, which received favorable reviews in national legal and technology industry periodicals.

The *Software Law Bulletin* once described Mr. Wilson as "one of America's most successful trial attorneys in computer cases" after

Clyde H. Wilson, circa 1934

Sarasota's first automobile

reviewing his national record verdict in technology litigation and other landmark cases he and the firm handled. An *American Banker* cover story named Mr. Wilson as one of two recommended "hired guns" available to banks dealing with the computer and software industry.

Mr. Wilson, Jr. served eight years as an adjunct professor at the University of Florida Levin College of Law, teaching intellectual property litigation. He has also served as a Trustee of that law school and on the Board of Overseers of Stetson University College of Law.

John Jaffer, a graduate of Harvard College and Law School, started his legal career as a research assistant to the Honorable John M. Scheb at the Second District Court of Appeal in Lakeland. He performs most of the firm's appellate practice, research and legal writing. Mr. Jaffer is the author of the chapter "Practical Considerations" in the Florida appellate practice manual published by the Florida Bar.

The Association of Trial Lawyers of America selected Wilson Jaffer to assemble and lead a team of lawyers to oppose limiting the role of juries in patent trials in the U. S. Supreme Court (*Markman v. Westview*). The resulting amicus brief was not successful. The Academy of Florida Trial Lawyers selected Wilson Jaffer to represent the association in *Bateman v. Mnemonics, Inc.* regarding Florida trade secret law. That brief succeeded.

The firm in 1994 sponsored a web page titled *The National Law Net* (nationallawnet.com), the first legal-related web page in the southeastern U.S.

Wilson Jaffer has handled legal controversies and cases in forty-four states, the District of Columbia and several foreign countries. Those cases have been the subject of articles in *The Wall Street Journal* and national television shows *60 Minutes*, *20/20* and *Inside Edition*.

Despite its national practice in technology litigation, the firm continues to handle local business and real estate litigation. The firm is proud of its 70-plus years of service to Sarasota.

Selected Bibliography

The following bibliography includes books which should be generally available in the central Gulf coast region. Much of the research for *Sarasota: Journey to Centennial* was conducted in primary sources - personal manuscript collections, interviews, diaries, government documents, public records, and newspapers. Major research libraries consulted include:

Smithsonian Institution, Washington, D.C.
Library of Congress, Washington, D.C.
National Archives, Washington, D.C.
P.K. Yonge Library of Florida History, University of Florida, Gainesville, Florida
Florida State Archives, Tallahassee, Florida
Manatee County Historical Society Collection, Eaton Room, Manatee County Public Library
Florida Collection: Monroe County Library, Key West, Florida
Florida Collection: Strozier Library, Florida State University, Tallahassee, Florida
Florida Historical Society Collection, University of South Florida, Tampa, Florida

Valuable secondary material on Sarasota and the central Gulf coast may be found in the *Florida Historical Quarterly*, *Tampa Bay History*, and the *Florida Anthropologist*.

Newspapers

Florida *Peninsular*
Sunland Tribune
Bradentown *Herald*
Tampa *Herald*
Fort Myers *Press*
Manatee River *Journal*
Nassau *Guardian*
Chicago *Daily-Tribune*
Palmetto *News*
Buffalo *Sunday Morning News*
Key West *Register*
Niles *Register*
Tallahassee *Sentinel*
Tallahassee *Floridian*
New York *World*
New York *Herald*
New York *Times*
The Venice *News*. 1927.
This Week In Sarasota. 1925
Sarasota *Times* (1899-1923)
Sarasota *Herald*
Sarasota *Herald-Tribune*

Books

Barrientos, Bartolomé. *Pedro Menéndez de Avilés, Founder of Florida*. (1567) Anthony Kerrigan, trans. Gainesville: University of Florida Press, 1965.
Bemis, Samuel Flagg. *Pinckney's Treaty, America's Advantage from Europe's Distress, 1783-1800*. New Haven: Yale University Press, 1960.
Bartram, William. *The Travels of William Bartram*. (1791) Francis Harper, ed. New Haven: Yale University Press, 1958.
Bickel, Karl A. *The Mangrove Coast*. New York: Coward-McAnn, Inc., 1942.
Boehme, Sarah E., Christian F. Feest and Patricia Condon Johnston. *Seth Eastman, A Portfolio of North American Indians*. Afton, Minnesota: Afton Historical Society Press, 1995.
Browne, Jefferson B., *Key West The Old and The New*. 1912. Reprint facsimile with introduction by E. Ashby Hammond. Gainesville: University of Florida Press, 1973.
Bradna, Fred, and Hartzell Spence. *The Big Top*. New York: Simon and Schuster, 1952.
Buker, George E. *Swamp Sailors. Riverine Warfare in the Everglades, 1835-1842*. Gainesville: University Presses of Florida, 1975.
Bullen, Adelaide K. *Florida Indians of Past and Present*. Reprint of *Florida from Indian Trail to Space Age*, Vol. 1, Chapter 24. Gainesville: Kendall Books, 1965.
Bullen, Ripley P. *A Guide to the Identification of Florida Projectile Points*. Revised. Gainesville: Kendall Books, 1975.
Cabeza de Vaca, Alvar Nuñez. The Journey of Alvar Nuñez Cabeza de Vaca. Translated by Fanny Bandelier. New York: Allerton Book Co., 1922. Chicago: The Rio Grande Press Inc., 1964.
Cantacuzene, Princess, Countess Speransky née Grant. *My Life Here and There*. New York: Charles Scribner's Sons, 1922.
Carter, Clarence Edwin, compiler, *The Territorial Papers of the United States*. The Territory of Florida, Vol. 22-26. The National Archives and Records Service, Washington, D.C.: U.S. Government Printing Office, 1959.
Canova, Andrew P. *Life and Adventures in South Florida*. Tampa: 1906.
Coe, Charles H. *Red Patriots*, 1898. Facsimile reprint with introduction by Charlton W. Tebeau. Gainesville: University Presses of Florida, 1974.
Covington, James. *The Billy Bowlegs War*. Chuluota, Fla.: Mickler Press, 1982.
Curry, Larry. Foreword by Archibald Hanna. *The American West, Painters from Catlin to Russell*, Viking Press, 1972.
Dippie, Brian W. *George Catlin and His Contemporaries: The Politics of Patronage*. Lincoln: University of Nebraska Press, 1990.
Eastman, Mary Henderson. *Dahcotah or Life and Legends of the Sioux around Fort Snelling*. (1849). Afton, Minnesota: Afton Historical Society Press, 1995.
Federal Writers' Project Guide to 1930s Florida. *The WPA Guide to Florida*. (1939) Reprint. New York: Pantheon Books, 1984.

The Florida State Gazetteer and Business Directory for 1884-1885. Charleston: Southern Directory and Publishing Company 1884.
Fogarty Ollie Z. *They Called It Fogartyville*. Brooklyn: Theodore Gaus, 1972.
Fontaneda, Hernando d'Escalante. *Memoir of Hernando d'Escalante Fontaneda*. C. 1575 Translated by Buckingham Smith, Edited by David O. True. Coral Gables: University of Miami Press, 1944.
Forbes, James Grant. *Sketches, Historical and Topographical of The Floridas; More Particularly of East Florida*. 1821 Facsimile edition. Gainesville: University of Florida Press, 1964.
Garcilaso de la Vega. *The Florida of the Inca*. Translated and edited by John Grier Varner and Jeannette Johnson Varner, 3rd printing. Austin: University of Texas Press, 1962.
Gilbert, Paul, and Charles Lee Bryson, *Chicago and Its Makers*. Chicago: Felix Mendelsohn, 1929.
Goggin, John M. *Indian and Spanish Selected Writings*. Edited by Charles H. Fairbanks, Irving Rouse, and William C. Sturtevant. Coral Gables: University of Miami Press, 1964.
Griffin, James B., ed. *Archeology of Eastern United States*. Chicago: University of Chicago Press, 1952.
Grismer, Karl H. *The Story of Sarasota*. Sarasota: M.E. Russell, 1946.
_____. *Tampa*. Edited by D.B. McKay. St. Petersburg, Fla.: St. Petersburg Printing Company, 1950.
Harllee, William Curry, *Kinfolks*. A Genealogical and Biographical Record of (Harllee, Fulmore, Curry Kemp, Bethes, Robertson, Dickey Families). 3 vols. New Orleans: Searcy & Pfaff, 1934-1937
Historical, Architectural, and Archaeological Survey of Sarasota, Florida. Bureau of Historic Sites and Properties, Division of Archives, Department of State. Miscellaneous Project Report Series No. 51(1977), 1982.
Hodge, Frederick W., and Theodore H. Lewis, eds. *Spanish Explorers in the Southern United States, 1528-1543*. New York: Charles Scribner's Sons, 1907.
Hoffmeister, John Edward. *Land from the Sea: The Geologic Story of South Florida*. Coral Gables: University of Miami Press, 1974.
Howard, O.O. *Famous Indian Chiefs I Have Known*. New York: The Century Co., 1908.
Hrdlicka, Alex. "Skeletal Remains Suggesting or Attributed to Early Man in North America," *Smithsonian Institution Bureau of American Ethnology*, Bulletin 33. House Document No. 816. 59th Congress, 2nd sess. Washington, D.C.: U.S. Government Printing Office, 1907.
_____. *Catalog of Human Crania in the United States National Museum Collections: Indians of the Gulf States*. Smithsonian Institution, Proceedings of the United States National Museum, Vol. 87. Washington, D.C., 1941.
Irving, Theodore, *The Conquest of Florida under Hernando de Soto*. Vols. 1 and 2. London: 1835.
Jarvis, Nathan S. *An Army Surgeon's Notes of Frontier Service, 1833-1848*. Reprinted from *Journal of the Military Service Institution of the United States*. (July 1906) 3-8, (Sept.-Oct. 1906) 275-86.
Larson, Lewis H. *Aboriginal Subsistence Technology on the Southeastern Coastal Plain during the Late Prehistoric Period*. Ripley P. Bullen Monographs in Anthropology and History, No. 2. The Florida State Museum. Gainesville: University Presses of Florida, 1980.
Laumer, Frank. *Massacre!* Gainesville: University of Florida Press, 1968.
Ludlum, David M. "The Tampa Bay Hurricane of 1848" in *Early American Hurricanes, 1492-1870*. Boston: American Meteorological Society.
Lyon, Eugene. *The Enterprise of Florida, Pedro Menéndez de Avilés and the Spanish Conquest of 1565-1568*. Gainesville: University Presses of Florida, 1976.
Matthews, Janet Snyder. "The Bidwell-Wood Histories - A Contrast." In *The Bidwell-Wood House*. Sarasota: Sarasota County Historical Society Inc., 1978.
_____. *Edge of Wilderness: A Settlement History of Manatee River and Sarasota Bay*. Tulsa: Caprine Press, 1983.
McClellan Park, Sarasota, Florida. n.d. Illustrations by Katherine D. McClellan. Sarasota, n.d.
McDermott, John Francis. *Seth Eastman, Pictorial Historian of the Indian*. Norman: University of Oklahoma Press, 1961.
_____. *The Art of Seth Eastman. A Traveling Exhibition of Paintings and Drawings*. Washington, D.C., The Smithsonian Institution, 1958.
McDuffee, Lillie B. *The Lures of Manatee*, 2nd ed. Bradenton, Fla.: A.K. Whitaker and Manatee County Historical Society 1961.
McKay, Donald B., ed. *Pioneer Florida*. Vols. 1-3. Tampa: The Southern Publishing Company, 1959.
McLeod, Hiram A., *The Escape of Judah P. Benjamin*. Tampa Fla.,1909, 3rd Ed., 1962.
Mahon, John K. *History of the Second Seminole War, 1835-1842*. Gainesville: University of Florida Press, 1967.
Manucy, Albert. *Florida's Menéndez, Captain General of the Ocean Sea*. St. Augustine: St. Augustine Historical Society 1965.

239

Marshall, Douglas W, ed. *Research Catalog of Maps of America to 1860.* In the William L. Clements Library, University of Michigan. Vol. 4. Boston: G.K. Hall, 1972.

Milanich, Jerald, and Samuel Proctor, eds. *Tacachale, Essays on the Indians of Florida and Southeastern Georgia during the Historic Period.* Ripley P. Bullen Monographs in Anthropology and History No. 1. The Florida State Museum. Gainesville: University Presses of Florida, 1978.

_____ and William C. Sturtevant. *Francisco Pareja's 1613 "Confessionario, A Documentary Source for Timucuan Ethnography."* Translated by Emilio F. Moran. Tallahassee, Fla.: Florida Department of State, 1972.

Morison, Samuel Eliot, *The Oxford History of the United States, 1783-1917.* 2 vols. London: Oxford University Press, 1928.

Morris, Allen. *The Florida Handbook.* Tallahassee: Peninsular Publishing Co.

Mowat, Charles Loch. *East Florida as a British Province, 1763-1784.* Gainesville: University of Florida Press, 1964.

Murray, Marian. *Florida Fossils.* Tampa: Trend House, 1975.

_____ and A.E. Austin. *Asolo Theater.* Sarasota: John and Mable Ringling Museum of Art, 1952.

Narratives of the Career of Hernando de Soto in the Conquest of Florida as told by a Knight of Elvas and in a Relation by Luys de Biedma, Factor of the Expedition. Translated by Buckingham Smith, together with an account of De Soto's Expedition based on the diary of Rodrigo Ranjel, his private secretary. Translated from Oviedo's *Historia General y Natural de las Indias.* (1535) Edward Gaylord Bourne, ed. Vols. 1 and 2. London: David Nutt, 1905.

Narratives of de Soto in the Conquest of Florida as told by a Gentleman of Elvas and in a Relation by Luys Hernandez de Biedma. Translated by Buckingham Smith. Gainesville, Fla.: Palmetto Books, 1968.

Nolan, John. *Report on Comprehensive City Plan for Sarasota, Florida.* Cambridge, 1925.

Norfleet, Barbara P, ed. *Killing Time, Photographs by Joe Steinmetz.* Cambridge: Amory & Pugh, 1982.

North, Henry Ringling, and Alden Hatch. *The Circus Kings: Our Ringling Family Story.* New York: Doubleday, 1960.

Official Records of the Union and Confederate Navies in the War of the Rebellion. 30 vols. Washington, D.C.: U.S. Government Printing Office, 1894-1927.

O'Daniel, V.F. *Dominicans in Early Florida.* United States Catholic Historical Society Monograph Series 12. New York, 1930.

O'Neil, Buck, with Steve Wulf and David Conrads. *I Was Right On Time.* New York: Simon & Schuster, 1996.

Parks, Arva Moore, *Miami: The Magic City.* Tulsa: Continental Heritage Press, 1981.

Patrick, Rembert W. and Allen Morris. *Florida Under Five Flags.* 4th Ed. Gainesville: University of Florida Press, 1967

Phillips, P Lee. *Notes on the Life and Works of Bernard Romans.* 1924 facsimile edition. Gainesville: University Presses of Florida, 1975.

Pinardi, Norman J. *The Plant Pioneers.* Torrington, Fla.: Rainbow Press, 1980.

Plowden, Gene. *Those Amazing Ringlings and Their Circus.* Caldwell, Fla.: Caxton, 1968.

Pratt, Richard. *David Adler.* New York: M. Evans and Company Inc., 1970.

Richards, John R., compiler. *Florida State Gazetteer and Business Directory,* Vol. 1, 1886-1887. New York: The South Publishing Co., 1886.

Ringling Bros. and Barnum & Bailey Circus Route Book. New York: Ringling Bros. and Barnum & Bailey Press Dept., 1964.

Ross, Ishbel. *Silhouette in Diamonds.* New York: Harper & Brothers, 1960.

Sarasota County, Florida. Sarasota: T.F. Arnold (c. 1922).

Sarasota County, Florida. Sarasota: Sarasota County Chamber of Commerce, n.d. (c. 1925).

Sarasota, Sarasota County of Florida including Whitfield Estates. New York: Sanborn Map Co., 1929.

Sarasota Visitors' Guide, 1932. Sarasota: Chas. E. Wadsworth, C.E., 1931.

Schell, Rolfe. *De Soto Didn't Land at Tampa.* Fort Myers Beach, Fla.: Island Press, 1966.

Simpson, Charles Torrey, *Out of Doors in Florida. The Adventures of a Naturalist, Together with Essays on the Wild Life and the Geology of the State.* Miami: E.B. Douglas Co., 1923.

Smith, Hale G. *The European and the Indian.* Florida Anthropometrical Society Publications, No. 4. Gainesville, 1954.

Smith, Julia Floyd. *Slavery in Ante Bellum Florida, 1821-1860.* Gainesville: University of Florida Press, 1973.

Soldiers of Florida in the Seminole Indian - Civil - Spanish-American Wars. Florida Board of State Institutions, 1903.

Solís de Merás, Gonzalo. *Pedro Menéndez de Avilés.* Edited by Jeannette Thurber Connor. De Land: Florida State Historical Society 1922. Facsimile ed., Gainesville: University of Florida Press, 1964.

Sprague, John T. *The Origins, Progress and Conclusion of the Florida War.* 1848. Reprint facsimile. Gainesville: University of Florida Press, 1964.

Sulzer, Elmer G. *Ghost Railroads of Sarasota County.* Sarasota: Sarasota County Historical Commission and Sarasota Historical Society, 1971.

Swanton, John R. *Early History of the Creek Indians and Their Neighbors.* Smithsonian Institution Bureau of American Ethnology Bulletin 73, 1922. New York: Johnson Reprint Corporation, 1970.

_____. *The Indians of the Southeastern United States.* Smithsonian Institution Bureau of American Ethnology, Bulletin 137. Washington, D.C.: U.S. Government Printing Office, 1946.

Tebeau, Charlton W. *A History of Florida.* Coral Gables: University of Miami Press, 1971.

_____. *Florida's Last Frontier: The History of Collier County.* Rev. ed. Coral Gables: University of Miami Press, 1966.

_____. *Man in the Everglades.* Coral Gables: University of Miami Press, 1968.

Tomory, Peter. *Catalogue of the Italian Paintings before 1800.* Sarasota: John and Mable Ringling Museum of Art, 1976.

True Relation of the Hardships Suffered by Governor Fernando de Soto and Certain Portuguese Gentlemen during the Discovery of the Province of Florida. Now newly set forth by a Gentleman of Elvas. 1557 Facsimile of the original Portuguese. Translated by James Alexander Roberts. No.11, Vols. I and 2. De Land: Florida State Historical Society, 1932, 1933.

Ware, John D., and Robert R. Rea. *George Gauld, Surveyor and Cartographer of the Gulf Coast.* Gainesville: University Presses of Florida, forthcoming.

Warner, Joe G. *Biscuits and Taters: A History of Cattle Ranching in Manatee County.* St. Petersburg: Great Outdoors Printing Co., 1980.

Warner, W.S., ed. and compiler. *Palma Sola, the Youngest and Largest Town in Florida.* New York, 1884.

Webb, David S., ed. *Pleistocene Mammals of Florida.* Gainesville: University Presses of Florida, 1974.

Webb, Wanton S., ed. and compiler. *Webb's Historical, Industrial and Biographical Florida.* New York: W.S. Webb & Co., 1885.

Williams, John Lee. *The Territory of Florida. 1837.* Reprint facsimile. Gainesville: University of Florida Press, 1962.

Willey, Gordon R. *Archeology of the Florida Gulf Coast.* Antiquities of the New World, Vol.18. Introduction by Ripley P. Bullen. Cambridge: Peabody Museum, Harvard University, 1973.

Wilson, Raymond. *Ohiyesa, Charles Eastman, Santee Sioux.* Chicago: University of Illinois Press, 1983.

Wright, J. Leith Jr. *Florida in the American Revolution.* Gainesville: University Presses of Florida, 1975.

_____. *The Only Land They Knew: The Tragic Story of the American Indians in the Old South.* New York: Macmillan, 1981.

Youngberg, George E. Sr., and W. Earl Aumann. *Venice and the Venice Area.* Venice, Fla.: Sunshine Press, 1969.

Selected Archaeological Articles

Bullen, Adelaide K. "Paleoepidemiology and Distribution of Prehistoric Treponemiasis (Syphilis) in Florida," *Florida Anthropologist,* Vol.25, No.4 (December, 1972), pp.133-73.

Bullen, Ripley P. "Test at the Whitaker Mound, Sarasota," *Florida Anthropologist* (1950)Vol. 3: 21-30.

Bullen, Ripley P, and Adelaide K. Bullen. "The Palmer Site," *The Florida Anthropologist,* Vol.29, No.2, Part 2. Florida Anthropological Society Publications, No.8, 1976.

Carr, Robert S., Janet Matthews, Katherine Rogers and Marion Almy for Archaeological and Historical Conservancy Inc. Archaeological and Historical Investigations at Indian Beach, for the City of Sarasota, 1989.

Clausen, Carl J., H.K. Brooks, and A.V. Wesolowsky. "Florida Spring Confirmed as 10,000 Year Old Early Man Site," Florida Anthropological Society Publications, No.7, edited by Ripley Bullen, 1975.

Griffin, John W. "Prehistoric Florida: A Review," *Archeology of Eastern United States,* edited by James B. Griffin, University of Chicago Press, 1952, pp. 322-34.

Heilprin, Angelo. "Explorations on the West Coast of Florida and in the Okeechobee Wilderness," *Transactions of the Wagner Free Institute of Science of Philadelphia* 1(1887): 1-133.

Luer, George M. "The Roberts Bay Site, Sarasota, Florida," *The Florida Anthropologist,* Vol.30, No.3 (September, 1977), pp.121-33.

_____. "Excavations at the Old Oak Site, Sarasota, Florida: A Late Weeden Island-Safety Harbor Period site," *The Florida Anthropologist,* Vol.30, No. 2 June, 1977), pp. 37-56.

_____ and Marion M. Almy. "The Development of Some Aboriginal Pottery of the Central Peninsular Gulf Coast of Florida." *The Florida Anthropologist* 33:207-25.

_____. "A Definition of the Manasota Culture," *Florida Anthropologist* 35:34-58.

_____. "Temple Mounds of the Tampa Bay Area," *The Florida Anthropologist,* Vol. 344, No. 3 (September, 1981), pp.127-55.

Milanich, Jerald T. "Excavations at the Yellow Bluffs - Whitaker Mound," *Florida Anthropologist* (1972) Vol. 25:21-41.

_____. "Indians of North Central Florida," *Florida Anthropologist* 31: (February 1976)131-40. Project Report Series #3, Florida State Museum.

Royal, William, and Eugenie Clark. "Natural Preservation of Human Brain, Warm Mineral Springs." *American Antiquity* 26:2, 1960, pp.285-87.

Sheldon, Elisabeth, and Marguerita L. Cameron. "Reconstruction of Prehistoric Environments: The Warm Mineral Springs Project." *Proceedings of the Thirty-Second Southeastern Archaeological Conference,* 1975, Bulletin No. 19, edited by Drexel A. Peterson Jr. Memphis: Southeastern Archaeological Conference, 1976.

Smith, Hale G. "Two Historical Archaeological Periods in Florida," *American Antiquity,* Vol. 13, No.4, Part I, pp. 313-19.

Index

A
ADP Group, Inc.: iv, 172, 176.
A.G. Edwards & Sons, Inc.: iv, 172, 175.
Abbe, Carrie: 49, 51, 74.
Abbe, Charles Elliott: 49, 50, 52, 74, 123.
Abbe family: 49-52, 58, 65, 74.
Abbe, Myron: 65, 74.
Abbe, Nellie Louise: 49, 51-52.
Abbe, Charlotte Scofield: 49, 50.
Abraham the interpreter: 31.
A.C.L. railroad station: 65.
Acacias (Palmer family home): 93.
Acton, A.C.: 58, 63.
Acton, Fla.: 74.
Adair Realty and Trust of Atlanta: 113, 122.
Addision, John: 42, 44.
Adler, Felix ("King of Clowns"): 138-139.
Alafia River: 44.
Albee, Dr. Fred H.: 96-97, 143.
Albee, Stephen: 97.
Albee Sanitarium: 97.
Alice from Dallas (circus performer): 136.
Almy, Marion: iv, 174, 245.
Amaryllis Park Primary School (Booker East): 130, 150, 158.
American Legion, Sarasota Bay Post No. 30: 128, 144.
American National Bank: 114, 129.
American Petroleum Institute: 112.
Añasco, Juan: 27.
Anderson, John Murray: 136-137.
Anderson, Joseph: 51.
Andrews, Leonard: 51.
Ange, Mr.: 65.
Angola (early Sarasota Bay settlement): 33.
Anna Maria: 164.
Apalachee (Indian village): 26.
Apalachicola, Fla.: 62, 65.
Apoxsee (land use plan): 160, 163.
Arana, Captain Juan de: 28.
Arbogast, E.M.: 124.
Arcade Building: 114.
Arcadia: 104, 123.
Archaeological Consultants, Inc.: iv, 172, 174.
Archaic peoples: 20.
Archers, Royal Company of: 55, 65, 82.
Arkansas Territory: 14, 35-36, 44.
Armada of the Indies: 29.
Armed Occupation Act: 49.
Armistead, Brevet Brigadier General Walker K.: ix, 35, 36.
Armistice Day: 92.
Arnold, T.F.: 126.
Artiaga, Pedro Jose: 33.
Arvida Realty Co., Miami: 159.
Ashton Road: 51.
Asolo Opera Association: 156.
Asolo State Theatre: 156-157.
Atkins, Fredd: 160, 166.
Atlantic Coast Line Railroad: 94, 95, 106.

B
Babcock Preservation Act: 171.
Badger Pharmacy: 86, 108, 129.
Baldwin, Fla.: 46.
Ball Construction, Inc.: iv, 172, 177.
Banana Avenue: 62, 90.
Bank of Sarasota: 92, 117, 129.
Baptist Convention: 73.
Barbastro, Father Luis Cañcer de: 28.
Baum, Dwight James: 114, 135, 160.
Bay Haven Inn: 114.
Bay Haven School: 119, 158.
Bay Island Hotel: 93.
Bayou Hanson: 125.
Bayou Louise: 125.
Bayshore Drive: 107.
Beall's, Inc.: iv, 167, 172, 178.
Bee Ridge: 19, 51, 93, 123, 150.
Bee Ridge Farms: 93.
Bell, Charlie: 138.
Belle Glade: 128.
Belle Haven Hotel: 63, 65, 68-69, 93, 108, 114, 125, 129.
Belle Haven observatory: 78.
Benjamin, Judah: 45, 47.
Bermudez, Jose Phillippi: 40-41.
Beteta, Father Gregorio de: 28-29.
Bethlehem Baptist Church: 123.
Bidwell, Alfred: 50-51, 74.
Bidwell, Mary: 50.
Big Cypress Swamp: ix, 14, 35, 97, 104.
Big Pass: 52, 78, 125.
Big Slough: 150.
Big Top (circus): 136, 140-141, 150.
Bird Island: 111-112.
Bird Key: 111, 124, 150, 153.
Birdsall, John: 143.
Biscayne Bay: 48.
Bispham, Cyrus: iv, 172, 179.
Black Bottom (black community): 123.
Black Legend: 24.
Blackburn Bay: 49.
Blackburn, Benjamin: 49.
Blackburn, George W: 82-83, 88.
Blackburn, John Slemans: 49.
Blackburn family: 98.
Blackburn Point: 49.
Blackburn Road: 49.
Blair, Marshal: 83.
Blair, T.F.: 82.
BLE Realty Corporation: 96.
Bloxham, Governor William: 54.
Bobadilla, Doña Isabel de: 26, 27.
Boca Sarazota: 32.
Boehme, Sarah: vii.
Bolding, Jeff: 48.
Bon Secours: 166.
Booker, Emma E.: 119-120, 130.
Booker Elementary School (Middle School): 150, 158.
Booker High School: 150-151, 158, 160.
Booker School: 120, 130.
Boone, Boone, Boone, Koda & Frook: iv, 172, 180.
Boston Red Sox: 148.
Bowlees Creek: 39.
Bowlegs, Chief Billy (see also Holata Micco): 14, 31, 40, 43-44, 46.
Boy Scouts: 128.
Braden, Dr.: 44.
Bradenton Christian: 167.
Bradenton Prep: 167.
Bradenton, Fla.: 94, 123, 150.
Bradenton roads: 114.
Bradenton-Sarasota airport: 152, 165.
Bradentown: 65, 84.
Braden, Virginia and Dr. Joseph: 42.
Bradna, Fred: 130-131.
Bragg, General Braxton: 46.
Branch, Dr. Franklin: 36, 42.
Bridgeport, Conn.: 130.
British: 32, 34, 54.
Broome, Governor James: 42.
Brotherhood of Locomotive Engineers (BLE): 95, 97, 99, 103 (demonstration farm).
Brown, J.C.: 123.
Brown, Dr. J.O.: 82.
Brown, W.W.: 48.
Browning, Alex: 57, 59, 62-63, 67.
Browning, Hugh K.: 90.
Browning, John: 60, 63.
Browning family: 59.
Bry Leod, Theodore de: 30.
Buchanan, Vern: 169, 170.
Buck O'Neil Baseball Complex: 166.
Buffalo Bill Show: 106.
Bunce, William: 33, 35, 40.
Bundy, Randy: 148.
Burket, John F.: 129.
Burns, Ken: 166.
Bush, George W.: 169-170.
Bush, Gov. Jeb: 169, 171.
Burns, Owen: 111.
Burns, I.R.: 13.
Burns Court: 111.

C
Cà d'Zan (Ringling home): 12, 107, 114, 130, 135.
Caldes Island: 33.
Caldes, José and Joaquin: 33.
Caldwell, Governor Millard F.: 157.
Caledonian Hunt, Royal: 55.
Calhoun, J.C.: 89.
Caloosahatchee River: 35, 40.
Calusa Indians: 22, 25, 30.
Canaveral, Cape: 46, 143.
Canova, Andrew P.: 35.
Caples, Ellen and Ralph: 107.
Cardinal Mooney High School: 167.
Carlos, chief of the Calusas: 29, 30.
Carlton, Alderman: 44.
Carlton, Lisa: 163, 169, 175.
Carlton, Mabry Ranch, Inc.: iv, 172, 204.
Carlton, T. Mabry Jr.: 164, 166.
Casa Bona Hotel (Belle Haven): 114.
Casey, Captain John Charles: 40-41.
Casey Key: 40, 67, 93, 125, 128.
Casey's Pass: 93, 99.
Caspersen Beach: 171.
Cattle Kings: 49, 77.
Ceasar, W. James: 56.
Cedar Key: 56-58, 62.
Cedar Point: 83, 111.
Celery Fields Project: 163.
Center for Sight: iv, 172, 181.
Central Avenue: 62-63.
Central Highlands: 18.
Chaires, Ferman: 42, 44.
Chapline, Asa: 88.
Chapline, Jake Jr.: 88.
Chapline, J.B.: 89.
Chapman, Danny: 138.
Charles V (king of Spain): 26.
Charlotte County: 119, 150.
Charlotte Harbor: 14, 22, 25, 29, 33, 35-36, 40-41, 48-49.
Chase, Robert: 169.
Cherokee Park subdivision: 123.
Chicago, Ill.: 91, 94.
Chicago *Tribune*: 91.
Chicago White Sox: 154.
Chidsey, John Tuttle: 132.
Christianity: 25-26, 28.
Church of the Redeemer (Episcopal): 190.
Circus Hall of Fame: 146.
Citizens Bank and Trust Company, Tampa: 129.
City Livery Stables: 88.
City Marina: 1, 11.
City of Sarasota: iv, 172, 182-183.
City of Venice: iv, 172, 184.
Civil Aeronautics Administration: 144.
Civil Air Patrol: 143.
Civil War: 45, 47-49, 51, 82.
Civil Works Administration: 132.
Civilian Conservation Corps (CCC): 132.
Clam Island: 32.
Clark, Jane: 123.
Clark and Calhoun: 89.
Clark Road: 147.
Clas, Shepherd and Clas: 109.
Clearwater, Fla.: 28.
Clower, Jesse Monroe: 49.
Clyde Butcher Gallery: iv, 172, 185.
Coacoochee (Wild Cat): 41.
Coakley, Rollins: 171.
Coastal Picket Patrol: 143.
Coastal Printing, Inc.: ii.
Cockrell, Barbara O'Horo: 18.
Cockrell, Wilburn A.: 18.
Cocoanut Avenue: 62.
Cody, Buffalo Bill: 107.
Coleman, Eddie: 83.
Collins, Jerry: 147.
Colonial Gables: 163.
Colony Beach: 148.
Columbus, Christopher: 25.
Committee of Lords on Plantation Affairs: 32.
Community Foundation of Sarasota County: iv, 172, 186.
Concello, Antoinette: 144, 146.
Concello, Art: 144, 150.
Concord (ship): 34.
Confederacy (Civil War): 46, 47, 48.
Congressional Armed Occupation Act of 1842: 39.
Congressional Homestead Act of 1862: 48, 49.
Conner, Secretary of Agriculture Doyle: 161.
Cooper family: 42.
Cornaro, Caterina, queen of Cyprus: 157.
Cortez Village: 164.
County Line Road: 161.
Courthouse subdivision: 111, 160.
Cowboy Cavalry: 46.
Cow Pan Slough: 164.
Crescent Beach: ii, 124.
Crescent Pharmacy: 92.
Crocker, Peter: 48.
Crosley, Powell Jr.: 144.
Cuba, Cubans: 26-28, 46, 67, 77, 78, 81.
Cunliff Richard: 52.
Cunliff Lane: 19, 51, 74.
Cunningham, Owen: 42.
Curry, John: 48.
Curry, Larry: vii.

D
Dade, Major Francis Langhorne: 34-35.
Dade City: 35.
Dade's Massacre: 35.
Dann, Harry: 138-139.
David (statue): 131, 157.
Davis, Arthur Vining: 150.
Davis, Doc: 125.
Davis, Jefferson: 42, 47.
De Mille, Cecil B.: 150.
Derr, Frederick: iv, 172, 197, 210.
De Soto, Hernando: 26-29, 156.
De Soto County: 48, 52, 93, 119.
De Soto Hotel: 59, 65-66.
Dearborn, Major Greenleaf: 35.
Depression, Great: 131-132, 142, 144, 147.
Detert, Nancy: 169.
Diocese of Venice in Florida: iv, 172, 188.
Dirty Mary (ship): 65, 67.
Disney World: 151.
Disston, Hamilton: 54, 56, 65.
Dixie Highway: 104.
Dodge News: 148.
Doll family (Daisy, Tiny, Gracie, Harry): 137.
Dominic, Father: 29.
Dons Bay: 49.
Douglass Street: 122.
Drew, Helen: 70.
Drumright, W.J.: 48.
Dry, Delores: 166.
Duany, Andres: 170-171.
Dunbar Street: 122.
Dunne, J.J.: 56.
Dupree, Jerome: 166.
DuVal, H.S.: 56.

E
Eastman, Charles Alexander: vii.
Eastman, Mary Henderson: vii-viii.
Eastman, Nancy: vii.
Eastman, Seth: vii-ix, 14.
Eastman sketchbook: viii.
Edinburgh, Scotland: 54-55.
Edinburgh Academy: 55.
Edmondson family: 124.
Edmondson Road: 125.
Education Foundation of Sarasota County, Inc.: iv, 172, 189.
Edwards, A.B.: 113.
Edwards Theater: 113, 156.
Egmont, Earl of: 33.
Egmont Key: viii, 44, 81, 143.
Egmont Lighthouse: 48, 58.
Eighteenth District: 42.
El Vernona Hotel: 111, 114.
Elizabeth Ann (ship): 42.

241

Ella M. Little (ship): 67.
Ellenton: 169.
Elliot, M. Leo: 119.
Elslander, Father: 140.
Elvgren, Gil: 148.
Elzuardi, Jose: 39.
Emathla, Fasatchee: 31.
Emma E. Booker Elementary School: 170.
Englewood, Fla.: 20, 123, 164-165.
Engling, Colin: 157.
English, W.H.: 107.
Entres Nous (teachers' club): 122.
Episcopal Church of the Redeemer: iv, 172, 190.
Evans, Chick: 111.
Evans, Merle: 122, 136.
Everglades: 42, 44, 104, 114, 129-130, 170.

F
Fairgrounds: 130-131.
Faubel, J.H.: 125.
Faubel Street: 125.
FCCI Insurance Group: iv, 172, 191.
Federal Building: 142.
Federal Economic Recovery Act: 132.
Feld, Irving: 156.
FEMA: 169.
Ferdinand (king of Spain): 25.
Fernandina, Fla.: 57.
Field, Mrs. Marshall: 91.
Field, Stanley and Sara: 92.
Field Club: 92, 151.
Fields, Herb: 148.
Fifth Street: 123.
Fillmore, President Millard: 40, 43.
First Bank and Trust Company: 129.
First Baptist Church: 89.
First Baptist Church of Sarasota: iv, 172, 192.
First Infantry: vii, 36.
First Presbyterian Church: iv, 172, 193.
First Street: 113, 152, 156.
Fish House Spur: 113.
Five Points: 19, 62-63, 65, 87, 92, 108, 111, 113, 116-117, 129, 142.
Five Points, Little: 164.
Flagler, Henry: 78.
Florence (ship): 65.
Florel, Hamilton: 88.
Florida Citrus Commission: 147.
Florida Cracker: 63, 77.
Florida Land and Improvement Company: 56.
Florida Mortgage and Investment Company Limited (FM&I): 54-56, 62, 64-67, 74, 81, 85.
Florida State University: 156.
Florida West Coast Land Development Company, Miami: 150.
Follett, Lieutenant: 38.
Fontaneda, Hernando Escalante: 30.
Fordville, Fla.: 94.
Forepaugh-Sells Circus: 106.
Forest Lakes Country Club Estates: 150.
Fort Armistead: ix, 14, 31, 33, 35-36, 39.
Fort Brooke: 34-36, 40, 41.
Fort Dade: 81.
Fort Fanning: vii.
Fort Jefferson: viii.
Fort King: 34-35.
Fort Meade: 44.
Fort Myers, Fla.: 42, 44, 46, 94, 104, 156.
Fort Snelling: vii.
Fort Taylor: viii.
Fourth Florida Regiment: 46.
Fourth Street: 62.
Francis Carlton Apartments: 113.
Franklin, G.W.: 124.
Fraser, Captain: 35.
Frazier, Mrs. E.L.: 92.
Frederick Derr & Company, Inc.: iv, 172, 194, 210.
Frizzell, Arthur C.: 150.
Fruitville, Village of: 62-63, 94, 123.
Fruitville Road: 119, 144.
Fuentes, Diego de: 28.

Fuller, Benjamin:. 39.
Furnessia, S.S.: 56-57.

G
Gainesville, Fla.: 48, 65, 75.
Gamble plantation house: 47-48.
Garcia, Father Juan: 28-29.
Garcilaso de la Vega: 10.
Gasparilla Pass: 48.
Gator Asphalt Company: iv, 172, 236-237.
Gauld, George: 33.
General Land Office: 48.
Genevieve Street: 125.
Gilchrist, Governor Albert W.: 90, 93.
Gilles, Jack: 88.
Gillespie, John Hamilton: 55, 64-65, 67-68, 74, 78, 82-83, 85-86, 88, 90, 93, 111, 113, 117, 129.
Gillespie, Mrs. John Hamilton (Mary): 65, 83-84.
Gillespie, Sir John Hamilton: 55, 65.
Gillespie Avenue: 65.
Gillett, B.D.: 82.
Glasgow: 56-57.
Glasgow (Scotland) *Herald:* 162.
Glasser/Schoenbaum Human Services Center: iv, 172, 195.
Glazier, Ezekial: 47.
Glenn, John: 169.
Godoya, José Maria: 33.
Goldberg, Arthur M. and Viola L.: iv, 172, 218.
Golden Gate Point: 83, 105, 111.
Golf Street: 65, 88, 119.
Gomez, Antonio: 33.
Gomez, Juan: 33.
Gonzales, Andrew: 33.
Gore, Al: 169.
Graham, Governor Bob: 161.
Grantham, Eliza: 88.
Grassroots Leadership Initiative Hall of Fame: 167.
Gray, Secretary of State R.A.: 157.
Greatest Show on Earth (movie): 150.
Gregorio, Father: 29.
Greycloud (ship): 44.
Griebling, Otto: 138.
Griffith, Clerk Robert: 48.
Grismer, Karl: 144.
Gulf Bay Land Company: 124.
Gulf Blockading Squadron: 46.
Gulf Gate subdivision: 150, 164.
Gulf Coast Community Foundation of Venice: iv, 172, 196.
Gulf Stream Avenue: 69, 73, 86, 90, 111, 152, 160.
Gulf Stream Avenue Park: 90.
Guptill, Eliza and Frank: 67, 85.
Gussie (ship): 67.

H
Haley, James A.: 141, 144.
Halton, Dr. Jack: 86, 88.
Halton, Dr. Joe: 90, 92.
Halton's Minstrel Show: 88.
Halton Sanatorium: 86.
Hamilton, Wilma: 170.
Hamlin, Captain Will: 67.
Hamlin, W.T.: 148.
Harbor Acres: 20.
Hardee County: 119.
Harding, Warren G.: 107.
Harpers Monthly: 44.
Harris, Katherine: iv, 163, 169.
Hartford, Conn.: 141.
Hartsuff, Lt. George L.: 42.
Harvard School of Land Architecture: 95.
Harvey, J.W.: 88.
Hassel, Daniel and Mañuel: 42.
Hatchet Creek: 93.
Havana, Cuba: 27, 30, 33, 46.
Hawkins, Henry: 52.
Hazzard Fountain: 164, 166.
Helena (gunboat): 78.
Herald-Tribune Media Group: iv, 172, 197.
Heron Lagoon: 128.
Higel, Frank: 95, 98.
Higel, Genevieve: 89, 167.

Higel, Harry L.: 13, 83, 87, 90, 124.
Higel, Louise: 117.
Higel Avenue: 125.
Higel family: 125.
Higel Hurst Hotel: 125.
Higel Street: 122.
Highlands County: 119.
Highsmith Turner and Co.: 85.
Hi Hat Ranch: iv, 172, 198.
Hill, W.J.: 82.
Hill Cottage: 16.
Hillsborough County: 36, 39, 49.
Hillsborough River: 58.
Hirrihigua (Indian chief): 26.
Historic Spanish Point: iv, 167, 172, 173.
Hitchings, Clarence E.: 88.
Hodges, L.D.: 71.
Hofheinz, Judge: 156.
Holcomb, Constance: iv, 172, 206-207.
Homer, Winslow: vii.
Honoré, Adrian: 91.
Hooker, William: 42, 44.
Horse and Chaise: 49, 95.
Hover Arcade: 92, 113.
Howard, Mr.: 47.
Hudson (early Sarasota Bay settler): 42, 44.
Hudson Bayou: 33, 39, 50, 52, 81, 85, 112, 128, 132, 163.
Huffman Aviation: 170.
Hurricane Charley: 168.
Hurricane Donna: 150.
Hurricane Earl: 169.
Hurricane Elena: 161.
Hurricane Georges: 169.
Husani, Neil Mohamed: 168-169.
Hyde Park: 48.
Hyde Park Citrus Grove: 123, 150.

I
Icard, Merrill, Cullis, Timm, Furen & Ginsberg, P.A.: iv, 172, 199.
Ice Age: vi, 19-20.
Ihrig, Chet: 132.
Immokalee: 91, 93, 118.
Indian Beach: v, 110, 119, 123.
Indian Beach Road: 42, 110, 114.
Indian mounds: 33, 36, 49, 79, 85, 123, 161.
Indian Nation: 41-42.
Indian River: 40.
Inn, The: 73.
Interstate-75: 161, 163-164, 166.
Irish-American Corp.: 171.
Isabella (queen of Spain): 25.
Island Park: 150.

J
J.P. Igloo Ice and Inline Sports Center: 169.
Jackson Road: 103.
Jacksonville, Fla.: 65, 75.
Jacksonville *Times Union*: 52.
Jacobs, Lou: 138, 146.
Jeffcott, Richard (home): 78.
Jelks Family Foundation: iv, 172, 200.
Jennings, Christine: 169.
Jerome, Paul: 138-139.
Jersey City *Journal*: 96.
Jesup, General Thomas: 35.
John Ringling Towers Hotel: 168.
Johnston, Patricia: vii.
Johnson, President Andrew: viii.
Jones, Bobby: 93.
Jones, C.M.: 88.
Joshua Creek: 44.
Jumper, Chief: 31, 35.

K
Kansas City Monarchs: 165.
Kantor, MacKinlay: 148.
Keith, Edson: 118.
Kelly, Emmett: 138-139, 146.
Kennedy, R.I.: 88.
Kentucky Military Institute Color Guard: 143.
Kerkering, Barberio & Co., P.A.: iv, 172, 201.
Kevin Daves: iv, 172, 187.
Key West: 33-34, 39, 47, 62, 65.

Kilties Marching Band (Riverview High School): 151.
Kissimmee, Fla.: 67, 78.
Kissimmee (ship): 65.
Kitson, Syd: 171.
Kleinoscheg, Anton and Carrie: 74, 75.
Kleinoscheg home: 74.
Knight, Jesse and Caroline: 49.
Knight, Joel: 49.
Knights of Pythias Hall: 119.
Krebbiel's Pharmacy: 92.

L
Lacey, Kathleen: 90.
Lake Okeechobee: 128.
Lakeland, Fla.: 62.
Lakewood Ranch: 167.
Lancaster, Louis: 107.
Landings subdivision: 93.
Las Casas, Bishop Bartolomé de: 24, 28.
Laurel Civic Association: 168.
Laurel, Fla.: 20, 123, 158.
Laurel School: 98.
Lee, Comptroller J.M.: 157.
Lee Street: 122.
Lee Weatherington Homes: iv, 167, 174.
Leffingwell, Dr.: 69.
Le Moyne, Jacques: 17, 19-20.
Lemon Street: 88, 113, 119, 141.
Léon, Ponce de: 25-26.
Leslie, C.R.: vii.
Lesley, John: 46.
Lido Beach: v, 124, 150.
Lido Beach Pavilion: 48, 132, 149, 153, 158-159.
Lime Avenue: 62, 65.
Lincoln, President Abraham: 46-47.
Lindsay, David: 124.
Lindsay, George D.: 124.
Links Avenue: 65.
Little Sarasota Bay: 16.
Live Oak, Fla.: 52.
Lizzie G: 167.
Lizzie Henderson (ship): 65.
Lockwood Ridge: 19.
London *Illustrated News*: 31.
London *Times*: 54.
Longboat, Fla.: 32, 50, 124, 160.
Longboat Key: 27, 111, 150, 164.
Longino Ranch, Inc.: iv, 172, 202-203.
Lord, J.H.: 113, 115.
Lord's Arcade: 128.
Lowe, Emma M.: 33.
Lowe, William: 46.
Luke Wood Park: 132.
Luzier, Bob: 143.

M
M'Auslan family: 74.
Mabry Carlton Ranch: iv, 172, 204.
MacArthur, John T. and Catherine: 164.
MacDonald, John D.: vi, 148, 208.
Madison Square Garden (New York): 134-136, 156.
Magdalena (Indian interpreter): 28-29.
Main Street: 19, 58, 62-63, 65, 72, 82-83, 87-90, 111, 113-114, 119, 125, 128-129, 142, 150, 155.
Manasota, Fla.: 94.
Manasota Lumber Company: 94.
Manasota Period: 20.
Manatee: 36, 42, 49, 52, 82, 91, 119.
Manatee *Advocate*: 82.
Manatee Community College: iv, 172, 206-207.
Manatee County: 42, 48, 59, 122.
Manatee High School: 167.
Manatee Junior College: 150, 166.
Manatee Methodist Episcopal Church: 42.
Manatee River: 27, 33, 35-36, 42, 46-47, 49, 65, 67, 72, 94, 104.
Manatee River *Journal*: 61.
Mango Avenue: 62.
Mansperger, Linda: 245-246.
Margaret Ann (ship): 65.
Martin, Governor John: 96, 104.
Mary Disston (ship): 65.

Mason, Walter, Jim and Luther: 63.
Matthews, Dr.: 132.
Matthews, Eastmoore, Hardy, Crauwels & Garcia: iv, 172, 205.
Maus, Edgar: 92.
Mayor's Court: 82.
McClellan, Katherine: 123.
McClellan Park: 50, 123.
McClellan Park School: 123.
McCullough family: 41.
McDaniel, Miss Blanche: 84.
McDermott, James: viii, 14.
McGinty, C.C.: 88.
McKenzie, Willie: 123.
McLeod, Hiram: 48.
McVeigh, Timothy: 170.
Meadowsweet Pastures: 93, 132.
Mediterranean fruit fly: 130.
Menéndez de Avilés: 29, 30.
Merrick, George: 125.
Messer, Zeke: 88.
Meuser, Stanley and Veronica: iv, 172, 216.
Mexico: 26, 28-29.
Miami, Fla.: 125, 129, 143.
Micanopy, Seminole Chief: 35.
Michael Saunders & Company: iv, 172, 208-209.
Micco, Holata (see also Billy Bowlegs): 31, 40-44.
Midnight Pass: 163.
Miller, Mel: 138.
Miller, Rep. Dan: 169.
Mira Mar Hotel and Casino: 113, 115, 122.
Mississippi River: 27.
Mistletoe (ship): 69.
Mizner, Addison: 125.
Moore and Dooley Inc.: 124.
Morrill, E.W.: 85.
Morrill, Mrs.: 124.
Morrill Avenue: 125.
Morrill Street: 83, 85.
Mosely, Governor William: 41.
Mote Marine Laboratory: iv, 172, 210.
Mound Island: 29.
Multi-Stakeholders Group: 165.
Municipal Auditorium: 164, 166.
Municipal dock: 90.
Municipal Services Taxing Unit: 160.
Muñoz, Juan: 29.
Murphy, Garrett "Dink": 76.
Museum of the Circus: 138.
Myakka: 39, 76, 123.
Myakka basin: 123.
Myakka Drainage District: 93.
Myakka Lake: 91, 132.
Myakka, Old: 20.
Myakka River: 37, 93, 96, 112, 150, 164.
Myakka River pump house: 94.
Myakka State Forest: 171.
Myakka State Park: 76, 93, 132, 166.
Myakka Valley Ranch: iv, 172, 211.

N
Naples, Fla.: 94-95, 104.
Narváez, Pánfilo de: 26-27.
National Estuary Program: 163.
National Guard: 130, 150.
National Tarpon Tournament: 96.
National Youth Administration: 132.
Nau, Katherine: iv, 172, 202.
Naugle, Edward: 124.
Neal Family, Pat: iv, 172, 212-213.
Nelson, Sen. Bill: 169.
Net ban: 164.
New Deal: 132.
New Edzell castle: 112.
New Pass: 111, 124, 150.
Newtown, Fla.: 122-123, 130, 133, 150, 158.
New York: 57, 94.
New York Central Railroad: 107.
New York Giants baseball team: 119.
New York Times Company: 160.
Ninth Street: 63.
Nixon, President Richard: 158.
Nokomis, Fla.: 49, 97, 103, 123, 129, 158.
Nokomis Street: 102.
Nolen, John: 95, 113, 119.
Nolen, John and Associates: 95.
Norris, Gary: 170.
Northampton Equal Suffrage League: 123.
Northbrook Cattle Company: iv, 172, 214.
North brothers: 156.
Northern Trust: iv, 172, 215, 228.
North, Henry "Buddy" Ringling: 134, 141, 156.
North, Ida Ringling: 134.
North, John Ringling: 134-135, 140-141, 157.
North, John Ringling II: iv, 172, 214, 222.
North Port, Fla.: 20, 150, 160, 164.

O
Oaks, The: 91, 93, 144.
Ocala, Fla.: 22, 27, 34.
Ocita Indians: 23.
Oglesby family: 42.
Okeechobee: 108.
Olivella, Mañuel: 35-36, 39.
O'Neil, John Jordan "Buck" Jr.: 165-167.
162nd Infantry Company: 81.
Orange Avenue: 82, 87, 90, 118, 123, 130, 150.
Orange Blossom Hotel: 132, 155.
Orange Period: 20.
Orlando, Fla.: 75, 130, 151.
Ormiston Colony: 53-54, 57, 60.
Ortiz, Juan: 23.
Oscar Scherer State Park: 165.
Osceola, Chief: 35.
Osprey, Fla.: 20, 48-49, 79, 91, 93, 104, 123.
Osprey Avenue: 19, 49.
Osprey Avenue bridge: 132.
Out-of-Door Academy: iv, 172, 216.
Otter Key: 150.
Overton, John W. and Pamela: iv, 172, 218.
Overtown, Fla.: 123.
Oyster Bay: 33.
Oyster River: 33.

P
Pacheco, Antonio: 35.
Pacheco, Luis: 34-35.
Pacheco, Señora: 34.
Pacheco family: 34.
Pahokee, Fla.: 128.
Palatka, Fla.: 39.
Palm Avenue: 65, 85, 113-114.
Palm Beach, Fla.: 125, 128.
Palm Island: 32-33, 148.
Palm Island development: 156.
Palms Theatre: 92.
Palmer, Bertha Honoré (Mrs. Potter): 16, 76, 85, 91, 93, 102, 125, 132, 193.
Palmer, Gordon: 245.
Palmer, Janis: 245-246.
Palmer, Honoré: 91, 93, 123, 132.
Palmer, Potter Jr: 91, 93, 123, 132.
Palmer estate: 93.
Palmer family: 93-94.
Palmer Farms: 123, 126, 130.
Palmer Ranch: 166.
Palmerville, Fla.: 94.
Palmetto Junction: 94.
Pan Massachusetts (ship): 143.
Panic of 1907: 90.
Park View Hotel: 101.
Parker, John: 42.
Parker, William: 44.
Parkland, Fla.: 94.
Paschal, Guy: 148.
Pascagoula, Fla.: 62.
Payne, Calvin: 112.
Payne, Christy: 108.
Payne, C.N.: 108.
Payne, Martha: 112.
Payne, Mr.: 41.
Payne, Oscar: 48.
Payne Park: 154.
Payne Terminal: 112, 133.
Peace River valley: 39.
Pearl Harbor: 143.
Pearson, Sheriff Clem: 142, 147.
Peas (Peace) Creek: 14, 35, 40.
Peas Creek Trading Post: 41.
Pei, Icoh Ming: 150.
Pelican Bay: 128.
Peñalosa, Father Juan de: 28.
Peninsula Telephone: 85.
Pensacola, Fla.: 46, 62, 112.
Pentagon: 170.
Perceval, John: 33.
Perlman Music Program: iv, 172, 217.
Peters, William Wesley: 156.
Phantom (ship): 65.
Phillippi: 42, 44.
Phillippi Creek: 48, 52, 65, 74, 91, 118, 123, 150, 163, 165.
Phillippi Plantation: 165.
Phillips, Rose: 82.
Phillips family: 98.
Pickett, Charlie: 112.
Pinard, Felix: 12, 61, 65, 67, 68, 70, 72-73, 94.
Pinard, Josephine: 70.
Pineapple Square: 168.
Pinelands Reserve: 166.
Pine Level, Fla.: 48-49, 52.
Pine Level courthouse: 63.
Pine Level *Times*: 48.
Pineapple Avenue: 62, 113, 156.
Pines of Sarasota: iv, 172, 218-219.
Pizarro, Francisco: 26.
Plant, Henry: 78.
Players Theatre: 156.
Plaza Restaurant: 130, 152.
Pleistocene Epoch: 19-20.
Pliocene Epoch: vi.
Poinsett, Secretary of War Joel: 35.
Point of Rocks: 128.
Police force: 117.
Polk County: 74.
Polly (Indian woman): 44.
Ponte Vedra Beach: 143.
Post-Archaic period: 20.
Poynter, Paul: 124.
Preservation 2000: 165.
Price, Senator Ed H. Jr.: 167.
Proctor Road: 51.
Professional Benefits, Inc.: iv, 172, 220.
Punta Rassa: 66.
Purmort & Martin Insurance Agency, LLC: iv, 172, 221.

Q
Quality Aggregates Incorporated: iv, 167, 172, 236-237.

R
Rae, Stu: 148.
Reagan family: 98.
Reagan, President and Mrs. Ronald: 151.
Reconstruction: 49-50.
Redd, Captain Isaac Alderman: 37, 42.
Redd, David: 42.
Redd, Preacher: 65.
Reed M.P., Sir Edward J.: 54.
Reid, Eddie Coleman: 120.
Reid, Ethel: 83, 120.
Reid, James Leonard: 83.
Reid, Ray Field: 83.
Reid, Viola: 83.
Remington, Frederic: 15, 77.
Republican: 49-50, 107.
Resort at Longboat Key Club, The: 221.
Rigby, W.F.: 83.
Rigby, William and Wade: 42.
Riggin, George: 65.
Riggins family: 58, 74.
Riley, Harrison: 51, 52.
Ringling, Aubrey: 141.
Ringling, Charles: 107, 109, 111, 112, 113, 130, 141, 150, 160.
Ringling, Edith: 107, 109, 111, 112, 130, 136, 141, 150, 160.
Ringling, Hestor: 107.
Ringling, John: 12, 105-107, 108, 111-113, 114, 125, 130-132, 150, 157.
Ringling, Mable Burton: 12, 107, 108, 135.
Ringling, Robert: 141.
Ringling Art School: 114.
Ringling Bank and Trust Co.: 130.
Ringling Boulevard: 111, 113, 140.
Ringling Brothers Barnum & Bailey Circus: 11, 115, 130-131, 134, 136-141, 150, 156, 165.
Ringling Brothers Barnum & Bailey Clown College: 138.
Ringling causeway: 111-112, 122-124.
Ringling Causeway Bridge: 167.
Ringling College of Art and Design: iv, 172, 223.
Ringling complex: 122.
Ringling Estates: 111, 114, 144.
Ringling family: 130.
Ringling Hotel: 111, 142, 150, 160.
Ringling Isles: 111, 124, 150.
Ringling Isles Real Estate Development Company: 107.
Ringling Museum of Art: iv, 131, 135, 146, 156-157, 172, 222.
Ringling Towers: 111-112.
Ringling Trust and Land Title Guaranty and Mortgage Savings Bank: 111.
Ringling Shopping Center: 140.
Ritchey, Jim and Shirley: iv, 172, 189.
Ritz-Carlton Hotel: 110, 150.
Ritz-Carlton, Sarasota: iv, 172, 225.
Riverview High School: 151, 159.
Rivolta, Piero: iv, 172, 224.
Road 120: 91.
Roaring Twenties: 123.
Roberts Bay: 49, 95.
Roberts, Captain Louis: 62, 124.
Roberts, Robert Rickford: 49, 95.
Roberts family: 98, 125.
Roberts Hotel: 124.
Roberts Road: 125.
Rogel, Father: 30.
Rogers, Roland W.: 150-151, 160.
Romans, Bernard: 33.
Roosevelt, President Franklin D.: 132.
Roosevelt, Rough Rider Teddy: 81.
Roseburn (Gillespie home): 83-84.
Rosemary Cemetery: 63-64, 85.
Rosenwald Fund: 119.
Roth's newsstand: 108.
Route Cl: 156.
Ruby (ship): 65.
Rudolph, Paul: 168.
R/UDAT: 165.
RU-27: 165.

S
Safety Harbor: 20.
Saint Armand, Charles: 111.
Saint Andrews: 65.
Saint Armands: 111, 114, 124.
Saint Armands Circle: 16.
Saint Armands Key: 151.
Saint Armands-Lido Realty Corporation: 107.
Saint Augustine: 29-30, 97.
Saint Johns River: 30, 57.
Saint Louis: 65.
Saint Marks River: 26.
Saint Petersburg, Fla.: 119.
Saint Petersburg *Times:* 124.
Sam Jones: ix.
San Carlo Opera Company: 113.
San Cristobal (De Soto's flagship): 26.
Sandbar Beach Hotel: 99.
Santa Maria de la Encina (ship): 28-29.
Santa Maria, Father Dominic de: 28.
Sapphire Shores: 123.
Sara de Soto: 13, 89.
Sara de Soto Pageant: 142, 145.
Sara Sota: 50.
Sara Sota Assassination Society: 49-50, 52.
Sara Sota Vigilance Committee: 51.

Sarasota Art Association: 155.
Sarasota Bay, Little: 79, 85, 91.
Sarasota Beach: 113.
Sarasota Board of Commissioners: 160.
Sarasota Conservation Foundation: iv, 172, 226.
Sarasota County Administration Building: 13, 111, 114, 160.
Sarasota County Commission: 114, 150, 158.
Sarasota County Chamber of Commerce: 123.
Sarasota County courthouse: 65.
Sarasota County Environmentally Sensitive Lands Protection Program: 171.
Sarasota County Fair Association: 119.
Sarasota County growth: 167.
Sarasota Family YMCA: iv, 172, 227.
Sarasota-Fruitville drainage district: 123.
Sarasota Grammar School: 119-120.
Sarasota Gun Club: 88.
Sarasota Heights: 123.
Sarasota Heights schools: 119.
Sarasota Herald Tribune: iv, 124, 129, 167, 218.
Sarasota High School: 119-120, 121, 167 (baseball and football teams).
Sarasota Hotel: 113, 115.
Sarasota Ice, Fish, and Power Company: 85.
Sarasota Kennel Club, Inc.: 141.
Sarasota Key, Little: 124.
Sarasota-Manatee Joint Airport Authority: 144.
Sarasota Memorial Hospital: 19, 49, 147, 158.
Sarasota Memorial Healthcare Foundation, Inc.: iv, 172, 228.
Sarasota Mosquito Squadron: 147.
Sarasota municipal auditorium complex: 19, 132-133.
Sarasota Oil Company: 107.
Sarasota post office: 65.
Sarasota Ritz-Carlton: 168.
Sarasota School of Architecture: 168.
Sarasota Terrace Hotel: 111.
Sarasota *Times*: 82, 87, 90, 124.
Sarasota Town Council: 84.
Sarasota, Town of: 56, 59, 64, 90, 92, 161-162.
Sarasota-Venice Company: 93.
Sarasota Yacht Club: 116, 124.
Saunders, Michael & Company: iv, 172, 208-209.
Savannah Normal School: 83.
Schoolcraft, Henry Rowe: viii.
Schroeder-Manatee Ranch, Inc.: iv, 172, 229.
Scotland: 54, 56, 58, 65, 78.
Scottish colonists: 54, 57, 60, 62, 65.
Seaboard Air Line Railroad: 81, 94, 95, 96, 129.
Secession Congress: 47.
Seibert Architects, P.A.: iv, 172, 230.
Selby, Bill: 108, 112.
Selby, Frank: 108, 112.
Selby, Marie: 108, 112, 116.
Selby, Marie, Botanical Gardens: 168.
Selby Library: 133.
Selby Oil Company: 108, 112.
Seminole Indians: viii, 31-34, 36, 40-42, 44.
Seminole War, Second: ix, 34-35, 39, 41.
Seminole War, Third: 36-38, 42.
Serwatka, Walter: iv, 172, 206-207.
Seventh Regiment, Company E: 46.
Seventh Regiment, Company K: 46.
Shake It Creek: 49, 93.
Shaw's Point: 27, 46.
Shell Beach: 106.
Shell Beach subdivision: 107.
Sherman Silver Purchase policy: 65.
Sherrill, Mary: 52.
Sidell, Fla.: 94.
Siesta Beach pavilion: 150.
Siesta Developments: 124.
Siesta Drive In: 150.

Siesta Key: 39, 93, 124, 128, 147, 156.
Siesta Land Company: 124.
Siesta subdivision: 124.
Sixth Street: 63, 112.
Smith College: 123.
Smith, Hamden: 88.
Smithsonian Institution: 18.
Snell, Hamlin Valentine: 36, 39-44.
Sophie (Ringling family cook): 130.
Sousa, John Philip: 101.
South Bay: 128.
Southeast Bank, NA.: 62.
Southeast High School: 167.
South Florida Bulldogs: 46.
South Gate subdivision: 150, 165.
Southgate, Katherine: 90.
South Links Street: 88.
Southside School: 50, 119.
South Venice 2010: 166.
Spanish: 20, 21, 23-26, 28, 30, 32, 39.
Spanish-American War: 78, 81.
Spanish fishermen: 35-36, 39.
Spanish Point: iv, 48-49, 67, 91, 172, 173, 245-246.
Spragins, Wendell and Lynda: iv, 167, 233.
Stafford, Governor: 58.
Stahl, Ben: 148.
State Board of Public Welfare: 130.
State Route 72 (see also Sugar Bowl Road): 132.
Steele, Bobby: 137.
Steinmetz, Joe: 139, 155, 157, 162.
Stephens, Wilson and Laura Virginia: 98.
Stephens family: 98.
Stewart family: 74.
Stickney, Uncle Ben: 125.
Stickney Point: 125.
Stickney Point Bridge: 125, 153.
Stickney Point Road: 56, 150.
Stottlemyer, Charlie and Dee: iv, 172, 193.
Stowe, Harriet Beecher: viii.
Strawberry Avenue (Ringling Boulevard): 62, 113, 132.
Sugar Bowl Road: 132.
Sun Debs: 158.
SunTrust Bank, Southwest, Florida: iv, 172, 231.
Super Bowl: 161.
Suwannee River: vii.
Suwannee Straits: 18.
Sweeting, Deputy: 147.
Syprett, Meshad, Resnick, Lieb, Dumbaugh & Jones: iv, 172, 232.

T

Tait, John Selwin: 54, 56-59.
Tallahassee, Fla.: 42.
Tamiami Trail: 104, 111, 118-119, 121, 156.
Tampa Bay: 26-27, 30, 33, 35, 39-40, 46, 49, 58, 75, 81.
Tampa, Fla.: 32, 34, 44, 46, 50, 65, 69, 78, 81, 90, 94-95, 104, 119, 125 131.
Tampa Southern Railroad: 94.
Tarpon Springs, Fla.: 20, 156.
Tarpon Tournament: 149.
Tatum, A.J.: 48.
Tatum family: 52, 58.
Tatum Ridge: 19, 52, 65.
Taylor, General Zachary: 35, 36
Temple Beth Sholom: 160.
Temple Emmanuel: 160.
Tenth Street: 42, 62, 81, 123.
The Robin (BLE ship): 99.
Thirteenth Street: 119.
This Week in Sarasota: 124.
Thompson, Charles N.: 106-107.
Thompson, Kenneth: 147.
Thompson, Thelma: 106.
Timucus Indians: 21.
Toale Brothers: iv, 172, 233.
Tocobaga Chile: 22, 30.
Tocobaga Indians: 20-21, 33.
Tornadoes (Booker High School football team): 151.
Treasure Island: 125.
Tresca, Frederick: 47-48.

Tresca, Will: 47.
Trust Company of Sarasota: 107.
Tucker family: 58.
Tuckers Sporting Goods: 116.
Turner, J.B.: 82.
Turner, J.P.: 83.
Turtle Beach: 128.
Tustenuggee, Chocote: 31.
Twiggs, General David: 41.
Twin Lakes Park: 166.
Twitchell, Ralph: 153, 159, 168.
The Twitchell Group Architects, P.A.: 24.
2020 Comprehensive Plan Amendment: 168.

U

Union blockade: 46-48.
Union Navy: 47.
United Way of Sarasota County, Inc: iv, 172, 234.
University of Florida, Agricultural Experiment Station: 147.
University of South Florida: 159.
Urology Treatment Center, The: iv, 172, 235.
U.S. Army Corps of Engineers: 42.
U.S. Army, First Infantry: 36.
U.S. Coast Guard: 143.
U.S. Department of Housing and Urban Development: 168.
U.S. Department of Treasury: 33.
U.S. House of Representatives: 141.
U.S. Land Office: 48.
U.S. Navy: 143.
Useppa fishery: 33.
Utopia, Fla.: 94.
Utz, Thornton: 148.

V

Vaca, Cabeza de: 26.
Valentine (Booker High School band conductor): 151.
Vamo, Fla.: 123.
Van Wezel Performing Arts Hall: 154, 156, 158, 168, 217.
Vandalia, U.S.S.: 34.
Velvet Highway: 104.
Venetian Waterway Park: 171.
Venice, Fla.: 18, 49, 91, 94-96, 98, 101, 104, 129, 138, 143-144, 147, 150, 156, 158, 160-161, 164, 166.
Venice Aerials (baseball team): 143.
Venice Area Beautification Inc.: 171.
Venice Avenue West: 102.
Venice airfield: 143.
Venice Beach: 161.
Venice Boulevard: 96.
Venice Chamber of Commerce: 97.
Venice Depot: 171.
Venice Golf Course: 99.
Venice High School (baseball title): 167.
Venice Hospital: 166.
Venice Hotel: 96, 100.
Venice Ice Company: 103.
Venice Inlet: 40, 93.
Venice Main Street: 165.
Venice Municipal Airport: 170.
Venice *News:* 97.
Venice-Nokomis: 96-97.
Venice Pharmacy: 102.
Venice Post Office: 102.
Venice Public Beach: 97, 99.
Venice Railway Station: 165.
Venice Tarpon Club: 96.
Venice Tile Company: 102.
Venice Trailer Park: 147.
Verna, Fla.: 20.
Viceroy of Mexico: 28-29.
Victory Avenue: 113, 119.
Vincent, Joe: 62.
Vincent, Rosa: 62.
Vincent children: 71.
Vincent house: 72.
Vision (ship): 65.
Vision 20/20: 165.

W

Walker and Gillette architects: 95.
Wallace, Dr. Robert: 63, 65, 74.
Walpole, Charlie: 143.
Walton Tract: 164, 166.
Wakaninajinwin: vii.
Warburton, Piers E.: 56, 74.
Warm Mineral Springs: 18, 25.
Warren, Dr.: 69.
Warren, Governor Fuller: 147.
Washington Boulevard: 63, 112, 122.
Washington Park: 111.
Watrous Hotel: 114.
Webb, Eliza Graves: 48, 49.
Webb, Henry: 104.
Webb, John: 48, 49.
Webb family: 49, 52, 91.
Weeden Island: 20.
Weir, Tom M.: 58.
Weir, Robert Walter: vii.
Wendel Kent & Company: iv, 172, 236-237.
West Coast Inland Navigation District (WCIND): 156.
Western Union: 92.
Whidden, Dempsey: 41.
Whidden, John: 44.
Whidden, Lott: 44.
Whitaker, A. Klein: 246.
Whitaker Bayou: 20, 33, 36, 39.
Whitaker, Charlie: 65.
Whitaker, Emile: 52, 59.
Whitaker, Dr. Furman C.: 47, 49, 65, 104.
Whitaker, Hamlin: 59, 65, 74.
Whitaker, Mary Jane Wyatt: 36, 42, 44, 47, 51, 59, 79, 89.
Whitaker, Nellie Abbe: 47.
Whitaker, William (Bill): 36, 39, 42, 44, 47-48, 89.
Whitaker family: 36, 42, 49, 58, 65, 74, 93.
Whitaker mules: 72.
Whitaker Smith Livery Stable: 63.
Whitehead, William: 33.
Whitfield, J.G.: 114.
Whitfield estates: 122, 144.
Wild Goose (ship): 65.
Willard, Captain Albert: 58.
Willard, Charles: 51.
Williams, Ted: 148.
Willys, John N.: 107.
Willys-Overland Automobile Company: 107.
Wilson, C.V.S.: 64, 82, 87, 124.
Wilson, Dr. C.B.: 90.
Wilson Jaffer P.A.: iv, 172, 238.
Wilson, Rose: 64, 87.
Wilson, W.G.: 65.
Windom, Robert E. and Lelia:, iv, 172, 218.
Windsor, Fla.: 75.
Withlacoochee River: 35.
Womans Club: 113.
Wood, Arthur M.: iii, 245-246.
Wood, Pauline Palmer: 246.
Woodmere, Fla.: 123, 164, 166.
Woodruff Joseph: 41-42, 46, 57.
Woodward tract: 112.
Worcester, Thomas M.: 112.
Works Progress Administration (WPA): 132, 144.
World Trade Center: 170.
World War I: 104, 116.
World War II: 143-144, 161-162.
Worthington, Edward L.: 96.
Wright, Frank Lloyd: 154.
Wyatt, Mary Jane (see also Whitaker, Mary Jane): 42.
Wyatt, Nancy: 42.
Wyatt, William: 42.

Y

Yarborough, Mrs. T.W.: 98.
Yellow Bluffs: 51, 93.
Yohola, Sarparkee: 31.

Z

Zarazote: 32.

Acknowledgments

Like *Journey to Centennial* (1985) and the Revised Edition (1997), this Second Revised Edition remains the work of many hands. The 1985 and 1997 Acknowledgments pages confirm, in specific detail, the debt I owe to many valued friends, co-workers and professional associates.

Documentary history is a continuum. Each successive edition builds on its predecessors in this, the longest continuously published reference history of Sarasota County.

Among those to whom great thanks are due, and with apologies for the inevitable, unintended omissions, I gratefully acknowledge: **Linda Williams Mansperger**, Executive Director, Historic Spanish Point, at whose instigation we embarked upon this publication; my Sarasota-born husband and Gator fan, **Lamar**, who outlines the tough game plan and gets our team across the goal line with the extra point kicked between the goal posts; and **Marion Almy**, President of both Archaeological Consultants and Sesquicentennial Productions, Inc. (SPI), whose academic and professional experience as well as native Sarasota perspective blend with passion and energy to interpret our regional history for present and future generations. In 1994, **Charles Baumann**, C.P.A., established SPI as a 501 (c) (3) corporation "to elevate public awareness of Florida's history and to inform Floridians of their diverse cultural heritage." Proceeds from these published works are reinvested in the community for projects advancing historical knowledge.

For many months, contributors to this effort have included our **Partners in Progress**, whose fascinating histories illumine this Second Revised Edition; our **SPI Advisors** *(see page iv)*; Senator Bob Graham and his wife, **Adele**; **Clyde and Niki Butcher**; **Kelley Nathan**, who became our first SPI Executive Director; and principal writer and co-author Allan H. Horton. Allan also elevated the content of the Epilogue by contributing his considerable photographic skills. Of equal importance are my committee of editors, critics, deadline producers and devil-is-in-the-details nerds, **Carolyn Kenney**, editor-in-chief, **Marion Almy** and **Lamar Matthews**. The labors of these special friends and colleagues infuse this volume. I am also grateful to my lifetime advisor and loving sister, **Vera Snyder O'Neill**.

Technical production is once again in the extremely capable hands of Coastal Printing, Inc. through President **Alan Guttridge, Jr.**, **Don Kopf**, and **Elsa Holderness**.

Finally, I wish to specifically mention in memoriam, **Arthur M. Wood, Sr.**, whose friendship, quiet encouragement and confidence-building skills have enabled me over the three decades we have pursued this project.

In fact, this project would never have materialized without **Mr. Wood**. I remember vividly the first time I met him.

How This Project (and Historic Spanish Point) Came To Be

Paulette Crabtree Schindler had wanted to have a Junior Science Museum like the one in Tallahassee, so the Junior League of Sarasota, Inc. started a committee to look for a suitable site. I was in the Junior League as a Provisional when I decided I wanted to write a book. They let that be my volunteer work in the community – to write a community history.

In 1974, we formed and incorporated as a 501 (c) (3) a group that later became the Gulf Coast Heritage Association.

I worked successfully to nominate Historic Spanish Point to the National Register of Historic Places in 1975. In the course of doing that, I had dealt extensively with **Webb** family descendants and the **Webb** family archival materials. At the same time, I was researching history with **Janis Hardage Palmer**, who had been the most recent, fulltime resident, with her husband **Gordon**, of the Palmer estate at Historic Spanish Point, until **Gordon** died in 1964.

In the 1970s, **John Detterick**, the Junior League, and I, were working to establish a county museum. **John Detterick** was chairman of the Sarasota County Bicentennial Commission and vice president of Sarasota Federal Savings and Loan, the successor entity of which became a part of SunTrust Bank, Southwest Florida. **Detterick** and Sarasota Federal had sponsored the publication of the manuscript which became the 1983 reference, *Edge of Wilderness*, which satisfied my thesis requirements for a Master's degree in history from Florida State University. We had been working with representatives of the **Palmer** family to set aside 25 acres, which was the area encompassed by the National Register boundaries. Archaeologist **Ripley Bullen's** material, from the Florida State Museum at the University of Florida, already had been incorporated in the 1975 National Register nomination.

Mr. Wood agreed to meet with **John Detterick** and me to talk about the property. I had heard and read a lot about him as the chairman and CEO of Sears, Roebuck and Co. who had completed construction of the Sears Tower in Chicago, at 110 floors the tallest building in the world. I expected him to arrive in a shiny, bright, chrome Rolls Royce or something – and he drove up in a 6- to 7-year-old, colorless Chevrolet with no chrome. Out stepped a tall, distinguished and very handsome man with bushy, red eyebrows. He came into **John's** office and sat down. John and I were both very nervous. Mr. Wood explained that whoever had represented themselves to us as having the right to extend an offer of land in the Palmer/Oaks property had no authority to do so – and he was there with the very bad news that none of that was possible.

John Detterick looked at me and I started babbling all about all the histories I had been researching over the past two or three years on the **Webb** family which nobody had put together with the **Palmer** family. The **Webb** family didn't know the **Palmer** family history, and the **Palmer** family didn't know the **Webb** family history. I had actually already met with **Mr. Wood's** wife – **Pauline Palmer Wood** – a couple times, and she had ordered a lot of the photographs from the Manatee County Historical Society archives that I had been having copied and accessioned by **Klein Whitaker**. **Pauline** was the last grandchild born during **Mrs. Palmer's** lifetime. **Mrs. Palmer** had written a letter from her Oaks estate acknowledging the birth of **Pauline**. I knew she was the last of a very important historic line of people in Sarasota's past.

As I started reciting all this history, **Mr. Wood** took out a rumpled business envelope from his inside coat pocket and started scribbling – in pencil. He scribbled notes probably for nearly an hour while I talked about the **Webb** family history and the **Palmer** family history on that site – histories I had learned while preparing the National Register nomination.

At the end of that time, he put the envelope back in his pocket and said: "I will see what I can do, but I can't make any promises."

So, every Tuesday morning at 10 o'clock, **John Detterick** called **Mr. Wood's** secretary, **Carolyn Link**, in **Arthur Wood's** office on the 98th floor of the Sears Tower in Chicago, and stayed on **Arthur Wood's** radar screen, faithfully. At the end of a long period of time, with the consistent advocacy of Sarasota attorney **Bill Strode**, their legal counsel, we were written into the **Palmer** family's Oaks estate plan that went before the Sarasota County Commission as part of the open, green space parcel stipulated within the Oaks subdivision development order. On December 30, 1980, **Lamar** hand-delivered to the County Commission a conveyance between the county and the predecessor not-for-profit of Historic Spanish Point. If the conveyance wasn't accomplished in 1980, it wasn't going to work. The county commission approved the conveyance.

When we met for the first time in the White Cottage, we changed our name to the Gulf Coast Heritage Association, Inc. **Bill Lonsdale** was the first president. We got a $40,000 grant from the State of Florida that enabled us to hire architect **Herschel Shepard** to develop a master site plan. That gave us credibility and a shopping list with prices for each component. **Pat Neal**, as Appropriations Chair in the Florida Senate, took that shopping list and earmarked a $785,000 grant for historic preservation in the state budget.

None of this would have happened without **Art Wood**. It took a CEO of his stature to pull it off; there were multiple **Palmer** family trust representatives who signed the agreement. And, **Art Wood** stayed very involved by serving as the **Palmer** family's consultant to **Linda Mansperger** until his death, at 93, in 2006.

Without **Arthur MacDougall Wood, Sr.**, there wouldn't be a Historic Spanish Point with which to celebrate this Silver Anniversary Second Revised Edition of *Sarasota: Journey to Centennial*.

1913-2006, Arthur M. Wood, Sr.